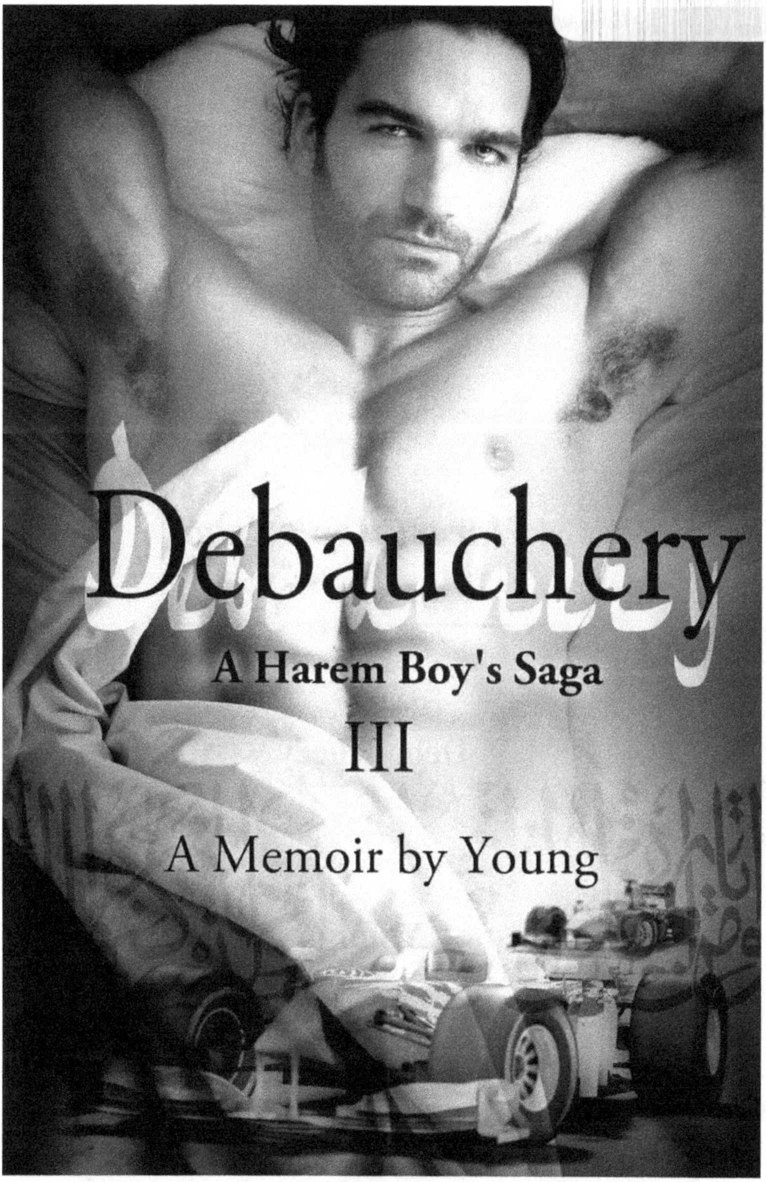

Debauchery
A Harem Boy's Saga
III
A Memoir by Young

A Harem Boy's Saga

———•◆•———

III

Debauchery

A Memoir by

Young

A Harem Boy's Saga III: Debauchery

Copyright © 2014 by Bernard Foong (Young).

All rights reserved. No part of this book may be used or reproduced in any manner whatsoever including Internet usage, without written permission of the author.

Author's Website:

www.aharemboysaga.com

Author's email:

young@aharemboysaga.com

The contents of this book constitute a work of NONFICTION. It documents the author's experiences, and is not intended as an expose'.

No portion of this book may be transmitted or reproduced in any form, or by any means, without permission in writing from the author or publisher, with the exception of brief excerpts used for the purposes of review.

This book contains substantial sexually explicit material and language which may be considered offensive by some readers.

Book editing by Ellen Fishbein

This book was copyright in July 2014.

This memoir is dedicated to teachers, educators, and tutors who had groomed and provided sound advice to students the world over.

"I was lucky that I met the right mentors and teachers at the right moment who taught me to believe in myself."

Bernard Tristan Foong

Prologue

In the three years since I typed the first words to *A Harem Boy's Saga – I – Initiation; a memoir by Young*, my journey of documenting my Middle Eastern harem experiences has both been emotionally exhilarating and empathetically solicitous. Although my time in the Arab Households was brief, it enlightened me: these experiences developed my strength, spirit and maturity, and because of them, I eventually became an independent individual with a voice of my own.

Doubtless, there are those who will proffer different opinions about my early induction into an adult world. Personally, I am still grateful to have been educated in love, sensuality and sexuality within the safely guarded environment of the Enlightened Royal Oracle Society (rather than on my own in the streets, without guidance or sound advice from learned mentors, teachers or big brothers).

Debauchery documents my harem experiences in my third household, the *Quwah*. It also chronicles my exotic travels with my entrepreneurial 'Master' and patriarch, Prince P. The Arab world in 1967 was vastly different from today's Middle Eastern societies. In certain aspects, the wealthy Arabian nations, especially the United Arab Emirates, have progressed, accumulating luxury products and a better standard of living for their citizens. Simultaneously, they have also regressed in their willingness to protect the rights of humanity that were passed down by learned Bedouin sages and savants of yore.

I hope, by revealing my harem experiences, my memoirs will reawaken the sanguine Arabian heritage of tolerance, acceptance and sufferance that was the epicenter of this historic culture. I applaud those whose valor and courage to regain Allah's universal truth has put them in harm's way, and I believe they can save the legacy that had been hijacked, its holy words transmuted to enrich the minority's personal gains and political agendas.

As was taught to me in the past, is remembered in the present and, I'm sure, will be recalled in the future:
"The truth will set you free."

Table of Contents

Part One:
Malaysia - Kuala Lumpur.
United Kingdom – London, Isle of Wight, Portsmouth.
French Riviera – Cannes, Antibes, Côte d'Azur.
Greece – Peloponnese, Athens, Isle of Lesbos, Mykonos.

Chapter 1	The Truth Will Set You Free
Chapter 2	The Beating Hearts
Chapter 3	The Illustrator
Chapter 4	The Differences
Chapter 5	At Le Gavroche
Chapter 6	Côte d'Azur
Chapter 7	Are You A Lesbian?
Chapter 8	Under the Cerulean Sky
Chapter 9	The Olympians
Chapter 10	The Four Loves
Chapter 11	The PARTHENON
Chapter 12	Sex & Nudity
Chapter 13	The Isle of Lesbos
Chapter 14	Eros & E.R.O.S.
Chapter 15	Pathway to the Sacred Way
Chapter 16	From Eromenos to Eraste
Chapter 17	The Superyacht Show
Chapter 18	Am I a Romantic?
Chapter 19	Dangerous Liaisons
Chapter 20	Let's Go Fly a Kite
Chapter 21	The Chapel of Love
Chapter 22	The Swimming Pool

Part Two:
France – Paris, Aubigny-sur-Nere.
Italy – Florence.

Chapter 23	In a State of Flurry
Chapter 24	Notre Dame de Paris
Chapter 25	An Aching Heart
Chapter 26	Zentology
Chapter 27	Grande Mosquée de Paris
Chapter 28	Musée National Gustave Moreau
Chapter 29	Wrestling with the Angels
Chapter 30	Hôtel de Crillon
Chapter 31	Église Saint-Sulpice
Chapter 32	French Frivolities
Chapter 33	Zensuality & Zexuality
Chapter 34	La Sainte-Chapelle
Chapter 35	Hôtel Le Bristol Paris
Chapter 36	Château Rouge
Chapter 37	La Chasse à Courre
Chapter 38	Museo delle Carrozze
Chapter 39	La Sala Bianca

Part Three:
Bahrain – Manama.
Monaco – Monte Carlo.
France – Eze Village, Cannes.

Chapter 40	Quwah
Chapter 41	The Kaneeth
Chapter 42	The Powers Behind the Throne
Chapter 43	The Carousel
Chapter 44	In the Altair
Chapter 45	The Investors
Chapter 46	Preying Wolves
Chapter 47	Solicitations
Chapter 48	An Expedient Resolution
Chapter 49	Hickory, Dickory, Dock
Chapter 50	Let the Games Begin
Chapter 51	Winners and Losers
Chapter 52	Loving Me, Loving You
Chapter 53	One Enchanted Evening
Chapter 54	The Artist & His Protégé
Chapter 55	The Laws of Attraction
Chapter 56	The Dissipated Mr. 'M'

Part Four:

Japan – Tokyo, Kyoto
United States of America – Pennsylvania
France – Paris.
United Kingdom – Isle of Wight

Chapter 57	Learning from the Best
Chapter 58	Japanese Homosexuality
Chapter 59	Naked Japan
Chapter 60	A Sacred Path to Enlightenment
Chapter 61	Lusting after Love
Chapter 62	The Tea Room
Chapter 63	From Kenzo, Yogji, Kansei to Hanae
Chapter 64	The Chigo's Way
Chapter 65	To the City of Brotherly Love
Chapter 66	The Vivacious Vicious Vixen
Chapter 67	Lone Rangers
Chapter 68	Matchmaker, Make Me a Match
Chapter 69	Andy, Where Are You?
Chapter 70	The Golden Pavilion
Chapter 71	The Pleasure Garden
Chapter 72	No. 11 Place Des Etats-Unis
Chapter 73	Naughty Bad Boys
Chapter 74	Cupids Disease
Chapter 75	Mirrors of the Soul
Chapter 76	The Boy Who Wouldn't Grow Up
Chapter 77	We Need to Talk Young Man, We Need to Talk!
Chapter 78	Auld Lang Syne

Part I

Malaysia - Kuala Lumpur.
United Kingdom – London,
Isle of Wight,
Portsmouth.
French Riviera – Cannes, Antibes,
Côte d'Azur.
Greece – Peloponnese, Athens,
Isle of Lesbos, Mykonos.

1

The Truth Will Set You Free

"I hope you have not been leading a double life, pretending to be wicked and being really good all the time. That would be hypocrisy."

Oscar Wilde

August 1967

Kuala Lumpur, Malaysia

It had been eight weeks since I last saw my beloved Andy. I was dying to get back to the arms of my lover. Andy and I were sad to see my 'big brother' leave, even though we had the opportunity to spend time cruising around the Greek islands before he left for *Medizinische Universität Wien (The Medical University of Vienna)*. Oscar's departure to Vienna had been heart-wrenching for the three of us. But we acknowledged that he must leave to pursue his life's other adventures, which only he could experience.

The thought of seeing my Valet again after eight weeks of absence and celibacy was reason enough for extreme excitement on my part. I only had a few days left in Kuala Lumpur before my departure to London.

Mother and my female relatives were delighted to see me, and I them, when I arrived home for my summer vacation. As far as Father was concerned, I dreaded the thought of having to go through his various grueling 'butch me up' experiences. Life back at the Methodist Boys' School wasn't much fun either. That year, the Malayan government was preparing for a major nationwide celebration. It was Hari Merdeka (Independence Day), the national day of Malaysia, which commemorated the independence of the Federation of Malaya from British colonial rule since 1957. Malaysia was formed on 16 September, 1963, together by the Federation of Malaya, Sabah, Sarawak and Singapore.

Students were selected from the Methodist Boys' School, along with other local schools to perform, at the Capital's national sports stadium, the *Merdeka Stadium*. Needless to say, I was one of the chosen performers even though I didn't care to participate; the school made it compulsory for those selected to attend rehearsals for this arduous celebration.

My task involved lifting and lowering a large red flag among a sea of other red cloth holders to the timing of Malaysia's national anthem. We were synchronized to raise the red cloths on command, therefore forming a representational pattern that resembled an oversized 'human' Malaysian flag. For two weeks, after-school time was spent on rehearsals. By the end of each day, my arms were sore from lifting and lowering the deplorable cloth.

During rehearsals I became acquainted with a pair of twins, Dorothy and Alice, from the Bukit Bintang Girls' School, our sister school, who were also performing at the event. We became friends. One evening, the sisters organized a birthday party at their parent's house. I was an invited guest. At the party, I was introduced to Andrew, a sixteen-year-old who was Alice's boyfriend. Although Dorothy was just my acquaintance and did not know the secret life I led at the other end of the world, she was latching onto me as a potential love interest. In her eyes, I was a boy with impeccable manners with whom she could discuss artistic and fashionable topics.

I had lost many of my effeminate traces during my year and half away from Malaysia. Outwardly, I was a well-groomed teenager. My experiences abroad had prepared me to be an educated young man, mature beyond my years, a feature which Dot (Dorothy's nickname) was attracted to.

Party Time

There were times when the twins invited me on double dates to the movies, but I politely refused. On the evening of their birthday party, Mother suggested I attend, since I was often a loner at the house. I accepted the birthday party invitation. As with many Kuala Lumpur teenage parties, my friend's parents had made it a point that there be neither alcoholic beverages nor recreational drugs available. They made the girls promise not to ransack their house when they were out for the evening, and they left their daughters and friends to party.

It was 1967, and the birthday twins did not want their parents around to keep vigilance. The house was left to a bunch of obstreperous teenagers. Although the birthday girls were by nature obsequious, they were easily malleable by others among them. As the party progressed, some guests became rambunctious after consuming a few intoxicating beverages and inhaling some recreational substances, which were smuggled in without our hostesses' knowledge. There were teenagers smooching in the living room and in other areas of the property.

After a series of jubilant dances with the birthday twins, I was ready to call it a night, but under Dorothy's insistence, I stayed. Nobody at the party knew of my sexual inclinations except me. During a slow dance, Dorothy leaned her head against my chest. Although this intrinsic way of dancing was not new to me, I had no intention of leading my friend on. I tried keeping a polite distance. Dot, thinking me shy, continued her aggressive approach. I had little choice but to go with the flow, since she held me tightly with no intention of releasing me anytime soon. The moment arrived when her lips almost touched mine. She looked into my 'eyes wide shut', expecting romance to sparkle between us. Though I did not feel the same as Dot, I did not back away, since it was her sixteenth birthday I did not wish to upset the teenager. I play-acted, much like I did during one of *"Sacred Sex in Sacred Places"* photography shoots. In my mind, it was the correct thing to do; after all, I'd be gone in a week's time, back to London town. I would not be seeing my Malaysian friends for another year. To me, this was simply a moment in time to make the birthday girl feel good about herself.

After a few dances, I excused myself to leave. Unfortunately for me, Ms. Dot had other thoughts, which were the complete opposite to mine. She insisted I stay and began introducing me as her boyfriend to those who came to wish her a Happy Birthday. I was astounded by such a proclamation. Yet, my politeness urged me to continue my impersonation and not to embarrass the hostess.

Before the night was over, Dot had pulled me to the bedroom she shared with her sister. Locking the door behind her she began to undress seductively. I was at a loss for words and actions. I was panicking within, but keeping my cool on the outside. My Bahriji training had taught me to be fearless. I told my hostess that we should take it slow and not jump into any drastic actions we may live to regret. In short, I was desperately trying to talk my way out of this awkward situation.

My tenacious hostess would not budge. She had stripped down to her sexy underwear as I perspired profusely, not from the excitement of seeing a semi-naked female but from the tension of figuring out an escape route from this unappealing dilemma. As Dorothy inched closer and closer, the only solution I could think of was to feign illness. I began with a series of gurgling noises as if I was sick to my stomach and needed to barf. She did not take my hint and continued heading towards the bed where I was seated. Unlocking the bedroom door, I ran towards the outside bathroom. It was occupied. Great! I thought to myself. Now I can leave the party on the pretense that I wasn't feeling well. Without turning around to bid my hostess farewell, I ran out of the house. I was glad Bakar was waiting for me in the driveway. The old chauffeur sped me home.

The Day After

At rehearsal the following day, I avoided eye contact with Dot in case she cornered me. As I was walking towards our family Bentley after rehearsal, Ms. Dorothy and her dear sister Alice appeared out of the blue. Taken by surprise, I had nowhere to run or hide except act complacent around both my friends.

Dot was the first to inquire, *"Are you alright? You ran off half-way through the party. I didn't know what happened to you!"*

Looking concerned, Alice added, *"Were you sick? Was it the food we served, or did you fall ill from consuming too much of the booze that the boys brought?"*

"I must have eaten too much and drank too many canned beverages; that always upsets my stomach." I lied. "Sorry I didn't have a chance to thank you for inviting me to such a delightful party. I had a wonderful time," I continued to be mendacious.

"Sorry you weren't feeling good. We hope you are better now?" The twins said simultaneously.

"I'm much better," I continued to lie.

"Tomorrow is Medeka Day. After our performance we are planning a picnic at the Lake Gardens. Will you join us?" Alice asked blithely.

Trying to think up a quick excuse, I replied, *"Unfortunately, my mother asked me to accompany her to visit some relatives. They, too, are having a holiday celebration. Thank you for the invitation."*

Before I could make my great escape to my waiting vehicle, Dorothy embraced me and kissed me on my lips. I was startled by such forwardness. The kiss lasted a brief second before she kissed both my cheeks to say goodbye. I was left speechless as the twins departed.

To this day, I regret not having had the courage to tell Dorothy the truth there and then. I had 3 days left before my flight to London. I decided to do the right thing. I ordered a dozen pink roses for Ms. Dorothy with an attached card.

Goodbye Ms. Dorothy

Mother thought I had finally turned over a new leaf when she saw me buying a bouquet of roses for a girl. As much as she accepted me as who I was, like most mothers she was hoping the day would come when I would leave my boyish 'boy-to-boy' love and turn heterosexual. With no intention of upsetting Mother, I gave her a loving smile but said nothing. If she thinks I'm a changed man, she has every right to her thoughts. I was never one to jostle nature's balance, let alone dishearten my mother's presupposition that I was turning 'straight'.

I did not see the twins after the celebratory performance at Medeka Stadium. On my departure day, both sisters came to the airport to bid me farewell. I handed Ms. Dorothy the dozen pink blossoms and a peck on both cheeks before boarding the BOAC flight bound for London. The card I gave to my 'girlfriend' read,

To my friend Dot,

By the time you open this card I will be miles across the ocean, on my way to reunite with my 'big brother' and lover. I am sorry to have misled you into believing that there was a romantic spark between us. I apologize for this misunderstanding. I am also sorry for not being honest. I sincerely hope I didn't cause you unnecessary distress.

I am gay and will most likely remain so throughout my life. I have been in a steady relationship with my nineteen-year-old BB for half a year, and our love grows stronger with each passing day. There are many things I am not able to confide to you or to anyone. I hope you'll come to accept me and love me as the person I am. I hope we can continue our friendship. Enclosed is my boarding school address if you wish to correspond with me. I would be delighted to receive news from you.

My best wishes to you and for your future endeavors. May blessings flow throughout your life unceasingly.

With love from your dear friend,
Young.

I never heard from Ms. Dorothy again.

2

The Beating Hearts

"Absence makes the heart grow fonder."

American Proverb

1967

London, England

It was close to midnight when my BOAC flight from Kuala Lumpur finally touched down at Heathrow. True to his word, Andy had arrived in London earlier that day from Germany to meet me. He had spent the summer with his siblings, Aria and Ari. His mother came to spend time with her children without her husband. The stubborn Herr Finckenstein had made a vow not to see or accept his gay son unless Andy apologized to the old man and promised to change his homosexual lifestyle. Only then would he accept Andy back into the fold. Of course, this was out of the question for my lover. He had no intention of living a lie, nor was he the type who would give in to please his father for the sake of keeping peace.

Although Uncle James was away on business, he had kindly agreed to let Andy and me stay at his Mayfair home for a day before his return. After all, we were in the city for 3 days before departing on the Simorgh to Monaco. Oscar would be meeting us in Cannes; he had to finalize his enrollment at The University of Vienna before accompanying us on our cruise around the Greek islands.

My beloved was waiting for me at the airport arrival lounge. I flew into his arms as soon I saw my Valet's handsome face. I couldn't wait to catch up on Andy's news, and neither could he resist embracing me. Lifting my face to his, he kissed me lovingly in front of the waiting crowd. Our eight weeks' absence had made our hearts grow fonder. Our souls were once again connected, and we did not care what people thought of our intimacy. We were utterly overjoyed to be together. As if he was afraid I would disappear, he wrapped his arms around my shoulders as we walked towards the waiting Rolls Royce, which Uncle James had so kindly arranged to collect us. As Jeffrey (the chauffeur) was loading my luggage into the booth, Andy ushered me into the back seat and we began French kissing. He, like me, had been celibate for the past eight weeks.

With the push of a button, the tinted windows and soundproof glass separating the driver and backseat passengers began to roll up. We were sealed in our private world. Andy's urgent kisses were too exhilarating to stop. In the heat of our passion, my lover reached his hands into my sweatshirt and fondled my sensitive nipples. I could feel my guardian's hardness straining against his jeans, waiting for release from its denim confines. I reached down to stroke his bulging crotch, teasing his urgency. I wanted our sensuality to last and to prolong our foreplay like we often did when we were practicing tantric sensuality. His delicious tongue began exploring my yearning oral orifice, jabbing desirously into my willing fissure, pleasuring me as much as I was gratifying him.

I unzipped his jeans as I continued to caress his bobbing organ beneath his dampening brief. Reaching in, I held onto my prized possession, squeezing its leaking tumescence onto my thumb before feeding us his viscidness. His intoxicating masculinity mixed with his deliciousness sent me yearning for more. Tearing our tops off, Andy lay atop, planting sweet kisses on my neck and nipples before devouring my ears voraciously with his lapping tongue. I squirmed uncontrollably beneath my aggressor. I was ready to receive him. I pushed his pants down to his ankles while he tore at mine. I pressed my eagerness against his. Holding both organs in my hands, I stroked them with burning desire. My lover lifted himself above and fed me his bulbousness. His delirious manliness had me craving my fill. I wanted him, and he desired me.

Lifting my legs above my head, he buried his face into my longing crevice; he was licking, suckling and wetting my opening, readying for unrestrained entry. My horniness had prepared me sufficiently to receive *mon amour* without further ado. I coveted him; I needed him, and I was ready to receive his engorgement as he slid inside me in a single gliding stroke. Involuntary tears of joy flowed down the sides of my face. I squirmed ecstatically. I was beneath the man I loved, and I was his treasure to behold. His length pulsated within as if our beating hearts had merged as one. We breathed in unison – his breaths were fast and furious, mine demanding and urgent.

Bending down, *mon ange* devoured my oral cavity ravenously. Our tongues met in ardent enthusiasm. Our love knew no boundaries except love's transcendent supremacy. We moved as an entity, our synchronicity watched only by the invisible Olympian gods, who supervised our every move with invincible directedness. My lover could no longer hold off his powerhouse; his protrusion burst forth into sparks of dispensable lightning, sending shock waves of ecstatic currents deep within my core. In reciprocation, I, the willing recipient, discharged my delirious energy from my obelisk of affection, shooting flames of molten liquid onto our heaving chests, faces, and hair. We could not get enough of each other. Andy stayed buried inside me until we heard the moving vehicle grind to a stop. Only then did we realize that Jeffery would soon be opening the passenger doors for us to disembark. We dressed hurriedly, but I was sure remnants of our passion lingered in the back seat for our chauffeur to wipe clean.

Jeffery did not utter a word when he let the both of us out. I detected a knowing smile on his well-schooled servant's face, informing me that mum was the word of our evening's sojourn. After all, it was his proprietary call of duty that the 'downstairs' staff never reveal the secret lives of what went on above stairs. Jeffery was a trusted aide from the old school and had been in Uncle James' service for god knows how long. He would never betray our trust. When he brought in our luggage, Andy offered to tip him generously, but he replied, *"That wouldn't be necessary Sir! Enjoy your stay. If you require my service, ring the bell and I will bring the car round. Good-night Sir, and have a good evening."* With those last words he left *mon trésor* and me to our own devices.

That night, Andy and I hardly caught a wink of sleep, yet we were happily contented the following day. Absence had indeed made our hearts grow fonder.

July 2012

My correspondence with Dr. Arius continued regularly. He had become my confidant and a trusted friend. In one of his emails he inquired, *How's your renewed friendship with Andy progressing? By the sound of your correspondence, you seem happily appeased. Has this to do with Andy being back in your life, or is Walter loving you more than he ever did? LOL!*

I wrote:
My dear friend,
You sure have a way with words. The grateful heart is a joyful soul, and the more we appreciate our blessings,

the more exulted we are, both among ourselves and with those around us. To me, this is the ultimate joy. I think on the words of English hymn writer Isaac Watts and his inspiration, Psalm 98.

'Joy to the world! The Lord is come'; the Lord has indeed returned and my friendship with my ex is going strong.

'Let earth receive her King'; the 'king' remains as alpha as he always is and always will be. He will have it no other way but to be himself; therefore, if I embrace him back into my life, I'll have to accept him as he is. :)

'Let every heart prepare him room'; well, even my beloved Walter is preparing him room. He's been talking unceasingly about my ex, as if he's the exalted one. Even though they haven't met, he already thinks Andy is god in human form. Hahaha!

*'And heaven and nature sing'; I'm sure heaven and nature will be singing his praises when **A Harem Boy's Saga** series is available for sale at major bookstores and online. My editors are already in love with the perfect Andy and with the image I painted of my benevolent ex-'big brother'. They were part of the group that spearheaded my search for my ex, not to mention my darling husband, Wally, who was determined to see me locate Andy.*

'And heaven and nature sing'; they (my cheerleaders) are more excited about what Andy is doing these days than I am. I'm not denying my own excitement, but I know to keep my distance. I am older, wiser, and more cautious now, and I don't throw caution to the wind as I did in my teenage years.

'And heaven, and heaven, and nature sing'. As you so eloquently observed through our correspondence, I am indeed happy to be able to tell the story that I kept hidden for years. The truth has indeed set me free, and that is reason enough for rejoicing.

In regards to, 'Joy to the world! The Savior reigns'; I'm not sure, at this point in time, whether locating my ex-lover is as positive as my friendly supporters make it out to be. I have my reservations as to this 'savior's' reign.

'Let men their songs employ'; me finding Andy could be a blessing in disguise or otherwise. It's too early to tell. Therefore, I'm not employing my song of complete joy just yet.

'While fields and floods, rocks, hills, and plains repeat the sounding joy, repeat the sounding joy, repeat, repeat the sounding joy'. Hmmm! I don't know. With two alpha-males in my life, there may be no room for me to breathe. It could be stifling, to say the least.

'No more let sins and sorrows grow'; I think I'm mature enough to know that this will not be the case, no matter how much I would like this line to be true.

'Nor thorns infest the ground'; about this line I definitely have my doubts. There may be jealousies between the two alphas if I don't play my cards right.

'He comes to make His blessings flow'; this can be true to a certain extent but certainly not in its entirety. His blessings are certainly flowing in abundance as I write. Let's pray this holds true as life progresses forward...

'Far as the curse is found, far as the curse is found, far as the curse is found.' This is debatable.

As to, 'He rules the world with truth and grace.' I can say with utmost conviction that Andy will rule the world with truth and grace. Of this I am without doubt.

'And makes the nations prove the glories of His righteousness'; yes, yes and yes. Knowing my ex, this, he'll unquestionably do to this very day if he sets his mind to the task.

Last but not least, 'and wonders of His love, and wonders of His love, and wonders, wonders, of His love.' There is absolutely no question about this. We have been searching for each other for our entire lives, and now we have reunited. We were soul mates in past lives and in this one. We have found each other again.

My dear doctor, you are a dear, dear friend. I hope our friendship will continue to blossom throughout the seasons.

Blessings and Love,
Young.

3

The Illustrator

"I did some artistic nudes when I was eighteen with a French-Canadian photographer while I was modeling. They were beautiful shots, and they were not about nudity."
Lexa Doig

1967

Portobello Road, London, England

The following morning, Andy and I left to explore the Portobello Road weekend market, the largest antiques market in the United Kingdom. We took the tube to Notting Hill Gate, walked a short distance before hitting the cosmopolitan and energetic mid-to-late Victorian terrace houses and shops that squeezed tightly into the available spaces, adding intimacy and a pleasing scale to the streetscape. Further down the road, lining both sides of the narrow pavements were makeshift stalls, erected specially during the weekends. They sold all kinds of Victorian and Edwardian bric-a-bracs, not to mention antiques that had made their way from the far reaches of the colonial British Empire of yore. This vibrant street was also home to the Grade II Electric Cinema Club, which showed artsy Avant Garde movies. It was also one of Britain's oldest cinemas. About a third of the way down the winding road, the market ran underneath a series of adjacent bridges of the A40 road and the Hammersmith &

City line of the London Underground. Here, the section focused on secondhand clothes as well as trendy couture wear. A passageway from Portobello Road all the way to Ladbroke Grove was filled with the hippest stalls on the entire market, where one could find fashion, fashion and more throwaway fashions.

Portobello market was also made famous by the cult British children's book character Paddington Bear, featured in Michael Bond's books. Paddington enjoyed visiting Portobello Market daily. His friend Mr. Gruber owned an antique shop on the Portobello Road, with whom Paddington has his elevenses (tea or coffee taken at midmorning and often accompanied with snack) every day.

I was simply delighted to be there with my lover. My childlike curiosity drew me into every shop. Everything on display was as exciting as the next. We were ready to rest our tired feet halfway through the market. Like any decent Brits would do, we stopped for a cup of tea at a side street cafe. Just as we were entering the shop, someone waved to us. It was none other than Orion, a 'big brother' we knew from Daltonbury Hall. He was also resting his weary feet, accompanied by his artist friend, Julian, who lived in a flat in one of the Victorian buildings adjacent to Portobello Road. Orion insisted we join them at their table.

Orion and the Illustrator

"What brings you guys to this part of the world?" the 'big brother' inquired after introducing us to his companion.

"We are in London for a few days before heading to Cannes. We are cruising around the Greek islands before returning to Daltonbury. What a surprise to see you here!" Andy exclaimed excitedly. *"What are you doing in Portobello Road, old chap?"*

"I'm visiting Julian. He is an accomplished illustrator. He asked me to be his model for an upcoming project. We came down here for some refreshments after a couple of hour's work at his studio."

Before the BB could continue, Julian chimed in, *"I'm working on an illustrated ad campaign for a casual wear company. Instead of the run-of-the-mill photography assignment of models wearing the clothes, the company commissioned me to illustrate a series of models in various provocative stages of undress, wearing only casual tops or bottoms.*

"I found Orion through an ad agency. That's how we met. How do you guys know each other?"

"We attend the same school," my Valet replied.

"My, oh my, your school sure recruits good-looking chaps," the illustrator commented. *"Will the two of you be interested in modeling for me? You'll be paid for your time. If you are available, I can take some Polaroid test shots and go from there. It'll be a half day's work at most. I illustrate from photographs I take of my models."*

I gave Andy an approving puppy look, indicating that I wanted to get my hands on that project. My guardian gave me an understanding smile. He knew what was going through my mind and said, *"I believe my charge has already given you his nod of approval. If he desires something, he usually gets his way. This young one has a way with me."*

"Fantastic! I take Young's nod as an agreement to my request?" Julian asked affirmatively. *"In that case, I'll take some pictures of the three of you at my flat after we finished our beverages. You can see some of my artwork and illustrations. This will give you some idea of the type of work I do."*

The Illustrator and his Flat

Proceeding down a side street, we arrived at a quaint Victorian building where Julian lived and worked from his second-floor studio flat. It was a charming and cozy space and provided sufficient room for a bachelor to live. He had been living there for the past three years. Julian's artwork hung on all the available wall spaces, and some leaned against the walls. His work bore an uncanny resemblance to the famous artist and illustrator Maxfield Parish, yet it possessed an original style that was childlike with hints of innocent eroticism. I was impressed by the attractive English-Frenchman's illustrations.

Julian was born in Cornwall to an English mother and a French father. He moved to London after graduating from Poole College of Art in Bournemouth. After working at an established advertising agency, he became a full-time illustrator. Commissions for his work came trickling in, and he was soon able to purchase a comfortable flat. By the time of his passing from AIDS-related illnesses in 1982, Julian had established a name for himself. He was known as an artist and illustrator in the United Kingdom and in France.

"Let's start by taking some individual Polaroid pictures of Andy, followed by Young. I've already photographed Orion, so we'll have him in the group shot when I photograph the three of you together. How does that sound?" The illustrator enquired?

"Fine by me," I replied.

Julian behaved professionally throughout our photo-shoot. Andy was given a pair of loose-fitting sweat pants without any top, while Orion and I wore only sweatshirts without trousers. While I was sandwiched between Orion and Andy, my lover sprouted a hard-on. He was standing behind me against my nakedness and began rotating his pelvis against my derrière, causing my libido to stir. My cock started to wake with each of Andy's gentle gyrating motions. I was soon standing erect and so was Orion's manhood. As we stood in close proximity and caressed each other, our organs began rubbing against each other as if performing an erotic dance. I could not subdue my bobbing erection with my Valet's hardness bouncing against my derriere. His encouragement stirred our trio's sensuality to a heightened state of arousal.

Julian took this provocation as a sign that he would be getting some superb photographs, both for his portfolio and for his personal enticement. Although the illustrator was clothed, his hardening genitalia peeked over the top of his jersey pants. Glistening strings of translucent fluid were leaking onto his hairy torso. He had on a sleeveless cropped top that displayed his well-defined six-pack. His bulbous pronouncement approved of our sensuality. He kept clicking as he viewed his three models through his camera lens. He did not stop circling the room as we propagated our concupiscence.

Orion wasted no time in his active persuasion. We kissed passionately for the camera and for our personal gratification. Andy urged me from behind as he pulled my waist towards his swelling protuberance. Orion's pulverizing protrusion pressed compellingly against my hardness from the opposite end. Bending forwards, I scooped his erection into my eager mouth, ablactating his lusciousness as if I was deprived of nourishment. His leakage tasted deliciously masculine and his groin smelled deliriously intoxicating. Andy dropped his pants. He was gliding his stiffness against my butt cheeks. Spitting to lubricate his curved member, he eased into my offering orifice. My lover and the 'big brother' filled me to the brim from opposite directions.

Julian could no longer hold off his desires. He discarded his sweatpants to join the party, feeding me his pleasurable inches together with Orion's jutting edifice. I was in seventh heaven, engulfing both shafts into my oral opening. Taking turns to satisfy our frenzied lust, I devoured them hungrily. I was a famished baby needing feed, and the men took turns weaning my esurient mouth. I promised them further satisfaction when Andy had consummated my rear. Our alluring sexuality took on an alternative flight when my lover could no longer hold off his sexual patronage. Letting out several cries, he filled me with his adoring emotions, depositing his virility deep within my person. He slumped his heaving chest against the small of my back while his waning length slid slowly away from my dripping hollow, only to be replaced by Orion's gluttonous engorgement. The model eased into my well-lubricated opening effortlessly. He began our love dance with a gentle foxtrot before progressing to a hot Peruvian salsa, reverting to an irresistible Buenos Aires mambo, and finally ending with the crème de la crème of dirty dancing, an Argentinian tango that filled me with his oozing Latino charisma. I desired more, more than my fill. Julian seemed to read my lascivious thoughts. He took over the model's position and was now pounding inside me with vigor. He could no longer hold off his exhilarating urgency. The artist unloaded into my obedient aperture. Their intoxicating virility mixed with my masturbatory actions sent me shaking uncontrollably; I exploded all over the floor. The BB and my beloved did not want any of my spills to go to waste. They lapped up every drop before feeding me my seed in a three-way kiss. We suckled, we caressed and we shared my delectable appetizer between us. Julian had moved behind to my back. He delved his tongue into my pulsating wetness, relishing on Andy's and Orion's deposits before plunging his salivating mouth onto my semi-erect boyhood, savoring the remnants of my ejaculation.

    The four of us spent the remainder of the day together in the warmth of Julian's flat before taking in a provocative movie at the nearby Electric Cinema Club. As Lexa Doig had professed, *"I did some artistic nudes when I was eighteen with a French-Canadian photographer while I was modeling. They were beautiful shots, and they were not about nudity."* I, like Ms. Doig, also did some artistic nudes when I was an adolescent with an English-French photographer while I was modeling. They, too, were beautiful shots, and they were not about nudity but artistic expressions of love.

4

The Differences

"The stupid believe that to be truthful is easy; only the artist, the great artist, knows how difficult it is."
Willa Cather

Late Summer 1967

London, England

Andy and I decided to go to a play the day before we were scheduled to depart to meet Oscar in the South of France. Uncle James was in town and invited us for dinner at *Le Gavroche*, a French restaurant that had just opened at 61 Lower Sloane Street. James knew the owners, Michel and Albert Roux, who were also my uncle's clients at the Hong Kong & Shanghai Banking Corporation. They had invited my London guardian to the restaurant's official opening, and James had decided to bring us along with him. We met him at his town house after attending the pre-premiere theatre performance of *Sweet Charity*, made famous by Shirley MacLaine in the movie of the same name. Andy had managed to obtain tickets through his friend, who was a set designer working on the production.

Taxi Dancers

As was the case, I was in awe during and after the musical. As we sat and enjoyed beverages after the performance, I couldn't help asking my beloved, *"What's a 'taxi dancer'? It was Charity's profession in the show."*

"A 'taxi dancer' is a paid dance partner in a partner dance. Don't utter a word. I know what your next question is going to be what's a partner dance?" Andy replied knowingly.

He continued, *"Partner dances are dances whose basic choreography involves coordinated dancing between two partners. Good examples are ballroom dances, during which two people dance in a coordinated manner.*

"During the 1920s and '30s in America when, taxi dancing enjoyed peak popularity, patrons in a taxi dance hall would buy dance tickets for ten cents per dance. That gave rise to the term 'dime-a-dance girl'. When a patron presented a ticket to a taxi dancer, she would dance with him for the length of a single song. The taxi dancers would earn commission on every dance ticket that they collected from their dance partners. Typically, half the ticket price went to paying the orchestra, dance hall, and other operating expenses, while the other half would go to the taxi dancer. The 'ticket-a-dance' system was the centerpiece of the taxi-dance halls where the taxi dancers worked. During the 20s, taxi dancers worked only a handful of hours per evening. They frequently made two to three times as much as women who worked in factories or stores did. After World War II, taxi dancing became less popular, and most of the taxi-dance halls disappeared by the late 50s, early 60s. That's why you don't hear of these types of establishments nowadays."

My curiosity got the better of me. I asked, *"Did taxi dancers and taxi dance halls go underground like E.R.O.S.?"*

My Valet burst out laughing before he spoke, *"Kind of like that, but you can still pay to dance with a female employee in some nightclubs in the United States, especially in Los Angeles. These contemporary clubs no longer use the ticket-a-dance system, but operate on time-clocks and punch-card systems. This allows the patron to pay for the dancer's time by the hour. Some of these modern dance clubs operate in buildings where taxi dancing was held in the early 20th century. They are now known as Hostess Clubs. In some cases, they do operate as prostitution rings.*

"You see, Young, taxi dancing is becoming more common in settings where partners are in short supply. This involves both male and female dancers. Male dancers are often employed on cruise ships to dance with single female passengers. The growth in 'Tango Tourism' to Buenos Aires, Argentina has led to an increase in both formal and informal taxi dancing services in the milongas (dance halls). Some proprietors are in the business of selling holiday romance." My Valet gave me a wicked wink.

"You mean prostitution?" I asked.

"That's correct. Much like the word Courtesan or Cicisbeo, the term 'taxi dancer' has morphed into a derogatory word meaning that refers to a prostitute. But the original meanings of these words are quite different.

"For example, a Courtesan was originally a female who was part of a royal entourage, usually as the mistress of a high-ranking man. On the other hand, the historical term of a cicisbeo refers to the escort or lover to a married woman in 18th-century Italy. They are not prostitutes in the usual sense."

Pederasty

I continued questioning, *"Is it a little like the way the word 'pederasty' has been bastardized?"*

"Yes, my boy. You are correct. You and I are sufficiently educated to know that pederasty is not a disparaging term, but many people do not understand it

that way. As we are taught, pederasty simply means a homosexual relationship between an adult male and an adolescent male outside his immediate family. The word paederasty derives from the Greek word paiderastia (love of boys), a compound derived from παῖς (pais) 'child, boy' and ἐραστής (erastēs) 'lover'. Now that we are on this topic, we may as well discuss the meaning of this word in greater detail.

"Historically, pederasty has taken the form of a variety of customs and practices within different cultures from the Eastern to the Western hemispheres alike. The status of pederasty has changed over the course of history. It has been idealized and criminalized. In European history, its most structured cultural manifestation was 'Athenian pederasty', which reached its zenith in the 6th century BC."

I chimed in before Andy could continue, *"Although I understand the meaning of pederasty; what exactly is 'Athenian pederasty'?"*

My big brother explained, *"Athenian pederasty entailed a formal bond between an adult man and an adolescent boy outside his immediate family, which often consisted of a sexual and loving relationship. As an erotic and educational custom, it was initially employed by the upper classes as a means of teaching the young and it conveyed important cultural values, such as bravery and restraint, to them.*

"Athenian society generally encouraged the erastes (a 'top' or active partner) to pursue a boy to love; he would sometimes even sleep on the youth's stoop and otherwise go to great lengths to make himself noticed. At the same time, the boy and his family were expected to put up resistance and not give in too easily. Boys who succumbed too readily were looked down upon. As a result, the quest for a desirable eromenos (a 'bottom' or passive partner) was fiercely competitive."

I chirped in, *"You mean, like the way you were pursuing me during the early stages of our relationship?"*

Andy gave me a wide grin, ruffled my hair and continued without attempting to answer my question. He continued, *"In regards to Greek pederasty – Plato, an early critic of sexual intercourse in pederastic relationships, proposed that men avoid all carnal expression of their love for boys. Instead, he advised them to progress from admiration of the lover's specific virtues to love of virtue itself in an abstract form. While copulation with boys was often criticized and seen as shameful and brutish, other aspects of the relationship were considered beneficial, as indicated in proverbs such as, "A lover is the best friend a boy will ever have."*

"A pederastic relationship had to be approved by the boy's father. Boys who entered into such relationships in their teens were around the same age that Greek girls were when they married. The mentor was expected to teach the young man and to see to his education. The boys were also given certain ceremonial gifts."

"Would you say it was similar to the way we are treated in the Arab Households harems we serve?" I queried.

"Yes, very similar. Although in Greek pederasty, the physical dimension ranged from full chastity to sexual intercourse. Greek pederastic art shows seduction scenes as well as sexual relations. In the seduction scenes, the man is standing, grasping the boy's chin with one hand and reaching to fondle his genitals with the other. In the sexual scenes, the partners stand embracing face to face, and the older of the two engaged in intercrural sex with the younger. Anal sex is almost never shown, and when it was, it surprised observers. The practice was ostensibly disparaged, and the Athenians often called it jocular names after their Dorian neighbors ('cretanize', 'laconize', 'chalcidize'). While historians such as Dover and Halperin

hold that only the man experienced pleasure, artistic and poetic depictions tell a different story, and other historians assert that it is 'a modern fairy tale' that the younger eromenos was never aroused."

I stopped my Valet to ask, *"What is intercrural sex?"*

My lover smiled at me seductively before answering, *"Intercrural sex is not something you'd like us to do, my darling boy. Trust me; you'll not enjoy this form of sexuality as much as the way we usually make love."*

He continued, *"Intercrural sex is a type of non-penetrative sex in which the man places his penis between his partner's thighs (often with lubrication) and thrusts to create friction.*

"Now, let me continue before you interrupt me again. *From the early Republican times of Ancient Rome, it was perfectly normal for a man to desire and pursue boys. However, penetration was illegal for free-born youths; the only boys who were legally allowed to be passive sexual partners were slaves or former slaves. They were known as 'freedmen,' and the exception was only made with regard to their former masters. For slaves, there was no protection under the law, even against rape.*

"The result was that pederasty largely lost its function as a ritual part of education. It was instead seen as an activity primarily driven by one's sexual desires and competing with the desire for women. In this way, the social acceptance of pederastic relations waxed and waned throughout the centuries. Conservative thinkers condemned it — along with other forms of indulgence.

"Tacitus (a Roman senator and historian) attacks the Greek customs of 'gymnasia et otia et turpes amores' (palaestrae, idleness, and shameful loves). However, almost all the Roman emperors indulged in male love — most of it of a pederastic nature.

"As Edward Gibbon (an English historian and a Member of Parliament) mentioned, "Of the first fifteen emperors, Claudius was the only one whose taste in love was 'entirely correct'." T*he implication is that he was the only emperor not to take men or boys as lovers.*

"On the other hand, Martial (a Latin poet from Hispania) appears to have favored it, going as far as to essentialize not the sexual use of the catamite (a boy who submits to a sexual relationship with a man) but his nature as a boy: upon being discovered by his wife 'inside a boy' and offered the 'same thing' by her, he retorts with a list of mythological personages who, despite being married, took young male lovers, and concludes by rejecting her offer since 'a woman merely has two vaginas'."

I couldn't help myself but interrupt, *"So, does the saying 'A boy for pleasure; a woman for procreation' hold?"*

"I'm afraid so, my love. You see, Greek pederasty in its various forms was often the subject of philosophical debates; thinkers would argue about whether the carnal type was proper as opposed to a more spiritual eroticism.

"Pederastic couples were also said to be feared by tyrants, because the bond between the friends was stronger than that of obedience to a tyrannical ruler. Plutarch gave us an example of the Athenians Harmodius and Aristogeiton. Others, such as Aristotle, claimed that the Cretan lawgivers encouraged pederasty as a means of population control, by directing love and sexual desire into relations between males. Whatever forms pederasty takes, it is definitely not the same as pedophilia."

Pedophilia

"My dearest Valet, what is pedophilia? I've never heard such a word. Please explain?" I said with great curiosity.

"This is a relatively new word. The first time I heard it spoken was by Dr. Nuein and Dr. Henderson, when they gave me advanced tutorials in my sexual education class. This word is not officially used in any professional medical studies papers. Currently, our sex education professors are doing preliminary research on this subject. It's a new field of study. In ancient times, nothing was called pedophilia because pederasty was an accepted form of homosexual relationship.

"Our teachers described pedophilia as a psychiatric disorder in persons sixteen years of age or older, typically characterized by a primary or exclusive sexual interest in prepubescent children (generally eleven years or younger, though specific diagnosis criteria for the disorder extend the cut-off point for prepubescence to age thirteen). An adolescent who is sixteen years of age or older must be at least five years older than the prepubescent child before the attraction can be diagnosed as pedophilia.

"In contemporary usage, pedophilia means any sexual interest in children or the act of child sexual abuse, a term also known as 'pedophilic behavior'. Pedophilia is the act or fantasy, on an adult's part, of engaging in sexual activity with a child or children. This commonly used application also extends to the sexual interest in and sexual contact with pubescent or post-pubescent minors.

"Although this 'abnormal' behavior is mostly documented in men, women can also exhibit it. They also mentioned that researchers assume the current available estimates underrepresent the true number of female pedophiles. No cure for pedophilia has been developed thus far, but there are therapies that can reduce the incidence of child sexual abuse. You see, Young, the word 'pedophile' is a contemporary term because in ancient times there was no such thing as a pedophile."

"Is that why E.R.O.S. is a secret society? Because it does not conform to the mid-20th century ideals of what a 'normal' sexual relationship should be?" I interrupted my guardian.

"Briefly, the answer is yes. The truth told before its time is a dangerous thing," my lover commented, and as he looked at his watch, he indicated that it was time to meet Uncle James for our dinner appointment.

5

At Le Gavroche

"There are three constants in life: change, choice and principles."
Stephen Covey

July 2012

Although I had not met Dr. Arius in person, I felt like we had known each other for a long time. Our regular correspondences had brought us closer as friends. I continued answering his questions from his survey as well and as truthfully as I could. In one of his emails, he inquired, *"Young, in **Initiation**, you mentioned that you missed home terribly during the first few weeks at Daltonbury Hall. It must have been a very different world compared to what you were used to in Malaysia. How did you cope with not having your family near you?"*

"That's an easy question Dr. A.S.; Nikee was there to help me through the lonely times. My ex-'big brother' was there to guide me and listen to my problems and heartaches. Without Nikee, I believe it would have been harder for me to cope in my new environment. That was one of the reasons I was infatuated with Nikee – he was a good listener, and he paid attention to my needs.

"As much as I missed my mother, aunties and female cousins, I was happy to be in England, a country I had always dreamed of living in since I was nine years old. I was totally delighted to be away from my tyrannical father. My fear of him caused me anxiety when I was living at home. Uncle James, my surrogate father, was a wonderful force in my life, because we could relate to each other. His stalwart advice and understanding of my harem life also furthered our relationship. I grew into a man under James' guidance. I could confide anything to my uncle, which I could never do with my biological father. A perfect example of Uncle James' unconditional love for Andy and me was in the summer of 1967. He had invited us to the opening of Le Gavroche, a new French restaurant in London..."

1967

The Journey

As always, it was wonderful to see Uncle James after several months of absence. On our way to the restaurant in his silver Rolls Royce, he told us, *"You boys look fantastic."* Turning to my Valet, he continued jokingly, *"I trust you are looking after this 'son' of mine well? If Young tells me otherwise, you will never hear the end of it."*

"How could I not look after this beloved boy? He's like a fluffy kitten. He's always curious, asking the most inappropriate questions whenever they come to mind. At times, I've had to apologize to our company for Young's inappropriate queries. He's a handful when it comes to inquisitiveness, but I love him dearly nevertheless." Andy replied.

Changing the subject, Uncle James inquired, *"How are your parents, Andy? The last time we met, you and your dad were not speaking. Have you made amends?"*

Shaking his head, my Valet replied sadly, *"I'm afraid not, Sir. My father refused to accept my homosexuality, and he does not even acknowledge Young's* existence. This is what bothers me the most. I cannot respect a man who doesn't respect and accept the person I love."

"I'm sorry to hear that, Andy. Many men from my generation or older have a difficult time with the way the younger generation lives. In many cases, it's out of fear and misunderstanding of homosexuality. That fear drives them to reject gay, lesbian, bisexual and transgender people. Although I'm not putting all the blame on religious indoctrination, in many instances, strict and overzealous religious teachings also breed fanatical clerics who organize 'witch hunts' against the GLBT population.

"If a person does not understand the culture or lifestyle of another, he or she often feels threatened by that person's presence. I'm not only referring to gay men or women, but also to foreign nationalities that are different from their 'accepted' cultural way of life. That's the reason so many insults and prejudiced comments get thrown at people of different nationalities. Many wars are fought due of the fear of the unknown."

Andy and I listened attentively to my uncle's words. My lover remarked, *"As much as I love my dad, I don't know how to deal with his small-mindedness. He made it clear to me that unless I turn from my homosexual life and become 'normal,' he will never accept me. This will never do for me – I cannot live a life of lies and deceit just to please my father."*

Uncle James shook his head and said with a sigh, *"I'm sorry to hear that your relationship with your dad has deteriorated. You know, son, it would not be a bad idea for you to reach out to him. As is often the case, an older a person gets into a set way of life, incapable of accepting new ideas and concepts. Many think they have lived through the prime of their lives and know all the answers. Many people become stuck in a certain time period and have difficulties keeping pace with the ever-changing world.*

"If you want my advice, I suggest you take the initial step to reach out to your dad. Actions speak louder than words. When your father sees you are the same Andy he has loved since the day you were born, and being gay changes nothing, his heart and mind will soften to accepting you back into his life. The healing process takes time, but be the first to reach out to him. He'll love you for that. You don't have to give in to his demands. Possibly, with some gentle persuasion from your siblings and mother, he'll see that his son has grown in strength and spirit.

"Nobody wins when both sides are unwilling to take the first step to reach out to the other. Be a true gentleman, but also be sturdy and firm when talking with your father. Show him you possess inner strength and chivalry. Let him be the judge to see how brave his homosexual son has grown to become – a man of his own."

Andy responded, *"You are so wise, Uncle James. I wish my dad was more like you."*

"In every situation, there are always choices. Choose and tread with courage; then you'll never regret the path you have selected." James advised.

"Does that mean I, too, have to reach out to my dad?" I queried.

Giving me a gentle smile, my 'surrogate dad' gestured his approval. He continued, *"There are basic human principles that we, as civilized human beings, stand by. When your principles are right, you should stand by your beliefs. But that does not mean being unrelentingly stubborn. Listen to the other people's opinions before comparing your belief system to theirs. You'll find that there are usually more similarities than differences. Don't make the mistake of trying to convince them to agree with you; allow them the benefit of the doubt and let them judge for themselves. Andy, more often than not, they will come around to your way of thinking if and when your actions derive from a genuine source. The universe has a way of rewarding the pure of heart."*

We were both grateful for Uncle James' advice when the Rolls arrived at the front entrance of Le Gavroche, aptly named after the character Gavroche from Victor Hugo's novel *Les Misérables*.

Le Gavroche

As soon as we entered the packed restaurant, Madam Alexis and Monsieur Albert Roux came to greet my uncle, who introduced his protégés to the couple. Madam asked, *"Young, your uncle has told me a lot about you. He said you are an incredible artist and an aspiring fashion designer. Which fashion school are you planning to enroll at?"*

Her comments caught me by surprise. I did not know how to respond. Instead, my Valet replied on my behalf, *"It's too early to determine that. He still has a few years in boarding school before he's ripe for college."*

"It's never too early to plan," Alexis commented. *"I can recommend several excellent fashion schools in London. In fact, one of our guests, who's here this evening, is a lecturer at one of the prestigious fashion schools in England whom I'd love to introduce to Young."* Turning to me, she continued, *"Your dear uncle suggested I recommend a few excellent fashion design schools to you."*

"That would be wonderful, thank you. I'd be delighted to listen to your recommendations."

"In that case, you'll have to sit next to me during dinner so we'll have a chance to talk," Madam pronounced before proceeding to greet the newly arriving guests.

Conversation with the Ladies

True to her word, I was seated next to Alexis and a lady by the name of Ms. Gay Yates. She was dressed in an electric green outfit with a matching hat and shoes. She was a fashion lecturer at The Harrow College of Technology and Art in London. Throughout dinner, which consisted of several courses, one being the restaurant's famous Le Caneton Gavroche (whole poached duck in a light consommé served with three sauces, for two) and Omelette Rothschild, Alexis remarked, *"Gay, this young chap is planning a career in fashion. His uncle says he's an excellent sketcher and a talented artist. He has organized fashion shows and designed garments for women in Malaysia and the Middle East. I think he'll make an excellent student at the Harrow College of Art."*

Ms. Gay smiled and looked me and Andy in the eyes before speaking in her trademark high-pitched sing-song voice, *"Really! Both these young men are simply too delicious to eat,"* she joked. *"Tell me more about yourself, Young."*

I was amused by her happy-go-lucky demeanor and sing-song voice. I remarked humbly, *"My uncle and Madam Alexis are too complimentary about my amateurish fashion accomplishments. Although I have designed stage costumes for a couple of musical revues at my father's nightclub, I can hardly call myself a costume designer. My aunty and cousin did teach me some basic sewing skills. There is much I need to learn in fashion, but I'm very interested in attending fashion school and becoming a professional fashion designer."*

Before I could expand, Gay posed another question, *"How did you land a designing position with Arab ladies in the Middle East?"*

My Valet quickly jumped in with an answer before I could disclose too much information to the woman, *"We are in a foreign student exchange program with the U.A.E.*

The women in one of the Arab households where we were stationed learned that Young was well versed in fashion. They asked him to style their wardrobes for their Eid al-Fitr celebration. As a token of appreciation for his excellent work, we accompanied them to Paris during Haute Couture week to visit the designers' ateliers so Young could experience what it's like to be a professional fashion designer."

"Excellent, this is a great starting point. When Young is ready to apply to a British fashion school and he decides to apply to Harrow College of Art, I'll make sure our principal, Mr. G. Lippmann, considers his application carefully." Ms. Yates resumed, *"Stay in touch with me when you are in London. I'd like to know about this boy's fashion progress. As educators, we like to encourage students who are genuinely interested in fashion at a young age.*

"There are several other excellent schools I'd be happy to recommend to him when he is ready to enroll. Make sure you keep me posted on Young's educational developments."

Just then, the restaurant's notable Soufflé Suissesse (cheese soufflé baked on double cream) arrived at our table. We consumed the scrumptious dinner and dessert to our heart's content, savoring the French classical delicacies and enjoying the atmosphere at Le Gavroche's grand opening.

6

Côte d'Azur

"Everyone has people in their lives that are gay, lesbian or transgender or bisexual. They may not want to admit it, but I guarantee they know somebody."
Billie Jean King

July 2012

Dr. Arius continued to question me during our regular correspondence. He asked, *"How did you feel the first time you met Andy at the Kipling Rowing Club boat house? Did he come on to you as soon as you were introduced, or did your chemistry develop over time? What was your impression of him when you were initially acquainted?"*

"My dear doctor, I remember that day very clearly. The memory of our first encounter never left my mind after all these years. The first time I saw Andy, he and four other naked rowing-team members were carrying their rowboats to 'Swan'. His imposing hands and tall, handsome physique stirred a longing within me that I had never felt before. It was love at first sight. As soon as our eyes met, sparks flew between us. I was too young and inexperienced to understand this kind of organic attraction. I was dumbfounded by his kind eyes and charming smile. For reasons unknown to me, I felt that I'd found my soul mate, but at the time, I'd never heard of a soul mate. I only knew I would have a loving relationship with this man, even before we had the 3-way forest rendezvous with Nikee.

"It was more than lust. My emotional stirring was similar to the feeling I had when Walter (my current life partner) and I first met. I just kept thinking, 'It would be wonderful if he were my boyfriend.' It wasn't logic; I just knew he was the one.

"Andy certainly did not come on to me the moment we met. In fact, he was extremely polite when we were introduced. He shook my hand and uttered some pleasantries while staring into my eyes. His gaze never left mine, even though my eyes occasionally strayed to glance at his endowment. I was too mesmerized by his outgoing ruggedness. That was what attracted me to him.

"Although he did not show any outward physical attraction to me, our magnetism drew us together. I guess he knew I was charmed by him, since he was already trained in the art of sensuality and sexuality, before I was inducted into E.R.O.S. He taught me the art of loving.

"I was too naive to understand the attraction we both felt. I thought Andy was just being his friendly self, since he behaved similarly around his friends and acquaintances. The occasional chance meeting we had at our school was always pleasant, cordial and courteous even though his gaze seldom left my eyes. His beautiful, piercing eyes have a way of stripping me naked. More often than not, I was the first to look away.

"My infatuation for Andy developed after my three-way encounter by the forest pond. The smell of his person intoxicated me, especially during our love-making session. I tried hard not to fall in love with him, because Nikee constantly instructed me to 'play the field'. I was afraid to fall in love with Andy in case it would upset my mentor.

"It was after the gym-room orgy that I realized he had set his sights on me. It was the longing way he glanced at me during our various entanglements with others within the group. He was watching me like a hawk, making sure I wasn't abused and that I was enjoying myself throughout *the sexcapade. If I had expressed any discomfort during the event, he or Nikee or both of them would have whisked me away from that situation. I stayed because I felt like Andy was making love to me through his loving watchfulness, even though we were making love with others. My lover's presence got me through my four years of service in the Arab Households with flying colors. It was his divine sequential love that provided stability in my young life. I'm extremely grateful to my ex-Valet and lover."*

A good example of Andy's unconditional love was during our Greek Island sojourn...

1967

Cannes, French Riviera

...The following morning, after attending Le Gavroche restaurant's opening soiree, Jeffery (Uncle James' chauffeur) drove us in the silver Rolls Royce to a private air field by Heathrow Airport to board the Simorgh, in which we would fly to the South of France. Upon arrival at Nice - Côte d'Azur Airport, we were chauffeured to the infamous Carlton Hotel, located on La Croisette where we stayed for a couple of nights before boarding the Kahyya'm, docked at Cannes Harbor.

The scenic beauty of the French Riviera was breathtaking as our Bentley rounded the winding roads towards the Carlton. Built during the Belle Époque era, this hotel was an imposing palatial structure where Grace Kelly had first met her prince charming, Prince Rainier III of Monaco, in the year 1955. She subsequently became Her Serene Highness, Princess Grace of Monaco.

Oscar was already waiting for us at the hotel's expansive lobby as our bell boys brought in our luggage. Standing beside him was a young couple whom my BB introduced as Mary and Alfonzo. They had met at the

Vienna University when my lover had gone to finalize some entrance paperwork to the medical school. They would soon be students at the same university. They had decided to go on an adventurous sightseeing vacation around the Riviera.

Mary & Alfonzo

The good-looking Alfonzo came from a wealthy Spanish aristocratic family in Barcelona, while eighteen-year-old Mary was a bright, aspiring model from America who had modeled for French Elle and Harper's Bazaar. She was also enrolling at the University of Vienna to pursue an economics degree. She'd met Alfonzo in Paris while modeling for Elle. The twenty-year-old Spaniard, a playboy of the western world, was smitten by Mary's beauty and had pursued her relentlessly. In turn, she persuaded him to return to university to pursue a law degree instead of drifting aimlessly as an international party boy. The two were fun-loving and easy to get along with, and we became better acquainted while people-watching at an outdoor cafe on the busy boulevard.

Mary asked, *"Are the three of you lovers?"*

Surprised by her remark, Andy replied, *"Do we look like we are?"*

"The way the three of you interact gave you guys away. When I was modeling for Elle in Paris, I met several gay designers, makeup artists and hair stylists, along with photographers and journalists. The artistic world is full of delightful gay, lesbian, bisexual and transgender talent.

"A leggy, gorgeous girl, Bryanna, whom I was paired with in a shoot, is transgendered. In fact we have been booked to do a photo-shoot in Athens in a few days' time. Bryanna is such a joy to work with. She knows all the trendiest and best places to visit in any major metropolis. I learned a lot from her. She taught me makeup and hair

styling tricks, in case an appointed artist and hairdresser didn't show. I can always fall back on her techniques for my beauty regime."

I couldn't help inquiring, *"Do I get to meet Bryanna if we 'happen' to be in Athens during the day of your shoot?"* I asked, while my inquisitive eyes told my Valet that I was up to one of my mischievous tricks.

Andy chimed in amusingly before Mary could continue, *"This young man is always trying to get himself invited to artsy projects, especially fashion-related ones. He is passionate about fashion. Knowing Young, if you don't extend the invitation, he'll invite himself anyway. He has a way of soliciting an invitation. He knows how to get into your vulnerable self when you least expect it."*

Mary answered laughingly, *"He's so cute when he gives me that boyish look. I can't resist inviting him to the shoot. I'll introduce you guys to Bryanna if you are interested in meeting her. She is certainly an eccentric character. I'm sure she'd love to meet you guys.*

"Alfonzo and I are leaving for Antibes tomorrow to spend the day sightseeing in this ancient Roman city. Would you boys like to join us?"

Alfonzo added, *"It would be great if you can. I've rented a Sunbeam Alpine convertible, much like the one Grace Kelly drove in 'To Catch A Thief.' I want Mary to experience what Her Serene Highness, Princess Grace, experienced while driving along the winding coastline of Cote d'Azur."*

"We don't want to impose ourselves on the two of you. You are here on a romantic holiday." Oscar interposed.

"Don't be silly, old chap, we'd love to have you guys join us, right, Mary?"

"Of course! That's why we flew here with you this morning. There's nothing like seeing the scenic Azure coast with like-minded friends."

Alfonzo's remark caused Oscar to give Andy and me a flirtatious glance, as if there was a hidden meaning to the man's words. We said nothing but nodded in agreement.

"We'll have to arrange with Captain Kasim to sail not tomorrow morning but the day after. The Kahyya'm is docked at the harbor waiting for us. To return the favor, will the 2 of you sail with us to Athens? Then we can be there for your photo-shoot. How does that sound?" Andy enquired of Alfonzo and Mary.

"That's sounds great! Then we can spend more time getting to know one another." Alfonzo gave Andy, Oscar and me a roguish smile, as if he had some amorous plan up his sleeves.

The Three of Us

That evening Andy, Oscar and I had dinner at a quaint restaurant in Marche Forville (Covered Market) to the west of Rue Meynadier. It continues to be the city's most popular fresh vegetable and flower market to this day. It was lined with gourmet eateries, famous for their pasta noodles. As soon as I'd ordered the restaurant's famous mussels and spaghetti dish with plenty of seafood-y saffron cream sauce, I spoke to Oscar, saying, *"Alfonzo and Mary seem fun to hang out with. What's their story?"*

Andy responded before my BB had a chance to answer, *"Young, you are always so inquisitive about people's life stories. I'm sure they are happily in love just like we are."*

Oscar smiled and replied wickedly, *"Well Andy, you may be quite mistaken by their outward show of lovemanship."*

"What do you mean by being mistaken by their outward show of 'lovecraft'?" My lover leaned to our other lover enquiringly.

"I bumped into Alfonzo when I was handing in my paperwork at the university's administration office. I caught him staring at me. He came over to borrow my pen when I was putting it away. It was his excuse to get acquainted with me – there were pens on the counter, but he made an excuse to borrow mine so he could start a conversation. During the course of our dialogue, he would accidentally and at times purposefully lay his hands on my shoulders or my waist. I've a funny feeling he may be using Mary as a cover-up for his other sexual liaisons. They may very well have an agreement to an open relationship."

"Did you confide this to Mary?" my Valet asked.

"I never mentioned anything, but I have a hunch that she is a femme lesbian. Since the both of them get on well, they could be using each other as a front, pretending to be lovers in front of their parents and friends. Beneath it all, they may be living completely different lives."

"What's a femme lesbian?" I questioned.

With a wide Cheshire grin on his face, my BB explained, *"A femme lesbian is a lesbian that takes the more receptive role in a sexual relationship, as opposed to a 'bull dyke.'"*

That word caused more confusion, so I continued questioning, *"What's a 'bull dyke'?"*

"A 'bull dyke' is a rather derogatory term for a masculine lesbian." Andy explained.

"They're sometimes referred to as 'Bulldiker', 'Bulldiger or 'Bulldagger'. They all mean a butch, masculine lesbian." Oscar expounded. *"Then there is 'Chapstick Dyke' or 'Chapstick Lesbian' which refers to a lesbian that is between a 'bulldyke' and a 'lipstick lesbian'."*

"I didn't know there were so many different kinds of lesbians! How did you know all these terms? And what in the world is a 'lipstick lesbian'?" I cocked my head, more eager than ever to remember all these new words.

"Young, a 'lipstick lesbian' can also be known as a 'doily dyke' – it's a pop culture variation of a feminine lesbian. Then there is 'baby dyke,' a young, immature, or recently 'out' lesbian. There are also 'Bi-Dykes', 'Bykes' or 'Half dykes'; these describe bisexual women who are more attracted to women than to men or lesbian or dyke-identified women who acknowledge some sexual or emotional affection for men. These terms are used by some women who identify themselves as being primarily attracted to genderqueer individuals."

"Good God! I didn't know there were such a variety of lesbians. And what in the world is genderqueer?" I exclaimed.

"There are more to come. There are 'Soft dykes,' who are also referred to as 'Soft Butch'. This, my dear boy, describes lesbians who dress in masculine clothing but retain a feminine appearance, such as having longer hair, chapstick, clear nail polish, feminine shoes so on and so forth.

"Last but not least, there is 'D.I.D', short for 'Dyke in Denial,' a term used by lesbians to refer to women who fit the stereotype of a lesbian in behavior or appearance but self-identify as bisexual, pansexual, or heterosexual. 'D.I.D' is also used as a referential identifier for a woman who is still in the process of coming out to herself as a dyke or lesbian." My BB explained animatedly.

"But you haven't explained what genderqueer means?" I persisted.

Before Oscar had a chance to answer, Andy raised an eyebrow and asked, "How do you know all these terms, Oscar?"

"Well, well my darling lovers, I was taught GLBT terminologies by Dr. Henderson during one of our private *tutorials."* Oscar gave us a supercilious grin. He was proud that he knew more than Andy did about something.

That night, our propitious lovemaking more than made up for my lovers' verbal combativeness over who was more knowledgeable about lesbian terminology. I was just happy to be sandwiched between both my Apollos. But the persistent question about the meaning of 'genderqueer' continued to bug me. I made it a point to find out from Oscar at another, more appropriate time.

7

Are You a Lesbian?

"Things are in their essence what we choose to make them. A thing is, according to the mode in which one looks at it."
Oscar Wilde

1967

Antibes, Côte d'Azur

Early the following morning, after a restful night at the Carlton Hotel, we packed ourselves into Alfonzo's rented blue Sunbeam Alpine convertible, heading towards the hilly resort town of Antibes in the Alpes-Maritimes department of southeastern France. This Mediterranean coastal resort lies between the cities of Cannes and Nice. Nestled among the communes of Antibes is the village of Juan-les-Pins. This holiday destination is popular among the jet-set, with its beaches of fine-grain sand and small inlets. It also boasts a famous hotel, 'Le Provençal', built in 1926, and had received guests like Charlie Chaplin, Lillian Harvey, Jack Warner and Man Ray, to name a few.

As our vehicle made its way along the scenic route, I couldn't help but exclaim how beautiful this part of the world was and that I wished to make a home here someday. Looking down the cliffs where luxury yachts cruised along the aquamarine waters, I exclaimed, *"I'm so looking forward to sailing these waters tomorrow. Our 'Master,' the Hadrah, has so kindly loaned the Kahyya'm to us for a week."*

As soon as I uttered the word 'Master', Andy and Oscar gave me an unsavory glance.

Alfonzo asked, *"Who is the Hadrah, and why do you call him your 'Master'?"*

Andy jumped to a response quickly, *"What Young is saying is that the Hadrah, our household patriarch where we were stationed, has kindly loaned us the use of his boat. This boy likes to refer to him as the 'Master'. It is a respectful way to address a host in the Middle East."*

"He is certainly a very generous man to loan his private yacht to you guys. Is he going to be here to meet with you?"

Quick-thinking Oscar chimed in, *"Yes, he'll be here for the International Boat Show in a week's time. We'll see him then."*

Alfonzo added, *"While we are on the topic of Boat Shows, I went with my dad to the first ever Boat Show in Barcelona, several years back, at the Fira de Barcelona Montjuïc Exhibition Centre. It was quite an exhilarating experience. This show is now an annual Barcelona benchmark event and a meeting point for nautical enthusiasts in Spain. You guys should come visit my city soon."*

"Of course we will. With a friend like you to be our guide, it'll be fun to visit Barcelona," my BB commented with enthusiasm.

"The three of you can always stay at my villa. I'll show you what my city has to offer. Why don't you come during the winter break? The city will be filled with festivities during that time of year."

I couldn't help but exclaim, *"That will be fantastic! We'll definitely come visit you this Christmas."*

Andy looked at me as if I'd put my foot in my mouth again. He replied, *"Once again this boy is so full of gusto, he has a knack of agreeing to go to places and events without considering if it would be inconvenient for our host or hostess. I apologize for his ebullience."*

"That's one of the reasons I like Young. He's so full of zest and sprightliness; it's difficult not to be charmed by him," Mary said delightfully.

"That's what the Hadrah said of me, too," I responded instantly. *"I'm glad you like me, Mary. My BBs often reprimand me for either saying the wrong things or jumping exuberantly into any given situation. The truth is; I can't help myself. Everything is so exciting and I'm eager to explore the world."*

My companions laughed at my childlike vivaciousness as we continued towards our destination.

Notre Dame de l'Immaculée Conception

We finally arrived at the Antibes Cathedral of Notre Dame de l'Immaculée Conception, located up the narrow street of Rue de la Paroisse in Vieil Antibes (the old city).

As we browsed the ornate baroque holy relics of the holy virgin, Mary commented, *"Did you boys know that this used to be the pagan temple of Diana and Minerva? In the fifth century, the temple was converted and rebuilt as the present-day cathedral."*

"I had no idea," Alfonzo replied.

"Who are Diana and Minerva?" I asked.

"They were Roman goddesses. Prior to their transformation, they were Greek Olympians, Artemis and Athena. Both were maiden goddesses, sworn to virginity. They represent the sacred purity of young women before the age of marriage."

"In my mythology class at Daltonbury Hall, I was taught that Diana was essentially the goddess of the woodlands and hunts. I've seen paintings of her being surrounded with wild animals." I added.

Mary continued as we walked round the church's periphery, *"Several cults were associated with Diana. Her most famous cult was at Aricia near Lake Nemi (derived from the word 'nemus', meaning 'scared wood or grove').*

This cult is also referred to as the 'mirror of Diana'. Women carrying torches and wearing wreaths conducted annual sacred rites to honor her after sunset at the sacred grove. They would leave offerings for this tutelary goddess.

"She is also known as a maiden huntress and protector of all that is wild and free. The ancient Romans worshipped her as a moon goddess, patroness of nature, fertility and childbirth.

"Much like Ceres, the goddess of corn, and Bacchus, a god of the wine, her sanctuaries were commonly located in groves. As mistress of the greenwood, Diana was thought to own the beasts, whether wild or tame, that lurked for their prey in its gloomy depths. Therefore, hunters and herdsmen would pray to her."

Before Mary could continue her explanation, Andy chimed in, "She was especially worshipped as a goddess of childbirth, who bestowed offspring on men and women, right?"

"You're correct, Andy, women worshipped Diana as the giver of fertility and easy births. She is often portrayed as a huntress accompanied by a deer."

"Why a deer?" I asked curiously.

"You see, Young, Diana believed her body was very sacred, and no man was to see her naked. One day, a wandering hunter came across Diana bathing. She became very angry and turned him into a stag. The man was now unable to speak, so no one would ever hear about Diana's naked body.

"Actaeon, the wandering hunter, was killed by his own hunting dogs, because he couldn't tell them he was their master. The goddess was always surrounded by *young, beautiful attendants, be they males or females, who used to hunt with her."*

Sappho on Lesbo

I couldn't help but ask, *"Was she a lesbian? She seems so butch to be hunting wild animals."*

Mary and the boys burst out laughing before answering, *"Maybe yes, maybe no."*

I burst forth with my forthright question, *"Mary, are you a lesbian?"*

Andy was now desperately trying to remedy my bluntness. Mary, taken aback by my unexpected query, answered without a substantiate response. She asked smilingly, *"My dear boy, have you heard of the poet Sappho?"*

"In my Greek literature class, my professor did mention Sappho briefly. He said she was one of the great Greek lyrists and among the few known female poets of the ancient world. She came from a wealthy aristocratic family and lived her life in the isle of Lesbos. Is that where Lesbians originated from?" I asked inquisitively.

My companions burst into another round of hysterical laughter as soon as they heard my question. Mary calmed herself before answering, *"Young, you ask the funniest questions. I'll do my best to explain. During the seventh century, Lesbos was a cultural center. Sappho was called a lyrist because, as was the custom of the time, she wrote her poems to be accompanied with a lyre. She was one of the first poets to write from the first person point of view; describing love and loss as it affected her personally."*

Oscar chirped, *"Didn't Sappho compose her own music and refine the prevailing lyric meter to what is now known as Sapphic meter?"*

"Yes, she did. She innovated lyric poetry both in technique and style, thus becoming part of a new wave of Greek lyrists who moved from the gods' and muses' perspectives in poetry to more personal poetic voices.

"Her style was sensual and melodic. Hers were primarily songs of love, yearning, and reflection. Many females sought her out for education in the arts, and she showed them affection. She nurtured these women, wrote poems of love and adoration to them. When they eventually left the island to be married, she composed their wedding songs. Sappho's poetry was not condemned in her time for its homoerotic content, although it was disparaged by scholars in later centuries. This suggests that perhaps love between women was not persecuted then as it has been in more recent times. Sappho has become so synonymous with woman-love that two of the most popular words to describe female homosexuality--lesbian and sapphic were derived from her."

"On our forthcoming Greek island sojourn, I'd like to visit the isle of Lesbos. Since you are so well versed in the history of Sappho, will you join us on our cruise?" I inquired.

"It's very kind of you to invite me. I'll be delighted to accompany you for a few days, but not for the entire trip, as I've my modeling job to attend to. Is Alfonzo invited along?" Mary asked.

"Of course Alfonzo is invited. We can't invite one without the other. After all, you are a couple, aren't you?" Andy extended the invitation.

Mary and her boyfriend shared reticent glance before accepting our invite.

Château Grimaldi

It was late afternoon by the time we arrived at Château Grimaldi. This castle was built upon the foundations of the ancient Greek town of Antipolis. It became a stronghold of the Grimaldi family in 1608 and has borne their name ever since. For six months in 1946 this was the residence of the artist Pablo Picasso. On December 27th 1966 it became home to the Picasso Museum.

As we browsed the numerous cubist works of art, I chanced upon a painting named; *Les Deux Amies*. I tried to decipher the angular lines, forms and shapes depicting two nude women before asking Andy, *"Why does Picasso paint women with such angularity?"*

My lover replied, *"I'm not sure the reason behind the cubist movement. For some reason, I've never been a great fan of Picasso."*

Mary overhearing my question came to join us. She commented, *"I on the other hand love Picasso's work."*

"Why's that?" I asked before continuing, *"I like women to look feminine instead of being angular. In his paintings the women seems to come from a different planet."*

Mary said laughingly, *"That's precisely the reason I like Picasso's art. He seems to see through the general ideology of how women are perceived by society of that era. I for one, am not soft and demure like others see me. I have a mind of my own and a fierce internal strength that many do not see outwardly. Picasso's paintings speak to me. I can identify myself with the women he paints."*

"You are certainly not angular or cubist looking in any way," I responded.

My friend continued laughingly, *"The artist's interpretation is not a literal depiction of women. For me it's the hidden emotional messages that I relate strongly with."*

"Does that mean you like women that are puissance and mighty; women that possess masculine qualities?" Oscar inquired.

"I like the 'take charge' kind of females. They fascinate me."

"Why?" I queried.

"I don't know why, I just do. Young, it's probably the same reason you like men that are manly and masculine. I happen to like women that are macho and butch."

Andy gave Oscar and me a cognizant grin, as if confirming their speculation that Mary may indeed be a lipstick lesbian.

As we continued viewing the artworks, Alfonzo commented, *"Did you know that Picasso is a fellow Spaniard? He was born in the city of* **Málaga** *in the Andalusia region of Spain. He came to Antibes in 1947 and painted one of his famous work here; the 'La joie de vivre' which we are currently looking at."*

Andy added, *"He lives in Vallauris with his wife Jacqueline Roque doesn't he?"*

"I believe so. Before he moved to this part of the world, he lived in the baroque city of Aix-en-Provence which is best known as the home of Paul Cézanne.*"* Alfonzo continued, *"He bought the Château de Vauvenargues at Mont Sainte-Victoire, the mountain that Cézanne returned to again and again to paint. It was there that he, Jacqueline and her daughter from a previous marriage settled. Although he was literally in Cézanne's backyard, it was the work of Manet's 'Le Déjeuner sur l'Herbe' that inspired much of Picasso's work at Vauvenargues."*

"Where did you obtain this information?" I asked.

"Look over there, it's written on the large wall placard detailing the artist's current and past life." Alfonzo said with relish in his voice.

Before long, our group agreed to head back to Cannes for a nice scrumptious dinner. One question remained unanswered that day. Was Mary a lesbian?

8

Under the Cerulean Sky

"A loving heart is the beginning of all knowledge."
Thomas Carlyle

Last Week of July 2012

Dr. Arius continued his inquiries through our regular correspondence. *"When your headmaster at Daltonbury Hall explained to you the details of the Middle East foreign exchange, were you shocked by the information that you have to provide carnal services within the male Arab Households? What was your initial reaction when you were told the news that you were one of the selected five to join a secret society?"*

"As far as I can remember, Dr. A. S.; I was more surprised than shocked. I couldn't fathom the idea that I was that special to be one of the selected few to enter this exclusive clandestine club. I kept wondering what was so special about me, that out of one hundred fifty to two hundred students, I was one of the lucky five.

"I felt privileged and special to be a part of an exclusive club. I would have agreed on the spot but the selection panel suggested I give the matter further thoughts. The school elders and my BB wanted to be absolutely sure that I knew what I was getting myself into rather than allowing me to make a spur of the moment decision.

"Looking back at the situation in later years, they were assisting me to grow to be a responsible adult; to decide and make my own decisions and not be coerced into the program through the influence of my teachers and mentor. They provided all the information for me to make my decision. They were very specific that the decision had to come solely and directly from me so there would be no disparity after my induction into E.R.O.S."

I continued to answer the doctor's queries with honesty, *"When I was told that I'll be trained in the art of carnal knowledge, I was eager to participate. At that age, my libido was working overtime and I was sensually and sexually curious. I believe many adolescents are curious, like I was, to learn everything there is to know about sex and the act of making love.*

"In my view, the strict American laws about statutory rape only make it harder to catch actual rapists. The fullest extent of the law comes down on adults who, in reality, are having consensual sex with young people. Lawmakers have their priorities all wrong.

"In many ancient cultures when males or females reach puberty, they were encouraged to express their sexual maturity as part of nature's phenomenon; unlike contemporary times when societal regulations and governmental laws forbade and hinder an adolescent's sexual growth. Hence, the ever increasing number of sexually misinformed teenagers; which leads to guilt trips and misguided sexual expressions, such as rape and bullying that are rampant these days.

"Please do not misunderstand me, doctor. I'm not pro rape or condone non-consensual sex between an adult and a young teenager. I'm merely stating the facts of life. Love comes in all shapes, forms, ages and expressions. It is a natural human behavior that humans are attracted to others of the same species, especially during puberty. Society can impose laws and regulations but a 'normal'

growing adolescent will find ways and means of releasing their sexual functions even if the law deems such acts as criminal offenses.

"An excellent example is the catholic church imposing celibacy laws for all priests and clerics. Such abominable bans will only result in unsavory criminal acts such as pedophilia and rape by religious zealots. My belief is: if any overly zealous religious institutions or governmental bodies exercises strict bans on natural human developments, the chances of their followers, congregations and or public finding ways of breaking the law would be greater than un-censoring the ban. It is human nature to be free to develop one's growth and freedom of expression.

"That said, I do agree that there should be laws governing a society to keep peace and order in the land. But as long as the sexual acts between the parties involved are consensual and not forced upon by another, then the 'sin' of breaking nature's law of physical attraction is no longer a sinful act but a celebration of love.

"What's your opinion on this topic, doctor?"

1967

On the Kahyya'm

The azure ocean loomed ahead as we sailed out of Cannes Harbor. I was invigorated to be on the Kahyya'm after eight months of absence. I could not help reminiscing the first time I sat foot on this luxury yacht while cruising along the tranquil waters of the Mediterranean. Andy had gone below deck to fuss with the luggage and our cabin allocations, while Mary and Alfonzo were spending some quiet moments reading at the rear of the vessel. Oscar was resting in the lounge deck as I stood on the boat's hull watching the foaming waves glide by. I couldn't help feeling appreciative and sad all at once.

I was wondering how on earth did I transform so rapidly from a shy, naïve and effeminate Kuala Lumpur boy to a well-travelled sophisticated young man within a short period of twenty months. I was thankful for all the wonderful people and circumstances that had manifested in my life, especially Andy, my beloved Valet, guardian and lover. I was sad because Oscar my other lover, 'big brother', and mentor would be leaving me soon. Like Nikee, he would be forging a life of greener pastures and the chances of us being together would be slim and far between. I was already missing Oscar before he was gone.

As I was in deep concentration, I noticed a school of dolphins swimming next to the boat. These beautiful creatures were frolicking without a care in the world, as if inconsistence was an eternity in their lives. I wanted to be like them, to live life freely and explore the vastness of the world.

I was lost in contemplation when a pair of hands reached around my waist. Taken by surprise, I turned to find my 'big brother' standing behind me. He held onto my waist as if he didn't want to let me go. I surrendered to his loving embrace as he lowered his head on my shoulder. The warmth of his closeness coursed through my pulsating heart. I leaned against his masculinity as he inhaled my boyish essence. Oscar began a slow dance kissing the side of my neck, before progressing to the tip of my earlobe. His intoxicating breath sent shivers down my spine. Time stood still as I savored this moment of loving tenderness. Turning the side of my face towards him, he kissed my lips, savoring the sweetness of its voluptuousness. My groin stirred to his tender touch. He moved his hand towards my crotch, slowly and gently he caressed my growing length within the tightness of fitted jeans.

I cupped my hands behind my lover's firm buttocks, pressing his hardness against my derriere as we continued our passionate kisses. He reached inside my T-shirt and brushed his nimble fingers against both my erect nipples. Ecstatic sensuality electrified my being. I relinquished my person to his control. His gyrating motion suffused that he desired me there and then. Unzipping my jeans, he reached his palm inside my briefs; massaging my leaking bubulous head; partaking my deliciousness from his fingers to my longing oral orifice. We shared my precum between us as we French kissed with abandonment.

He couldn't wait to yank my jeans and briefs to my knees exposing my nakedness to the warm soothing breeze that was caressing against my delicate skin. I reached my hands behind, unbuttoned his pants to let them drop to his ankles. He continued rotating his pelvis against my behind while his quivering length bounced in rhythmic motion to my pinning gyrations. I needed him and he wanted me.

Relinquishing myself to this enticing sensuality, I backed myself against his protrusion. Through the corner of my eyes, I noticed a figure observing us from the upper deck. It was my beloved Valet. He stood watch, making sure that I had my alone time with Oscar. I knew my lover's unconditional love would never disrupt my intimacy with this lover that would soon be leaving our midst. My guardian was allowing me the opportunity to bid my farewell to my BB. Andy was truly one of the most enlightened souls I've ever known.

As my mentor stood guard gazing with expectancy from above, my lover knelt between my butt cheeks, kissing them adoringly before delving his tongue deep within my yearning orifice. The electrifying sensation sent tremors through my body. I desired him not to stop. I backed against his face while my hand pushed him towards my craving slit. Wetting my opening with his saliva, he bent me against the railings as he eased himself into the depth of my person. Loosening my passageway for his unbridled entry I bared my love to my handsome 'big brother'. He glided into my soul, slowly and easily, transporting my spirit to an ecstatic realm of blissfulness. I received him readily. He held tightly onto my slender waist, stoking, caressing my core to euphoric riotousness. At times fast and furious and at other times unhurried and ponderous, he enraptured our last dance with ease and grace as we moaned to the spirit songs of the frolicking dolphins that were swimming next to the boat. We were at one with god as 'God' watched approvingly from above deck. Staring into Andy's beloved eyes, his unconditional love reached out to the both of us as if Zeus was blessing us with his nod to our enraptured copulation. I was at once filled with love for both lovers. Andy was making love to me mentally from above. Both lovers were within my mind and my soul simultaneously. I had reached nirvana with no intention of being there. The emotional enchantments blew me over the edge. I came without eliciting any actions on my part. It was as if some magical potion had been sprinkled on my physique which I had no control over. I spilled onto Oscar's hand as he strengthened his grip on my washboard stomach. My release was too tantalizing for my lover to withhold his passion much longer. His amorous love filled me with affection that only the three of us had the privilege to experience. My lover stayed in me until his passion subsided, only then did he loosen his grip around my waist. We kissed with veracity as I gazed upon our other lover standing above deck. Andy gave me a loving smile before vanishing from view beyond the setting sun against the deep blue cerulean sky.

Dinner Conversation

As the four of us gathered at the pristine deck watching the last rays of sunset disappear over the horizon, the Kahyya'm's private chef had painstakingly prepared a Moorish meal for us to enjoy.

Andy commented, *"Early tomorrow morning we'll be arriving at the peninsula of Peloponnese."*

Alfonzo exclaimed before my Valet could progress, "Sparta here we come!"

"Here's a quiz for you. Does anyone know what *Peloponnesos* means?"

Mary answered, *"The name Peloponnesos means "Island of Pelops"."*

"And who is Pelops?" Andy queried.

"In ancient Greek mythology, Pelops was the king of Pisa. He was also the founder of the House of Atreus through his son bearing the same name.

"His cult developed into the unifying founding myth of the Olympic Games for all Hellenes and he was highly honored at Olympia. Chthonic night-time libations were offered to the 'dark-faced' Pelops in his bothros (sacrificial pit) at the Olympia sanctuary. These rituals were performed before the offerings were proffered to Zeus, the sky-god, the following day." Oscar venerated.

"Very good old chap! Did you also know that The Greek War of Independence actually started in Peloponnese?"

"Is that the reason why Sparta is well known for generating excellent warriors over the centuries?" Alfonzo questioned.

Andy explained, *"There's a long history to Spartans being brave warriors. It is a known tradition that male children are revered and were brought up under severe military discipline. Boys aged seven were taken from their parents' control and were then organized into small bands. The most courageous became captains. They were drilled daily in gymnastics and military exercises and were taught that retreat or surrender in battle was disgraceful.*

They also learned to endure pain and hardship without complaint and to obey absolute orders without question."

Oscar added, *"Discipline grew even more rigorous when the boys reached manhood. All male Spartans between the ages of twenty and sixty served in the army. Although they were allowed to marry, they had to belong to a men's dining club and eat and sleep in the public barracks after their marriage ceremony was over."*

Alfonzo remarked, *"I read in a Greek history book that pederasty and military training were intimately connected in Sparta, as in many other Hellenic cities. Is that true?"*

Oscar supplemented, *"It is a well-documented fact that Spartans made sacrifices to Eros before every battle because they believe that their safe and victorious return after battle depended upon the friendship of the men that were drawn up. Unlike other cities which stationed lovers side by side in battle to encourage each to fiercer efforts, Spartan youths were so well trained that they fought nobly regardless of where they were positioned. And yes to answer your question, Alfonzo; the lover was responsible for the boy's training."*

"So it is true that Spartan pederasty and military training were intimately connected," the Spaniard declared.

Andy continued, *"In order to understand the social mores of the ancient Greeks, you have to realize that there were heavy sanctions on pre-marital sex between men and women. Men usually married late, after they had proven themselves in battle. It was therefore not uncommon for a young man to take a boy as a lover, in the interim before he married and adopted a heterosexual life.*

"Similarly for the boy; when he becomes an adult, he will take a boy as a lover, before marriage and soon after resumes a heterosexual life himself. Some societies still practice this to this day. It is generally a temporary

expedient and rather different to those who prefer an ongoing homosexual life."

Mary chimed in, *"They are unlike Athenian boys, who spent little time in military training and are well versed in learning the art of music and literature. That's why Athenians are known for their artistic pursues such as the art of poetry and lyrical compositions."*

"Ooh, how very exciting! I can't wait to visit Sparta tomorrow to witness for myself if Spartan men are truly macho, rugged, strong, brave and courageous." I chimed, breaking the seriousness of our conversation.

My companions could not resist laughing at my cheekiness. Andy turned to me and said, *"Wouldn't you like to find out you saucy young chap. You are so full of yourself."*

As the Kahyya'm sailed below the cloudless starry sky heading towards the deep blue Aegean sea, our group continued debating and discussing the topic of Grecian homosexuality late into the tranquil Mediterranean night.

9

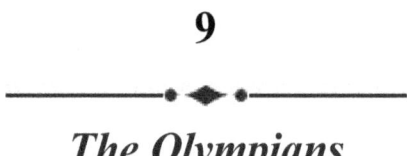

The Olympians

"Deep experience is never peaceful."
Henry James

1967

Ancient Olympia

    We arrived in Peloponnese early the following morning. The Kahyya'm was docked at the Messanian Gulf near the lively ancient fishing village of Xirokambilies, which is close to the Ancient city of Sparta and the Byzantine castle of Mystras. The picturesque beauty of the majestic peaks of Mount Taygetos rose above, covered richly with olive and orange groves. The four of us decided to hire an English-speaking guide, Patros, to chauffeur us round the various parts of the peninsular for the day. The first stop on our itinerary was Ancient Olympia, located at the foot of the Kronion Hill. It is in a valley between two rivers and has become one of the most famous sites in Greece. As we explored the ruins of the 'Gymnasium', tears began to stream from my eyes for no apparent reason. A sense of nihility overcame my person. As I stood weeping, Andy who was accompanying me; reached over and wrapped his arms around me. He asked with concern, *"My dear boy, what's the matter? Why are you crying?"*

I leaned against my Valet but did not utter a word. *"Are you alright, Young?"*

I burst into tears without reason. My beloved embraced me with loving tenderness. *"Shhh, shhh, don't cry my boy. What's making you so sad? Tell me,"* Andy comforted.

I replied, choking, *"I'm very sad. I feel that I've been here before. It's as if I'm witnessing a death scene being reenacted."*

Hyacinth & Apollo

Just then, Oscar came to join us and overheard my pronouncement. He said, *"Legend has it that Hyacinth, a beautiful youth about your age, Young, died when hit by a flying discus thrown by his lover, the god Apollo. Hyacinth was trying to impress his beloved by running to catch the moving disc. Unfortunately, he tripped, fell and was hit on the head by the swiftly flying object. He died instantly.*

"Zephyr, the god of the West Wind, was also in love with the youth. He was jealous that Hyacinth preferred the radiantly handsome archer god, and he created a feud between Apollo and himself. To take his revenge, Zephyr blew Apollo's discus off course to injure and kill Hyacinth in the process.

"The grief-stricken Apollo refused to allow Hades (God of the Underworld) to claim the deceased youth. He drew the beautiful boy's spilled blood and fashioned a flower from it, today known as a hyacinth. As a sign of his grief, he stained the newly formed petals with 'ai' from his tears. Since then the mythological Hyacinth has been identified with a number of plants other than the Iris, the true hyacinth flower."

Patros chimed in, *"Last but not least, according to our local Spartan myth, Hyacinth and his sister Polyboea* were taken to heaven by Aphrodite, Athena and Artemis to become a god and goddess on Mount Olympia."

"What has that got to do with Young's sudden melancholy?" Alfonzo asked.

Oscar continued dispensing his theory. *"I believe this beautiful boy is experiencing a moment from a past life in which he witnessed the death of Hyacinth, and possibly at the very site we are standing on. His apprehension is probably his unconscious memory of the fateful event."*

Andy answered logically before our lover could continue, *"Perhaps Young is already missing you, Oscar, before your departure from our midst? Grief has already set in before you have even gone."*

Silence fell over our group before Mary spoke, *"Love is such a beautiful thing. Obviously, this young man loves you deeply and truly, Oscar. Can you not see that?"*

Both of my lovers wrapped their arms around each of our shoulders, and the three of us embraced, forming a circle of love and affection. Patros exclaimed with propensity, *"The beauty of young love! How sweet and charming."* He added, *"During my years of driving visitors around the island of Pelops, I have witnessed many such cases. There are energies in this land that seem to affect lovers deeply. Perhaps the ghosts of history return to bless the lovers of the present. They are reminding us that true love is the most precious part in our lives."*

"I think you are correct Patros. I think you are correct," Mary affirmed the Greek's proclamation.

At the Palaestra and the Baths

We arrived at the Palaestra, the ancient sports ground built in the third century BC. Although the building was now a courtyard encircled by a line of columns, in the ancient days it was a gymnasium partitioned into dressing rooms, baths, classrooms with attached benches, and rooms specially designed for the eleothession (a place where athletes were coated with olive oil) and the konistrion (an area designated to dust or sand the athletes' bodies before they entered their respective competitions).

Patros promulgated, *"During ancient Olympic Games, men competed naked in different sports. That is why their bodies were oiled before training and competitions.*

"After their aggressive training, the athletes would then enter the baths. These early Greek baths were located by the bank of the river Kladeos, where oblong wells were installed at the end for them to draw water. In the fourth century BC, this room here with mosaic floors was erected with hot water bathtubs. During the firt century BC, a large room built with hypocausts – a system of central heating in which hot air from an underground furnace circulated beneath the floors and between the double walls – was constructed."

Alfonzo asked, *"I've seen movies of ancient Greek athletes scrubbing their bodies with a curved, bladelike instrument, to clean off the dirt from their perspiring physiques."*

Oscar responded laughingly, *"That instrument is known as a scraper."*

"You are wrong, Sir. That instrument is not called a scraper but is known as a strigil." Patros corrected my BB.

At the Temple of Zeus

We had arrived at the most renowned building in this historical site, the Temple of Zeus. Our guide continued, *"This sanctuary was built between 470 and 456 BC by Libon of Elis. Although the original building is now a ruin, in its heyday, it boasted thirteen supporting columns* on each side. You can still see the Hellenistic mosaic floors, which we are currently standing on."

Alfonzo added, *"Is this the place where the victors of the Olympic Games were crowned with wreaths of laurels beneath the gigantic gold and ivory statue of Zeus?"*

Mary supplemented, *"Wasn't the statue moved to Constantinople and later destroyed in a fire after the ancient Olympic games where abolished?"*

"Both of you are correct. Zeus' statue was burned down in AD 475. As to the fate of this temple, Theodosius II set fire to the structure because the Christians deemed it a place of pagan worship. Also, natural disasters, such as earthquakes, did incredible damage to the place. The remaining structures, those that were left standing, are what you see lying in ruin on the ground. Some pieces of the remaining statue are on display at the Louvre in Paris." Patros advised.

Mary turned to me and inquired, *"How are you feeling, Young? Are you feeling better?"*

Andy replied on my behalf, *"He's fine now. He's been in a pensive state since we set sail."*

"This boy is such a romantic. Hopefully when we reach Athens, Bryanna will be able to cheer him up. She knows all the trendy and chic places to go. She is an excellent 'blues' disperser."

"I'm doing my best to cheer him up and to affirm that I'm here for him when Oscar leaves. He's so sentimental. My heart can't help but reach out to him when he is sad. Luckily, most of the time he's very cheerful. It's only when his 'big brothers' leave that he feels depressed." My Valet continued, *"When Nikee, his first BB, departed for further studies, I took him under my wing. It took him some weeks before he recovered from his downheartedness. I practically had to sing and dance to get him back on track."*

Mary stressed, *"It is difficult when someone we love dearly leaves our midst. Time will heal our wounds. Deep experiences are never peaceful."*

At the Archaeological Museum of Sparta

Lining the walkway toward the entrance of Sparta's Archaeological Museum were life-size, headless stone statues in Hellenistic tunics and togas. This relatively small museum housed the famous torso of King Leonidas, who with an army of three hundred Spartan warriors fought off a huge Persian army of several thousand in the famous Battle of Thermopylae. As we walked around the museum viewing the exhibits, we came upon a stone carving with the inscriptions that read;

English translation:

The Law of Sparta

Let it be written in the laws of the city on a pillar in a central place in stone: for each free man, it is his sacred duty to choose a boy and love him as his own, for how will boys become the best of men without a lover as a guiding light? Who but a lover can nurture them, and what but love can teach the sense of right? Boys must honor and obey their lovers be faithful to them as a wife; they must inscribe within their heart what love discovers and let it light them on the path of life, for only the free can the free mind secure and only love is free and will endure.

After Andy read the transcripts aloud, Patros commented, *"My school taught to us that in ancient Sparta, any eligible man of 'excellence' who did not take on a boy lover could be fined by the ephors (the democratically elected 'overseers' of the community) for neglecting his duty to the polis. The first responsibility for any leading citizen was to nurture a boy with love in order to pass on his own good qualities to the lad.*

"And every year we celebrate the Hyacinthia. The festival last for three whole days."

"What is the Hyacinthia?" I asked.

Oscar interjected, *"You remember we were discussing Hyacinth and Apollo when we were at the Gymnasium in Olympia? This is a festival celebrating the death and rebirth of these two tutelary deities, and it's one of the principal Spartan festivals in this region."*

"You're right, Oscar." Patros affirmed and continued, *"The first day is for mourning the death of our divine hero Hyacinth. On that day, we offer simple sacrificial banquets to our deceased loved ones without pomp or circumstance. On the second and third days, we celebrate his rebirth as Apollo Hyakinthos or Hymenaios, meaning 'Of the Hymns'. Young people in the local villages play the cithara (an instrument resembling the lyre) and the aulos (a simple double-reed woodwind with only four or five finger holes), singing songs of praises to Apollo. There are horse races and choir competitions with lots of rejoicing and street dancing. It's also a time for joyous celebration for the town's womenfolk, who decorate carts and participate in parades. Visitors, friends and relatives are welcome to participate with our countrymen. It's like a festive county fair."*

"What happens on the third day?" I questioned.

"The third day is more solemn. It is customary for our womenfolk to weave a chiton (tunic) to offer to the Goddess Athena, although this tradition is rapidly dying out.

"There is a poem which is taught to us through our oral tradition. I'll recite it to you." Our guide began;

"You Ebàlide (spirit),
without the bloom of youth,
and I see your wound,
oh my beloved!
My crime is your pain,

*your death my right is guilty,
I am author!
But it is my fault?
Guilt of having played it?
Amato?
If I could, dying with you,
with my life to pay!
Because they are prevented by law of fate,
always in my heart I will have eternally on the lips!
You celebrate the lira from my fingers crossed,
you my songs celebrate and you,
new flower figurerai my complaints."*
We applauded when he finished his recital.

In the Museum's Courtyard

A life-size bronze statue of King Leonidas stood in battle position, ready to attack any intruder that dared induce him to combat. Patros, in a happy mood, continued enlightening our group. He began, *"There is another ancient Spartan festival that is celebrated annually. It is called the Gymnopaedia. In the ancient days, naked youths displayed their athletic and martial skills through a series of war dances."*

"Naked dancing through the streets in public?" I exclaimed.

Our guide said laughingly, *"The custom of naked dancing started in 668 BC with the introduction of naked athletes oiling their bodies for exercise to highlight their physical beauty."*

"Do boys still dance around naked at this celebration nowadays?" I asked with intense curiosity.

"Unfortunately not. These days, they wear a tunic that resembles the ancient costume. But, during the festivities, there are always groups of drunken youths who

will adhere to the naked tradition. Why don't you guys stay for another few days to enjoy this festival? Then you'll be able to experience firsthand if the boys take off their clothes to dance." The Greek grinned amusingly.

"Can we stay for the festival?" I pleaded emphatically.

Andy soon put a stop to my excitement, *"My darling boy, as much as you'd like to stay, we are sailing to Athens tomorrow. Mary has to attend to her modeling assignments. Besides, she promised to introduce us to Bryanna, and you wanted to attend the fashion shoot, don't you remember?"*

I was saddened by the promise I had made to Mary, so I kept silent. Patros continued, *"Gymnopaedia is a festival dedicated to the god Apollo. Spartan youths dance vigorously with musical grace and with warrior-like grit in the summer heat. This festival is also to celebrate the defeat by Argos in the year 669 BC at Hysiai, in the hope to appease the gods and to prevent another such disastrous occurrence. In the past, military style dancing emphasized military success and support of the Spartan military campaign. The kind of dance we perform today is very different to that of the past."*

"Why did youths dance in the nude?" I questioned inquisitively.

"In ancient Greece, sports were generally reserved for men, and would be performed 'gymnos' (naked). Men were the only spectators when such sports were performed publicly. However, in Aristophanes' plays, he indicated that women also exercised naked in public. Some historians have suggested that this festival included young women dancing in order to show their strength and worthiness in giving birth to healthy strong men. It was also to promote eugenic marriage and population growth, with which our city struggled in later years.

"Public performance of such sports was generally in a ceremonial setting, such as for the occasion of a religious feast. Although not all ceremonial sports were competitive, some included an element of competition for the most beautiful movement, speed and strength. In ancient days many of the sport categories resembled dance more than modern track and field events. That was probably the reason for displaying their nudity; it was a beautiful expression of the beauty of the human form."

As I pondered Pathos' last statement, I was again tossed into the throes of dispondency. I was sad that my time with my physically and mentally attractive lover would be coming to an end.

10

The Four Loves

"Love will find a way through paths where wolves fear to prey."
Lord Byron

Early August 2012

In response to my question, Dr. A.S. replied:
Young,
I couldn't agree with you more in regards to the social and governmental rules and regulations that are currently governing the American continent and some parts of the western world in regards to assisting the sexual growth and maturity of our young adults. In some aspects the law had become a hindrance.

I remember back in the old days the age of consensual sex used to be when a person reaches puberty (between the ages of twelve to eighteen). Nowadays, it seems ironic that the current age of consent is set as high as eighteen years especially in America when many young adults in the 'real' world are already having sexual experiences much earlier.

In many European countries the age of consent is around fourteen to sixteen although there are some liberal continental countries that have ruled the age of consent at thirteen.

Of course in some Asian countries, they are as young as twelve or thirteen (marriageable ages) which are more in keeping with the 'real' world when children reach puberty.

Changing the topic, there are questions I have for you regarding your induction into the Bahriji (Oasis) school:

- *Did you fancy the other 'big brothers' and Valets that were in the Bahriji?*
- *If you did, how were you taught to control your sexual urges not to desire or solicit their attention and affection? Or is there an open to all policy?*
- *Were all the students at the Bahriji highly sexed?*
- *If so, how were students taught to restrain their sexual urges without the educational system getting out of control?*
- *Did the students from the boys' and girls' schools have sexual relationships before being allocated to the various Arab households?*

1967

Athens, Greece

Sailing into the Piraeus Mikrolimano, the second largest yacht marina in Athens was an experience in and of itself. Luxury boats of all shapes and sizes docked alongside one another were as opulent as their owners.

Along the bustling shoreline were fish restaurants offering the best of the day's catch.

According to mythology, Piraeus is protected by the goddess Artemis and her temple was built on its naval foundations. This section of Athens has inspired many Greek writers; the likes of Nikos Psathsas (Ta Pedia tis Piatsas) and film makers like Jules Dassen (Never on Sunday). Piraeus is the city in Greece that many songs have been written about by famous Greek composers, the likes of Zambetas, Xarhakos, Mikis Theodorakis, and Manos Hadjidakis. Well-known songs such as 'Ta pedia tou Pirea', 'Drapetsona', 'Kato sto Pirea', 'Lemonadika', were sung by popular singers of their day such as Gregoris Bithikotsis, Vicky Mosholiou to name a few.

This fishing port reflects the Greek word 'Nostos', meaning 'missing my country'. Thousands of Greek immigrants migrated to America and Australia, and thousands of seamen had traveled the seven seas from this port town; leaving behind pining wives, mothers and children as their ships left to sea.

We arrived to the welcoming fanfare of restaurant keepers, bidding us enter their establishment to dine, rest and to be merry. Unfortunately we had an appointment to keep or rather Mary had a meeting at the modeling agency to meet the photographer and the cosmetic company's representative who has hired her for the job. Off our entourage trooped to a modern high rise building in the middle of Athens.

Annika

The moment we stepped through the agency's door, the infamous Bryanna was already waiting Mary's arrival. Our group of men was introduced to Annika, the beautiful owner of the agency; Sepheaon, the Revlon representative and last but not least the charming photographer, Bruce.

All eyes gravitated to us. They were obviously accessing our assets to see if we were potential male model materials to be recruited into the agency's fold. While the female models were discussing their forth coming shoot with Sepheaon and Bruce, Annika took the opportunity to inquire of us, *"What brings you good-looking guys to Athens?"*

Andy replied politely, *"We are here on vacation before returning to our respective school and university."*

"Greece is a marvelous place to visit this time of year. Are you enjoying yourselves?" Annika asked.

"Very much so. We just arrived from Peloponnese. There are many historical places to visit, and insufficient time to see them all." Alfonzo responded.

"Young men, you'll enjoy Athens. There is plenty to see. If you stay long enough, I'll be able to organize some modeling assignments for the four of you. Will you be interested to sign with my agency?"

"I can stay since I'm accompanying Mary but I can't speak for these three guys (directing his gaze at Andy, Oscar and me). I believe they are planning to sail to Mykonos and Lesbos after Athens."

Oscar added, *"We are spending a week in Greece before I head back to university in Vienna. I'm afraid I will not be here long enough to work on any modeling assignments."*

Before Andy could comment, I chimed in quickly. *"Andy and I can always return if you have assignments for us during our school breaks. I'll love to learn and participate in the modeling world."*

My Valet looked at me as if I had spoken too quickly. Shaking his head he added, *"This boy is so quick to jump into any potential fashion related projects before considering the consequences of our previous commitments. He is very keen to learn all he can about the fashion world."*

"I don't blame him. When I was his age, I couldn't wait to enter the modeling business. He seems to have a fashion eye, judging from the way he dresses." The proprietress replied smilingly before continuing, *"What about you, Andy? Will you be interested in doing some modeling work during your school holidays?"*

My lover looked at me. Seeing my hankering stare, he nodded his head and replied, *"It's very difficult to say no when this boy gives me his longing puppy dog look. He has a way of softening my heart into giving in to his wishes. I suppose I wouldn't mind doing some modeling assignments if and when the opportunity presents itself. I'm doing this because of him, as long as Young can accompany me to the modeling assignments."*

"That shouldn't be a problem. Young can always be on the sidelines watching you work. I may also be able to get work for him so the both of you can be on the same projects. I know 'Greek Love', remember I'm from this part of the world." She smiled and gave us a knowing wink.

I couldn't help blabbing out loud, *"What is Greek Love?"*

Bryanna, Mary, Sepheaon and Bruce who were in the midst of their project discussion, turned towards my direction, they burst out in laughter at my innocent remark. Bryanna said jokingly, *"Wouldn't you like to know what 'Greek Love' is young man. I'll take you to places where you can best locate 'Greek Love'."*

Bruce supplemented, *"I'll be happy to show you what 'Greek Love' is,"* he jested mischievously.

Puzzled by their comments I searched the group for a definitive answer. Instead they continued amusing themselves facetiously at my ignorance. Finally, Annika sat me down and explained, *"In order to understand the meaning of 'Greek Love', you must understand the history of Greece. In historical memory, Greece of a treasured past was romanticized and idealized as a time of a culture when love between men was not only tolerated but encouraged. This form of classical homoeroticism was expressed as the high ideal of same-sex camaraderie.*

"You'll find that many of us that are in the fashion/modeling industry generally have very liberal views

about homosexuality between men and men or woman and woman."

My guardian sitting beside me chirped, *"Young, do you remember when I read you 'The Art of Loving' by Edmund Fromm? There is another famous writer, C.S. Lewis who wrote 'The Four Loves'. Although he presents love in a Christian point of view, I believe there are valuable lessons to be learned from this author."*

"What are the four loves," I questioned.

"There are four Greek words for love; 'Storge' (affection), 'Philia' (friendship), 'Eros' (romance), and 'Agape' (unconditional love or charity)." Annika sufficed.

"I thought Eros was the Greek god of Love. How can he be lumped with affection, friendship and charity?" I asked eagerly.

My mentor continued, *"Let me break down and explain the four different kinds of love to you.*

"Starting with 'Affection'; 'storge' is fondness through familiarity (a brotherly love) that is usually applied between family members or people who have otherwise found themselves together by chance. It is described as natural, emotive, and the most widely diffused of the four types of loves. Its naturalness is present without coercion; emotive because it is the result of fondness due to familiarity; and it is widely diffused because it pays the least attention to those characteristics deemed 'valuable' or worthy of love. This form of love is able to transcend the majority of discriminating factors. Ironically, its strength is also what makes it highly vulnerable. Affection has the appearance of being 'built-in' or 'ready-made', and as a result most people come to expect, even in this mythical, non-hormonal presence, its presence irrespective of their behavior and its natural consequences."

"Wow, what a mouthful of words to take in." I declared. *"Go on, I'm all ears, I'm listening."*

My Valet continued, *"The second form of love; 'Philia', is the love between friends. Friendship is the strong bond that exists between people who share common interest or activity. The way Lewis describes Friendship; 'the least biological, organic, instinctive, gregarious and necessary of our Loves, because our species do not need Friendship in order to reproduce. He then went on to explain that Friendship is exceedingly profound because it is freely chosen."*

"So how did the Greek god Eros play a part in these four loves?" I asked with immense curiosity.

"Hold on, let me finish before you jump the gun to question about Eros.

"Like the friendship between David and Jonathan in the Bible, Lewis explains that true friendship, is almost a lost art. He goes on to express a strong distaste for the way our modern society ignores Friendship and notes that he cannot remember any poem that celebrated true Friendship like those between David and Jonathan, Orestes and Pylades, Roland and Oliver, and last but not least, Amis and Amiles. Lewis also explained, "To the Ancients, Friendship seemed the happiest and most fully human of all loves; the crown of life and the school of virtue and by far the modern world, seems to have ignored it.

"Lewis then went on to assert that few people in modern society appreciate true Friendship because very few have experienced it."

I interjected, *"Isn't this the kind of loving friendship that you, Oscar and I share?"*

"I'm sure Lewis will beg to differ on your statement."

"Why?" I questioned.

"To answer your question will bring me to Eros; 'romantic love'. It is love in the sense of 'being in love' or 'loving' someone sexually. According to Lewis' point of view, he concludes that Eros can become a god to people

who fully submit themselves to it. He also stated that it can be an extremely profound experience for people, up to the point of suicide pacts and furious refusals to part. Much like the way you are sad because of Oscar's imminent departure.

"That is why Eros, the god is depicted as an archer. His arrows are known to pierce through the thickest of hearts and blind them with romantic love. So much so that those blinded by this type of love will and can commit murder, thus causing mayhem and collateral damages to those they love."

"I love you and Oscar romantically but we don't go round murdering each other or inflicting harm to each other." I affirmed.

Annika thought my affirmation diverting. Oscar and Alfonso listening in also gazed at me beguilingly.

My BB chimed in where Andy left off, *"This brings us to the final form of love; 'agape'. Charity is the love that brings forth caring regardless of circumstances. According to Lewis, he recognizes this as the greatest of the four loves, and believes it to be a specifically human virtue. He focuses on the need of subordinating the natural loves to the divine love of God, who is the manifestation of charitable love."*

"You mean like the kind of love I felt during my 'Initiation' ceremony at the school's chapel?" As soon as I uttered the sentence I knew I shouldn't have, but it was too late to withdraw my declaration.

Alfonzo and Annika asked almost simultaneously, *"What kind of 'Initiation' ceremony is he referring to?"*

Quick witted Andy jumped in to my defense. *"Young is referring to the pact Oscar, he and I made, that we remain inseparable through our unconditional love for one another.*

"We made promises that we will remain loyal friends throughout eternity. We did a ceremonial pact in

our school chapel when no one was watching. We made a vow to be there for each other in good and bad times; kind of like a 'blood-brothers' initiation ceremony."

This explanation seemed to satisfy Annika's and Alfonzo's curiosity. They soon let the matter drop.

11

The Parthenon

"Debauchery is perhaps an act of despair in the face of infinity."
        Edmond De Goncourt

1967

At The PARTHENON

True to her word, that evening after their project meeting at the modeling agency, Bryanna, with our entourage in tow, arrived at an industrial section of this vibrant city. Dressed in our latest disco gear, we were ready to paint the town red. Although The PARTHENON was a fancy dance club, it also boasted a voguish restaurant where the city's fashionistas came to wine, dine and chill. This establishment was a place to see and be seen.

The exterior of The PARTHENON was nondescript except for the ostentatious cars parked in the vicinity. The inside was an entirely different world where the magniloquent lifestyle of the nouveau riche and famous came alive nightly.

The latest dance music blared as we entered through a series of ornately draped reddish-gold velvet curtains. Our hostess, Bryanna, seemed to know everyone in the establishment. A good-looking gentleman by the name of Eugammon came to greet us. After a round of 'kissy-face' introductions, he showed us to our dining table above two flights of stairs. As my eyes adjusted to the atmospherically lit interior, I was amazed to discover an expansive space which appeared relatively small for the exterior. Doric columns stretched high above this three-storey structure. I felt like I had entered an Olympian temple of the Gods. At the far end of the hall sat a gigantic statue of Poseidon, trident in hand; his presence lorded over his dominion of mortals, who were delightfully boogieing on the dance floors below.

Situated on the western part of the building, where we had originally entered, stood a floor-to-ceiling alabaster Athena, guarding the club's entrance with hounds on the left and a spear on her right. All along the peripheral walls and dividing corridors were busts and statuettes of Grecian mythological deities, inviting partiers to an evening of Bacchanalian debauchery.

As we sat ordering our food, I was completely mesmerized by the opulent display of affluence. Bryanna, seeing me dumbfounded, asked, *"What do you think of the place, Young?"*

I stared at her, speechless, while my Valet responded on my behalf. *"The last time he set foot inside a dance club was several months ago. The CLUB bears no comparison to this venue."*

Our hostess replied, *"As you saw upon entering, there is a long line of people waiting for the opportunity to glimpse this voguish establishment. The management here is very picky. This is a playground for the international elite only."*

Before Bryanna could finish her sentence, a hand was upon her shoulder. Surprised by this sudden interference, she turned to face her intruder only to discover a dashingly handsome gentleman in his early 30s, bending down to kiss her cheeks.

The Aga Khan

"How wonderful to see you, B," the man greeted our transsexual model.

"Goodness gracious, Aga, when did you arrive in Athens? Who are you here with?"

The men in our group stood as Bryanna introduced us to Prince Karim Aga Khan.

"Do join us, K. What have you been up to since I last saw you in Rome?"

Karim replied, *"My dear, I've been keeping busy. You, of all people, should know I never stop working. I just arrived from Pune. I was overseeing the renovation of the palace. It's been a long and tedious project, but you know, B, I'm enjoying every moment."*

A waiter brought a chair for His Highness. He sat beside Bryanna and continued jokingly, *"Are all these beautiful creatures your model friends?"*

"Mary and I are working on a Revlon shoot at the Acropolis tomorrow with Bruce," she said, nodding in the photographer's direction. *"Sepheaon is a fantastic make-up artist for Revlon, and these four virile young men are visiting Greece before heading back to their respective school and university."*

The Imam directed his question to the youngest person at the table, *"Where are you studying, young man?"*

"I'm a student at Daltonbury Hall in England, Sir. Andy and I are on a foreign student exchange program to the Middle East. When school term begins in a week and a half, we'll be stationed in Bahrain." I replied timidly.

My Valet continued on my behalf, *"His Highness, the Prince, has kindly taken me and Young into his Household. We are most grateful to him for his hospitality."*

"P is a good friend of mine. When are you boys scheduled to be at the Quwah?" he asked, referring to P's palatial home.

"Three weeks from now, Sir."

"Very good! I've invited P to spend time at Aiglemont, my French country estate. I'm sure I'll be seeing the two of you soon. P likes to travel with his entourage wherever he goes."

Andy responded on our behalf, "Thank you, Sir! I'm sure we'll meet again."

"Bryanna, you must come to see me at Aiglemont. Get away to rejuvenate in the country; fresh air will do you good."

"That will be splendid! I'd love to visit Aiglemont again. The last time I visited was a year ago."

K chirped in quickly, "I'll send my plane to pick you up when you are ready to come for a visit. Call me. Maybe you can come when Young and Andy are visiting with the Prince. Have you met P?"

"I don't believe I have. It'll be fun to visit when the boys are there. These two make a cute couple, don't you think?"

"They are indeed an ardent duo, and they are so charmingly polite. I like them already." His Highness agreed with Bryanna.

As our scrumptious dinner arrived, Prince Karim excused himself to return to the company he had arrived with. I couldn't help but ask, "Who is the Aga Khan?"

Oscar looked at me in shock. My BB went on to explain, "He is Aga Khan IV, international business magnate and a well-known racehorse owner and breeder."

Mary added, "He is the reigning Imam of Nizari Ismailism, a denomination of Ismailism within the Shia Islamic faith with 15 million adherents worldwide."

Alfonzo cut in, "Ten years ago, he succeeded his grandfather, Sir Sultan Muhammad Shah Aga Khan III, when he had just turned twenty. Their family claims direct descent from the Prophet Muhammad. Ali, the Prophet's cousin and son-in-law, was supposedly the first Imam in Shia Islam. Ali's wife, Fatima az-Zahra was the Prophet's daughter from his first marriage."

Andy took over, saying, "Aga Khan IV is considered by his followers a 'huijah', or proof of God on earth. He is believed to be infallible and totally immune from sin."

Mary resumed, "He is also considered by his followers to be the carrier of the eternal 'Noor of Allah', 'Light of God', a unique concept to a certain Shia denomination."

"Whoever and whatever he is, he is a very powerful man both in international political and social arenas. He's very influential and a well-connected person to be friends with," Bryanna supplemented.

"If you ask me, I think he is interested in you romantically. Don't you agree?" I said with gusto.

The model laughed heartily at my remark, knowing that there was an element of truth to my statement. She did not answer; instead she changed the subject when our delicious desserts arrived.

Poseidon's Cave

The dance music was too inviting for me to stop my happy feet from thumping to the rhythm of the disco beat. I had to dance, and dance I did with Mary, Sepheaon, Annika, Bryanna, Bruce, Alfonzo, Oscar, and of course, my beloved Valet and guardian, Andy. After the sixth song of whirling and twirling on the dance floor, I was ready for a break. While dancing, a certain smell permeated through the rotunda of this great hall. I could not decipher what the pungent smell was until I asked my lover.

Andy took my hand and guided me away from the disco floor to a less noisy section of the PARTHENON. Under the dimly lit ambience lighting and segregated from the noisy dance area by layers of purplish golden organza drapes, we entered Poseidon's Cave.

Upon entry we were greeted by an abundance of luxurious cushions strewn over a sea of oriental rugs covering every inch of the floor. As my eyes slowly adjusted to my new surroundings, I was unfazed to find an ocean of naked or semi naked bodies intertwined in heated passion.

Andy guided me to several empty seats where I could rest my tired feet. He headed to the bar to get me some water. The moment my guardian moved away, a hand reached over to pass me a rolled cigarette. The grinning man had a dazed look in his eyes as he leaned over and said, *"Give it a try, you'll like this. It's good."*

"Thank you for offering. I don't smoke."

"Give it a try, boy; you'll see things you've never dreamed of seeing." He pressed my hand to take the burning stub.

"Don't be such a spoilsport, puff on it." He pressured.

Reluctantly, I inhaled. Before I had a chance to take another puff, I was choking and coughing uncontrollably. Suddenly, the room became vibrantly distorted. I felt myself floating as if some unseen force had lifted me off the ground. The entire room turned psychedelic. Everything around me was intensely bright, as if I had entered a mythological realm or a different reality.

The man who had handed me the smoke had suddenly sprouted a pair of gargantuan emerald wings. His fiery, pernicious eyes were staring at my heart, and I thought he might tear it out of my chest. I backed into a corner in fear. With my hands across my face, I made a desperate attempt to avoid his claws while he pawed at my helplessness. I tried running, but my legs would not move. I dodged his evil grasps at every angle, yet he kept attacking me relentlessly. I rolled around in the sea of cushions, afraid that this terrifying monster would snatch me to his cave of horrors. I did not desire to be held captive by this flagitious teratism.

In my depth of despair, a pair of colossal white wings descended to shelter me from harm. The benevolent angel from my Daltonbury Hall dream had manifested to my rescue. Peeping through his feathery downs, he was at once Andy and Oscar. They appeared to be one and the same, and yet they were different, depending on the angle from which I observed this celestial being.

The warmth of his touch washed away my fears; the coziness of his musculature and the beauty of his entrancing gaze brought peace and tranquility back to my injured soul. I held onto him tightly before falling into a deep, trance-like slumber.

When I awoke at dawn the next morning, I suffered a splitting headache and an extremely dry mouth. Andy was giving me water from our bedside glass, while Oscar slept soundly next to me. I found myself back at our cabin on the Kahyya'm. How I got there I had no idea. *"What happened?"* I asked my guardian.

"You blacked out at the PARTHENON. Oscar and I had to carry you back to the boat. You tell me what happened?"

"I don't know? The last thing I remember was being cradled in the bosom of an altruistic angel who resembled both you and Oscar simultaneously. Then I fell into blackness, wrapped in the comfort of the spirit's soothing wings."

My guardian whispered, *"Try to recall what happened after I left to get you a glass of water at the bar?"*

"A man handed me a rolled cigarette of sorts and insisted that I take several puffs. I choked on the inhalation before plunging into a series of hallucinations. . ."

"Ahh haa! That man must have given you a dose of marijuana and LSD rolled as a joint."

"What is marijuana and LSD?" I questioned.

"They are recreational drugs, popular among hardcore partygoers. It often produces a temporary high and hallucinatory experience. It is addictive when used regularly.

"You, young man, I can never leave you alone. You must be more careful and not so trusting of strangers. A time will come when I won't be there to assist you." Andy reprimanded me for my imprudence.

I fell back onto the bed without contradicting my mentor. My head was pounding with excruciating pain. I had no wish to argue with my lover; I knew what he said was correct. Instead, my Valet said, *"I'll get you some Alka-seltzer. You better get some rest before we troop off to the fashion shoot, which you, boy, promised Mary you'd attend."*

Melancholy

After my Valet departed, I stared at my 'big brother' and lover lying next to me. His serenity reminded me of the angel I had seen the night before I fell unconscious. I was thrown into a dismal state of melancholy once again. Tears of sadness filled my being as they slid down the corners of my eyes. My heart reached out to my handsome lover. I stretched out my hand to touch his flawless face as illimitable love flowed from my palms to his skin. He did not stir. I detected a complacent smile on his upturned lips. *"Oscar, Oscar, Oscar, why do I love you so?"* I muttered quietly. *"Why is parting such a difficult task?"*

12

Sex & Nudity

"Sex ought to be a wholly satisfying link between two affectionate people from which they emerge unanxious, rewarded, and ready for more."

Alex Comfort

August 2012

Hi A.S.,

I'll jump straight to the point to answer your questions:
- *Did you fancy other 'big brothers' and Valets who were at the Bahriji?*

Yes, I did fancy the Bahriji Valets but not necessarily Daltonbury Hall's 'big brothers.' Every student at Daltonbury was allocated a BB, but not all Freshmen were groomed to enter E.R.O.S. Most of the BBs at the English boarding school had to satisfy certain criteria before they could be accepted into the 'big brother' stewardship program. Most were selected for their academic excellence, character, and their personal achievements.

Those Freshmen who had the potential to enter E.R.O.S. were allocated attractive 'big brothers,' because these BB recruits were also members of E.R.O.S. They had once been E.R.O.S. Freshmen. Aesthetically pleasing appearance was vital to their recruitment selection process. This was not the case with the 'regular' BBs who were not training Freshmen as potential E.R.O.S. members.

On the other hand, when I arrived at the Bahriji, in my young eyes, all the Valets and accompanying BBs were handsome and possessed a certain je ne se quoi that was extremely pleasing and attractive to the eyes as well as the intellect.

Of course I fancied many of the Bahriji Valets. How could I not? Any homosexual adolescent boy in the early stages of his sexual explorations would have felt the same way.

That brings me to your next question:
- If you did, how were you taught to control your sexual urges and not to desire or solicit their attention and affection? Or was there an open-to-all policy?

We were not so much taught to control our sexual urges; rather, we were instructed to use our rational judgment and body language to analyze whether the people we were interested in would respond to our intended desires. There were no written rules that officially restricted Freshmen, Juniors and Valets from forming strong 'Philia' bonds. If that bond stretched into a romantic liaison, that was okay, as long as it was consensual.

That was the reason Andy asked if I would welcome him into my bed when he was assigned as my Valet. If you remember, I did not invite him into my bed until after our return to the Bahriji after our Red Sea Riviera sojourn. If he had forced himself on me, he would have been eliminated from the BB/Valet program.

As I also mention in **Initiation**, there was a kind of unspoken rule of thumb for Freshmen and Valets not to overstep the boundaries of other Valets or Freshmen when an adolescent boy was in training, unless the trainer (Valet/BB) invited the said Valet into their inner sanctum *as part of the boy's sensual and sexual training programme.*

For example, it was acceptable for Nikee to have invited Andy to participate in our three-way forest rendezvous and to help instigate the gym-room orgy. The BBs were there together as our trainers.

- *Were all the students at the Bahriji highly sexed?*

I suppose Bahriji students were sexually active, although I wouldn't consider them "highly sexed." We were taught to enjoy sex as part of natural adolescent growth. We were taught not to harbor guilt regarding the sex act. As Pat Paulsen so rightly said, "In opposition to sex education: let the kids today learn it where we did - in the gutters." Thank God I was one of the lucky few who did not have to learn it in the gutters but was expertly taught by professional mentors.

- *Did the students from the boys' and girls' schools have sexual relationships before being allocated to the various Arab households?*

Officially, the answer is no. Students from the boys' and girls' schools were segregated unless we were brought together for practical sensual and sex education lessons.

Unofficially, like most adolescents in regular schools, there were bound to be situations in which the teenagers would meet on their own without guidance from elders. This is inevitable; from the onset of puberty, males and females have always found ways to copulate throughout the history of mankind. It is in our natural human DNA to sexually desire another.

Although I'm not a hundred percent certain, I am fairly positive that Bahriji boys and girls would find an outlet for their sexual experimentation, be it lawful or otherwise, prior to being relocated to their respective Arab households.

1967

The Acropolis

By the time Andy and I arrived at the Acropolis, it was late afternoon. The Revlon photo-shoot was well on its way since Bruce wanted to catch the beauty of the evening sun before it set over the distant horizon. Bryanna and Mary, beautifully made up by Sepheaon, were draping themselves over the ruins of the Temple of Athena Nike. Posing this way and that, they moved in synchronicity like a pair of ethereal butterflies fluttering in and out of different chiffon dresses, which they wore throughout the shoot.

Fortuny

Several finely pleated dresses caught my attention. I was curious to find out who the designer was, so I asked, *"Who is the designer who created these beauties?"*
Bryanna replied while moving gracefully for the photographer, *"These are vintage Fortuny."*
"Who is Fortuny? I've never heard of this designer's name."
Sephoean chimed in, *"Mariano Fortuny y Madrazo was a turn-of-the-century creative genius. He was the true Renaissance man of his time; although he was trained as a painter, he was also an accomplished designer, architect, inventor, couturier, and lighting technician.*

"The man is most remembered for his innovative pleated silk dresses.

"He was also an excellent interior, stage designer and photographer. In the early 1900s, Fortuny invented a unique method of dyeing and printing fabrics. This technique often produced rich, vibrant colors resembling ancient brocades, velvets and tapestries."

Mary added, *"I read an article in Vogue Italia that mentioned that he was born in the ancient Spanish city of Granada, but he made his mark in Paris, Venice and Rome. He died in his Venetian Palace in the late 1940s and was buried in the Verano Cemetery in Rome."*

"Whoever he is, his designs are superbly and delicately luscious!" I exclaimed as I reached over to feel the luxurious fabric on Mary's body.

"In his early years," Bryanna explained, *"the designer created a rectangular silk scarf with geometric and asymmetrical patterns we know today as the 'Knossos scarf.'*

"The items that made him famous were his Art Nouveau dresses, which he designed and made for theatrical legends, the likes of Isadora Duncan and Sarah Bernhardt. These dresses were known as 'Delphos robes.' They were inspired by ancient Grecian gowns."

"You mean like the clothing depicted in Sir Alma Tadema's paintings?" I inquired. *"I love his paintings. All his figures are so ethereal, as if they don't do any active work except drape themselves around and pose on marble floors all day long."*

The women laughed at my critique before Sepheaon continued, *"Fortuny's simple, long, and loose-fitting gowns were both artistic and functional. You may say it's a one-size-fits-all garment. These clothes are unique in their detailing.*

"Young, take a look at these beautiful glass beads that are so eloquently trimmed around the edges of the hems. They are both ornamental and practical. The colors of these dresses change according to the light and movement of the body. Aren't they fantastic works of wearable art?"

"Is that why Fortuny designs are evergreen?" I commented with confidence.

Bryanna gave me a loving wink, said, *"You're correct, boy. A good designer designs clothes that are of the moment, whereas a great designer designs clothes that are relevant forever."*

Test Shots

The sun was rapidly disappearing over the distant horizon when the Revlon shoot came to a close. Bruce, the photographer, was eager to ask Alfonzo, Oscar, Andy and me if we would pose for some test shots he wanted to present to an upcoming contemporary artist, Vittorio.

Bruce informed us, *"Vittorio is a painter friend of mine. He asked me to scout for suitable male models for an upcoming mythological Greco-Roman series he's planning to paint."*

Bryanna chirped, *"I've been invited to the unveiling of his new exhibition this evening. Would you guys like to come see his work? This will give you an opportunity to view his painting style."*

I was the first to respond, *"Yes! I'll accompany you."*

Alfonzo added, *"It'll be fun to attend an art exhibition. I'd like to see his work, too."*

Andy inquired, *"What kind of paintings does he do?"*

"He does mainly male nudes. They are tastefully done," the photographer responded.

"I'm sure you guys will love his art. He combines photography and paint. His art has an erotic quality that is both classic and contemporary. I like his work very much," Bryanna assured us.

"Let's get cracking on the test shots before I miss the gorgeous sunset. You guys can discuss Vittorio's paintings later," Bruce reminded the group.

The photographer took some amazing nude shots of Alfonzo, Andy, Oscar and me against the ruins before we called it a day.

Vittorio's Men

After an authentic dinner at Filippou (Φιλίππου), we were ready for an evening of art. The gallery was located at Kolonaki at Haritos, just off the main shopping street of Patriarchou Ioakim, in a classy area of Athens. The venue was already filled with guests, art aficionados and beautiful people *ooh*ing and *ahh*ing at the paintings hanging against the white walls.

As soon as we entered, the gallery owner came to greet Bryanna, who, like Mario (remember Count Mario Conti in **Initiation** and **Unbridled?**), knew everyone who was anyone in the international social circuit.

As our entourage stood and admired the exotic male specimens displayed on the walls, a gentleman in his early 30s came over to introduce himself.

"I am Vittorio. Welcome to the gallery. Bruce had mentioned to me earlier that you would be coming to my exhibition." The artist said. *"Do you like my work?"*

Alfonzo complimented, *"I like the way you make the photographs resemble oil paintings. The men in the pictures are beautiful!"*

"Thank you! I hope you guys will be my models as well in the not-too-distant future. You are the type of men I like to photograph and paint."

I couldn't help asking, *"Your painting looks so realistic. We know a couple of photographers who work in similar genre to yours."*

"Oh, really? You have to introduce them to me. I'd like to see their work." Vittorio responded.

I looked at my Valet to make sure I hadn't said the wrong thing. Andy answered politely on my behalf, *"I'm sure our photographer friends will love your art. They too love to photograph models in the nude."

I chimed in before my Valet could continue, *"We modeled for them in Italy and the United States recently. I'm sure they'd love to meet and talk shop with you."*

Oscar added, *"You may already know or have heard of them, or at least the socialite Count Mario Conti from Venice?"*

"Ahh, the name rings a bell. After all, the male-nude art world is not very large. I'm sure, at one time or another, we are bound to encounter each other."

"We'll definitely introduce you and your art to our friends. You do fantastic work. I, for one, will be delighted to be your model." I commented delightfully.

"Once again, this boy is jumping the gun. We are leaving for the isle of Lesbos tomorrow before heading to Mykonos. I don't know if we'll have the time to model for you," my guardian riposted.

"I'm also travelling to Mykonos to stay with some friends in a couple of days. I'd be happy to meet you there to show you the island. Maybe I can photograph you guys there?" The painter offered his solution.

"That would be splendid! It's always good to have someone who knows the place as a guide, instead of us stumbling around, clueless, not knowing where we are heading," Oscar responded before Andy could answer no.

"Okay then! I'll meet you in Mykonos two days from now."

Before we had departed from the gallery, we had already scheduled a date with the artist.

Beneath The Twinkling Stars

I awoke in the middle of the night to the gentle sway of the Kahyya'm. Andy, sleeping soundly next to me, did not stir. I reached over to cuddle my other lover, but he was not in bed. I tossed and turned for a few minutes before venturing onto the deck, wrapped in a large cashmere shawl.

Under the silvery moon, a couple of shadows oscillated in the dark. I crept quietly to have a closer look. Wrapped together intimately were two figures that I recognized. Alfonzo was French-kissing my BB under the twinkling stars. Oscar responded passionately. He gripped the Spaniard's head, pulling his friend towards him. Their tongues pried open each other's mouths with sensual abandon. Under the silvery moon their nakedness glistened with sensuality. I was mesmerized by the erotica unfolding before me. I stayed silently to watch. They moved in unison, as if two ephebes were training for combat, but in the art of love. It was a beautiful sight to behold, and I wished their actions not to stop.

They wrestled each other to the floor, each combatant intransigently trying to gain the upper hand. I was watching an erotic movie of two fine specimens of manhood in the throes of passion. Jealousies did not enter my mind; in their place, I felt admiration and veneration. Surprised by my own response, I observed the unfolding scenario unobtrusively, allowing nature to take its course.

The soft moans echoing on the deck stirred my libido to attention. My cock began growing beneath my wrap. I reached to stroke my throbbing erection; little did I notice the tall figure standing behind me, watching my every action. The more I watched, the more I was aroused. I discarded my covering and began masturbating to the rhythm of my own love dance.

The homoerotic flowering of the two beauties triggered my explosion. My eyes closed, I spewed my seed onto my belly and thighs.

Suddenly, I felt an ardent tongue lapping up my spill. I opened my eyes in bewilderment, only to find my Valet's handsome face staring back at me. Before I could utter a word, Andy had inserted his sperm-covered finger into my mouth, keeping me silent. He fed me my sweet deliciousness. I licked and suckled at his length, tasting the gooeyness until I drank the last drop from its tip.

My lover reached to kiss me, feeding me more of the nourishment he had just imbricated from my stomach. We kissed passionately, exchanging our appetizing fluids with tacit enthusiasm. We had no wish to disrupt the lovers' copulation.

Andy lifted me into the air, my legs straddling against his chest; he spread my buttocks open with his firm hands before easing his curvaceousness into my tender core with precision. I held onto his neck firmly as he bounced into me repeatedly. I yearned for Andy's love. His lusciousness, now buried deep within, further affirmed his desirousness, and I knew that we were fully merged in a sensually sexual journey towards spiritual nirvana.

My lover leaned me against a balustrade, and we sealed our union as we had on our first encounter. His love was too enticing an enchantment; I could not bear my lover to hold off his imperium over my being. I was emboldening his urgencies into my willing orifice. I coveted my soul mate, willing him to stay within me for as long as he could before his amorousness could not stifle his attraction towards my person any longer. He released himself inside me, whimpering inaudible words of love softly into my ear.

We stayed immovable until his member slid out involuntarily. Only then did my winsome lover carry me back to our cozy bed.

We fell into peaceful slumber. When I awoke the following morning, Oscar was sleeping soundly next to me, his hand draped nonchalantly across my naked chest.

13

The Isle of Lesbos

"I've always known I was meant to dominate your sex and avenge my own."
Marquise de Merteuil
(Dangerous Liaisons)

1967

Molivos/Mithymna/Molyvos

The Kahyya'm was docked at Molivos, located at the northern tip of Lesvos, more famously known as the Isle of Lesbos. The tranquil village of Molivos, also known as Mithymna or Molyvos, is arguably the most beautiful village on this island, with its picturesque harbor dominated by a medieval castle and tiers of red-tiled stone houses that line the slopes, away from the cerulean sea.

Music has always been the beloved activity of the Mithymnians, and, true to form, we were greeted by popular Greek music when we stepped ashore. It has also been said that the grapes of Mithymna were unequalled in their aroma and nectars; hence, the worship of Zeus, Dionysus and Hercules included delicious wine from this part of the world.

Our group, which consisted of Mary, Bryanna, Alfonzo, Oscar, Andy and me, rented scooters to tour this island of their native daughter Sappho. As we cruised along the costal roads, I couldn't help but marvel at the wonders I had seen since my recruitment into E.R.O.S. I held my lover's waist adoringly as we scooted towards the Petrified Forest.

At the Petrified Forest

I was surprised to find a barren, rocky hill instead of a lush, dense forest. Under closer observation, I was amazed to find the fossilized remains of local flora, and fauna imbedded in the solid rocks. I asked our entourage, *"How did these leaves and small animals get crystalized into these gigantic boulders?"*

"Young, this used to be a dense forest filled with lush vegetation. One day, the Amazon warriors arrived. As soon as they neared the trees and animals, the wildlife withered and died. That's why this place is called the Petrified Forest." Bryanna said with mock seriousness.

"Really? Did the animals in the forest die because they saw the Amazon warriors coming? Where did these warriors come from? And why were they here?" I responded shockingly.

Oscar added with a sly grin on his face, *"Bryanna is telling the truth. The Amazon women warriors came to petrify the forest."*

"You guys are pulling my leg. There were no Amazon women here to petrify the forest, were there?" I turned toward my mentor with an inquiring look.

They burst out laughing at my gullibility before Andy replied, *"Young, you are so credulous. Don't believe everything these guys tell you. They are having fun with you."*

I looked at Andy for further explanation, but Mary chimed in, *"Actually, it was the Spartan women who terrified the forest and not the Amazonians. Historians over the centuries had been debating the differences and similarities between these two groups of warrior women."*

I looked at the female model with doubt. I wasn't sure if she was telling the truth or teasing me. She continued, *"You see, Young, Spartan females were influenced by Amazonian women. It is a known fact that the Amazonians lived within a matriarchal society as compared to the patriarchal Spartan women. But it is also true that Spartan females were expected to be fierce and be able to defend their land at the spur of the moment."*

Bryanna added, *"You may or may not know that the patroness of both societies was Artemis, the goddess of the hunt, the protector of animals, women, young girls and youth."*

"Are you telling me that Spartan females and Amazonian women were butch dykes?" I asked.

Our entourage broke into loud, uncontrollable laughter. Finally Oscar commented after much merriment, *"Young, Young, Young, I'm sure not all the women were 'butch dykes', as you put it. But it is a fact that women of ancient Sparta were a special breed. They were athletic and educated, and they had quite a high social status."*

"The best-known Spartan female was the legendary Helen of Troy. She wasn't really from Troy. Paris abducted her and caused the ten-year Trojan War.

"Contrary to contemporary society's image of Helen, portrayed as a beautifully made-up and delicate, obedient lady, ancient Spartan women were forbidden to wear any kind of make-up," Bryanna explained. *"Instead, they were encouraged to pursue natural physical perfection and self-dependence. They could own land and slaves as well as lend money.*

"Adolescent girls were known to go through hours of vigorous physical education daily, which was similar to the regimented training that their brothers and boy-cousins had. They raced, wrestled, threw discus and javelin, and fist-fought. They also coached themselves in the courage of withstanding pain. To them, birching was not just a

punishment; it was training in "maternal power." They knew that with each whip, their legs and hips would become stronger; moreover, the more scars they had, the more their girlfriends and adult peers would respect them. Girls who didn't have visible scars were mocked as weak boys and were called 'milksop' and 'coward'. Therefore, they were by no means meek and genteel, nor were they glamorous as they are in Hollywood movies.

"The poet Ovid painted a young Helen in 'Heroides' wrestling naked outdoor in palaestra (ancient Greek wrestling school). She wielded weapons and also fought in hand-to-hand combat. Spartan women were always involved in their combative culture."

Mary interjected, *"Oohh! I'm beginning to like the Helen you are describing."*

I exclaimed, *"You like macho warrior women?"*

They laughed at my childlike naivety. The transsexual model continued, *"Mary, Helen was definitely not a weak, submissive and romantic woman who buckled under brute force. It is highly probably that the self-dependent, strong and physically trained Helen was hijacked by the effeminate Priam's son against her will; perhaps Helen attracted the dandy to her and departed with him to Troy.*

"One thing is for sure, don't believe everything Hollywood shows you. The real Helen of Troy can well be compared to an Amazonian woman."

Once again, I couldn't help asking, *"Mary, are you a lesbian?"*

Andy gave me a slap on my buttocks, looked at me sternly, and said, *"That's none of your business, boy. You can't go round probing into people's sexual preferences."*

I kept quiet, not daring to query further. Mary replied smilingly, *"My dear boy, when the correct opportunity arises, you'll be the first to know."*

My Valet changed the subject. He responded, *"It is common knowledge that young Spartans were not locked up, waiting for marriage. Youngsters of both genders competed and trained together in the nude. During their mating games, both sexes participated in gymnastic exercises, athletic contests, and celebrations with song and dance.*

"And Spartan women rarely married before twenty, while the men started their mandatory military training at twenty-one, which could last for as long as ten years."

Bryanna chirped, *"Therefore, Helen and her coeval girls participated delightfully in the mating games, looking for future partners. Male youths often stared at the strongest and deftest girls..."*

Before the transsexual model could continue, Alfonzo said, *"So much for this history lesson on Amazonian warriors, Spartan women and Helen of Troy. I want to know the real reason why this forest was petrified?"*

"It's a simple natural phenomenon, Alfonzo. The forest was covered with volcanic ashes after eons of volcanic eruptions. Over time, the remains of the flora and fauna became imbedded between layers of hot molten lava. They fossilized, and today we have the Petrified Forest." Andy put the matter to rest.

Skala Eresou

The charming sleepy village of the Skala Eresou was like any other Greek village. We found a quaint cafe to rest our tired feet and to take in the beautiful scenery.

Mary, Andy and I took a walk round the village; we wanted to explore the birthplace of Sappho, one of the most famous Greek poets from antiquity. The two boys, Oscar, Alfonzo and Bryanna wanted to take in some sun, and they enjoyed the tranquility of the pristine beach situated in front of the cafe.

As we approached the village square to view Sappho's bust, perched in the middle, I inquired of Mary, *"How do you know so much about ancient Greek women?"*

"I'm interested in women's roles throughout history, she continued, *"Just as you are intrigued about the history of homosexuality."*

"Do you really like masculine-looking women?" I asked inquisitively.

Andy gave me another implacable look but said nothing. Mary did not answer my question until she had circled around Sappho's bust. *"Young man, have you heard of another Greek legendary female athlete by the name of Atalanta?"*

"No," I replied.

"Atalanta was born in Arcadia and was a realization of strength and courage combined with femininity and eroticism. She is best known for her participation in male activities such as hunting, warfare, wrestling, and running. At the same time, she also possessed an aura of femininity and sexuality. That is the kind of woman I admire."

"Is she your role model?" I queried.

"Yes, she is. That is the type of woman I love: strong, powerful yet romantic and exotic. I'm drawn to these kinds of women."

"Doesn't Alfonzo mind you having affairs with women?" I blabbed without giving my question a second thought.

"Young!" Andy reprimanded.

"It's okay. I may as well be honest with the both of you. Although, on the surface, our acquaintances think Alfonzo and I are lovers, we have an agreement in which we can see other people on the side. I'm attracted to males and females. Alfonzo has the same inclinations." Mary

continued, *"The reasons we are together are several. First and foremost, we are very good friends and we understand each other well. He is like my brother and I his sister. We are each other's confidants."*

"So I was correct all along. You are a lesbian," I chirped.

"Young! Stop your insolence at once," my Valet scolded.

"It's okay, Andy. This boy just can't help being himself. He wants to know everything there is to know about life. I don't blame him for his out-rightness. That's what makes him charming and loveable. Don't be so hard on him, Andy. I know you love him as much as I adore him."

Before my guardian could respond, I chimed, "Mary, please continue." I was hoping she would continue telling us her other reasons for being with Alfonso.

Instead, she said, *"According to Greek Mythology, Atalanta sailed with the Argonauts to find the Golden Fleece. She was the only brave female who traveled with the men. She suffered injuries in the battle at Colchis but was healed by Medea.*

"Legend also has it that Atalanta's father wanted a son. When he found out she was female, he exposed his daughter in the forest, where a bear suckled the infant until the goddess Artemis sent hunters to rescue her. Raised by her rescuers, she grew to be a huntress. *She was the most fleet-footed mortal alive, perhaps with the exception of the mythical Euphemus, who was rumored to be able to walk on water.*

"When her suitors sought her hand in marriage, she gave them a choice – they could defeat her in a footrace and earn her hand, or they could be executed. She outran all of them except one: Hippomenes. He had prayed to Aphrodite for help, and the goddess gave him three golden apples from Hesperides to bowl across Atalanta's path

during the deciding race. The undefeated sprinter noticed the golden fruits and reached down to gather each apple. In so doing, she gave her suitor time to run ahead to win the race."

Andy mentioned, *"This story bears resemblance to Puccini's famous opera Turandot, in which the Chinese princess challenges her suitors to solve her riddles. Those who failed were also executed."*

"Maybe Puccini copied the Atalanta's myth and adapted it to Turandot?" I remarked confidently.

"You, young man, are too haughty for your own good," my Valet rebuked light-heartedly.

Mary resumed, *"Atalanta's most famous feat was her victorious wrestling match against Peleus during the funeral games of Pelias. Atalanta managed to defeat the male hero, who later used his experience of wrestling with a woman to marry the giant sea-nymph Thetis. Peleus managed to defeat her in a wrestling match, and he fathered Achilles.*

"Interestingly, the most widespread Greek representation of the female form was the nude portrayal of Atalanta wrestling Peleus in Palaestra. This portraiture indicates that Spartan women athletes were held in great esteem as competitors against men."

Andy added, *"The ancient Olympic Games were almost entirely male-only events. Women were forbidden to attend the main stadium at Olympia, where running and combative sports were held. Women were allowed to participate in equestrian events only if they owned their own horses."*

"But Atalanta defied these man-made rules by competing in the running competition. She inspired the creation of the Heraea or Heraia Games, the women's version of the Olympic Games, dedicated to the goddess Hera," Mary interrupted quickly. *"These races were supposedly run between virgin girls who ran in accordance*

to their age groups. The winner was presented with a crown of olives and a share of the cow sacrificed to Hera. The winners were dedicated statues.

"There is a statue of 'a runner girl' from Sparta on display in the Vatican Museum. On a stump beside the statue is a palm branch symbolizing her victory."

"It's getting late and I'm hungry. Let's find our group and go for dinner," I suggested vehemently.

14

Eros & E.R.O.S.

"Whatever else can be said about sex, it cannot be called a dignified performance."
Helen Lawrenson

1967

Mykonos, Greece

Vittorio and his friend Argos came to meet us at the dock. Hopping onto the Kahyya'm, he directed captain Kasim to a remote part of the island where one could see the bottom of the pristine aquamarine sea from above deck. We arrived at the artist's lavish private residence, which was sheltered by hilly cliffs on either side.

Earlier that morning, Bryanna and Mary had returned to Athens for a modeling assignment, leaving Alfonzo to join Oscar, Andy and me on the last leg of our Greek islands sojourn.

The deck hands began lowering a small sailboat for us to row ashore in. Our host suggested, *"Let's swim to the beach."* He had stripped naked before even finishing his sentence. He plunged into the cool inviting water, followed by Argos, Alfonzo and Oscar. Andy was left to instruct the Abds that the sailboat was no longer necessary. The two of us dove into the sunlit ocean. It was refreshing to swim in the buff. Alfonzo challenged us to race to shore as Argos remarked, *"We'll claim our prize from the last one out from the ocean."* On that declaration, we clamored towards the shoreline. Who was the last one out of the water? *Moi.*

As we lay panting on the white sand, Argos announced merrily, *"Young, you've lost. We'll be claiming our prize before you leave Mykonos."*

"What's the prize?" I asked.

Vittorio answered laughingly, *"You'll find out soon enough. For now, it remains a secret."*

At Super Paradise

After a refreshing outdoor shower, we headed to Super Paradise for a late lunch. Super Paradise was one of the three public beaches on which one could strip bare to sunbathe naked; it was also a busy center where an array of bars and taverns served delicious salads and traditional Greek meals.

Vittorio guided us to a stylish restaurant. The waiter found us a quiet courtyard table at the back of the house, overflowing with orangey pink bougainvilleas and pergolas dripping with grapes. As soon as the good-looking waiter took our orders, Vittorio announced, *"I love Mykonos. I've been coming to this island for the past six years. The house I rented is an ideal place for me to paint and to work on my art in solitude.*

"Although the island is fairly small, I get the modern amenities I require. Most importantly, I love the people who vacation on this island, especially the men. I discover most of my models on the beaches."

Andy inquired, *"What is there to do besides watching handsome naked men frolic around?"*

Vittorio laughed heartily, *"Of course there are places of interest to visit. Mykonos is more perfect than its postcards. We'll take a stroll and you can see the houses, churches, and windmills that stand along narrow alleyways, where overfed cats love to gaze serenely at passersby."*

"I'm already in love with the beauty of Mykonos. Did you guys notice the door frames and window shutters? They are painted in splashes of sky blues and jade greens," I babbled excitedly.

BB Oscar ruffled my hair, saying, *"You are the only boy I know who would not miss details like that. You are such an observant little artist."*

I smiled but said nothing. Vittorio asked, *"What kind of art do you do?"*

For reasons unbeknownst to me, I blabbed, *"I design ethereal-looking clothes. Just like those worn by women in Sir Alma Tadema's paintings. And those that Mariano Fortuny designs."*

My Valet looked at me with astonishment. He hadn't expected me to pronounce that I was a full-fledged fashion designer, let alone a designer of Grecian dresses. Vittorio countered, *"So, young man, you are a fashion designer."*

"Yes, I am!" I claimed.

Andy chimed in before I could continue, *"This boy is so full of himself. He loves to brag about his fashion work. He still has a way to go before I would officially call him a fashion designer..."*

I added quickly, *"That is not true, Andy. I had my first fashion show six months ago in Kuala Lumpur, and I styled the Kosk and the Sekham women's wardrobes. That makes me a legitimate fashion designer."*

The group found my proclamations amusing. Oscar chirped, *"Young is a pretty good designer. I've seen him dress the Sekham women, and they do look very stylish."*

Argos queried, *"Who are the Kosk and Sekham women?"*

I stared at Andy, knowing that I might have let too much out of the bag. As always, my quick-witted Valet had a suitable answer to everything. He said, *"We have been on a student exchange program to the Middle East for the past six months. The Kosk and the Sekham were the households where we were stationed.*

"It is true that Young did act as a fashion consultant to both households, and I have to give him credit for doing a fantastic job dressing the women during their weddings and festive celebrations."

Our host commented, *"I'd love to see some of Young's fashion work. I have friends in the fashion business, and they are always scouting for new talents to work as apprentices in the established ateliers. I'd be happy to introduce them to you."* The man looked at me for a response.

"I don't have any work here to show you, but I'll be happy to draw you a few sketches, so you can see what kind of clothes I design," I twittered delightfully.

"Okay! When we return to my villa, you can show me your sketches, and I'll show you my etchings," he grinned evilly.

At Paraga Beach

After a stroll along the narrow alleyways of Platis Yialos, where houses were sandwiched closely together, we arrived at a small, secluded beach where the younger crowd hung out. The bodies of gay nude bathers dotted the far end of the shoreline as they soaked up the Aegean sun.

Vittorio motioned us to follow. As we walked along the sand, he said, *"I'll show you where I find most of my models."*

True to his word, flecked out of public view, nestled among the trees and shrubberies, were couples or groups of men gathered together in the throes of passion. They seemed oblivious and many did not mind voyeurs or onlookers observing their licentious actions. These men were exhibitionists showing off their sexual prowess to whomever wished to watch. Some would move from one group to the next as if playing a game of musical chairs.

As we watched, several men started edging closer to our entourage. They began rubbing their crotches to see if anyone of us would respond in kind. Although I was fascinated by this sexual wantonness, Andy did not care for such brazenness. Pulling on my arm, he led me towards a slightly more public section of the beach, leaving our friends to their devices.

As my Valet and I sat admiring the dramatic sunset reflected on the turquoise water, I couldn't help but lean my head against his shoulder. No words were needed as we marveled at nature's romance.

Suddenly, I felt a pair of hands on my shoulder and warm breath down the back of my neck. Without turning around, I knew that Oscar was behind me. His coziness never failed to ignite my passion. My groin stirred at his touch. Andy kissed my longing lips as I opened willingly to both lovers.

My BB reached his hands into the front of my T-shirt, caressing my already aroused nipples as I reached to fondle Andy's growing organ, concealed behind his denim jeans. I could feel Oscar's throbbing member against my spine while he continued kissing gently at my tender neck.

This erotic foreplay was too titillating for the three of us. We did not care if there were people watching; we went with nature's flow as the ocean waves lapped gently against the rolling sand. I closed my eyes and surrendered to my lovers' adoring embraces.

A short distance away, a camera was clicking unobtrusively at our love-making scenario. I did not open my eyes to see the photographer. My instinct told me that it was none other than the artist whose work we so admired. He was capturing the essence of our heated ardor, the spirit that differentiates a good photograph from a great one. Our host was seizing this rare moment to capture the unravelling sensuality, where affection merges with sexuality, the place where divinity converges with spirituality. Vittorio, the artful conjurer, knew he was onto something special, something more than what his regular models could provide him. Our trio gave him the magical enchantment he desperately craved to propel his artistic endeavor to a new level of artistry. We furnished him with an unbridled honesty where many fear to tread, afraid that their openness may lead to heartbreak.

Unbeknownst to our skilled photographer, we were no ordinary boys. We were fearless E.R.O.S. boys, groomed in the arts of sensuality, sexuality, and most significantly in the Art of Loving.

Our fervent desires propelled us to unimaginable heights of emotional ecstasy. Stripped naked, the three of us had amalgamated into a single entity. I felt Oscar in the core of my being while our beloved Andy lay buried deep inside my BB. We moved in synchronicity to the oscillating motion of our rhythmic breath: Gaia's breathe of life, the life of God, the life of the universal truth.

The hedonisms of our being soon brought us to uncontrollable depths of deliverance. We could stave off no longer our desires for each other. Oscar froze as his love poured into the kernel of my soul. My Valet released his masculinity deep within the mystic tunnel of our lover. I could not hold off the flame of my essence and spewed my flowing fountain onto the powdery sand, and the ocean cleaned away my remnants with each lapping wave, returning my seed to timeless eternity.

The three of us stayed motionless while Vittorio's shutter snapped away, as if Poseidon had granted him permission to document our amour.

We lay, spent, on the edge of the ocean as the last ray of evening light disappeared over the horizon. Only then did we plunge into the sea to wash away the final traces of our union, reverting our primal call back to nature's humanity.

Our photographer approached as we were drying ourselves. *"The three of you are amazing. I believe I caught some priceless pictures in this equipment."* He gazed at his camera before glancing at his groin, which was standing at attention.

"Young, I'm ready to claim my prize." He pushed me to my knees. His manhood throbbed against my face as he pushed my head against his crotch. His bobbing length was too enticing to forego. I plunged my oral orifice onto his bulbousness in a single gulp. I teased and I sucked on the prized possession. I was more than happy to serve my victor his prize. The artist's pulsating equipment was too scrumptious to let loose. I wanted to taste the fluid of this Eraste, who I knew was on the verge of deliverance. He shot on my face before I could inhale another whiff of his masculinity. Andy, Oscar and I shared Vittorio's deposits with the zeal that only seasoned lovers know before I finally opened my eyes to stare at the handsome victor.

Early September 2012

I continued answering Dr. Arius' questions wholeheartedly. He inquired:

Dear Young,

- *Is there a reason why you chose to call the clandestine society "The Enlightened Royal Oracle Society" (E.R.O.S.)? What prompted you to give it that name?*

My answers are several-fold. Let me begin by telling you:

- *I wanted a name that reflected the nature of the secret society without coming close to exposing the actual name of the organization.*

- *Secondly, the Enlightened Royal Oracle Society to me seems an appropriate title, since the program is truly an enlightened education based on ancient Greek philosophies and psychology, especially that of the philosopher Plato. His idealistic concept of Eros spurred much of the program's development, even though Plato did not consider physical attraction a necessary part of Eros. According to his philosophy, "Platonic love" in its original sense can be attained by the intellectual purification of Eros from carnal to an ideal.*

In the case of E.R.O.S., romantic and sexual love does play a vital role in our education. The secret society acknowledges that the full meaning of love should comprise not just the idealized form in Plato's teachings but also that which originated from the divine source since the beginning of mankind.

In his Symposium, Plato argues that Eros is initially felt for a person, but it can become an appreciation for the beauty within that person, or even an appreciation for beauty itself in an ideal sense. Plato also expresses that Eros can help the soul to 'remember' beauty in its pure form. Therefore, it follows that Eros can also contribute to an understanding of truth. For the philosopher, Eros is neither purely human nor purely divine: it is something intermediate, which he terms a 'daimon' (a good or benevolent nature-spirit, a being of the same nature as both mortals and gods).

Adding to Plato's ideology, E.R.O.S. differs in a desire to possess the physical and the physical attraction is vital; therefore, this form of love transcends the divine and the sublime simultaneously. In my experience, the name I chose could not be more apt.

Nevertheless, Eros remains, for Plato, an egocentric love, tending toward conquering and possessing the object that represents a value for mankind. To love the good signifies a desire to possess it forever. Love is therefore always a desire for immortality.

According to my E.R.O.S. education, I was taught to embrace both types of love without fear and with honesty and an open mind. We were to accept the higher form of divine, unconditional love as well as the earthly, carnal love which is inherently built into our human DNA.

Paradoxically, in Plato's theory, the object of Eros does not have to be physically beautiful. This is because the object of Eros is beauty, and the greatest beauty is eternal, whereas physical beauty is in no way eternal. However, if the lover achieves possession of the beloved's inner (i.e. ideal) beauty, his need for happiness will be fulfilled, because happiness is the experience of knowing that you are participating in the ideal.

E.R.O.S., on the other hand, teaches that physical and inner beauty can co-exist simultaneously. When this combination happens, it transforms into a divine experience. The Enlightened Royal Oracle Society also taught me that inner beauty often reflects the outer beauty (physical beauty) and vice versa.

Dear Dr., I will continue to discuss the topic of 'Eros and E.R.O.S.' in my next correspondence. For now, I bid you adieu.

All the best,
Young.

15

Pathway to the Sacred Way

"Boys will be boys."
English proverb

1967

Villa Αγάπη (Love)

"Rise and shine, my beautiful one," my beloved Valet whispered in my ear.

I opened my sleepy eyes to the image of handsome Andy staring down at me. He gave me a tender kiss. *"Time for a morning dip, my darling boy,"* he commanded before lifting me onto his broad shoulders and carrying me like a sacrificial lamb in the direction of the inviting ocean just outside our bedroom. I pretended to struggle against his firm grip but was enjoying the affectionate attention my lover was showering me with. I landed in the cooling aqua with a big splash, waking every cell of my being to the new day.

Oscar and Alfonzo were already frolicking naked in the pristine water. Andy lifted me onto his shoulders as we waddled toward our friends. Before long, Alfonzo was on Oscar's shoulders as I wrestled the Spaniard in the refreshing sea. Our loud screaming and carrying on caused such a racket that Vittorio and Argos came to see what was happening. They too joined us in our naked fun and games. I, being the youngest and most vulnerable, was the first to fall into the ocean, followed by Alfonzo. As was the Villa Αγάπη rule, the losers had to pay the winners their prize. And pay we did.

Clothing was optional at Villa Αγάπη, since none of us wanted to be encumbered in any way, shape or form. Our accompanying Abds were used to seeing us in the raw, so it came as no surprise when we sat down for the breakfast in the nude.

"I'd like to do some shots of you guys running around naked in the house; that is if you don't mind?" Our host said at the table.

"That's fine by me," Oscar responded, seconded by Alfonzo, Andy and me.

I commented, *"I can run around naked all day. The weather is so gorgeous; it's refreshing not to wear any clothes."*

"You little devil, you just like to see us in the buff so you can ogle at our you-know-what all day long." Oscar tickled my waist for a confession, sending me squirming and shrieking from my seat onto the floor. My BB tickled me relentlessly, causing my cock to jump to attention. We were wriggling on the carpet in uncontrollable laughter. Vittorio, not letting this spontaneous moment pass, got his camera and started our first photo-shoot of the day. By the time we had finished breakfast, we were already posing naked and in compromising positions for the artists. We twisted and turned every which way to our photographer's beck and call.

Camera in hand, Vittorio suggested, *"Let's go to Delos for the day. There are several interesting historical sites that I'm sure you boys will love to visit."*

"What's there to see?" I asked.

"You'll know when we get there," Argos responded.

"This boy is so eager and inquisitive to know everything," my Valet added. *"And he often asks the most*

inappropriate questions when we are in conservative company."

"But we are not in conservative company," I answered.

"*That's what makes him adorable,*" the artist responded wittily. "*This is what makes Young, young.*"

The Journey

We hopped onto the Kahyya'm and sailed on a two-mile journey to the island of Delos. As we sat watching the aquamarine water ripple past, Andy queried, "*Argos, how did you end up in Greece?*"

The German Jew replied, "*Our family escaped Berlin before the wall was erected. My father is Greek and my mum's family is from Berlin. They live on the island of Delphi and my older brother and I are in Athens.*"

Alfonzo chirped, "*I remember when I was in school in Barcelona; one of our history teachers mentioned the work of the German art historian Johann Winckelmann. He was a major influence on gay German literature.*"

"*I'm not familiar with Winckelmann's work. What did he say?*" Oscar asked with great interest.

"*According to Winckelmann, he observed the inherent homoeroticism of Greek art but had to leave much of this perception implicit; he is known to have said, 'I should have been able to say more if I had written for the Greeks, and not in a modern tongue, which imposes on me certain restrictions.' He was a homosexual, and his homosexuality influenced his response to Greek art, which often tended toward the rhapsodic: 'from admiration I pass to ecstasy...' he wrote of the Apollo Belvedere. Then he goes on to say, 'I am transported to Delos and the sacred groves of Lycia, a place where Apollo was honored. His statue seemed to come alive like the beautiful creation of Pygmalion.'*

"Nowadays, this writer is regarded as 'historical and utopian' in his approach to art history. He provided a 'body' and 'set of tropes' for Greek love. His was a semantics surrounding Greek love that fed into related eighteenth-century discourses on friendship and love."

"It's surprising I have not heard of this writer," my BB commented.

Argos remarked, *"He's known mainly in Germany. He inspired many a German poet in the later eighteenth and nineteenth centuries, including Goethe, who pointed to Winckelmann's glorification of youthful male nudes in ancient Greek sculptures as an inspiration for the new aesthetic of his time. Winckelmann was a model of Greek love as a superior form of friendship, just like the male nudes in Vittorio's art."*

The artist added cheerfully, *"Although Winckelmann did not invent the euphemism 'Greek love' for homosexuality, he, like me, had been characterized as an 'intellectual and artistic midwife' for the Greek model as an aesthetic and philosophical ideal that shaped the homosocial 'cult of friendship.'"*

Andy couldn't help but include himself in the conversation. He reasoned, *"Mid sixteenth and seventeenth century German literature had often included the term 'griechische Liebe', or 'Greek love', along with 'socratische Liebe', 'Socratic love', and 'platonische Liebe', which is 'Platonic love' in reference to male-to-male attractions.*

"German 18th-century works from the 'Greek love' milieu of classical studies have also included academic essays by Christoph Meiners and Alexander von Humboldt, the parotic poem of 'Juno and Ganymede' by Christoph Martin Wieland, and One Year in Arcadia: Kyllenion (1805), novel about an explicitly male-to-male love affair in a Greek setting by August, Duke of Sachsen-Gotha."

I couldn't help asking, *"How did you guys know so much about German homosexuality?"*

Andy answered, *"Don't forget, I'm part German and so is Argos..."* Before my Valet could continue, Vittorio chimed in, *"I'm a quarter German. My grandfather has German blood."*

"Just because you have German lineages doesn't make you knowledgeable about German homosexuality studies," I replied.

The three part-German men gave me three sly grins as if oblivious to my question, while Vittorio continued. *"Did you know that in 1897, Magnus Hirschfeld, a German doctor and writer, formed the Scientic-Humanitarian Committee to publicly campaign against 'Paragraph 175'; a notorious law which deemed sex between men illegal?"* Before anyone could respond, he conferred, *"Adolf Brand, a member, later broke away from the group, disagreeing with Hirschfeld's medical viewpoint of 'intermediate sex.' He saw male-to-male sex as merely an aspect of manly virility and male social bonding. He was the first to use "outing" as a political strategy, claiming that a certain German Chancellor, Bernhard von Bulow, had engaged in homosexual activity.*

"There was also a female Uranian activist in 1904 by the name of Anna Rüling, who saw 'men, women, and homosexuals,' as three distinct genders, calling it an alliance between the women's and sexual reform movements. Unfortunately, this was her only claim to fame and her only known contribution to the Hirschfeld cause.

"This was when women began joining the previously male-dominated sexual reform movement, around 1910. The German government tried expanding Paragraph 175 to outlaw sex between two women as well as between two men. Soon a man named Friedrich Radszuweit started publishing a lesbian magazine in Berlin known as Die Freundin (The Girlfriend)."

I decided to jump into this discussion without any knowledge in the subject, saying, *"What happened to Hirschfeld and the Scientic-Humanitarian Committee?"*

Argos filled in the blanks, *"Hirschfeld's life was dedicated to social progress for transsexuals, transvestites and homosexuals. In late years he formed the Institut fur Sexualwissenschaft (Institute for Sexology). This institute conducted an enormous amount of research and consulted many transgendered and homosexual clients, thus championing a broad range of sexual reforms, including sex education, contraception and women's rights."*

Alfonzo queried, *"I thought the Nazis were anti-LGBT?"*

"That's why, with the rise of Nazism, the stride Germany made in LGBT reforms soon came to a drastic reversal. The institute and its library were destroyed in 1933. The only part of the movement that managed to survive through the Nazi era was the Swiss journal Der Kreis."

"If the Nazis were anti LGBTs, how did Der Kreis survive the scrutiny?" I questioned.

Before anybody could give me a definitive response, our conversation came to an abrupt end when captain Kasim announced our arrival at the birthplace of Artemis and Apollo.

Δηλος (Delos/Dhilos)

Dhilos, the "Brilliant" island was a major sacred site for the ancient Greeks, second in importance to Delphi. This island was once covered in a variety of temples and sanctuaries, which were dedicated to the many Gods. According to Greek mythology, this was also the birthplace of Artemis and Apollo, the twin offspring of Zeus by Leto. When Leto discovered she was pregnant, Zeus' jealous wife Hera banished her from the earth. Poseidon took pity on the maiden and provided Delos for her to give birth to the demigod and goddess.

At the Sanctuary of Dionysus

The moment we stepped off the Kahyya'm, we were welcomed onto the entrance to the Sacred Way; the Agora of the Competitors. As our entourage proceeded towards the Sanctuary of Apollo, we passed many fallen statues and ruined monuments. These ruins lined the path towards the Great Temple of Apollo. Against the north wall stood the base of a colossal marble Statue of Apollo. Part of the trunk and the thighs were located behind the temple of Artemis, while a piece of the statue's gigantic foot had been carted off to be displayed at the British Museum in London, England.

Argos, acting as our tour guide, began his commentary, *"Did you know that the myth of Apollo dates back to the earliest development of the Greek religion, while that of Dionysus only acquired importance at a later date?"* He pointed in the direction of Sanctuary of Dionysus, which consisted of two huge broken phalluses sitting on top of a couple of stone columns. Our guide continued, *"Nearby is a small temple dedicated to Dionysus."*

I queried, *"Why are these giant penises guiding the pathway to the Theatre Quarter and the Temple of Dionysus?"*

"You see, Young, Dionysus had a rather effeminate appearance. He was often associated with uncontrolled sexual excitement. That's why two gigantic phalluses were placed at the sides of the god's statue," Argos explained.

Alfonzo declared, *"I thought the ancient Greeks like boys with small penises instead of large phalluses."*

"That is indeed true. If you look at most of the male nude statues, their members are often tiny compared to

their well-proportioned physiques. The Greeks believed that sperm has a shorter distance to travel when it moves through a small penis," Andy asserted.

Vittorio chimed in jokingly, *"Is that why you like Young's little boy penis?"* Our group laughed at the artist's statement.

The man continued, *"The Greeks were horny buggers. Haven't you seen the Greek vases depicting pictures of boys courting boys, boys playing sexual games, and adult men having sexual intercourse with boys? All the boys are depicted with tiny penises."*

Alfonzo replied laughingly, *"I've come across pictures of ancient Greek martial arts schools in which combatants exercised naked. They were considered to be a fine place to meet sexual partners."*

"You mean like modern-day gyms, like the one at our school?" As soon as I uttered the last word, I remembered I shouldn't have. It was too late; I had stuck my foot in my mouth again.

Argos asked curiously, *"What kind of school do you go to, boy?"*

Andy jumped to my rescue, *"What Young meant was, in our school, after vigorous work-out exercises, some boys in the shower room are known to sprout hard-ons. I'm sure there are sensual and sexual innuendos that go on behind closed doors. After all, boys will always be boys."*

"We are horny teenagers after all. We are always ready for action," Oscar said amusingly. He was assisting Andy in dissipating Argos' curiosity.

Vittorio commented lightheartedly, *"In these Greek martial arts gymnasiums, there was a law prohibiting grown men from entering the dressing rooms. Judging from the behavior of Socrates, the philosopher, this law seems to have been altogether ignored. It is a known fact that when he was around young men, he lost all senses of propriety.*

He was a sucker for youthful beauty, a true-to-form Eraste."

"In fact, much of Athenian love life took place in public places: many vases show people watching when two people are having intercourse. There is no written evidence that people objected to sex in public places."

"Aren't you the same way, like Socrates?" I noted of the painter.

"Young! You can't make such an inappropriate comment to our host." My Valet reproved.

The artist gave a loud belly laugh, said, *"Well said, young man. I am not a hypocrite, and I am the first to admit that your observation is entirely correct (unlike Hitler's high ranking homosexual officers)."*

"What about Hitler's homosexual officers? Tell us more," Oscar expressed. *"I didn't know there were homosexuals in the Nazi party at all, let alone high-ranking officers."*

"Oh yes! There were. The Nazis were some of the greatest hypocrites in the history of mankind." Our host continued, *"I'll relate a funny episode to you: The old bugger, Hitler, had to have an aide pick out the right color socks, ties, and other matching articles before he could go out in public.*

"In a secret Nazi April 1944 report, an aide was severely disciplined for playing a practical joke on the dictator during Das Vashenborger day (Fascist Fun Festival or April Fool's Day), which embarrassed him in front of Italian Fascist Bennito Mussolini. The aide switched Hitler's normal dark green uniform for a bright pink color. The aide, Corporal Karl Kraggs, had bribed a homosexual concentration camp inmate to fabricate a pink Nazi uniform in exchange for some unnamed 'sexual pleasures.' He knew Hitler was colorblind.

"The event was caught on film when the two heads of state met briefly on a balcony in Rome to address a party

gathering of loyal Italian Fascists. Once rippling laughter broke out within the crowd, SS guards escorted a very angry Hitler away from the balcony and hustled him to his room for a wardrobe change.

"Afterwards, the paranoid German leader refused to wear anything except green, including his underwear. The practical-joker corporal was later sentenced to hanging with a pink rope.

"It's also well known that many of Hitler's closest aides were secret homosexuals. Ernst Roehm, the virile and manly chief of the SA and the buddy of Adolf Hitler from the beginning of his political career, was as gay as they come.

"A certain Peter Granninger, who had been one of Roehm's 'partners,' was given cover in the SA Intelligence Section. For a monthly salary of 200 marks, he kept Roehm supplied with new 'friends'; his main hunting ground was Geisela High School Munich. He recruited no fewer than eleven boys from this school, whom he first 'tried out' and then took to Roehm.

"Then there is Gruppenfuhrer or Obergruppenfuhrer (Lieutenant General) Karl Ernst, a militant homosexual, who had been a hotel doorman and a waiter before joining the SA. He was appointed as the commanding officer of several hundred thousand Nazi Storm Troopers when he was not yet 35. There are more, but I'll leave that for another time."

16

---•◆•---

From Eromenos to Eraste

"Men are wise in proportion, not to their experience, but to their capacity for experience."
George Bernard Shaw

2nd Week of September 2012

I continued my email to Dr. Arius.
Dear Dr.,
I'm sorry I had to end our last correspondence abruptly. It was late, and Walter was calling me to bed. With an assertive partner, there are times I have to comply with his wishes. Otherwise, I'll never hear the end of it. :)

Regarding other reasons I named the clandestine society the Enlightened Royal Oracle Society: the word 'royal' refers to the household members to whom we were assigned. The majority of our 'Masters' or household patriarchs were either of aristocratic ancestry or were bestowed honorary titles by their governments, tribes or kingdoms. Therefore, we were in royal services, in the truest sense of the word.

Secondly, many of the Bahriji students were of aristocratic bloodlines or were born into wealthy lineages. That is another reason I chose the word 'Royal' to represent all members of the secret society.

This brings me to 'Oracle,' as described by The Free Dictionary:

- *A shrine consecrated to the worship and consultation of a prophetic deity, as that of Apollo at Delphi.*

E.R.O.S. was like a shrine dedicated to the teachings and lifestyles of ancient Greeks and other pre-Christian cultures, and it integrated different expressions of love. It was unlike today's overzealous religious teachings, which impose strict regulations that denounce alternative forms of erotic love.

An oracle is therefore much needed to dispel the demonization of other forms of sexuality besides heterosexuality.

- *A person, such as a priestess, through whom a deity is held to respond when consulted.*

In many ways, our 'big brothers'/ 'big sisters', Valets, mentors and teachers did take on the roles of 'priests' or 'priestess'. They acted as benevolent 'deities', making sure their charges were cared for and no harm befell them.

- *A person considered to be a source of wise counsel or prophetic opinions.*

Our BBs or Valets were educated and trained to be sources of wise counsel and, at times, to provide prophetic advice to their young charges so they could experience life's varied pitfalls with caution and circumspect.

As Freshmen and Juniors, we were learning to be respectful and well rounded, so we could one day also provide wise counsel and prophetic advice to the next generation of E.R.O.S. members.

- *A command or revelation from God.*

In regard to an oracle being a command or revelation from God: as E.R.O.S. members, we believe that we are made in the image of God; therefore all humans are gods and goddesses. As benign deities, we were taught to respect and revere others if we are to be treated similarly.

We also believe that all beings are interconnected; therefore, if we mistreat others, the circle of life will return our actions to us.

- *The sanctuary of the Temple.*

Our bodies are sanctuaries. Hence, at the Bahriji, we were educated in the art of honoring the sacredness of our bodies, from grooming to looking after our health and fitness through to tantric sensuality and sexuality. The temple of God is within and without every individual.

These are the reasons I chose the Enlightened Royal Oracle Society (E.R.O.S.) as the name to represent the actual clandestine society.

You've probably guessed; E.R.O.S. is pronounced similarly to 'Eros,' who is:

- *The ancient god of love and the agent of natural sexuality. He was the eldest of the Erotes born at the creation of the universe and the most mischievous. He, who randomly shot out love-inducing darts from his golden bow.*

As E.R.O.S. members, we were schooled to not be afraid and not be encumbered from experiencing love in all its varied forms, from storge, agape, and phila through to the erotic. Hence, the Enlightened Royal Oracle Society (E.R.O.S.) is the most appropriate name I could have picked to best represent the kind of education I was inducted into without exposing the clandestine society's name.

I will answer the other questions you posed in my next correspondence. For now, be well, be safe and take good care of yourself.

Your beloved friend,
Young.

1967

Elia Beach, Mykonos, Greece

The evening before we sailed to Cannes to meet Hadrah Hakim at the boat show, we realized that our weeks' vacation had flown by quickly. Vittorio had invited us to a beach party at Elia Beach the evening before our departure. We could hear faint echoes of distant drumming emanating from an otherwise serene ocean scape as we strolled towards the direction of the 'Rave'. Our host had advised us to 'dress casual'. For us, casual meant our swim trucks or speedos without anything besides our flip-flops or open-toe sandals.

On the opposite side of a valley, speakers were blaring out loud dance music. This venue has been temporarily set up for a nude beach party. It was obvious that it was a gay party; there were not many women in sight except a sprinkling of lesbians and fag hags, gyrating in the midst of a hundred homosexual men. A temporary stage had been erected for the performers, who were already singing and dancing in their birthday suits. Many "revealers" looked like they were in a trance, and booze and recreational drugs flowed freely.

I recognized the pungent smell from Poseidon's Cave. Andy wrapped his arm around my shoulders immediately. It was a protective gesture he often made to ward off potential intruders who dared venture too close, a signal that he was in charge and that they'd have to obtain his permission if they wanted to chat with me. I was eager to explore and run free. I was mesmerized by the good-looking men who were bouncing naked, dancing to the pulsating beat. Their bobbing members of varied shapes and sizes flopped every which way as they oscillated on the sandy beach.

It was a free-for-all party. Alfonzo, Oscar and Vittorio had disappeared into the crowd, leaving Argos, Andy and me to our own contrivance. As much as I would have liked to break free from Andy, I had little choice in the matter; my guardian would never allow me out of his sight. He was apprehensive that I would blunder as I had at Poseidon's Cave.

Argos inquired, *"Why aren't you guys out on the dance floor?"*

"Why aren't you?" My Valet asked in turn.

"I've been to this sort of party before, and usually Vittorio turns up needing me to cart him back to the villa."

"So you act as the artist/bodyguard besides being his boyfriend?" I queried.

Argos answered smilingly, *"Something to that effect. One of us has to be the sensible one."*

"Andy is not my bodyguard; he's my Valet. There are times I like to go exploring on my own. I like to be able to experience things without assistance."

My lover chimed in quickly, *"If I left you alone, you wouldn't know what to do with yourself. You, boy, like to fantasize that you are capable of looking after yourself but in reality you'll be running back in my direction if I do leave you alone."*

"Give me a chance to be my own person," I replied stoically.

"Andy, you do have to let Young go exploring. You can't shield him forever. Maybe tonight is a good time to give him the benefit of the doubt," the Greco-German advised.

"Ya! Give me a try. I promise I will return to you in one piece," I assured my guardian.

Andy thought for a moment without uttering a word. He wasn't sure if our persuasions were a good presage. The music began thumping faster and more urgently. Suddenly, Argos pulled me to my feet to dance, leaving Andy to contemplate.

At the end of my exhausting dance, Andy agreed to liberate me for an hour. He said, *"You, young man, if you want to go traversing, make sure you're back in an hour. If*

I don't see you on the dot, I'll be sending a search warrant after you. And don't go smoking dope or drinking liquor," my Valet said authoritatively.

I bent down, gave my lover a big kiss and disappeared into the crowd, leaving Andy and Argos to their own devices.

Elebe

It was a liberating feeling to be on my own. Since entering boarding school, I had never been alone, except for the one time when Andy flew with Ramiz to bring Ubaid back to Dubai from Florence. But then I had Husni (my Persian cat) to keep me company while my guardian was away. Now, I was allowed an hour alone. What did I do but stand, watching naked partiers frolic while tapping my feet to the cadence of the disco music.

I was enjoying dancing to my own rhythm with my eyes closed. I did not notice the man twirling in front of me until I opened my eyes and returned to reality. He had a naughty Cheshire grin on his face, which resembled an attractive feline. He stared at me but said nothing. His gaze never left my eyes or my body. I was beginning to feel uncomfortable when Vittorio danced to my side. *"Young, where's your bodyguard?"* he asked.

"Andy was with Argos when I left them a moment ago." I answered.

"This is Elebe; he's one of my regular models." The artist shouted over the loud music. I extended my hand to shake his; instead, he bent over and gave me a lingering bear hug. I could feel his penis stirring under the heat of his perspiring body. He did not let go of me but continued squeezing me affectionately. I tried pulling away, but the man would not let his grip loosen. His phallus, now erect, was pressing against my torso. I looked to Vittorio for succor. The artist gave me a wicked grin, said nothing and

disappeared off into the crowd. My heart thumped wildly. The model gripped my hand, pulling me away from the maddening crowd. I found Elebe's naughty-boy machismo tantalizing, yet I wasn't sure if I should go with this guy. Would Andy send a search party out for me if I didn't return within an hour? I was torn between staying and moving. Elebe made the decision for me. The model lifted me onto his broad shoulders and carried me to a quieter section of beach. He deposited me on a sand dune. My heart was racing in anticipation of what was to happen.

Elebe lay on top of me as our lips met in desirous kisses. I could smell his intoxicated breath as he explored my oral orifice urgently. His bad-boy demeanor aroused me tremendously. The model's demanding sensuality was different from Oscar and Andy's love-making. Eager to traverse the rawness of his coitus, I surrendered to his actions. His excitement leaked onto my belly as he slid our hardness against our pressing torsos. This liaison stimulated my libido to a state of heightened loftiness I had never experienced before. My erection sandwiched itself between his ass cheeks while he straddled to keep me pinned on the ground. Spitting a wad of saliva onto his palm, Elebe smothered it into his anal opening. My length was guided into his compliant orifice as he cried pleasurably. The young man began gliding back and forth on my yearning rod. The sensation was too titillating for me to forgo as the model bounced on my throbbing phallus. It was a sensation I had never experienced – I had always been a passive recipient. Now the reverse was happening to me and I opened myself to this new experience. I spread Elebe's buttocks open and pounded into his being unyieldingly; causing him to groan in ecstasy.

Flipping the model onto his stomach, I entered the man's behind, riding him furiously at times and slowly at others. I wanted my newfound ecstasy to last. I didn't want this erotic sensation to end, and time moved more quickly than I had ever felt before. I could not hold off my orgasm any longer. Just as I was about to ejaculate, Elebe let out a series of rapturous roars as he shot his passive fury onto the powdery sand. I poured my rhapsodic deposits into his hungry cavity before slumping onto the man's back, heaving into him my final residue before my subsidence eased out involuntarily from his receiving orifice.

Elebe stuck his finger inside his being, scooping up the remaining nectar that had been lodged between his cheeks. He savored the last of my sediment to his lips like a thirsty feline lapping on water. The model consumed every drop of my delirious seed before turning onto his back to share my tastiness with me in a lingering French kiss.

For the first time in my young life, I felt empowered, as if I could do more than I ever could. I liked my role as an Eraste. I promised myself that I would share this newfound experience with my guardian and lover when the opportunity arose for me to test my strength again.

17

The Superyacht Show

"You don't buy a superyacht because it makes sense; in fact, that is the last thing it does."
Hein Velema
(Chief executive of *Fraser Yachts*)

1967

The Intercontinental Carlton, Cannes

We arrived back at Cannes on a Saturday, a day before Andy and I was due back at Daltonbury Hall to commence my Fall 1967 term. Oscar was returning to the University of Vienna the next day, Sunday. Our last evening together was a farewell rhapsody of sadness, especially for me. I knew I would miss my lover and BB after 3 months of a blissful triplet relationship. Fortunately, Andy was there to dissipate some of my melancholy and assist me to readjust to as 'normal' a life as possible.

We checked into the Carlton Hotel, where we had stayed a week ago. Hadrah Hakim had arranged dinner with us at one of the hotel's restaurants that evening. We didn't have to wait long before my ex-'Master' walked in. We stood to greet the patriarch.

"Sit down boys. It's good to see you three. Your friend...?" Hakim extended his hand to Alfonzo.

Oscar introduced Alfonzo to our host. *"How was your holiday?"* The Arab enquired.

"We had a fabulous time. Thank you for allowing us to use your luxurious yacht and the Simorgh." My Valet said appreciatively.

"We had a wonderful time! Thank you, Sir!" Oscar added.

"Did you travel with the boys, Alfonzo?" The Hadrah asked.

"I did and had a fantastic time learning the myths and legends of ancient Greece. Thank you for accommodating me on the Kahyya'm."

"Andy and Young are like family, and they are good boys."

My guardian chimed in quickly to thank Hakim for his compliment. *"You are very kind, Sir."*

"Tell me, Alfonzo, how did you get to know the boys?" the Hadrah queried.

"I met Oscar when I was registering at the University of Vienna. He asked me and my girlfriend, Mary, to join him on the cruise. I was coming to Cannes to meet my father for the boat show. He'll be here tomorrow from Barcelona," our friend replied.

"Excellent. I hope to meet your father. I'm also here for the boat show. Is your father an ardent sailor?" Hakim conferred.

"He is; I went with him to the first Barcelona boat show at Fira de Barcelona Montjuïc Exhibition Centre a few years ago. It was quite an experience. I'm looking forward to the Superyacht show tomorrow."

"Do you sail, son? I'm an avid fan of luxury boats, as you already know."

"Unfortunately, I'm not as zealous as my dad. I'll introduce Lorenzo to you and the boys. They haven't met him either," the Spaniard answered.

Last Night Together

Andy, Oscar and me, lay on the king, each of us feeling the strain of our lover's imminent departure. I, sandwiched between my 'big brothers', held onto Oscar's waist while Andy held mine. It seems our minds drifted in the same direction – sex, one of love's many manifestations.

I felt my Valet's groin stir as his palms cupped my scrotum. He began inching his fingers towards my sex, gently stroking me to erection. I performed the same action for my other lover, whose back was pressing against my chest and torso, as mine was on Andy's.

I could feel my Valet's intoxicating breath on the side of my neck as he began nibbling my ear. I imitated his actions on my BB, causing him to moan, desiring more. Oscar leaned his body sideways for my easy access. I planted a lingering kiss on his inviting lips. Andy glided his hardness against by derriere, stimulating my stiffness to unimaginable longing. I was happy with my newly discovered role as an active partner, and this was a perfect opportunity for me to again be a 'top'. I wanted to give Oscar's behind a try. I knew he would be open to receiving me, unlike sturdy Andy, who would never relinquish his masculinity. My Valet, a sworn top, was attracted to me because I was his eromenos and would always remain so in his eyes. Our idiosyncratic roles suited us, but with my newfound excitement, I wanted to experience uncharted territories. My 'big brother' lover was the consummate partner, since his bottom was tilting sensually at my engorgement. Andy wasted no time gyrating against my backside. He knew I would never refuse him entry. He firmly acknowledged that I would always be 'his boy' in our relationship.

My bulbuousness, sticky with natural lubrication, was knocking at Oscar's door. He was aware that I could not hold off my exhilaration any longer, he guided me inside him. Rapturously I eased into his willing orifice, his tightness wrapped round me. The tantalizing sensation was too provocative; I found myself pushing all the way into his being. Just then, I felt the tip of Andy's arousal easing into my core. This double entry was a sensation I had never felt before. This invigoration elevated my sensuality to a virgin level, driving me to insanity.

Andy wasted no time to stroke into my person. He recognized my passion and I his. Our union presided before we were aware of our individual needs. Our love had no boundaries except our hearts' desires for each other's blissful attainment.

As we voyaged towards our eventual release, I was transported on a tantric journey that Dr. Henderson had taught me so eloquently about at the Bahriji. His words rang in my head, *"Tantra is an ecstatic consciousness and a spiritual awareness of one's erotic nature. Its sexuality is a dimension of spiritual growth, in every moment of our embodied lives. It is the Supreme flow of the sacred life force, the Sacred Trinity of Love."* The three of us were experiencing 'Maithuna,' the realization of the void in all things. We were attaining enlightenment and perpetual bliss; we were in nirvana through our act of unselfish loving.

Electric arrows flashed, traversing our bodies. Rainbows of color struck our eyelids while foams of music fell over our ears. It was the gong of our simultaneous orgasm, as described so fluently by Anais Nin in her erotic book, Delta of Venus.

My palm, covered with Oscar's seed, was overflowing onto the king; my deposits, released into my lover's hollow, lay buried as a remembrance of our triplet love. Andy's forceful surrender shot deep in my heaving soul, reminding me that my benefactor had filled me with his unconditional love once again. His ponderous breathing on my tender neck told me that he would soon reclaim my love for himself. He and he alone would always be here for me.

We did not release our hold until our heightened consciousness induced us into states of hypnagogic hallucinations. Only then did we separate.

Port Pierre Canto, Cannes

The new Port Pierre Canto was completed in July of 1965 with a capacity to house several hundred boats along twenty-two hundred meters of mooring space, making Cannes' new port Europe's biggest private marina. Ranked among the best in the world, it was awarded by the State to 'S.A. International-Yachting Club de la Mer-Second Port de Cannes'. To mark its inauguration, the Sea World sent an emissary in the form of a young dolphin, christened Tiburce. The dolphin frolicked in the waters, accompanying the boats to the harbor limits. Adopted by pleasure boaters and sailors alike, Tiburce frolicked closer and closer to the boats until one day he got too close to a propeller. The injured dolphin was immediately transported to Monaco's oceanographic center. Unfortunately, he did not survive his multiple injuries. Nowadays, it is no longer a dolphin that welcomes boats into the harbor, but the goddess of the sea in the form of a statue. Amphitrite, Poseidon's wife, elected Port Pierre Canto as her permanent home.

Back in late summer of 1967, Tiburce was the harbor's mascot. Scarves, key rings, flags, mugs and other paraphernalia were stamped with his cute image. These were the early years of the Cannes international boat show, which has now morphed into Le Festival de la Plaisance de Cannes. Back then, the exhibition was held at Port Pierre Canto. For boat and luxury-yacht enthusiasts, the latest models from the world's leading shipyards and international premiere editions were put on display at this three-day event. International visitors from around the world came to buy, sell and admire the latest in yachting designs and innovations. Many nouveau riche buyers were from the wealthy United Arab Emirates.

We are Late,
We are Late
For a very Important Date

Andy, Oscar and I were scrambling like madmen to be ready to meet Hadrah Hakim, Alfonzo, and his dad, Lorenzo at the hotel lobby. We were scheduled to go to the boat show that Sunday morning. Unfortunately for the three of us, our last night with Oscar had engaged us in less than sufficient sleep. One or both of us were often awakened by the third. It was a heavy-duty sexual marathon.

We ran downstairs to our meeting with empty stomachs. Tell-tale signs of our sexual debauchery caused Alfonzo to inquire as soon as he saw us. *"You guys look like you were up all night, partying!"* He gave us a mischievous grin while his dad and the Hadrah were busy chatting about lavish boats and opulent yachts.

Oscar gave his friend a sagacious look before commenting, *"We are starving. Is there anything to eat at the exhibition?"*

Lorenzo, overhearing my BB's question, replied, *"I'm sure there is. Usually the major boat companies entertain their potential clients lavishly. I'm positive we can find something for you to eat.*

"I'm Lorenzo, Alfonzo's dad," the Spaniard greeted us. *"You must be Oscar, Andy and Young,"* he extended his hand to shake ours.

"It is nice to meet you, Sir." My Valet spoke on our behalf.

Just then, the hotel concierge came to guide Hakim to our waiting Bentleys.

The Superyacht Show

The port was already jammed with yachting aficionados, boating enthusiasts and paparazzi, walking around the pier *oohing* and *ahhing* at the latest models in the nautical world. Rows of colorful flags flew in the breeze as our entourage, guided by a Superyacht show executive, entered a cordoned-off red carpeted area. Reporters were lining the periphery, waiting to snap pictures of celebrities who were attending this ostentatious event. We were guided to our assigned seats, ready for the opening ceremony to begin. At the far end, caterers were busy working on final touches for the food arrangements. An open bar served champagne and other alcoholic beverages to the mingling guests.

As soon as the last word of the official opening ceremony was spoken, Oscar, Andy and I headed straight to the hors d'oeuvres tables. As we munched greedily at the delicious finger food, an unexpected guest tapped my shoulder. It was Aziz, the distinguished *Sacred Sex in Sacred Places* photographer. We exchanged nose-rubbing greetings with our Arab friend.

"*Hakim told me that I'd find you here,*" Aziz stated.

Oscar spoke while Andy and I gobbled greedily at the food we had piled onto our plates. *"We are starving. We haven't eaten this morning. We were rushing to get to the event on time. I'm so glad they serve food here."*

Andy asked, *"Are you with the Hadrah's entourage?"*

Just then, our ex-household 'Master' came over to greet us, and with him, Sheikh P. Thabit was looking to make his first luxury yacht purchase and P came to dispense advice to his friend. Thabit inquired, *"How was your Greek island vacation?"*

"*Thank you,* we had a wonderful time. *How are you, Sir?*" Andy responded politely.

"*Come, walk with us, I'd like your opinion on the boats.*" Thabit commented.

Accompanied by Pascal, one of the show's executive organizers, we made our round to view the opulent yachts on display. P whispered into my ear, "*I miss you and your perky ass.*" I smiled, not knowing how to respond to his saucy comment. Before I knew it, he gave my bottom a playful smack in full view of our guide. Pascal pretended not to notice and continued conducting our tour.

P was enjoying his brazenness, he continued, "*I'll have your voluptuous bottom again. You, boy, better keep it nice and tight for me.*"

I was getting embarrassed by the sheikh's bodacious commentary on my derriere. Andy came to my rescue; he tried changing the topic by asking, "*Your Highness, which boat will you recommend for the Wazir to purchase?*"

P took this opportunity to tease me further. "*The 'Superking' of course; where we can have lots of tantalizing fun and games.*"

The Arabs laughed at P's comment but said nothing. "*Which one do you like, Young?*" His Highness asked.

"*I like the one with the golden stripes painted across the royal blue hull. It is so regal and majestic. . .*" Before I could continue, P chimed, "*I know how you like it: regal, majestic, with a full body and magnificently huge.*" The men continued laughing at P's sexual insinuations.

My face turned red with embarrassment. The sheikh was obviously taking great pride in his feistiness. He continued loudly, "*Come, boys, I'll fly you to my palace after this insipid boat show.*"

My guardian took this opportunity to jump in to my deliverance, "*Thank you for your kind offer, your*

Highness. Unfortunately, we have to report to Daltonbury Hall this evening before we are advised regarding our next student exchange assignment."

"Nonsense! Return to the Quwah with me; I'll contact your school authorities to let them know you are already at my palace."

Thabit pitched in, *"P, let the boys do what they have to do. They'll be allocated to the Quwah in no time. Let's go to Monte Carlo after I've made my purchase. We can have a good time."*

"I'd like the boys to join us. It'll be more pleasurable." The sheikh would not let up.

Andy was exasperated, but he kept his composure, saying, *"Your Highness, I promise we'll be at your disposal the following week. There are formalities we have to attend to at Daltonbury. I know you'll understand our position."*

P did not answer. He was reluctant to let us out of his grasp. Luckily, Pascal took the opportune silence for his sales pitch. *"Since this young man likes the boat with the golden stripes painted across the royal blue trunk, maybe we should take a second look at this vessel."*

I supplemented quickly, *"What a good idea. I'd like to take another look at this elegant craft."*

As we went through the boat, Aziz suddenly exclaimed, *"I have a great name for this craft: Bettawfeeq (Good Luck)"*.

Andy and I remarked simultaneously, *"Bettawfeeq is a fantastic name. What a great idea."*

"It has such a noble ring to it," I added.

"I like the name, too. I do love the interior of this vessel. Consider it done, Pascal. Send me the paperwork for this vessel and I'll discuss the customizations I desire," the Wazir announced proudly.

"Yes, Sir! I'm at your service anytime. I'll have the design consultant with me when you are ready to meet us," Pascal propounded, joyful that he had made a sale.

My Valet whispered assertively to the prince when no one was paying attention. *"Get yourself ready for me, 'slave.' You are mine during my duration at the Quwah."*

P gave my lover a roguish grin; he nodded and disappeared to join his cronies at the extravagant event.

18

Am I a Romantic?

> *"It's time to say goodbye, but I think goodbyes are sad, and I'd much rather say hello. Hello to a new adventure."*
> Ernie Harwell

1967

Time to Say Goodbye

That Sunday flew by very quickly. Before I knew it, Oscar, Andy and I were packing our bags. The Simorgh returned Andy and me to Daltonbury Hall, while Oscar departed to Vienna to start his new life as a university freshman. Alfonzo stayed behind, accompanying his dad to Saint Topaz and joining Mary for a short vacation before heading back to university.

An overwhelming sense of loss hit me as I watched Oscar pack. It was the same sorrow I had felt when Nikee left for Saint Andrew's in Scotland. Now, it was Oscar's turn to leave. The three of us had bonded tightly during the few months we had been together. We had sated each other's needs in full when our triplet relationship was at its zenith.

Andy and I wrapped our arms around our lover to say our farewell. We kissed passionately as our tears trickled down our cheeks. We promised to visit one another in the not-too-distant future, but, as with most well intended assurances, we knew that the chances of being together would be few and far between.

We did see Oscar and Alfonzo in the winter of 1967, when Andy and I visited the Spaniard in Barcelona to spend Christmas with the couple, but time had moved us in different directions. As intimate as we pretended to be, our relationship lacked the magical quality that we had once shared during our time at the Sekham and in Greece. We had grown apart.

Early Fall 1967

Isle of Wight, England

The solid oaks lining the country roads were turning into shades of golden yellow and the maples a reddish orange. We arrived at the Isle to a fanfare of colors; only the English countryside heralded fall's glory so beautifully. I stuck my head out of the school's Rolls Royce, which was ferrying us from the runway tarmac towards Daltonbury Hall. A sense of felicity overcame me as we drove past the tranquil landscape, yet the scenic beauty stirred a melancholic sadness within me. Once again I started weeping for the loss of Oscar's presence in our midst. Andy held onto my waist, leaned his head against mine and whispered, *"It breaks my heart to see you so wistful. Don't cry, my dear one. I'm here for you. I will never abandon you."*

Little did I know that it was I who would eventually leave my Valet. Andy would never have abandoned me. He was a man of integrity, a man of his word. I, on the other hand, was the fickle-minded individual who wanted to conquer the fashion world. I was the boy who was too proud to return the love my mentor had so unconditionally offered, but in the early fall of 1967 I did not know what I know now. If I had, I would have chosen differently.

"I miss Oscar," I uttered.

"I'm here for you, my beautiful one. I'm always here for you," Andy vouched.

"Why is parting so difficult?" I cried.

"Goodbyes are such sad affairs. I'd rather consider goodbyes as new beginnings. Every goodbye is a new hello. Hello to our new adventure!" my Valet declared.

I stared into my lover's kind eyes before replying, "You have the correct words for every occasion. How do you do that? I want to be like you. Will you teach me? I love you very, very much!"

"I love you more," Andy answered smilingly. "Young man, 'nothing that is worth knowing can be taught'." He quoted Oscar Wilde. "You already have the answers within; all you need is to tap into your soul for the correct response. I'm afraid I cannot teach you how to be you."

"There you go again. You have the correct answer again. How do you do it?"

He laughed, "I don't know how! That's just the way I am."

I looked out at the passing scenery. I did not retort but kept admiring the natural pulchritude that flew by the car's window. My guardian inquired, "Young, have you heard of the Romantic period?"

English Romanticism

"I've heard of the term, but I don't know much about this era. It sounds romantic," I commented.

"Come, sit by me, and I'll explain. This period in history is often referred to as Romanticism. It was an artistic, literary, and an intellectual movement that began at the end of the eighteenth century. People during this period revered the visual arts, music, and literature above most other things. Romanticism also had a major impact on education and the natural sciences.

"This movement validated strong emotion as an authentic source of aesthetic experience, placing emphasis on emotions such as apprehension, horror, terror and awe; Romantics especially explored the emotions related to confronting the sublimity of untamed nature and its picturesque qualities. They often felt much as you feel now."

"Am I a Romantic?" I asked cheerily. My Valet's words were beginning to chase my gloom away.

Andy responded amusedly, *"Let me continue. In a lot of cases, this movement elevated folk art and ancient customs to that which we now consider noble. It also made spontaneity a desirable characteristic. It is arguably a 'natural' explanation of human activities as conditioned by nature in the form of language and customary usage."*

I sat mesmerized listening to my Valet's every word. He continued, *"Romanticism reached beyond the rational and classical ideal models and elevated a revived medievalism. It also embraced the exotic, unfamiliar, and distant in modes more authentic than Rocco chinoiserie, harnessing the power of the imagination to envision and escape the drudgery of the mundane."*

"Then I'm definitely a Romantic!" I exclaimed.

"Calm down and don't get yourself so excited. Please allow me to continue," Andy implored. *"Romanticism also elevated the achievements of what it perceived as heroic individualists, especially artists, whose pioneering examples would elevate society. It also legitimized the individual imagination as a critical authority, which permitted freedom from classical notions of form in art. There was a strong recourse to historical and natural inevitability."*

"Was Lord Byron a Romantic?" I questioned.

"Yes, and so was Shelley. The concept of Greek Love was important for these two significant poets. You must realize, Young: during Byron's lifetime, Regency England was characterized by hostility and a frenzy of persecution of homosexuals. The terms 'homosexual' and 'gay' were not used during this period, but 'Greek love,' at least among Byron's contemporaries, became a way of making homosexuality more palatable. That was an otherwise taboo subject within the precedents of a highly esteemed classical past.

"The philosopher Jeremy Bentham, for instance, appealed to social models of classical antiquity, such as the homoerotic bonds of the Theban band and pederasty. He demonstrated how these relationships did not inherently erode heterosexual marriage or the family structure."

"Was that how E.R.O.S. came into existence – during this period in history?" I chirped excitedly.

E.R.O.S. Formation

Andy continued, *"I'll come back to your question. Let me explain. During the eighteenth century there was a high regard for classical antiquity, which caused some adjustment in homophobic attitudes on the continent, but not so in England. In Germany, the prestige of classical philology soon led to more honest translations and essays that examined the homoeroticism of Greek culture, particularly pederasty, in the context of scholarly inquiry rather than of moral condemnation. Meanwhile religious and nationalist sentiments in England remained hostile. An English archbishop penned what may be the most effusive account of Greek pederasty available in English at the time. This was duly noted by the then 19-year-old Byron on his 'List of Historical Writers Whose Works I Have Perused'.*

"That brings me to answer your question regarding the Enlightened Royal Oracle Society, founded by Lord Byron. Let me give you a brief background of Byron's England. Plato was rarely read in Byron's time, in contrast to the later Victorian era, when translations of the Symposium and Phaedrus would have been an easy way for a young student to learn about Greek sexuality. The only English translation of the Symposium was published in two parts, first in 1761 and later in 1767. This was an ambitious undertaking by a scholar named Floyer Sydenham, who took pains to suppress his own homoeroticism: Sydenham regularly translated the word eromenos as 'mistress', and 'boy' often became 'maiden' or 'woman'. During that time, the classical curriculum in English schools often passed over works of historical and philosophical value, especially Latin and Greek poetry that dealt with erotic themes.

"Byron gives a catalogue in his poem Don Juan:
Ovid's a rake, as half his verses show him,
Anacreon's morals are a still worse sample,
Catullus scarcely has a decent poem,
I don't think Sappho's Ode a good example,
Although Longinus tells us there is no hymn
Where the sublime soars forth on wings more ample;
But Virgil's songs are pure, except that horrid one
Beginning with Formosum Pastor Corydon.

'That horrid one', by Virgil is Eclogue 2, a bucolic expression of frank homoerotic yearning.

"E.R.O.S. came into existence as a secret poet society precisely because of the repression of homoerotism during Byron's time," my mentor explained diligently.

"What was Shelley's role in all of this homoeroticism?" I asked my guardian.

"In regards to Shelley, he complained that contemporary reticence about homosexuality kept those modern readers who did not know the original languages from understanding a vital part of ancient Greek life. His poetry was amorously influenced by the 'androgynous male beauty' represented in Winckelmann's art history.

"Shelley wrote his Discourse on the Manners of the Ancient Greeks Relative to the Subject of Love on the Greek conception of love during his sojourn in Italy, which was concurrent with his translation of Plato's Symposium. He was one of the first major English writers to treat Platonic homosexuality, although neither of his works was published during his lifetime. His translation of the Symposium did not appear in complete form until 1910.

"Shelley asserts that Greek love arose from the circumstances of Greek households, in which women were neither educated nor treated as equals. As a result, they were not suitable objects of ideal love. Although Shelley recognizes the homosexual nature of the love relationships between males in ancient Greece, he argues that homosexual lovers often did not engage in erotic love. Rather, Greek love was based on the intellectual component, in which one seeks a complementary beloved. He goes on to maintain that the immorality of the homosexual acts is on a par with the immorality of contemporary prostitution, but I disagree."

"*Me too,*" I seconded.

My lover wasn't done talking. He went on, *"Shelley cited Shakespeare's sonnets as an English expression of the same sentiments, and he argues that they are chaste and platonic which I also disagree with."*

Before he could continue further, our vehicle came to a complete halt. We had arrived at the entrance of our boarding school, and our footmen were waiting to unload our luggage.

Mid-September 2012

Dr. A.S. supplemented the series of questions he posed:

Hello my friend,

I am here to pester you again. I hope you are enjoying our regular correspondence. It is certainly a joy for me to interview such a "distinguished author." :)

Thank you for the clarifications regarding the name of the Enlightened Royal Oracle Society (E.R.O.S.). Without further ado, I'll jump to the point with my next set of questions:

- *When you were at the Bahriji and were taught sensual and sexual topics, were you at any moment uncomfortable with the practical lessons?*
- *In **Initiation**, you mentioned the grotto being used for sensual training. Was it used for other purposes? It seems lavish to have so many fancy gadgets installed just for sex education lessons.*
- *Were regular school subjects taught to Bahriji students besides those that were erotic in nature?*
- *Did the students know each other while you were at the Bahriji?*
- *Did your parents or other Bahriji students' parents visit their children in their respective boarding schools while you were stationed there?*
- *Did your mother come visit you during term time at the boarding school?*

*On a different note; it will be interesting to know your **Initiation** readers' opinions! Are you planning to have **A Harem Boy's Saga** made into a movie, TV mini-series and/or a staged production?*

After reading Book 1, I can envision it as a big-budget movie. It has all the ingredients for a major production, like the 'Lifestyles of the Rich and Famous'.

Well Young, keep up the writing. I'm waiting to read Book 2.
As they say in Hawaii,
Aloha!
A.S.

19

Dangerous Liaisons

"Love grows. Lust wastes by Enjoyment, and the Reason is that one springs from a Union of Souls, and the other from a Union of Sense."
William Penn

1967

At Tolkien Brotherhood

Andy returned to Yates Fraternity while I shared a room with Duc, a French Canadian 'big brother,' and Samuel, a half Portuguese, part Austrian Freshman at Tolkien Brotherhood. Since I was no longer a Freshman but a Junior, I didn't need the constant guidance that Sam required. Duc was assigned to the Austrian/Portuguese as his 'big brother'.

Samuel's inviting smile captivated my attention as soon as I entered the room. I was attracted to him immediately. His gentility reminded me of myself when I first entered the boarding school. I extended my hand to greet him and detected a sense of timorousness in his boyish handshake. Duc was the opposite of his charge; instead of shaking my hand, he embraced me, kissing both of my cheeks before welcoming me into their midst.

"Good to have you in our den," he announced with pleasure. *"I heard you were in Greece."*

"How did you know?" I queried.

"Ah! I have spies stationed everywhere," he joked. *"How was your vacation?"*

"Thank you for asking. We had a phenomenal time learning about ancient and present-day Greek cultures. We met many interesting people. Have you been to Greece?" I asked.

"A couple of times; I had many enthralling experiences during my travels."

I took a liking to the French Canadian who spoke with a heavy French accent similar to Jacques and Gaston's, whom I knew from the Kosk household. Samuel kept quiet throughout our conversation. My heart reached out to the cute and demure young man. I could feel his innocent apprehension from not knowing enough to participate in our jovial pleasantries.

I turned to Sam to inquire, *"Where are your from, Samuel?"*

The boy answered timidly, *"I'm from Lisbon. This is my first time away from home."*

Duc chirped before his charge could continue, *"I'm showing him the school tomorrow. Will you care to join us, since classes don't start till Wednesday?"*

"I'd be delighted." I was happy to be included in their company. Some unknown force had smitten me, and my heart reached out to this shy lad. I wanted to protect him as Nikee had sheltered me when I first arrived at Daltonbury. Sam exuded a charming sensitivity, which I myself had exhibited nineteen months prior. My immediate instinct was to shield the boy from harm, even though he was not under any threat. A strange psychological transformation had coursed through my being. I wanted to be his 'big brother'.

Sleepless

In the middle of the night, gentle sobbing awoke me, coming from Sam's bunk. Duc was fast asleep on his twin. The adolescent continued weeping until I reached for him, inviting him to join me in my bed. I wrapped my arms around his slender waist and whispered, *"Don't cry beautiful one; like you, I was homesick when I first arrived at the school. I'm here for you."*

His crying ceased soon after we cuddled. Like a frightened rabbit, he eased his tender face against my chest as I hummed him a sweet lullaby. He fell into peaceful slumber. I climbed up to his bed, leaving him to dream sweetly on mine.

Samuel

The first bell of the day roused us. Duc, like Nikee, gave the freshman a prep talk before venturing into the communal bathroom for our ritualistic morning shower. I could detect Sam's uneasiness as we proceeded towards the bathroom. Before we entered, I said to Duc, *"Give me a minute with Sam. Go on ahead, and we'll be in shortly."* Our BB agreed, leaving Sam in my charge.

We sat on a bench outside the bath while I held onto the boy's tightly clasped hand. I advised, *"I know it is a daunting task to enter a room full of naked boys, especially when no one has seen you without clothes since you were a small lad. Remember, boy, there is nothing to fear except fear itself.*

"Let's close our eyes and inhale deeply. This will help you relax."

When we opened our eyes, Sam had calmed considerably. I led him through the door. Before long he was enjoying the company of the other boys, whacking at each other playfully with their washcloths and towels. I couldn't help feeling a sense of attainment from being allowed the privilege to assist in Sam's growth, even if it was in a minor way.

The campus tour went on in much the same way. The three of us became better acquainted. Although Duc and I did most of the commentary, the Freshman hung onto our every word, in case he forgot a detail and would later be quizzed on the subject. I found myself more drawn to this winsome young man the more time I spent with him.

Conversation With My Valet

Duc was as immaculate as they came; he was a perfect match to Sam's boyish charisma. My intuition told me that Sam was being groomed to be a potential E.R.O.S. recruit, and the French Canadian was preparing him for the role. Later in the day, when Andy and I met for high tea, my Valet inquired, *"How are your roommates?"*

I burst forth surreptitiously, *"I like both of them. Sam reminded me of myself when I first arrived at Daltonbury. He is so beguiling; I can't help but desire to take him under my wings.*

"As for Duc, his friendliness is entrancing beyond description. We spoke at length about our Roman and Grecian experiences while we were showing the newbie around campus."

"I see you've found a couple of distractions from missing Oscar," Andy quipped mischievously.

"There are, indeed, temporary mellifluous distractions to my melancholy," I confessed to my lover.

"What did I tell you yesterday when we were on our way to Daltonbury?" he teased.

"What exactly did you tell me, Mr. Valet?" I minxed.

Andy laughed, knowing full well I was bedeviling him, *"I said, 'Goodbyes are sad, but I'd much rather say 'Hello' to a new adventure.' I detect a new adventure coming your way, 'son'!"*

"You may well be correct, 'daddy'," I responded mockingly.

I continued my confession, *"I feel drawn to be a big brother to Sam. I've never felt this way before. What am I to do?"*

My guardian laughed loudly, *"You are such a Narcissus. I think you see yourself in Sam, and you'd like to nurture him like we BBs nurture you."*

"Don't be absurd, I'm not self-absorbed," I defended, although in reality there was an element of truth in my Valet's words.

"Oh yes you are, you enchanting Dickens. You love to play the devil's advocate whenever you have a chance. You, young man, better not go breaking the adolescent's heart like Vicomte de Valmont did to Cécile de Volanges."

"Who are Vicomte de Valmont and Cécile de Volanges?" I queried inquisitively.

Andy laughed louder. *"We only have a week before we leave for the Bahriji. You, young buckaroo, better leave Duc to care for his charge and not go barging in like a rakish amoral chevalier. By the sound of it, you are smitten with lust rather than genuinely caring for the welfare of the boy."*

"Nonsense, I'm not smitten with lust! I'm enamored by his dulcet personality, and I believe that I'll make a good big brother to Samuel," I answered resolutely.

"We'll see; time will be our arbiter," my lover affirmed.

Courtship

For the next couple of nights, after Duc was asleep, I took the opportunity to console my 'little brother' by sneaking into his bed or sneaking him into mine. I, like Nikee, would sprout an erection when Sam held me close. His youthfulness was too irresistible for me to control my libido. Sam, who was bashful and coy, was curious about his own sexuality. He was waiting for me to make the initial move; he was not versed in the art of seduction. I wanted to make sure that the young man was ready before I made my move.

Little did I know that Andy was covertly watching from the sideline, like the Marquise de Merteuil in Dangerous Liaisons. In his daedal way, he was tarrying to witness if I was genuinely ready to be a 'big brother' or if lust was the reason for my interest in Sam.

In my young mind, I wanted the best of both worlds. I felt on top of the world, having somebody look up to me as if I was his pillar of strength. On the other hand, I was ardently attracted to his artless innocence, a trait I had possessed not so long ago. Without knowing it, I had become the seducer and the seduced.

Duc

Duc was the quintessential 'big brother'. Like Andy, he was attentive, attractive, fraternal and ethical. Unbeknownst to me, he, like Andy was in love with me. Like Andy, his love was so cleverly concealed that I saw him as a friend instead of a lover. Duc knew our love could not be consummated when I was under Andy's charge. He would have to be gratified with dispensing his amorous energies in the education of his adolescent Sam, with whom he was equally captivated.

The BB was always conscientious during our time together. That week, Andy, Duc, Samuel and I became the best of friends. Samuel was homesick, and I was missing the feeling of Andy and Oscar in the same bed. There were times Sam and I would crawl into our big brother's twin, playing and cuddling before falling asleep in each other's arms. When we awoke, our erections were visibly obvious, yet none of us took any action to respond to nature's call. We were mindful of our positions.

After all, I concluded that the adolescent was under observation by Duc and the E.R.O.S. authorities; until the appropriate time presented itself, our reverent BB and I would have to keep our amatory desires to ourselves. The moment did arrive a few days into my week's residence at Tolkien Brotherhood.

End of September 2012

Dear Dr. A.S.
Greetings from Maui. I hope you can make it to the Valley Isle for a vacation. Fall has arrived, and Munich must be chilly during this time of year.
Below are the responses to the questions you asked;
- *When you were at the Bahriji and were taught sensual and sexual topics, were you at any moment uncomfortable with the practical lessons?*

The answer to this question is straightforward. I don't recall being uncomfortable when sensual and sexual lessons were taught. It was part of our regular school curriculum. To me, it was just another topic in our course of study.

It was after I arrived in America that I discovered that Americans, especially in the middle of America, would consider sensuality and sexuality taught in school a taboo. In the European continent, sensual and sexual subjects were non-issues; they were considered natural parts of the human experience. American Puritanism seems to have reverted to the dark ages. The mention of sensuality and sexuality to adolescents is often considered sinful, much like in Victorian England, where teenagers were seen but not heard, and eroticism was brushed under the carpet. As is often the case, adolescents are labeled too juvenile to make up their own minds. I am baffled by this adult mentality. I, as an adolescent, knew what I was doing, and I took responsibility for my actions.

Many adults and elders take comfort in finger-pointing; instead of teaching young people to take personal responsibility to re-evaluate their actions, when an adolescent makes the wrong choice, they look for scapegoats.

- *In **Initiation**, you mentioned the grotto being used for sensual training. Was this venue used for other purposes? It seems lavish to have fancy gadgets installed solely for sex education.*

The Bahriji grotto was constructed mainly for students' sensual and sexual practical training. These were cave-like structures used for romantic rendezvouses. Students were taught not to harbor hang-ups when making love outdoors. Although indoor privacy remains a dominant domain for erotic liaisons, sensual and sexual activities outdoors are often more therapeutic than indoor copulations. As humans, we seek to be one with nature when we mate.

- *Were regular school subjects taught to Bahriji students besides those that were erotic?*

Yes! We were taught regular school curricula, such as geography, mathematics, etc. I chose to highlight certain subjects in my book because these erotic topics were not taught in regular schools.

At the households I was stationed in, foreign students were homeschooled by excellent and highly qualified teachers. This was a prerequisite for every Arab Household that participated in the E.R.O.S. student exchange programme.

- *Did the students know each other when you were at the Bahriji?*

I knew most of the students at the Bahriji during my time there, since the student body was not large. There were some students whom I knew better than others, as I imagine is also true at regular schools.

- Did your parents or other Bahriji students' parents visit their children while you were at Daltonbury Hall?

My dad never came to visit me in school, but Uncle James did. When James came to Saudi Arabia on business in 1968, I was also stationed in the gulf state. We met, and I introduced him to the patriarch of the household I was stationed.

I am sure parents came to visit their children when I was at Daltonbury Hall. Do bear in mind that not all students at the boarding school were E.R.O.S. recruits. A handful of five were selected annually. Therefore, during the four years I was at Daltonbury, only twenty boys were recruited into E.R.O.S., and I was one of them.

In one of my other Arab households, a female E.R.O.S. recruit had to return to her boarding school temporarily because her mother was taken ill in hospital. She did not return to that household after she left. She was replaced by another female E.R.O.S. recruit after her departure.

- Did your mother come visit you during term time at the boarding school?

Mother did come to visit me at Daltonbury Hall in the Spring of 1968. She requested permission before students went on their Spring break. I had already returned to Daltonbury Hall from the U.A.E. before she arrived at the school. She stayed a day in the Isle of Wight before we departed to London to stay at Uncle James' residence.

You mentioned that it will be interesting to know my readers' opinions and questions. You asked me, am I planning to have ***A Harem Boy's Saga*** made into a movie, TV mini-series and/or a staged production?

Yes! I do envision ***A Harem Boy's Saga*** as a series of movies, a television mini-series and/or a staged musical.

*A producer will manifest who will take this project and run with it, I'm positive. That said, I would like to act in an advisory capacity and as a costume designer/consultant, since I've lived **A Harem Boy's Saga**. Who better to consult than the autobiographer, don't you agree?*

Well, Sir! I eagerly await your next questionnaire.

My regards to Pepsi and Cola; your beautiful hairy companions. :)

Young.

20

Let's Go Fly a Kite

*"Beauty is truth's smile when he beholds his own
face in a perfect mirror."*
Rabindranath Tagore

1967

Portsmouth, Hampshire, England

     The week flew by rapidly after classes commenced that Wednesday. When Saturday arrived, Andy, Duc, Samuel and I made a day trip to Portsmouth, the second-largest city in the ceremonial county of Hampshire on the southern coast of England. It is a ferry ride across the English Channel from the town of Ryde on the Isle of Wight. Although I had been through Portsmouth to catch the train to London to visit Uncle James, I had never stopped long enough to visit any historical venues in the city.

     That Saturday was Portsmouth's annual Kite Festival. Kite enthusiasts around the British Isles flocked to Southsea Common to enjoy a day of fun, games and kite flying. Since none of us had been to a kite festival, Duc suggested we spend the day visiting the kingdom's one and only island city.

Ferry Across the Channel

It seemed like other Daltonbury Hall students had the same idea. On board the ferry, we met several of Andy's rowing friends, who were also going to Portsmouth. I had met Tony and Steward at the boat house when Nikee first introduced Andy to me. Although we had exchanged pleasantries, they remained Andy's friends, since they were on the rowing team and I wasn't. Whenever my Valet was at Daltonbury Hall, they would rekindle their friendships through the activities of the Kipling Society's Rowing Club. It therefore came as no surprise that Andy and his friends' conversation drifted to their rowing activities.

Duc, feeling left out of their conversation, turned to me and asked, *"How long has Andy been your BB?"*

I jested amusingly, *"I thought you have spies stationed everywhere and know all of my secrets?"*

The BB played along. He remarked, *"I do have spies everywhere, but my secret agents don't tell me everything. They often leave me guessing."*

"In that case, make a guess. If you are correct, you'll be rewarded handsomely," I teased.

"Is that correct? I'll hold you to your promise. I'm a good guesser."

"I'll give you three tries," I replied.

"If I guess it the first time, what's my reward?" Duc asked.

"What would you like your reward to be?" I smiled.

He gave me a comely grin before answering, *"You've been together for under a year?"*

"That's a wily reply. It's not an accurate enough response. You are to guess the exact number of days, months or years, not give me a rough estimation of years," I preempted.

He grimaced trickily, *"You've lost your bet, boy. I'll be claiming my reward before you leave for the Middle East."*

"How did you know I'm leaving for Bahrain?" I gave a surprised chirp.

"Ah! So you are going to Bahrain," He responded.

I covered my mouth immediately, knowing full well that I had said too much. Duc continued laughingly, *"Don't worry, your secrets are safe with me."*

Although I wasn't a hundred-percent certain, my gut feeling told me that this BB was an E.R.O.S. member. I could tell by the way he was flirting with me. Samuel, his charge, was definitely training as a potential E.R.O.S. recruit.

Before our conversation could develop further, Samuel, who was till now enjoying the scenery by the boat's railing, came to join us. He inquired, *"What are the two of you discussing?"*

His BB answered smilingly, *"You, young man, will find out soon enough. For now, get ready to leave the boat. We have arrived at Portsmouth pier."*

At the Kite Festival

Back in 1967, Portsmouth was not the buzzing city it is today. Since we were going to a kite festival, we went to a local store to purchase a couple of kites. We wanted to join in the fun instead of being bystanders and watching the festivities unfold. Little did we know that kite enthusiasts the world over had come, elaborate kites in hand, to compete for the title of the best original design and show off their latest flying creations.

A crowd of onlookers and participants had gathered at the open field. Judging by the turnout, it was going to be a family event. There were many kinds of kites, from traditional paper kites to others made from lightweight plastic materials. There were kites resembling bobbing jellyfishes, swimming fishes, supernatant sea creatures, flying dragons, soaring mythical birds and crawling land creatures such as pouncing tigers and hopping rabbits. I had never seen such an array of rainbow colors blowing in the wind.

    We found a secluded spot in this expansive field to lay our belongings down for a picnic. Before long, our kites had joined the rest of the flying gaggle. Samuel and I were having a fun time maneuvering the strings of our individual kites while our 'big brothers' sat chatting some distance away, enjoying tea and finger sandwiches. They didn't notice when the adolescent tripped and fell backwards while pulling on his kite string. He had bumped his head on the ground, and for a brief moment the boy looked as if he had been knocked unconscious. His knee and ankles were bleeding. In a panic, I leaned down to see if he was alright. His eyes were closed, and he did not speak when I called out to him. My immediate thought was to give him mouth-to mouth-resuscitation. To my surprise, during the process I found myself kissing the boy passionately, like prince charming awakening the sleeping beauty. I held onto his limp body while tears streamed down my face. I wasn't sure if I made the correct revival move. Our BBs came running in our direction when they noticed what had transpired.

    Suddenly, Sam opened his eyes as if coming out of a daze. Duc carried his charge posthaste to the nearby first aid tent, which had been set up for emergencies. We followed behind. As he was being carried away, the adolescent turned and gave me an adoring look, as if he remembered the amorous kiss I had planted in his mouth some moments ago.

    Andy enquired, *"What happened?"*

    "We were having fun flying our kites, and the next thing I knew, Samuel was on the ground unconscious. He must have tripped while running backwards," I replied but omitted the part about the kiss.

The attending doctor soon gave Sam a clean bill of health after bandaging his minor wounds. Duc wanted to take his charge back to Daltonbury Hall immediately, but the Freshman insisted that he was fine and wanted to continue our day's sojourn. The six of us trooped off to 393 Old Commercial Road to the Dickens Birthplace Museum.

At the Dickens Birthplace Museum

This charming museum was the original house in which the famous Charles Dickens had lived during his childhood (besides his other residence at No. 16 Hawke Street, Portsmouth). Fortunately, young Charles was spared prison life, whereas his father John Dickens and the rest of his family were sent to the debtors Marshalsea Prison in Southwark, London for not being able to pay John's debts. This experience later inspired the novelist to pen Mr. Micawber's character in *David Copperfield*.

As we proceeded to view the exhibits in the museum, I was at once transported back in time to the harsh living conditions of the destitute during Victoria's reign. As our guide began to relate Dickens's life, I was reminded of the inhospitable conditions I had witnessed in the Malayan fishing village I had visited nine months ago with my ex-classmates.

Tears of sadness began trickling from my eyes as we progressed on the tour. Andy and Duc, noticing my woefulness, came to ask whether I was all right.

Andy, thinking I was missing Oscar, commented, *"You romantic boy, why are you crying again?"*

I leaned against my guardian sobbing uncontrollably.

"Hush, don't cry. Tell me what's wrong?" Andy queried, *"Are you missing Oscar?"*

Duc, seeing my melancholy, consoled, *"Don't cry Young, we are here for you. What's the matter?"*

I turned to the French Canadian BB, wrapped my arms around him and continued weeping. Duc and Andy lead me to a nearby bench with Sam in tow while Tony and Steward continued on with the tour.

"I'll miss you and Sam when Andy and I leave to the U.A.E. in a few days. I've grown very fond of the both of you," I sobbed.

"Hush now. We'll be seeing you again in three months, when you and Andy return to Daltonbury Hall. Time will fly by so quickly that you wouldn't notice we're apart," Duc comforted my aggrieved soul.

"Why do the people I love come and go so quickly?"

"I'm always here for you," Andy reiterated. *"You know I'll always be here for you, my dearest one."*

"Aw! You are so sweet, Andy," the BB remarked. *"Like the two of you, I'll be here for Samuel whenever he needs me."* He turned towards his charge and planted a kiss on his forehead, indicating his care and concern for the young man.

Samuel held my hand rapturously as we continued browsing in the museum. Duc gave Andy a smiling acknowledgement when he saw his charge being so lovey-dovey with me. Once again, a presentiment came over me that this BB had seen what had transpired between the freshman and me after Sam's fall.

Bedtime

It had been a fun, exhausting day, but early morning, we were scheduled to attend Sunday service at our school's non-denominational chapel. That night, when the lights went out and students had retired to bed, I lay awake, reliving the day's event. I began to miss Andy and Oscar next to me. I couldn't help but reminisce about the fervent kiss I had planted on the boy who was sleeping above me. I was unaware that the adolescent was also tossing and turning on his bed, as I was. He, like me eighteen months ago, was falling in love for the first time, not with his 'big brother', Duc, but with *moi*.

I had incognizantly taken on the role of the Vicomte de Valmont to my own Cécile de Volanges, just as my Valet had predicted. My Austrian Portuguese roommate was my object of affection. My Valet was correct to warn me to leave Samuel to his 'big brother's' charge instead of toying with the young man's tender affections.

Just as sleep was beginning to beckon me, I felt a warm body crawl into my bed. I did not stir when he wrapped his hands around my slender waist. Since the room was pitch dark, I could not see the person. My immediate thought was Sam must be lying next to me. Yet his grip was strong and powerful, lacking the fragility of an adolescent's touch. Whoever it was, I did not wish him to relinquish his hold on my being. I leaned my back against the warmth of his musculature. His intoxicating breath on my youthful neck sprang my organ to life. He pressed his lengthy hardness against my derriere, sending electric spasms through my being as I pressed against his muscular physique. His hands reached for my nipples, tenderly caressing them to attention. I tried not to make any noise as he continued his sensual foreplay. I turned my face to my side and our lips met in a libidinous kiss. I desired to explore his oral orifice as much as he craved for mine. My amorous lover rotated his nimble fingers around my leaking member, arousing me to heights of ecstasy I had no desire to waive.

I buried my face in his athletic pectus, covered with a light dust of hair. His musky scent was that of my French Canadian 'big brother'. I remembered it from when Sam and I were in his embrace. Without opening my eyes, I knew my lover. He had secretly longed for me, and now we were finally consummating our love. His sensuality was stimulating me to the verge of release as he lubricated my opening and his throbbing erection with my emissions. He eased into me.

My legs wrapped around his waist, I surrendered to his gliding onslaught as his stiffness plunged deep into my existence. I bit into his shoulders to stop myself from making unnecessary noises that might wake our 'little brother'. His puissant strokes sent me spewing my release onto our chests and bellies while he continued rocking until he could no longer hold off his orgasm. Jets of creamy fluid flowed into my core. Its fervent intensity aroused our fiery kisses, which lingered even after his mighty propensity had simmered to a heaving whimper. He had no intention of ceding his prize; he protracted within until his manhood slithered out involuntarily. He sheathed me into his loving cocoon until I fell into tranquil slumber. Only then did he leave my bed for his own.

Unbeknownst to us, our 'little brother' had been listening quietly above.

21

The Chapel of Love

"Experience is the worst teacher; it gives the test before presenting the lesson."
Vernon Law

End August 2012

Dear Dr. Arius,
I am flattered that you have so many questions for me regarding my early life. One question you asked:
- How do you or any of the E.R.O.S. recruits deal with jealousy, envy and other emotional negativity when it comes to dealing with sensuality, sexuality and love?

I am answering each of your questions by relating them to examples that I've encountered in the course of writing my life experiences in a chronological order.

1967

Sunday Service

That Sunday after our kite-flying outing was a beautiful day in the Isle of Wight. The autumn sunshine had cast a hazy glow over the lazy blue sky, reminding residents at Daltonbury Hall that Sunday service would soon be commencing at our school's non-denominational 'Chapel of Love'. As the church bells tolled, Sam, Duc, and

I were getting ready to meet Andy in the chapel. Throughout the entire morning, Sam had been unusually quiet. He went through his morning routine in a pensive state, replying only when spoken to. Duc and I did our best to cheer up the adolescent, only to be greeted with polite smiles and nods of acknowledgement. He went about his ritualistic chores as if he had a lot on his mind.

At The Chapel of Love

The first part of Chaplin Samuel Hollinger's message that morning was on the topic of 'Honor'. *"The reason why all men honor love is because it looks up, and not down; aspires and not despairs,"* the reverend quoted Ralph Waldo Emerson. As Dr. Hollinger continued his sermon, I couldn't help but glance over at the ruminative Samuel. I noticed that he was placidly wiping trickles of tears from his eyes. He was hiding his unsettling feelings from Duc, who was sitting next to him. Our 'little brother' quickly turned away when he saw me watching.

The pious doctor proceeded to speak on the subject of 'Respect', and he quoted Lao Tzu: *"When you are content to be simply yourself and don't compare or compete, everybody will respect you."* Samuel could no longer hold back his tears. He got up and headed towards the boys' room. Duc followed; by the time they returned to our pew, the adolescent had calmed. This time, he was able to make eye contact with me without turning away. He gave me a weak smile before listening attentively to the remainder of the sermon.

A Sunday Stroll

Andy suggested that the four of us take a walk around the tranquil countryside after the service. It was beautiful; we felt beckoned by the golden glow of the

English autumn landscape. Sam and I walked a little ahead of our guardians while they chatted away, animated by a heated discussion. I reached to hold Samuel's hand. He did not pull away. Instead he held onto mine as we had yesterday at the Dickens birthplace museum. I took my time before querying, *"Is something bothering you, Sam? You seemed forlorn this morning. You know we are here for you. Do you want to tell me the reason for your melancholy?"*

He kept silent as we continued to walk some distance. He leaned towards me and planted a kiss on my lips. Although taken aback by his unexpected gesture, I did not pull away. I returned his adoring affection while giving both BBs a cursory glance. They smiled and continued their debated dialogue. Sam finally blurted, *"I'm sorry I was mad with you this morning."*

Surprised by his apology, I was speechless. He continued, *"Will you forgive me?"*

"Forgive you for what?" I remarked.

It took the adolescent a while before he answered choosing his words carefully, he replied, *"I heard the two of you making out below my bed last night."* He paused before continuing, *"I was jealous and felt betrayed by you and Duc. I wanted to partake in your passion, but I didn't know what to do. I wanted to pry the two of you apart, yet my desire to partake in your lovemaking left me jealous. I didn't want to be left out, and I felt like we had created a loving triangle when we were mucking around in Duc's bed. I was afraid and unsure if I should pick a fight or. . ."*

I wrapped my arms around the Freshman, giving him a responsive hug. This time around I gave Sam a lingering French kiss in view of our guardians. No words were required as I led the young man into a clearing in a nearby forest. Leaning my friend against the tree trunk of a large elm, we continued our adolescent sensual exploration, awakening every fiber of our beings. Sam imitated my actions as we discarded pieces of our clothing. His smell reminded me of me. For the first time in my young life, I saw myself in Sam's refection and vice versa.

Andy and Duc laid a blanket on the leafy ground. They were excited as they watched our actions yet did not interfere with our youthful sensuality. They stood observing our every move, enjoying the titillation that unfolded before their eyes. I bent to engulf Sam's inviting nipples with my tongue; caressing and fondling them to hardness. He moaned ecstatically as I nibbled his pink knobs. Our boyish scents drove us wild with yearning. I wanted to savor every part of his freshness and he, he couldn't wait to explore every crevice of my youthful smoothness.

Unzipping his pants, I reached to cup his engorgement, teasing its bulbous tip to rapturous leakage. He wasted no time in pushing my trousers to my ankles. He held my buttocks firmly as I pressed my length against his slender belly. I thrust him against the tree as he surrendered his passion to me. Soon I was lying on top of him on the blanket while prying my longing tongue into his willing mouth. Our erections jousted and resisted one another, but the more they fought, the more aroused we became. I had no desire to leave Sam's receiving orifice. Our passionate foreplay had stirred our BBs to strip bare. Their stimulations pointed skywards as they joined in our circle of galvanizing sensuality.

Duc's delectable hardness was too irresistible for us not to share. Sam and I devoured his masculinity with unbridled devotion. My Valet reached to fondle our boyish globes, rubbing them before savoring our sweetness into his yearning mouth. Before long he was lapping at our openings with abandonment. He was delighted to take turns, enjoying our compliant crevices. Sam and I mirrored one another's actions like Narcissus did when he saw his own reflection in the water. Sam, like me, was unwilling to relinquish any part of our 'big brother's' organ; we suckled in unison until he could no longer stave off his passion. Duc spewed his abundance on our youthful faces before sharing his deliciousness with us.

Andy tilted our buttocks skywards, spat into our orifices and mounted our yearning bottoms with loving precision and tenderness. He knew it was our 'little brother's' first and he made sure not to hurt the boy. My Valet's sweet devotion never ceased to amaze me as he alternated between Sam and me. We received him desirously, ardently offering our ardors to our handsome Apollo without reservations. We welcomed him, we cherished him and most importantly we wanted to share his gratification between the both of us.

Our lover could hold off no longer; with a mighty vociferation, he spilled his amour inside the Freshman before plunging into my derriere for his final climax. Our BB was already lapping at Andy's flow, distributing our lover's releases to his 'little brothers'. Duc fed us as if we were hungry orphans in *Oliver Twist*.

This divine act of carnal flamboyance tripped Samuel and me over the edge. Our sexual boy-play finally propelled the two of us to disgorge simultaneously. Our stickiness bonded our beings into a single entity as our lips stayed locked in pleasurable kisses. We were unwilling to relinquish the savory feeds that our French Canadian guardian had so sensually fed his Freshman and Junior.

By the time we dressed, Sam was back to his normal cheerful self. It is therefore veracious to say that sex is no small feat, and it can chase the blues away (if only temporarily).

What did you say to him?

I managed to catch Duc on his own the following day when Sam was in class. My curiosity got the better of me, I asked, *"What transpired between you and Sam in the boys' room yesterday during chapel?"*

"I had a little chat with the lad to put him at ease," Duc responded.

"What did you say to him?"

The BB gave me a puckish wick, smiled but said nothing. He was obviously teasing me to probe further.

"Well? Are you going to tell me?"

"You inquisitive devil; I'll tell you if you'll go for a swim with me this evening at the pool..." Before he could complete his sentence, Andy walked up to us in the corridor. Our conversation terminated immediately. Duc excused himself, bid us *au revoir,* and off he trotted in the direction of the library. When Andy was not watching, he gave me a stealthy grin, pointed at his watch and spread out ten fingers, indicating for me to meet him at ten P.M. at his appointed location. I nodded before my Valet escorted me to the *Hobbit* for our lunch.

Andy Told Me

I opined to Andy over lunch, *"It was strange that Samuel apologized to me yesterday. He asked my forgiveness, but I wasn't even aware that he had offended me."* That said, I omitted telling Andy that Duc and I had made love the night before.

"I chatted with Duc when the both of you walked ahead. He was planning to give you the opportunity to be a part of Sam's secret training as a potential candidate for E.R.O.S. recruitment program. Before I could agree, the two of you were already going at it. I didn't expect you to jump into the big brother's shoes so soon. You are a constant amazement and a quick learner." He gave me a pat on my back.

"It seems Sam has passed his first test. There are several to go before he can be shortlisted," my Valet advised.

"Do you know what transpired when Duc followed the weeping boy into the men's room during chapel?" I queried.

"His BB used Emerson's quote to explain to the lad that love is an honorable act, and it befits a person to look upwards to all things positive rather than allowing jealousies to eat at the fabric of the boy's soul.

"He also explained that one always has a choice; we can always change our perspectives or the way we think. Positivity and negativity dwells in his mind simultaneously. Therefore, at any moment, he can change his thoughts. Duc also explicated that Sam can continue to feel less or more of whatever he chooses. The choice is his alone, and no one can alter his negative or positive thoughts. He is the only person who has the power to get him out of his depression."

"Wow! What a mouthful. I wish to be more like you and Duc. The both of you seem to have everything figured out." I looked at my mentor reverently. *"No wonder when they returned to the chapel, Sam lightened up tremendously. Now I understand."*

"Now, do you have anything personal you want to tell me?" Andy stared at me unmoving.

"No! Except that I love you very much." I lied, telling one half of the truth.

"You should know by now, 'The truth will set you free'." My mentor shook his head and propounded, giving me a second chance to come clean. I did not.

22

The Swimming Pool

> *"Experience, which destroys innocence, also leads one back to it."*
> James Baldwin

Early September 2012

I continued to answer Dr. Arius' questions regarding the way most E.R.O.S. students dealt with jealousy, envy and other emotional negativity. I cited an example.

1967

At the Swimming Pool

At ten P.M. sharp, I arrived at our school's heated swimming pool. There was no one around; the premise was officially closed for the day. Students could still enter the vicinity to use the shower stalls and toilets. As soon as I entered the building, the only person on the spectator's bench was Samuel. I went over to greet him. *"Where's your BB?"* I asked.

"He told me to come to meet you alone," the boy replied.

Surprised by his answer, it took a while for me to respond. *"Did he mention why he wanted us to meet alone?"*

Sam shrugged his shoulders and shook his head. I sat down next to him. *"Did you enjoy our forest rendezvous yesterday?"* I asked.

He gave me a timid smile, indicating that he had enjoyed our four-way liaison, but said nothing. I put my hand around his shoulders and drew him close to me. He did not resist. Instead, he leaned his head against my shoulder and whispered, *"I love you, Duc and Andy very much."*

I kissed him tenderly on his lips before replying, *"You are a very beautiful boy and one of the sweetest I know. You know Andy and I are leaving for the Middle East the day after tomorrow. We'll be there for three months. Duc will take excellent care of you while we are away."* I paused and looked the adolescent in the eyes. I continued, *"I'm going to tell you a story."*

Sam listened attentively. *"Not so long ago, when I was a Freshman, I fell in love with my 'big brother', Nikee. I wanted him to myself, but he said, 'Love me, but don't be in love with me. There are many exciting experiences in your future.' He continued, 'True love is not selfish; on the contrary, to love me, you must share me with others.' As much as I did not like sharing Nikee, I did as was told. He, in turn, shared me with others without jealousy.*

"Samuel, you must understand that unconditional love is a noble act, and to love someone unconditionally, we must at times make personal sacrifices for the better good for the object of our affection; jealousy being one of them."

Samuel chimed before I could continue. *"How do you control jealousy? It eats away at my being."*

I gave the boy another kiss on his lips before continuing, *"First and foremost, you must believe in yourself and be secure within your being. Learn to love and respect yourself. It is only then that others can do the same to you. Every action you take is a reflection of the person you love.*

"*There will be times when others will be jealous or envious of you as you sometimes are of others. Master the art of transforming your negative emotions into positive energies. Your lover or lovers will notice that and they will love you back the way you loved them: with respect and reverence.*" After a pause, I continued, "*I'm sure Duc can explain this better than me. I'm still a novice in conquering my jealousies and learning to keep them at bay.*"

Sam remarked, "*Duc did explain it to me yesterday in the boy's room. That's why I asked your forgiveness after our discussion.*"

I added, "*Jealousies are brought on by our injured pride and shattered ego. When you can view the larger picture, you'll understand that the person we love is always sharing his love with others; only then can you understand that hurt is created by our inner insecurities and fears. It has nothing to do with the people we love outwardly.*" I paused before speaking, "*You and I are so alike. I know you have the ability to subdue the green-eyed monster. Everyone has the capabilities to conquer, control and master their own fears and insecurities. Don't allow your moment of confusion to obstruct your better judgment. Always think before you act. My beautiful boy, you can do this; you have proven it to me. Yesterday morning, you did not lash out at Duc and me in the chapel. You walked out quietly and did not disrupt the sermon. Your action prompted Duc to come to you. We knew something wasn't right, but we wanted to see your reaction to a tumultuous situation. You did well. Now, do you understand what I'm saying?*"

"*You are so wise. I want to be like you.*" The Freshman responded, wrapping his hands around me.

I squeezed closer to him. "*You are already like me; you don't have to want to be like me. You don't even have to try; it's in your DNA. All you have to do is master the technique. Practice makes perfect."*

On that note, I gave the adolescent a lingering kiss. A surge of electricity coursed through his skin. Euphoric, I remembered when Nikee and I were at the pier by Swan; he had reached into my shirt to titillate my delicate nipples. I did the same to Sam. He gladly opened his mouth to receive my probing tongue, offering himself to me, as I had to Nikee when we made love for the first time.

The Plunge

We stripped naked, and I led us both to the pool's edge. His hand in mine, we plunged into the warm water. We frolicked playfully; splashing water at each other. I wrapped my arms around Sam and planted a passionate French kiss on his lips. He surrendered himself to me. The excitement of making love in the enticing aqua tantalized our erections to bob uncontrollably; encasing my hardness and his in his soft palms, the adolescent began stroking our erections in synchronicity. Our closeness sent frissons through our physiques. We were two adolescents exploring our sensuality in the heat of passion.

I turned Sam around to probe his tenderness with my nimble fingers, prying him open to receive my throbbing member. He squirmed, backing into me as I slid seductively against his compliant orifice. I needed him, and he desired me. I eased into him gently. The boy succumbed to my forcefulness. His beauty entranced my organ to quivering vibrations, which pleasured him as he accepted me eagerly. He gave me rein of his entirety as we merged into a celestial apparition, where our souls fluttered to heights of amorous ecstasies on imagined wings. I bit fervidly into his venerable neck, leaving my mark of proclamation in that moment of fervency. I desired to own him, yet I knew I had to practice what I preached. I had to release my control over the adolescent but his ardor captivated my soul. I could not quench my élan vital but to release my potencies into this fresh bloom, who so trustingly and genuinely desired my love's deposits.

My ferociousness sent the Freshman into uncontrollable tremors; he could no longer hold off his spill as he ejaculated in the warm aqua. I slumped onto his back in exhaustion, yet my manhood did not relinquish our coitus. I continued thrusting into his core until I released another fill into his embracing aura. Only then did I release my hold on the beautiful youth.

I grabbed us a large communal towel and wrapped our boyishness into a cocoon of affectionate warmth. We resumed our boy play until the clock struck midnight. Only then did we sneak back to our room into our separate beds, cherishing our amour before sleep took hold of our being. We were young and in love.

Little did we suspect the man lurking in the dark shadows by the swimming pool: our BB, Duc. He was recording our performances to present to the E.R.O.S. selection board.

Conversation with Duc

The following day, the day before Andy and I were to depart to the United Arab Emirates, I had a chance to speak to Duc privately. I inquired, *"What happened to you last evening? You asked me to meet you at the pool, but you didn't show, instead you sent Samuel."*

My BB grinned and responded mischievously, *"I wanted to give you a chance to be alone with Sam. Did you guys have a fun time?"*

"Why did you arrange that?"

"I set up the rendezvous as a test for Sam and for you," Duc continued amusingly.

"For me? Why am I involved in Sam's training? I'm not a BB."

"Andy and I had a lengthy discussion. It was he who suggested that we give you a chance to see if you can qualify to be a 'big brother' candidate."

"How will you or Andy know if we passed our tests when the both of you were not present to witness what transpired at the pool?" I remarked testily.

"We know."

"How? I didn't see either of you there."

"That doesn't mean we were not present!" Duc replied.

"If you and Andy were present, then tell me what transpired between Sam and me."

The French Canadian proceeded to relate in detail what he saw at the swimming pool. I was astonished by his information, so I queried inquisitively, *"Where were you hiding to document all this information, you crafty devil?"*

He gave me a wicked smirk, but gave me no answer. After a brief silence, I couldn't wait to pressure him for an answer: *"Did Sam and I pass our tests?"* I asked.

He maintained his lengthy silence, determined to preserve the suspense. By now my curiosity had gotten the better of me; I demanded, *"Are you telling or not? I'll ask Andy if you refuse to answer."* I pretended to walk away, hoping that I would entice the BB to speak.

Duc responded knavishly, *"Ok! I'll tell, I'm only teasing you. You are so gullible."*

"Well, go on."

"The two of you did better than expected. Observing you is like watching Narcissus making love to himself. You both are so alike; the only difference is one has darker skin than the other. Otherwise, it's like scrutinizing a pair of fucking twins," Duc jested.

"The two of you did put on a great show! I got excited watching. I'm sure your future Household Masters will have a field day watching you and Sam go at it," he remarked.

"You voyeuristic pervert!" I started thumping my BB, but Andy arrived, looking for me.

"What are you two playing at?" Andy inquired cheerfully.

"I was just telling this little fella that he did well last night at the pool, and he started beating me," Duc proclaimed.

My Valet chimed, *"Now, now, the two of you, stop being so childish. I have a serious announcement to make."* We stared at my guardian.

"I've just been informed by our Headmaster that Young's and my next household assignment is at the Quwah: P's palace, just as I had predicted. We must get our butts to the 'Rabbit Hole' for our medical check-ups. Once we have a clean bill of health, we fly tomorrow afternoon to Heathrow, where the Al-Fayoum will be waiting to take us to Bahrain."

Sure enough, Andy and I passed our routine medicals with flying colors. The following day we departed Daltonbury Hall en route to Bahrain airport.

Sadness

That evening, while Duc, Samuel and I were lying in bed together, we were filled with an unspoken dispiritedness. Although we knew we would be seeing each other in three months, we had grown intimate during the ten days we had been together. The time had arrived for us to say good-bye. Each of us had his own downheartedness; I was the boy's first love, and my parting proved more difficult for him than for Duc or me. Lucky for Samuel, his BB was there to assist him through his emotional desolation, and Duc guided him back to his chirpy self soon after Andy and I left.

I'm glad Daltonbury Hall provided us with 'big brothers' and 'Valets', who assisted Freshmen and Juniors in times of emotional trials and tribulations. Our assigned guardians lend their shoulders and listen with their attentive ears, making sure their charges are cared for. This, to me, is the beauty of man/boy love and affection at its best.

Part II

France – Paris, Aubigny-sur-Nere.
Italy – Florence.

23

In a State of Flurry

*"Life is like playing a violin solo in public and
learning the instrument as one goes on."*
Samuel Butler

1967

Aboard the Al-Fayoum

As soon as our school's helicopter touched down at the private airstrip near Heathrow Airport, the emerald-green plane was already waiting for Andy and me. Alongside the two uniformed stewards welcoming us aboard the Al-Fayoum, a man in his mid-twenties greeted us as soon as we entered. He introduced himself as Monsieur Alain Dubois. He was a newly appointed private tutor to the Quwah Household. This debonair gentleman was my tutor throughout my three months' service at the prince's ménage.

Monsieur Alain Dubois

Monsieur Dubois graduated from Cambridge University in England with an Arts & Humanities degree in Latin and English Literature. He had answered an E.R.O.S. advert seeking a private tutor for a Middle Eastern household while scouting for a job. He beat out the eleven other candidates by flaunting his well-bred and dashing charm during his interview with Asban, the Quwah's governor. I was Alain's first student on the first day of his new job.

We liked each other instantly, and he and Andy got on splendidly. He was six-and-a-half years older than my Valet, and they had a lot in common, since he had been a 'big brother' during his time at his boarding school. Andy later confided to me that Alain was actually training to become a Bahriji teacher. The first step to being considered as a Bahriji educator was through being a private teacher in an E.R.O.S. member's Household. All Bahriji teachers were ex-E.R.O.S. members.

My new teacher spoke English with a French accent. Although in the beginning I had difficulty understanding Monsieur Dubois' English, I was soon used to his linguistic delivery. His quirky communication was as attractive as his person. He also exuded a scent of fresh eau de cologne whenever I was close to him. He reminded me of spring rain in an Alpine forest. I was secretly drawn to Alain, but even I was not yet aware of it.

The Journey

Before we could have a conversation, our pilot asked us to fasten our seat belts for landing. Andy and I looked at each other in surprise. We had not anticipated arrival in Bahrain so soon. My teacher informed us that we were descending into Roissy instead of the Bahrain airport.

My Valet inquired, *"Why are we in Paris? I thought we were heading to Bahrain?"*

Monsieur Dubois replied informatively, *"I'm enjoined by my boss to accompany you to Paris. He will provide further instructions after we check into the Penthouse."*

"The Penthouse? How long are we staying in Paris?" I queried excitedly.

"That I cannot tell you; I have no idea. Asban gave me specific instructions to deliver you here. A car will be waiting for us when we alight from the plane."

True to my teacher's words, a green Rolls Royce was already waiting for us at the tarmac, driving us to an urban 3-story penthouse in the heart of the Saint-Germain-des-Prés.

L'Appartement de Terrasse (The Penthouse)

A couple of Abds from P's entourage deposited Andy's and my luggage in one of several guest suites in the eight-room penthouse, which the prince had rented for our two weeks stay. As I rummaged through my bags for a change of clothing, I discovered the brown envelope the Wazir had given me before I left the Sekham. I had neatly stored the package away and forgotten about it for several months. It sat untouched in the bottom compartment of my luggage.

"Oh my goodness! Look what I found!" I exclaimed to Andy.

"What did you find?" My Valet commented.

"I just discovered the envelope Thabit gave me when we left the Sekham. I had forgotten about it. Have you opened yours?"

"I did, and I deposited the check he gifted me into my Swiss account. I should have asked you about your package, but we were so busy prepping for our summer vacation, I forgot to remind you. Open it," Andy advised.

Folded into a note card was a $35,000 check addressed to me. The "Thank You" note read:

You are an excellent apprentice and model for my brother, Aziz. Please accept this token of appreciation from my brother and me. We will see each other at the Cannes Boat show.

Tread with caution in your next household.

(God Bless!)

Wazir Thabit

I was flabbergasted by the amount of money on the check. Andy inquired, *"What did Thabit say?"*

I handed the check and the note to my guardian without responding. After a brief silence, Andy remarked, *"I'll deposit this into your Swiss account tomorrow."*

"Thank You. Why did the Wazir say to tread with caution in our next household?" I burbled.

"He's just being cautious. You already know of the prince's ways. You have to be mindful when you are around him. I'll do my best to be near you when you are being summoned by his Highness."

"I'll be lost without you," I cried.

"Now, don't be silly; I'll never leave you in harm's way," my protector affirmed with conviction in his voice.

Just then, an Abd came to inform us that we were needed in the living room.

Why are we in Paris?

The prince had gathered a crowd in the spacious room. Besides Aziz (the photographer), Alain (my teacher) whom we already knew, we were surprised to see Bryanna, our model friend we had met in Greece, Caroline (a friend of Bryanna), Christophe (an attractive French model), Driss (a handsome French Moroccan model/actor), Suliman (the French/Arab cultural attaché based in Paris) and last but not least Count Mario. I was indeed astonished to see such a gathering of beautiful people in my 'Master's' entourage. Neither my Valet nor I had expected to see Aziz, Mario and Bryanna so soon. We had no idea that P knew Mario or Bryanna.

After casual introductions, P announced, *"I'm here to let you know I'm now a part of the 'Sacred Sex in Sacred Places' photography project. The reason we are here for two weeks is to film the historical French religious sites.*

I've dispatched Al-Fayoum to collect Elizabeth and her chaperone, Didee, from Amsterdam. They will be joining us when we dine at 'Le Meurice' this evening."

Andy and I were indeed astounded by P's pronouncement. We had no idea that we would be back on Aziz's team so soon. As we mingled and became acquainted before dinner, I cornered Bryanna. *"I didn't know you are friends with his Highness! How did the two of you meet?"*

"I've known P for a while. The Aga Khan introduced us. I have kept in touch with his Highness whenever he has been in town," the model replied.

"I thought you lived in Athens?" I queried.

Bryanna said cheerily, *"I'm based all over Europe. I travel a lot for my job. The world is my home."*

"I wish I could claim the world as my home. It sounds so exciting," I riposted enviously.

The transsexual model continued, *"You will, darling, when you become a famous fashion designer. The world is yours when you claim it as your reality. Don't let anybody tell you otherwise."*

"You are so confident and self-assured. I wish I could be like you," I chirped.

"Of course you can, young man. Be true to yourself in what you desire out of life, and the universe will respond to your calling. Stay focused and don't be sidetracked by the distractions that surround you. Most importantly, listen to your heart, it will show you the steps to take to reach your goal."

"Not only are you alluring to look at; you are also gorgeous on the inside," I remarked.

"You sure know how to flatter a woman. You charming devil!" Bryanna teased.

My Valet, who was talking with Alain, came over to join us. The model turned to Andy and continued cheerfully, *"This charge of yours is quite a beguiler. He knows how to make a woman feel good about herself."*

"I know, I'm already charmed by him," my lover responded, wrapping his arms around my shoulders.

"I'm not flattering you, Bryanna. I'm telling the truth, as Andy tells me to. He said, 'The truth is the first lesson in the Book of Wisdom'," I quoted my mentor.

"You certainly taught him well. You don't need me as your teacher; Andy can take over my job," Alain teased amusingly.

"This fella has a way with words. I give in to him too easily. He knows how to wrap his fingers around me, especially when he gives me his puppy-dog look. I should be harder on him. Maybe Alain can educate him better than me?" my Valet responded with a mock bristle.

"Can I use the cane on him if he misbehaves?" my teacher joked.

"I'm afraid he'll fall in love with the cane. That's my dilemma. He's unafraid of pain," Andy jested.

"Oouh, that's good to know. Thanks for the tip. Now I know how to deal with him if he's naughty," my teacher continued his flirtatious teasing.

There was more to his words than winsome small talk, but little did I suspect.

"Le Meurice"

This opulent restaurant within the vicinity of L'Opéra and the Louvre was and still is an amazing French-style gourmet restaurant situated within the well-known Le Meurice hotel. Besides the scrumptious food, the setting was as opulent as only the aristocratic French could create. Crystal chandeliers hung above white linen tablecloths. I felt as if I had entered the salon de la Paix at Chateau de Versailles. As soon as I walked through the majestic gilded glass door, I was greeted by huge ancient mirrors and a variety of bronze and marble frescoes. This fine dining establishment, decorated in pure white and silver, was romantic elegance at its best. When you looked out the French windows, you could see the picture-perfect manicured Tuileries Gardens. I felt as if I was part of Queen Maria Antoinette's court that entire evening.

Below the Table

I was seated between my teacher and P at the round dining table. Next to the prince was Elizabeth, the new arrival to our entourage. Didee, the adolescent's 'big sister' sat across from us beside Andy. Scattered around us were Aziz, Mario, Suliman, and the male and female models.

As the men's discussion turned to our photo-shoot schedules, one of P's hands landed nonchalantly on my thigh while his other found its way into Elizabeth's lap. We did not move away. Further down, I felt my teacher's foot inching its way around my ankles. Alain was playfully testing the waters to see if I would move my legs away. I did not. As dinner progressed and our conversation became more engaged, so did P's hand and so did Monsieur Dubois's foot became fierier. I was getting turned on by this secret seduction played out below my waist.

I looked to my Valet. He was in deep conversation with the Moroccan model/actor about his life in Marrakesh before arriving in Paris. Before long, my 'Master' had cupped my groin with his palm, and his other was fondling Elizabeth's crotch. The girl was getting excited, as was I. Our faces flushed pink, but no one around the table seems to notice what was happening. The adolescent and I froze. We did not move except to give occasional knowing glances at each other. We were both enjoying the attention showered upon our youthful libidos and had no intention of creating a commotion to embarrass our host. By now, my teacher had discarded his shoes and was caressing my ankles with both feet. My face grew red as my erection strained against my underwear. Before I had time to gather my thoughts, P had inserted his hand into my pants, fondling my erection through the slit of my underwear. I was getting inordinately excited as his Highness rotated his thumb around my bulbous head. My precum was oozing onto my 'Master's' fingers as he jerked my hardness. He had also inserted several fingers into the girl's opening, caressing her clitoris in silent furore. Neither of us uttered a word. Elizabeth and I were doing our best to maintain polite decorum in light of this highly charged sexual stimulation. Although we were from different 'oasis' schools, we had both been taught the arts of sensuality and sexuality. Now was the time to put our sexual education into practice. I believe we passed our tests, because we came, almost simultaneously, without creating suspicion. This enticing sexual secrecy was too titillating; I shot on P's hand as Elizabeth's orgasmic fluids covered his other hand, which the prince nonchalantly tasted in his mouth as if gulping down fresh oysters from his golden plate. He proceeded to devour my gooey release, as if savoring creamy sauce from the fish entrée that was before him.

To my amazement, nobody seemed to have noticed our orgasmic interlude. Our entourage continued their conversations without a hint of suspicion. I looked at Elizabeth, and she stared back with a cheeky grin on her pretty face. We discreetly adjusted our clothes, smiled and resumed polite conversation, I with my teacher and she with our host.

Alain's feet continued caressing my ankles after I ejaculated. I suspect he must have felt the uncontrollable tremors coursing through my body, yet he did not give me any indication that he knew what had transpired below table. After zipping up my trousers and feeling more composed, I did something I've never done before. I reached my hand out to tantalize my teacher's groin, just as P had done. I felt his throbbing hardness beneath his pants. I stroked his member without unzipping his trousers. Just as Professor Henderson had taught me during my art of seduction class, I enticed the Frenchman to desiring more while maintaining polite conversation above the waist.

By the time we finished dinner, I could tell Monsieur Dubois was in a state of sexual flurry. He was actively pursuing me, desiring further amore, but Andy carted me away for a word in private.

24

Notre Dame de Paris

*"Make me understand the lesson, so I'll find myself.
So I won't be lost again."*
Bernard Tristan Foong

1967

Conversation with Andy

My Valet questioned me as soon as he got me to a quiet corner after dinner. He asked, *"Are you alright? You were fairly quiet throughout the later part of dinner, and your face was flushed."*

I didn't want to tell Andy what had transpired below the dinner table, so I lied, *"I took a few sips of the wine that was placed before me. That's why my face turned red."*

"You know you are not of age to drink. Besides, I've known you to black out with a single sip. Why do you do that to yourself?" My guardian reprimanded.

Maybe I felt a sense of guilt for lying to my Valet. I retorted, *"I was in the midst of such entrancing company, and I felt the urge to celebrate the beauty around me. Tonight is such an enchanted evening, I wanted to re-experience the time we spent on Count Mario's gondola, floating on the Grand Canal in Venice."*

"You are such a sentimental fella. You have a knack of softening my stance when I am firm with you," my

schmaltzy facade had obviously convinced my Valet of the truth of my fable.

Maybe I was maturing and wanted to take responsibility for my actions instead of having Andy make my decisions, or maybe I was unconsciously falling in love with my French tutor. Whatever the reason, I had no idea why I had lied to the person to whom I could confide my secrets. That night, I lay awake on our Queen, brooding over my self-imposed guilt until fatigue took hold; only then did I fall into a disquieting slumber. It seemed only a moment before my lover rustled me awake to be ready for my morning lesson with Monsieur Dubois.

Morning Tutorial

Although I had a quick morning shower before my lesson, I was rubbing my sleepy eyes when Alain entered the study. Elizabeth seemed to be as somnolent as me. My teacher inquired, *"What's the matter with the two of you? You two look torpid. Did you not sleep at all last night?"*

I gave my professor a sluggish look and said nothing. He turned to his female student for an answer. She did not reply. Nevertheless our teacher began the morning lesson. Before long, I had lain my head on the table and dozed off. When I woke, I was lying on the sofa. Elizabeth was nowhere to be found. Monsieur Dubois was sitting by my side, watching over me. I asked, *"What happened? Where is Elizabeth?"*

Alain cupped my hands in his and murmured, *"She is sleeping in her bedroom. She, like you, fell asleep as soon as lessons began. I tucked her in bed."*

"Where's Andy?" I asked.

"He left with the entourage to help set up this afternoon's photography shoot after you came to class. He doesn't know you fell asleep during tutorials. I'm in charge of you and Elizabeth. The two of you are supposed to be

awake, not fall asleep on me. I'll have to punish you for being impertinent in class," he teased. *"Why are you so lethargic? What were you up to last night?"*

I closed my eyes dreamily and kept silently still. My hands lay in his, and he stroked them gently as if he was venerating a sleeping baby. I was enjoying the soothing touch. Suddenly, I felt his lips kissing my palms before suckling on each of my fingers. I dared not open my eyes in case he discovered I was still awake. As tired as I was, this gentle sensuality kept me desiring more, yet I did not stir. I pretended to have fallen back to sleep.

I was surprised when I felt his mouth on my toes, suckling them lovingly, one at a time. It felt like baby fishes nibbling for food as Alain progressed to caressing three toes in his ravenous devotion. He was definitely a connoisseur in the art of sensuality and I could not resist – I had to surrender to his erotic arousal with silent acceptance. This snogging left me pining for more, but to my chagrin, he left me desiring as I had him the evening before. He was playing my game, our game of deception: it was a challenge to see who would be the first to succumb to our fatal attraction.

Notre Dame de Paris

This famous Roman Catholic Marian Cathedral is located on the eastern half of the Île de la Cité in the fourth arrondissement of Paris. The imposing structure is often reputed to be one of the most prominent examples of French Gothic architecture, both in France and in all of Europe. It is also among the largest and best-known churches in the world. The naturalism of its sculptures and stained glass are in contrast with earlier Romanesque architecture.

How we obtained permission to photograph '*Sacred Sex in Sacred Places*' in this distinguished site remains a mystery to me. I guess our host's princely and political connection with the French government had much to do with obtaining our photography permission. The term, "I'll scratch your back and you'll scratch mine" would most eloquently apply to both countries' political, economic and social alliances. To top that, P's generous financial donation to the upkeep and maintenance of France's historical treasures was delightfully welcomed by the French religious governing body. After all, P had already set his sights on making France his second home and a playground for his wealthy and elite partisans; that alone was sufficient cause for the French authorities to cater to the wishes of his Royal Highness.

Mario, like many artistic fashion photographers of his generation, preferred to capture his naked and/or semi-naked subjects posing against the great Gothic backdrop high above ground. Ladders and scaffolding were already in place when I arrived with Elizabeth and Monsieur Dubois in the late afternoon. The male and female models, doing a group couture fashion shoot were already posing above and in Notre Dame de Paris. Their fancy outfits, arranged sexily on their sinewy physiques, were practically falling off them. As the shoot progressed in intensity, these expensive coverings were shed, only to be used as transparent, seductive shielding for their private areas.

Fatal Attraction

I was glad to be back by Andy's side. That morning after my sensual pretend-sleep foreplay with Alain, I was left with a kind of unrequited sexual thirst I had seldom experienced. In the past, my liaisons had progressed all the way. Now Monsieur Dubois had stirred in me to euphoria similar to the sensual hunger I'd had for Andy when I was in Nikee's care. I had unconsciously fallen prey to a parlous liaison, and I dared not speak its name. I was slowly descending into a psychological trap, which only my professor had the audacity to set. Alain was secretly testing my emotional strength, silently observing to see if I would pass the 'big brother' test. It was an examination I had no idea was being bestowed upon me.

For the moment, I was overjoyed to be with my Valet again. He was my protector, and like the couture outfits we were using as our last protective divide, I was clinging onto my lover for life, afraid to bare the last vestige of my vulnerability. This Frenchman was already gaining a precarious grip on my unquenched soul.

Posing for the Camera

When my turn arrived to pair with Andy and Alain, I was in a state of panic. I was afraid my libido would show through my faux pretense when sandwiched between my semi-naked Valet and the half-clothed Dubois. As much as I tried to calm myself, my thumping heart pounded rapidly. I was afraid that Andy would sense my perturbed state. He whispered in my ear as the photographers clicked away at our 3-way liaison, *"Young, are you alright? You haven't been yourself since we arrived in Paris. Tell me what the matter is."*

I did not reply, instead I pressed my face against my protector's muscular chest. I did not want him to see my flushed cheeks. Alain, aware of our sexual game, began pressing his growing groin against my derriere. He knew I desired him, and he also knew I was at a loss around him. I held my lover tightly; I did not know how to respond to this alpha male, who was sensually gyrating his pelvis against my buttocks. He was toying with my emotions, trying to gain control of my soul. I needed Andy to rescue me from my inner turmoil, a chaos I did not know how to deal with.

Alain's excitement grew as he witnessed my Valet and my passionate kisses. I dared not turn to face my teacher. I was afraid I would lose my propriety and give in to him. Most importantly, I did not want to jeopardize my love for Andy, who had nurtured and loved me unconditionally; I was his boy. Besides, this simulated sensuality was a photography exercise. It was not meant to be real.

The Gargoyles

Mario & Aziz wanted to do some adventurous shots. They had Andy and me lie in compromising positions on top of several grotesque-looking gargoyles that jutted out from the roof. As much as I was afraid of heights, I also wanted to overcome my fear, so I agreed to climb onto the back of the creature. As we twisted this way and that for the camera, I couldn't help stealing secret glances at Alain, who was standing on a nearby balcony to observe our performance. I was unconsciously falling head over heels for this alluring man. The harder I resisted his temptation, the further I descended into his charismatic grip. I clung passionately to my lover, causing him to query with concern, *"Young, are you alright? Are you afraid of the gargoyles? Of falling?"*

I replied, *"These creatures are scary, but I'm determined to overcome my acrophobia."*

Andy replied, *"You don't have to be scared of these sculptures. Gargoyles are said to frighten off evil and harmful spirits and protect those whom they guard."*

In truth I was more afraid of Monsieur Dubois than the gargouilles (gargoyles). I was already infatuated with the Frenchman without having to consummate our union. Like a creature in the legend of the gargouille, my professor was swallowing me into his garganta (gargoyle's "throat"). I was trapped like a butterfly in a spider's web, desperately struggling to get free from this psychological sadomasochistic bondage. My professor had encased me into an emotional cataclysm.

When Mario suggested I pose for some pictures with Alain, my heart pounded more furiously than it already was. As hard as I as tried to keep my composure, I had a hunch that he knew he already had me in his clutches. Our lips were close to touching, yet he hesitated, determined to drive me provocatively insane with his sensual titillation. I pressed my eyes shut, afraid to look him in the eyes. I was frightened by this attractive specimen that had so conspicuously taken hold of my person. I hated the feeling of not being in control, yet I wanted to understand Monsieur Dubois, the person behind the mask he so cleverly wore to disguise the real Alain. Posing erotically with my teacher had sent me into a tailspin.

The Stained Glass Windows

When Aziz suggested Dubois and I pose seductively against a large stained glass window, my heart missed several beats. Without my lover in between, Alain became more brazen. His closeness intimidated me as I leaned onto his bare chest. His intoxicating masculinity sent currents of pulsating shivers through my body. He held me tighter, as if I would dissipate from his already firm grip. I stole a glance at his handsome face. A pair of piercing blue eyes stared back at me adoringly. For a fleeting moment, the reflection of the colored stained glass cast an ephemeral golden halo around his resplendent hair. Suddenly, I envisioned a multifaceted celestial being in Dubois. His flawless skin radiated a shimmering glow, as if God were beside me. I was awed by such an unearthly beauty. Goosebumps formed on my skin. His lips were almost touching mine, yet he refrained from kissing. Everything around swirled, yet I remained motionless, suspended in mid-air. Time stood still. When I finally snapped out of this apotheosis, I was even more unnerved by my professor than I had been before our photo-shoot. I did not understand the cognitive hold he had on me. I dared not tell my beloved Andy of my evanescent experience. I was petrified of this empyreal individual.

25

An Aching Heart

"Do not try to run away from trials and tribulations, but endure them with patience. They cannot be avoided, and there is nothing for it but to endure them with patience."
Shaykh Abdul Qudir Jilani

September 2012

My psychiatrist friend asked in one of his questionnaires, *"Young, when you discovered that Andy had strong feelings for you, did you have similar feelings for him? Were you unsettled? Did the Bahriji School teach you techniques to deal with moments of inner turmoil, such as your infatuations with teachers, Valets or big brothers?"*
Hi Dr. A.S.,
In response to your questions, I'm citing a couple of examples to you as I relate my stories chronologically.

1967

At Tutorial

The following morning, lessons with Monsieur Dubois went as one might expect. Neither Elizabeth nor I fell asleep on our teacher, but his closeness sent me into a state of flurry. I had difficulty concentrating on my lessons. Although I pretended to hang on his every word, I was hypnotized more by the man's presence than his teachings. I did not know what had come over me, but throughout tutorials, my mind drifted to everything that had transpired over the last two days. My teacher's proximity induced a psychological threat within my adolescence. I dared not look him in the eye, so I avoided eye contact with him at all cost. I stole glances at his handsome face when he wasn't looking. I was trying to decipher the man behind the facade.

Elizabeth, oblivious to my secret, acted as if everything was as it should have been during our daily lessons. After class, I cornered her privately. *"Monsieur said you fell asleep in class yesterday morning. Why were you so exhausted? Did you have problems sleeping?"*

She bent over and whispered in my ear even though there was no one around. *"I was summoned by the prince to his private chamber. He wanted to see me alone."*

"And?"

Elizabeth giggled foxily, *"Wouldn't you like to know, you naughty devil."*

"Yes I would. Tell me," I pressed.

"You'll find out soon enough. That's all I've to say," the girl teased.

Just then, Didee arrived to collect her charge. She greeted me charmingly. *"Good morning, young man. Are you better rested today than yesterday?"*

"Oui, Mademoiselle! I'm alert, alive and ready to start afresh today," I answered.

"Very good then. We'll see you later at Basilique du Sacré-Cœur." On that note, she and Elizabeth disappeared in the direction of their chamber.

I was left to ponder to what would happen at the Basilica of the Sacred Heart.

'Mount of Martyrs'

Traditionally, this was the place of Saint Denis' martyrdom. He was the first bishop of Paris in the late third century. Many saints, including Saint Germain, Saint Clotilde, Saint Bernard, Saint Joan of Arc, and Saint Vincent de Paul have come to the hill of Montmartre, not to mention Saint Ignatius of Loyola and Saint François-Xavier who, with their companions, founded the Society of Jesus (Jesuits) on this very site in 1534.

A big Benedictine abbey occupied the entire hill until the French Revolution, where resident nuns were guillotined and the original abbey was destroyed by rioting peasants. Today, the cathedral is one of Paris' national treasures, visited by thousands of tourists and locals alike.

This was also the same basilica in which I had confessed to a French-speaking monsignor a few months ago about my love for Oscar, which I had kept from Andy. Once again, I relived a similar turmoil, which growled at the core of my being. Instead of me pining for BB Oscar, the object of my affection was now a Frenchman by the name of Monsieur Alain Dubois, who happened to be my private tutor. Unbeknownst to me, yet another emotional debacle was waiting to hoist me off the cliff of my adolescent innocence.

Sacré-Cœur Paris

Jesus the savior, outstretched hands inlaid into the gigantic mosaic dome, welcomed our entourage into this massive basilica. As had become routine during our *Sacred Sex in Sacred Places* photo-shoots, the basilica's rotunda around the dome was closed to the public that afternoon. We had private access to the dome's exterior, where we began the initial shoot. In Paris, our photographers took a different perspective, capturing the sacred venues from above ground. Models posing high above these imposing architectural wonders gave the photographs an intangible lightness, as if we were celestial beings ascending or descending to and from the heavens.

    For this particular shoot, our coverings were lengths of transparent cloth, draped seductively around our nakedness and barely covering our privates. In my pairing with Christophe, the attractive French model, I lay on my stomach against a see-through fabric that scarcely covered my buttocks. Christophe stood naked on the stone railing, facing me, his organza drape concealing only his manhood while he scattered rose petals onto my naked skin. Mario wanted us to look adoringly into each other's eyes like angels in love. For some strange reason, whenever we made eye contact, the model would break into uncontrollable laughter. He had too much difficulty maintaining composure to continue. Since Andy had I had often teamed together, the photographers required a different model to couple with me, and I was perplexed when Christophe's replacement was none other than my teacher. The pictures Mario and Aziz took of us at Notre Dame had turned out as the photographers had envisioned: a diffident boy leaning against an autocratic man for certitude. The professionals had captured the esoteric turbulence I had thought was hidden beneath my sprightly demeanor. Once again, I was forced to confront the man I feared. I had no choice but to go along with it. As Dubois took position in front of me, my consternate eyes avoided his penetrating gaze, afraid to look him in the eye. He lowered himself to a squatting position, turned my face towards his and stared affectionately into my timorous self. I tried turning away, but his firm grip refused to let go of my chin. I lowered my eyes and caught glimpses of his engorged manhood peeking from beneath his loincloth. My heart palpitated as if it would jump out of my chest. I closed my inner eyes, returning a glaring stare back into his piercing blues. I was lost in space as rose petals rained down onto my head and back. His nose touched mine, yet he again made no effort to kiss. I did not know how long my teacher held my chin to his; all I could hear were the sounds of resonating shutters clicking far away. I felt flaccid, as if my body was sliding off the balcony's edge, yet I could see myself floating above my person. I saw our intimate liaison as Alain held me tightly in his arms. He was desperately rocking me back to consciousness, like Apollo cradling Hyacinthe after he was hit by a flying discus. One of my teacher's tears fell on my cheek. I was again back in my body, awakening dreamily to the sounds of fluttering noises.

When I finally opened my eyes, Andy's hand was clasped firmly on mine. I was lying on the balcony floor. My lover had rushed to my aid the moment I had lost consciousness. He and Alain had lifted me off the balcony in case I fell to my demise. Andy lifted my hand to his tearful face, kissing my palms, but he said nothing. Only when I had fully recovered did he say, *"You, young man, are an enigma. I can never have you out of my sight. Whenever my back is turned, you faint on me. What vision did you see this time around?"* my Valet cried with concern.

I took my time to reply. I dared not tell Andy the truth about the vision I witnessed of Monsieur Dubois and me. *"I had an out-of-body epiphany. I felt like an angel floating above my body. Tears were streaming down your face, and you were distraught. Your unceasing love brought me to reality."*

My lover held my hands as Alain had when I had pretended to be asleep. He lifted them to his lips and kissed them lovingly. *"My dearest, please do not leave me in such discomposure. I can't bear to lose you."* Andy wept.

I stared at my Valet, speechless. Just then, Monsieur Dubois came over with Mario and the prince. Mario enquired, *"Are you feeling better now?"*

"Yes, much better. Thank you," I responded as my usual cheerful self.

"Good. Come to my chamber at ten P.M. this evening. I have something I'd like to discuss with you," P said soberly.

"I'll be there, Sir, at ten sharp."

The rest of the shoot went without a hitch. I was my enthusiastic self as long as I didn't pair with my professor. He unnerved me.

Dinner Conversation

As was the norm, Mario, the prince, the two female models, the Arab photographer, and the two male models, had dinner reservations at a fancy bistro in the heart of Paris. Andy thought it best for me to rest before my meeting with P. Didee and her charge stayed behind, since Elizabeth and I had early tutorials with Monsieur Dubois the following morning. My teacher wanted some alone time, so he too stayed with us in the Penthouse. A scrumptious private dinner was specially prepared for the five of us by P's personal chef. As we sat with our coffee and desserts in the cozy living room, Didee inquired of our professor, *"How are you enjoying the company of your students, since this is your first full-time teaching position?"*

Alain answered **humorously**, *"Besides my students falling asleep on me the first day of class, everything seems to be going peachy keen."*

Elizabeth and I were embarrassed that he had let the truth out. Our teacher continued, *"What happened to them? Did neither catch any sleep the night before last?"*

Andy gave me an unsavory look as if I had committed a grave misconduct. *"I didn't know Young fell asleep in class. He didn't tell me,"* my Valet remarked sternly.

Before Monsieur could continue, Didee chimed in, *"I have to apologize on behalf of Elizabeth. The prince summoned her to his chamber the evening before last. She wasn't released until the wee hours of the morning."*

"That's why she was exhausted in class," Dubois replied as if that excuse was sufficient. He continued, *"As for this young man, what's his excuse?"*

Andy looked to me for an answer. I added quickly, *"I had a lot on my mind. I tried to meditate to calm myself that night, but I had difficulty sleeping."*

"What's bothering you? Tell us! We'll try to help solve your problems so you can have a restful slumber tonight," my professor questioned; he was testing my honesty to see if I would tell the group the truth.

"Oh, nothing important. I have trouble concentrating in mathematics and physics. These subjects are so boring and are my least favorite subjects. That's why I fell asleep in class." Once again, I lied, telling only half-truths.

"Well, in that case, stay for an extra hour after we finish group tutorials tomorrow morning. I'll give you a one-on-one tutorial to get you up to par in these 'boring' subjects," my teacher asserted.

Andy chirped, *"That's an excellent idea. This boy definitely requires extra lessons in mathematics and physics. These are my favorite subjects, but not for this young fella. It's good of you to assist him with extra lessons."*

The thought of spending time alone with my French teacher again sent shivers up and down my spine. I did not utter a word in response. By the end of our dinner conversation, it was decided by my guardian and professor that I would have an extra hour in class after regular tutorials, without Elizabeth to act as my shield.

Zensuality & Zexuality

As our conversation continued, Didee turned to Monsieur Dubois and asked, *"During our photo-shoot yesterday you mentioned that you're working on your PhD research project... on an advanced form of progressive sensuality and sexuality studies? Can you enlighten us, professor?"*

Dubois replied lightheartedly, *"My project is in its infancy. I can't reveal too much. I'm almost done with the theoretical studies, and am currently conducting the practical aspect of my research. I have a lot more to do before I can present the finished papers to the E.R.O.S. examining board."*

My Valet enquired, *"Is E.R.O.S. funding your research?"*

"A third of the funding is from our organization, another third from private sources and the rest is from wealthy individuals."

Andy continued, *"What and who are these private sources and individuals?"*

"Sorry, old chap, I can't reveal this information. They have requested to remain anonymous."

Once again, curiosity took hold so I asked dexterously, *"Can you reveal the title of your research thesis? Then I can brag that you are my professor once you obtain your doctorate."*

"You artful dodger. You do have a way with words, as your Valet warned me," my teacher responded.

"Why are you so tight-lipped about your project? After all, we are E.R.O.S. compatriots; we can keep secrets. Your secret is our secret," I was inveigling the Frenchman.

Didee added, *"At least tell us the name of your research, then we can form our individual conclusions about the nature of your project."*

"Yes! Enlighten us! You are our learned professor," I chirped before Elizabeth seconded my pronouncement.

"OK! I'll reveal the title. Nothing more, nothing less."

We sat, waiting attentively for Monsieur Dubois to speak. *"The name of my project is 'Zensuality & Zexuality.'"*

"Is it related to Zen Buddhism?" my Valet queried.

"I knew you guys would ask more questions! That's it. I say no more!"

Didee pleaded, *"Now that you have piqued our interest, enlightened us further."*

"It will be revealed when my research is complete. For now, you have the title to contend with," my teacher's final words put an end to our inquisitiveness.

26

Zentology

> *"All beings by nature are Buddha's, as ice by nature is water. Apart from water there is no ice; apart from beings, no Buddha."*
> Hakuin Ekaku

End September 2012

In reply to your question, Dr. Arius, as to whether I have strong feelings for Andy: the answer is yes.

As I mentioned in **Initiation**, it wasn't until after our Daltonbury Hall gym room orgy session that I discovered he had strong feelings for me. At that point, I had decided that I needed to keep my emotional feelings in check; after all, Nikee had reminded me to play the field and not be emotionally attached to anybody, let alone a tall handsome stud like Andy.

In the beginning I was intimated by my ex-Valet. I never fathomed he would fall in love with ordinary me (that was the way I saw myself during those adolescent days). Andy, like Nikee, was every female's heartthrob and every gay boy's dream lover. In my mind, I would be the last person he would have a long-term loving relationship with. He could have anyone he desired.

In those early years, I was unsettled, insecure, and like any young person, I had doubts about my looks as well as my physical and mental capabilities. To me, Andy was an untouchable god-like Adonis whom I could admire only from afar. Little did I know he was genuinely in love with me.

The couple of times we did hook up, but other participants were involved; to me, he was a casual fling. Nothing serious would come of our liaisons. I never dreamed he had eyes for me.

The Bahriji School did teach us basic meditation techniques with which to calm ourselves when we were under stress. Over our three months of intensive studies, we were also taught basic theoretical and practical techniques to cope with inner turmoil. Among the reasons students were recruited into E.R.O.S. were our happy-go-lucky personalities. E.R.O.S. recruits took their lives in stride. We were open-minded, and we were personable around others. If any recruit displayed excessive signs of stress and nervousness or bipolar traits, the student would immediately be discharged from the program.

Think about Srihan, the Sri Lankan boy I mentioned in book II – **Unbridled.** He was dismissed from the secret society after exhibiting irrational and anxious behaviors.

In regard to students being infatuated with Bahriji School teachers: this would depend on the people involved. If they were attracted to one another and the relationship consensual, the E.R.O.S. elders would consider that an 'eraste and eromenos' relationship.

To illustrate, I use my affair with my fencing professor, Dr. Lichman, whom I willing gave myself to. I was attracted to him, and he felt the same way about me. We both agreed to have no strings attached between us. We knew we were free to see other people, since I was being groomed to enter Harem services. My role was to experience life to the fullest, and my professor expected me to enjoy sexual relationships with others. It was a creed we were mutually aware of, even if we did not discuss it.

This concept did not apply to Daltonbury Hall teacher/student relationships, since this was a regular boarding school and not an E.R.O.S. establishment.

Freshmen and their Valets and 'big brothers' were allowed to fall in love as long as their relationships did not jeopardize their services in their assigned households. If a Freshman or Junior found himself or herself in love with another student's BB or BS, that would not be advisable. However, the students could arrange a triplet relationship agreeable to everyone. Communication was paramount, as it was in my relationship with Andy and Oscar. On the other hand, it would not have been wise if Andy had barged in between my BB, Nikee, and me without invitation.

At the time, I had no idea I was being groomed to enter E.R.O.S.; therefore, it would have complicated matters if Andy had forced himself between my 'big brother' and me. That would have jeopardized my secret grooming set-up.

1967

In P's Chamber

Andy knocked on the door of the prince's private chamber at ten P.M. sharp. We were surprised when confronted by Monsieur Dubois at the opposite side of the entrance. He invited us in. P was nowhere to be found. As soon as we sat in the comfortable settee, Alain began, *"His Highness asked me to meet with you. He wanted me to inform you a little about my research project."*

We were astonished by my teacher's pronouncement. He had sworn to us that he would not reveal his PhD studies to anyone until his thesis was finalized and approved by the E.R.O.S. examining board. We stared at Alain, wanting him to continue. *"This may come as a surprise, but His Highness is one of the financial benefactors for my project."*

Andy queried, *"Why is the prince interested in Zentology?"* Andy and I had invented the word out of the blue.

Monsieur responded amusingly, *"That, my friend, is not of great concern. His Highness has kindly given me permission to approach the two of you. I am to enquire if Young is agreeable to being one of my research subjects."*

"You mean as a human guinea pig for your test run?" I blabbed.

My Valet shushed me quiet so my professor could continue. *"Young, you said you have difficulty sleeping and have a lot on your mind. Maybe my experiment will assist you with a good night's rest,"* Dubois suggested. *"Andy, you had inquired earlier if Zensuality & Zexuality derive from Zen Buddhism. Your assessment is close. You see, the essence of Zen is the attempt to understand the meaning of life directly, without being misled by logical thought or language."*

He continued, *"Zen often seems paradoxical; it requires intense discipline, which, when practiced properly, will result in total spontaneity and ultimate freedom. But this natural spontaneity should not be confused with impulsiveness."*

My Valet questioned, *"What has Zensuality & Zexuailty to do with Zen Buddhism?"*

"My topics of study have a lot to do with Zen Buddhism," Alain replied.

Enlightenment is Inside

"The essence of Zen Buddhism is that all human beings are Buddha, and all we have to do is to discover that truth for ourselves. Therefore, Zen has us looking inside ourselves for enlightenment. There's no need to

search the exterior for answers; the answers are found where the questions originated." My teacher persisted, *"Human beings cannot learn this truth by philosophizing or through rational thought. Neither can a person obtain the truth by studying Buddhist scriptures or participating in religious rites and rituals.*

"The first step in controlling the mind is through meditation and other techniques that involve the mind and body. We must give up logical thinking to avoid being trapped in a web of words."

"So, professor, has your research to do with Zen meditation?" I remarked.

"In short, the answer is yes, but my research reaches beyond to include sensuality and sexuality in the meditative equation." Alain explained further, *"Meditation is mental and physical action used to separate one from one's thoughts and feelings in order to become fully present. It plays a part in virtually all religions, although some don't use the word 'meditation' to describe their particular meditative or contemplative practices.*

"Although meditation does not always have a religious element, it is a natural part of the human experience and is increasingly used therapeutically to promote good health and boost the immune system.

"Anyone who has looked at a sunset or a beautiful painting has had the chance to understand: it is the feeling of calm and inner joy, while the mind becomes clear and perception sharpens." The Frenchman promulgated. *"Therefore, successful meditation means simply being - not judging, not thinking – just being aware and living at peace in each moment as life unfolds."*

My professor affirmed, *"I will monitor Young's progress if he is willing to undergo my Zensuality & Zexuality experiments."*

"Will Andy be present if I agree to give your experimentation a try?" I questioned. I reasoned, if my

guardian is nearby, he will protect me from my feelings for Alain.

Dubois explicated, *"It is best demonstrated without the presence of your Valet, because I want to monitor the solitary Young, without a bodyguard to influence the experience. Andy is more than welcome to wait in the adjoining room. If you feel uncomfortable, your guardian will be summoned to your aid. I need you alone to practice this meditative art with me as your guide."*

My lover looked to me for an answer: it was my choice to take or decline the challenge. After contemplating for a few minutes, I gave my nod of approval, even though my palms were already perspiring from anxiety. But I wanted to be brave, to confront my fear with courage. I needed to trounce this Frenchman who had gotten a mental hold on me.

"How long will the process last?" I asked.

"That will depend entirely on you, my friend. In my vocabulary, time does not exist," my teacher responded with certainty. *"Shall we begin?"*

Closing the door behind him, Andy disappeared into the adjoining parlor.

Meditation

As soon as the door closed, Dubois pulled out a Bahriji school leather harness. It was a burka harness we students used when approaching or departing from an Arab household. He motioned for me to sit across from him. He spoke. *"Zen meditation involves the body and the mind merging to be a single entity. In my work, I use the vim, an ebullient energy that expresses the life force, as a way to control the mind and guide it toward peace and focus. In this way, the meditator can be more alert, aware and alive. The purpose of this meditation is to stop the mind from rushing in either an aimless or purposeful stream of* thoughts. Therefore, I'm going to get you into a hypnotic state. In some cases the meditator could envision angels or supernatural entities," my professor prevised.

I interrupted before Dubois could progress further, "*I presume I have to wear this harness so I can concentrate better, without distraction?*"

"*Clever boy,*" he replied excitedly.

In truth, I was glad to don the eyeless mask so I didn't have to see the piercing blue eyes that frightened me.

"*Young, there are several methods of Zensual & Zexual meditation. I will not go into all the varied forms. Let's start with "Concentrative Zensuality" before progressing to "Regenerative Zexualilty". Remove all items of clothing, don the harness and lie flat on the floor.*"

I did as was told.

'Concentrative Zensuality'

My professor instructed in a gentle voice, "*Concentrate on your breath. Stay focused. Breathe in and out slowly. You can also concentrate on a physical sensation on your body...*"

As my body began to relax, I felt a tingling sensation, like a light caress on the surface of my skin. Although there was nothing touching me, my body responded involuntarily to this sensuality. This reverberant energy was igniting a fiery excitement within my person. My mind turned to sensual and sexual thoughts. Monsieur Dubois uttered softly, "*Concentrate on your breathing. Don't allow your mind to run away. Bring your thoughts back to your breathing.*"

As the vim encircled the erotic sections of my person, my aroused libido grew in stiffness. Sensual and sexual images continued to cross my mind and body, even though Alain continued to remind me to control my thought patterns and to concentrate on my breath. I was pulled in opposite directions. I tried to remain calm and still yet the unseen sensual and sexual energy demanded my undivided attention. I had difficulty focusing on my breath work.

"Go with the flow. Allow your thoughts to be your destiny. Release control of your mind and body. Go with the flow," my mediator advised. Dubois was channeling his sovereignty over me through mind control, a secret discourse I was not aware of at the time.

'Regenerative Zexualilty'

I followed his instructions, allowing the Frenchman to manipulate my person without laying a finger on my body. We were already making love without physical contact. His sexual vim radiated through his aura; he had encased me. I responded wholeheartedly to my 'Master's' invisible cocoon. My hardness bounced uncontrollably under his spell. Erotic currents coursed through my being when his warmth traversed across my nipples, around my scrotum and penis. My body gravitated towards the invisible energy as I plunged deeper and deeper into Dubois' hypnotic sexual web. I was held spellbound by this Zensual and Zexual master of disguise.

Dubois continued to coax me into the rhythmic flow. *"What do you see besides the tantalizing sensation you feel on your body?"* he whispered.

My body palpitated as my spirit drifted weightlessly outwards. I flew through the French window, soaring into the night sky before glancing down through the window. Monsieur's maneuvering palms were gliding effortlessly a few inches above my skin. His seductive fingers simulated caressing motions around my twitching nipples, my bouncing erection and my quivering scrotum. I surrendered my physique to this erotic sorcerer. He had my flesh begging for more. I desired release but also longed for this covetous sensation to last. His indefatigable potency was too irresistible for a young soul like mine. I was trapped within his aura, enraptured in a swaddle I could not elude.

Hypnotic Reverence

My mind took on an opposing temperament. Surging heavenward, I glided higher and higher. The Parisian nightlights twinkled dimmer in the distance until darkness engulfed me. Basked in the remoteness of timelessness, a glimmer of light appeared. I floated buoyantly towards the incandescence as the illumination grew in intensity.

A blink of my eyes – a host of masculine angels had surrounded me, spiriting me to their larkish love cavern.

I was in a rhapsodic euphoria as the angelic host escorted me. Their scantily draped amorousness aroused me as we frolicked with abandoned dalliance. Their masculinity drove me insane with desire. Their conquering force was almost too ferocious. I could no longer stave off my emission. Squirts of amatory nectar gushed onto my belly, onto my chest, and over my head. I had no control over this omnipotent rapacity. My rapid breathing continued to heave in synchronicity to their heavenly chorus. Electric bouts of orgasmic entr'acte sheathed me in a series of incessant convulsions before I finally simmered to apathy floating in an ocean of nothingness.

"Return to us, Young," a distant voice pulled me to reality. I drifted toward the soothing sound. The twang of a snap woke me to the present. A mess of gooey semen laid on my slender abdomen as my professor detached my contraption. He stared at me unflinchingly, as if to assert that I was his, and I was now his property. Throughout my service in the prince's household, Monsieur Dubois never laid a finger on my person, but I was already his. This mind-controlling wizard had utilized Zentology to

manipulate me like a string puppet, dancing to the rhythm of his bidding.

It was past midnight before Andy and I returned to our chamber. That night, I slept like a rejuvenated child in the cradling bosom of my physical lover, but my mind was now restrained by another.

27

---·◆·---

Grande Mosquée de Paris

"Life is not complex.
We are complex.
Life is simple, and
The simple thing is the right thing."
Oscar Wilde

1967

Private Tutorials

Needless to say, my unruffled sleep left me rejuvenated enough to commence my morning tutorials with Monsieur Dubois the following morning. As soon as Elizabeth left our company after regular lessons, my teacher inquired, *"I presume you had a good night's rest, judging from your bubbly qui vive."*

"Thank you, Sir. I slept right through the night without any disturbance."

"Wonderful! You should practice 'Zentology' three times a week. This will keep your mind, body and spirit in balance."

"That will be fantastic. I'd like to be a practitioner of this art form!" I exclaimed.

"Tell me your experiences under hypnosis. I would like to document your visions for my research project," my professor said calmly.

I hesitated before confiding to my teacher, *"I was heralded away by a host of beautiful angels. We frolicked in the buoyancy of space. Time did not exist, and my wishes manifested instantly – the moment I thought of them. I had no desire to leave that celestial realm."*

"You must have had a marvelous 'Zexual' rendezvous with the beatific ones," Alain jested.

I smiled and stared coyly at my books. I was too bashful to look directly at my teacher.

"Let's have another session tomorrow evening, shall we?" The Frenchman suggested.

I nodded my approval without uttering a word. For the remainder of the tutorial, I absorbed my mathematics and physics lessons with agility and vigilance, even though I hadn't had any particular interest in those subjects prior to my 'Zentology' experience.

Grande Mosquée de Paris

The prince, Aziz and Driss were praying at *La Grande Mosquée de Paris* while Elizabeth and I were having our regular tutorial. The trio had left the Penthouse early that holy Friday, in part to observe the religious liturgy, but also to secure a filming schedule with the mosque's acting mufti (deacon), **Dalil Boubakeur**. The Grand Mosque was his *endroit de convocation* whenever the prince was in Paris. Unlike the conservative Islamic institutions in the Middle East, this Muslim community held a more liberal stance on the interpretation of the Quran. The Dalil Boubakeur, a close friend of His Highness, granted filming permission for'*"Sacred Sex in Sacred Places'* without hesitation.

A serene fountain and a landscaped courtyard greeted our entourage as we entered the expansive site. We were not allowed to set up our filming equipment until after the last of their devotees had left the premises and the building was closed to the public.

While we *oohed* and *ahhed* at this splendid Moorish architectural wonder, several models decided to lounge in the scrumptiously decorated Moroccan tea salon while Mario, Alain, Christophe, Driss, Andy and I went exploring the ornate Tunisian foyer and the tranquil courtyard.

The Courtyard Garden

As we sat on the garden benches, my teacher addressed our group, *"Did you know that this mosque was built for North African Muslims by the French government in gratitude for their loyal service against the Germans during World War I, when much of North Africa was part of colonial French territory?"*

Mario chimed, *"I know this structure is a rampart against fundamentalist Islam, and its rector is in favor of integration of Muslims into mainstream French society."*

Andy queried, *"Is that a reason we can film here without hassle?"*

Dubois added, *"That's one of the reasons. The prince has also been a generous donor to this Islamic community; Paris is his second home."*

Driss quipped, *"An openly gay Muslim scholar friend of mine worships in this progressive mosque. He is planning to start a gay-friendly mosque in Paris, devoted mainly to GLBT Muslims."*

"That is indeed a progressive move, even for a Muslim living in Paris," I remarked.

"What's his name? I'd love to meet your friend. Maybe I can do a feature article on his GLBT activism in an Italian magazine," Mario the opportunist inquired.

*"I'm sure **Ludovic Makmud Albriem** would be delighted to talk with you about his GLBT work. I'll call to arrange a meeting. For all I know, he may be here*

worshipping as we speak. He is a devoted Muslim and an expert in the Quran," Driss replied.

Just then, Bryanna came to join us. *"I discovered a beautiful hammam on the other side of the mosque's entrance. It's open to women of all religions twice a week. Caroline, Didee, Elizabeth and I are returning on Sunday to use it,"* the transsexual model twittered excitedly.

"I want to go too!" I exclaimed.

"Sorry fella, Sundays are for females only. You'll have to come back another day when it's for men," Bryanna cooed.

I looked towards the men in our group for a response. Before Andy could answer, my professor announced exuberantly, *"I'll come with you, boy,"* before adding, *"We'll all go to the hammam on Monday. Who'll care to join us?"*

The Tea Salon

As I sat eating the delicious French Moroccan pastries in the tea room, Monsieur Dubois came to sit with my Valet, Driss and me. He began, *"Besides this tea room serving savory pastries, this place has a courageous history not found in French textbooks."*

I asked curiously, *"What is the courageous history?"*

Alain turned to me as if giving me a once-in-a-lifetime history lesson. *"This grand mosque, under the founder and the then acting Imam, Si Kaddour Benghabrit, provided refuge and assistance to a number of Jews, helping them escape Paris when the Nazis occupied the city during the second World War."*

Unflinchingly, Andy questioned, *"I thought Muslims collaborated with the Nazis. This information is new to me. I had no idea that Muslims assisted Jews in escaping Hitler's clutches."*

Alain continued, *"You must understand, in the early 1940s, France was home to a large population of North Africans, including thousands of Sephardic Jews. The Jews spoke Arabic and shared many traditions and daily habits with the Arabs. Neither Muslims nor Jews ate pork, Muslim and Jewish men were all circumcised, and their names were often similar.*

"This mosque is a huge walled fortress. Besides serving as a prayer sanctuary, it was also an oasis of equanimity where visitors were fed, clothed and bathed. They could talk freely and rest in the tranquil gardens without the German troops suspecting counter-revolutionary activities within its walls. Therefore, the Sephardic Jews, under Arab protection, managed to flee this Nazi occupied city."

Driss responded, *"I'm a French Jew, and I've heard this story from my parents."*

"Do they live in Paris?" my teacher inquired.

"They live between Paris and Marrakesh, where I was before I returned to Paris. You guys should visit Marrakesh. I'd be happy to show you around." The French Moroccan model extended us his invitation.

"I want to visit Marrakesh. Can we go, Andy?" I gave my Valet my lovey-dovey puppy dog look, trying to convince my lover to accept the invitation.

Monsieur Dubois replied instantly, *"Let's all go. His Highness will fly us there. He's always ready for an adventure, especially when the place has religious and historical significance."*

Andy and I looked at Alain in bewilderment, wondering how he could make such an impulsive decision on behalf of the prince without prior consultation.

Ludovic Makmud Albriem

A little before the worshippers and visitors left the **Grande** Mosquée for the day, Driss introduced a fashionably attired exotic male to our group. He was the first person I'd ever encountered who wore a cream-colored fedora and carried an exquisitely crafted ivory cane as an accessory to match his off-white ensemble. He looked like a character who had just stepped out of *The Great Gatsby*.

"Look who I found in the foyer? This is **my friend Ludovic, whom I mentioned to you. I had to drag him over to meet you."** Driss addressed his last sentence to the Count.

"Hello! I'm delighted to meet you. I'm Count Mario Conti." The photographer extended his hand to shake the French Arab's hand. Instead of returning the handshake, Monsieur Albriem took off his hat and kissed the ladies' hands like a nineteenth-century debonair before leaning across to greet the men with traditional Arabian nose rubs. *"It's a pleasure to meet all you beautiful people. My dear friend,"* he shot a smile at Driss, *"told me you are doing a photo-shoot on the premise."* Before the Count had a chance to reply, he continued, *"Do you mind if I stay to observe this delightful happening?"*

Mario responded quirkily, *"Yes, do stay! It'll be a while before the photo-shoot is done. I have to do my job before the mosque authorities throw us out. Would you like to join us for dinner after the shoot?"*

"That is not a problem, monsieur. I can amuse myself while I watch you all work. Yes, I would be delighted to join you beautiful people for dinner." The dandy riposted politely before draping himself comfortably on a chaise lounge.

The Photo Shoot

Monsieur **Ludovic** observed with keen interest as we stripped naked to pose provocatively for the cameras.

Several hours into the shoot, after I finished my turn, I joined Andy, the prince, Driss and my teacher. P was already talking animatedly in Arabic, French and English with our new acquaintance and with Dubois, who was also versed in all three languages; leaving Andy and me to eavesdrop when English and French were spoken.

"*De quelle partie de la Turquie êtes vous?*" P inquired (Which part of Turkey are you from?).

"*My family is from Konya, in Turkey's Central Anatolian heartland, Sud-Est d'Istanbul (South East of Istanbul). La maison du poète Sufi Jalal Al-enfonce dans la tête Rumi (The home of the Sufi poet Jalal al-Din Rumi). I came to France with my older brother when I was a little boy,*" Ludovic answered.

The prince continued questioning, "*J'entends dire que vous commencez une mosquée gaie à Paris, est-ce que c'est vrai?*" (I hear you are starting a gay mosque in Paris, is that true?).

"Yes, I am. I will not mention anything to Dalil Boubakeur until I'm fully funded on this project."

"Tell us more! We find your project intriguing." Alain spoke on His Highness' behalf, which P didn't seem to mind.

Andy and I gave each other bewildered glances, wondering why P would allow Dubois such commanding prerogative over his person. I had an unsettling presentiment that His Highness was under my professor's bewitching spell.

Before long, the photographers announced that we were wrapping up the shoot, and dinner would be served at our Penthouse.

Dinner Conversation

As always Jafar, P's chef prepared a delicious meal for our entourage. During the course of dinner Mario inquired of our guest, *"Enlighten us further about your controversial project?"*

Ludovic confessed, *"You must have figured out by now that I'm a gay Muslim. When I was a student at La Sorbonne I became interested in Théologie Sacrée Islamique (Islamic Sacred Theology). I graduated with un degré de doctorat dans la Théologie Sacrée Islamique (a doctorate degree in Islamic Sacred Theology). Throughout the course of my theological research, I discovered that from the 10th to the 14th century, Muslim society had a far richer mix of legal, rational and mystical views on sexuality and its numerous possibilities as an aspect of life. The Islamic community viewed sexuality as a way to access enlightenment and spiritual insight. For centuries, Muslims did not consider homosexuality to be the supreme abomination it is condemned as today. There are no references in classical Islamic ethics that scorn people's sexual orientations. Neither does the Qur'an forbid homosexuality.*

"Renowned Muslim poets had written odes glorifying handsome boys, and some were interpreted as metaphors for their love of God. Others referenced gay intimate relations as spiritual pathways to Allah."

"Much like the ancient Greeks?" I chirped.

"Yes, that is correct, but under European colonialism, homosexuality became criminalized, as it is to this day," Monsieur Albriem said sadly before continuing. *"The Parisian mosque I'm developing is inspired by the work of Muslims for Progressive Values in North America, who practice common prayer in an egalitarian setting without gender discrimination."*

My professor remarked, *"What a noble and exalted cause."*

"Please allow Monsieur Albriem to continue. I am interested in your cause and the steps you are planning to

take to bring this place of worship into reality." His Highness encouraged the gay Arab to proceed.

"Common prayer, practiced in an egalitarian setting without any form of gender discrimination, is one of the pillars supporting our proposed reforms and progressive representation of Islam," he explained. *"This contemporary mosque will honor some Islamic traditions, like Friday prayers (Jumu'ah). The Muslim marriage contract (Nikah) will bless same-sex unions. It will also perform funeral rites (Janazah) for those who have been denied traditional Islamic funerals because of their sexual orientations.*

"This will also be a safe place of worship for our gay and transgender brethren who fear aggression as well as for Muslim women who do not want to wear headscarves or sit in the back of the mosque like second-class citizens. This will be a place where no religious questions will go unaddressed. Our Imams will discuss and speak about taboo topics, and this 'Unity' mosque will be a safe venue for people who feel uncomfortable or ill at ease in traditional places of Islamic worship. I'm positive that this project will bring hope to many believers in our contemporary Muslim community."

Andy remarked, *"I'm sure this will be the first GLBT mosque in Europe."*

Driss answered smilingly, *"Although this will be the first openly gay mosque in Paris, there are approximately six gay mosques sprinkled throughout the United States, Canada and South Africa, although the majority of our gay brethren worship in secrecy. They are worried about being ostracized by their families, friends and peers."*

"Even if this mosque offers newfound freedom," P commented, *"gays will continue to remain in the closet, especially in extremist fundamentalist Islamic countries, where punishments against homosexual activities are*

harsh, and not to mention, advocacy for gay rights is severely punished."

Ludovic countered reverently, *"What you say, your Highness, is indeed correct, but if the Prophet Mohammad were alive today, he would marry gay couples. In the Qur'an, our prophet defended men who were effeminate and who were not attracted to women. He banned any violence against them and accepted everyone as God's creations. It is my hope for all men, women and children to pray together in unity."*

28

Musée National Gustave Moreau

"It is the Void that is the Spiritual Existence, the Incorporeal Unity, revealing itself in thousands of forms."

Shinto-Gobusho

1967

In my Journal

Since I first started keeping a diary, I had been documenting my thoughts, experiences and travels diligently in my personal book of secrets. That evening, before I retired to jot down my day's experiences at the Grande Mosquée de Paris, Baron Pierre Laroche's calling card fell out of my journal. (I had met him at the Eiffel Tower; he was Edouard's friend and ex-schoolmate).

The baron had invited Andy and me to visit **Chateau Rouge** whenever we returned to Paris. I showed my Valet the card and he said, *"Let's give the baron a call tomorrow. Maybe we can meet him this weekend."*

"That would be splendid. I'd love to visit **Aubigny-sur-Nere***. The French countryside must be enchanting this time of year,"* I said excitedly.

"Maybe he'll take us on a **pheasant hunt***. It's the time of year for this sport,"* Andy remarked.

"Don't we need to get permission from His Highness if we are going on our own?" I queried.

"Maybe Pierre would like to meet the Prince and our entourage? Let's give him a call tomorrow morning and we'll play it by ear."

The baron was delighted to receive our call. He invited Andy, me and our friends for brunch that Sunday.

A Saturday Outing

After a hearty breakfast, my professor suggested, *"I'm going to take my students on a field trip to a special place in the ninth arrondisement, in the heart of the Nouvelle Athènes (New Athens), where a famous nineteenth-century artist used to reside."*

"Who is this famous artist?" I raised my hand to question.

Dubois answered amusingly, *"You'll find out soon enough. One thing I'll tell you: this venue is filled with surrealist hallucinogenic canvases that depict jewel-like mythical beasts and magical landscapes."*

"It's right up my alley!" I exclaimed at the prospect of visiting such a captivating place. *"I love fantastical and magical wonderlands. Is it anything like Alice in Wonderland?"*

"Well, boy, it is a place similar to Charles Lutwidge Dodgson's children's storybook land, but this venue is infinitely more sophisticated. This outing will be an educational experience for the two you," proclaimed my teacher. *"Are you ready? Let's go."*

The Musée National Gustave Moreau

Our entourage consisted of Bryanna, Didee, Elizabeth, Mario, Aziz, Monsieur Dubois, Driss, Andy and me. We arrived at the bohemian quarter, where artists, musicians and writers used to reside in the mid-nineteenth century. A three-story building had been made into a museum to celebrate the life of Gustave Moreau, a symbolist painter whose work was a major influence on the surrealist movement.

This house was converted into a museum in 1903 and contains over six thousand works by the artist. The gallery was his own design: Moreau had spent a lifetime working on a museum layout for his work. This apartment building has since become one of the best-organized museum collections in Paris.

Psychedelic Dream

As soon as we entered the foyer, we were greeted by a tall, spacious salon covered from top to bottom by humongous artworks. I felt as if I had stepped back in time to old Paris. Located at the far end, situated in the center of this expansive salon, was a uniquely crafted spiral staircase. It was one of the most enchanting art nouveau masterpieces I had ever set eyes on. My jaw dropped as I gawked at this extraordinary architectural wonder. My exploratory curiosity drew me towards this inordinately beautiful structure, and I wanted to climb its steps to investigate what lay hidden within the upper floors. I stared, mesmerized at this imposing spiral, until a hand touched my shoulder. Andy spoke, *"Young, has your spirit disappeared to another realm? I've been talking to you for the past few minutes, but you do not respond. You seem lost in time and space. Are you alright? Or are you experiencing another nauseated out-of-body experience?"* my Valet queried seriously.

"Uuh! What did you say?" I questioned.

"I said, are you alright?"

"Yes, I'm fine. I feel as if I've stepped back in time." My teacher was standing by my side before I could fully comprehend my disposition. He stared at me with his intense blue eyes and a bemused look on his flawless face. I

felt disconcerted. Monsieur Dubois's hypnotic regard, together with a plethora of Moreau's surrealist works, sent my mind and body spinning. I followed my professor as if in psychotic rapture. He led me in front of several paintings that depicted scantily clad youths leaning against winged angels; the paintings were Hesiod and the Muse, The Voices and Saint Sebastian and the Angel. He began to explain, *"Young, Symbolist art is almost indistinguishable from Art Nouveau, Aestheticism, Decadence, Impressionism and Post-Impressionism. The definition lines are blurred between these categories.*

"When I look at a 'typical' Moreau painting, I see layers upon layers of symbolic meaning. The first theme is one he shares with the Renaissance masters but portrays in his own style. On top of these paintings is a layer of black henna-like gel, which is often invisible from a distance, yet the darkness dominates the paintings when viewed closely. How the artist managed to make the two layers interact and complement each other is one of his greater achievements. When I study the interaction of these layers, I often arrive at the conclusion that this is artistically impossible, but somehow it worked for Moreau."

Bryanna came to join us before Alain could continue. *"Moreau's paintings are so rich that it is a visual overload to my senses. The central figures are almost lost in the abundant and the excessive detailing,"* the model critiqued. *"Each square inch of the canvas is filled with minutiae that compete for my attention."*

Andy remarked, *"I'm so visually bathed by the image in front of me. I find myself moved to a different state of mind."* I nodded in agreement.

"His art has an ethereal quality – it forces us to see angelic visions and fairies from 'the beyond,'" I commented.

My teacher looked at me; his glance resembled a sharp arrow penetrating my abdomen as in Moreau's painting of Saint Sebastian. My legs grew weak. I excused myself to sit on the steps of the spiral staircase. Like one of the angels in the paintings, Andy came to my rescue, putting his arm around my waist as I leaned against his shoulder for comfort. He asked with concern, *"You have been rather odd lately. Is anything bothering you?"*

I waited until Dubois was out of earshot before I responded to my lover's question. *"Monsieur Dubois has a formidable stare. I can't put my finger on his intention."*

"Are you frightened of your teacher?"

"No, I'm not afraid of him. But I feel like he has cast a spell on me. He exudes a certain magnetism that seems to hypnotize my person. I feel drawn into an unfathomable web; I can't find my way out. He has not lain a finger on me and has been a gentleman, yet I feel unsettled when I am alone in his presence."

"Your active imagination must be working overtime. Alain is probably absorbed in his 'Zentology' research, causing you to think he has a hypnotic hold on you." My guardian brushed off my concerns.

I added, *"This evening, Alain is conducting another Zensuality and Zexuality session with me. He said I should get into the habit of practicing it three times a week."*

"Don't worry my boy. I will be vigilant in the adjoining chamber while he is working his magic on you," my Valet assured.

As we rejoined Bryanna, Driss, and my professor for the remainder of the tour, Alain interposed, *"Did you know that Moreau was a loner known for his individual style?"*

Bryanna interjected, *"Very much like you, Dubois. You are an enigma to us."*

"How so?" Dubois raised an eyebrow.

"Moreau's interests ranged from India to Africa, from the Middle East to Japan, from the ancient Greeks to Medieval times. You, Dubois remind me of Casaubon in

George Eliot's Middlemarch, who spends his days trying to compile a Key to All Mythologies." The transsexual model moved from amusing sarcasm to seriousness with her voice.

The Zentologist retaliated, *"The curator Ted Gott quotes one of Moreau's critics who praised his version of Salomé, with the words, 'She is feminine beauty itself, eternally fatal and cruel.'"* He stressed the sentence before continuing, *"'She is the crystallization of every secret fear the Victorian male may have held about womanhood. Salomé inspired both lust and horror. She was given a suitably sinister treatment by Oscar Wilde, Aubrey Beardsley, and later, by Richard Strauss.'"*

Bryanna countered, *"I'm sure you are aware that Moreau remained single throughout his life, devotedly living with his mother until her death. Then he met Alexandrine Dureux, which the artist describes as his 'best and unique friend'. Although she had been labeled his 'mistress', I believe she was really his muse, if not his soul mate. They were united for twenty seven years, but never married. All his correspondence with Alexandrine was burnt by the painter himself, and their relationship was discovered decades later.*

"I think Moreau had a fear of women and, in my opinion, was a latent homosexual who exalted the tragic homoerotic youthful males he depicted in his numerous paintings. I think he could not come to terms with his own sexuality." The model was obviously using Moreau to hint at my teacher's irresolute sexuality.

The Key to All Mythologies

My professor rebuffed facetiously, *"My dear Bryanna, the search for explanations is a normal and healthy function of the mind, but it can become pathological if it is allowed to develop in excess. The problem arises when one pushes the desire for explanation too far and imposes his or her wish on the world so as to make it conform to their own imagined outcome. You see, my dear gal, a characteristic feature of the Casaubon delusion is the belief that the universe is constructed as a sort of giant cipher, a cosmic intelligence test set for mankind by God for we individuals to puzzle out. As illustrated by your good self, Monsieur Casaubon is a product of this tradition, and I must admit that complete esoteric systems have been founded on this very belief."*

Driss chimed before Alain could push the debate further. *"Personally, I am into theosophy, the body of truths that form the basis of all religions and which cannot be claimed as the exclusive property of any one."*

Andy seconded, *"I couldn't agree with you more. Theosophy offers philosophy that renders life intelligible and demonstrates the justice and the love which guide its evolution."*

The Frenchman responded with a defensive vengeance to Bryanna's playful accusation of his life's outlook. *"It puts death in its rightful place, as a recurring incident in an endless life, opening the gateway to a fuller and more radiant existence. It also restores to the world the Science of the Spirit, teaching man to know the Spirit as himself and the mind and body as his servants. It illuminates the scriptures and doctrines of religions by unveiling their hidden meanings, thus justifying the existence of humankind."*

I couldn't help but ask, *"Is that the reason you are so absorbed in 'Zentology'. You want to be God?"*

Before Monsieur Alain Dubois could answer my question, Mario answered on everybody's behalf, *"We are all gods and goddesses made in the exact image of the one true God."*

That statement brought our heated debate to an end as we proceeded to our next educational destination, headed by none other than my professor, Monsieur Alain Dubois.

29

Wrestling with the Angels

"Artistic temperament sometimes seems a battleground, a dark angel of destruction and a bright angel of creativity wrestling."
Madeleine L'Engle

1967

Lapérouse

This historical restaurant located at 51 Quai des Grands Augustins in the sixth arrondissement began its life as a bar, wine shop and eatery in 1766. By 1860, a certain Jules Lapérouse took over the eatery and named it after himself. His first act was to create the famous 'private salons' located on the first floor and expand the dining facility to broaden the views across the Seine to the Ile de la Cité. The 'petite salons' or 'salon privé' rapidly became in demand by the Parisian social and political élite; they were ideal for illicit liaisons with the infamous French courtesans of the period.

It has been rumored and, in some cases, documented that courtesans, upon receiving payment for their services duly rendered in diamonds, would scratch the mirrors in the'"salon privé' and dining room to ensure that the precious gems were not fake. Those scratches still adorned the walls of the salon in which we now found ourselves. We were joined by Caroline, Christophe, Aziz,

His Highness and Monsieur Ludovic Albriem. The gay Muslim had wiggled his way into the prince's good graces.

As soon as we were seated, Christophe disclosed, *"Did you know that these scratches are famous, left by courtesans?"*

My French teacher responded wittily, *"Of course I do. I also happen to know that Monsieur Lapérouse established a series of secret passages and stairways from the restaurant to a former convent and to the back streets within the vicinity, so that the patrons could make their escape if their wives arrived unexpectedly."* He continued grinning wickedly, *"There is also a secret tunnel that runs beneath the qui des Grands Augustins to a landing jetty on the banks of the Seine, which without doubt is another escape route."*

"That's why I love Paris. So much sexual intrigue lies within the subterranean French society," Monsieur Albriem exclaimed amusingly.

Alain added, *"There is more to this irrelevant gossip. According to French laws at the time, adultery was not considered illegal if carried out in public places, such as restaurants."*

Andy chirped humorously, *"I presume Monsieur Lapérouse made all these improvements to allow high-ranking officers, politicians and high society to visit the 'petit salons' pleasure chambers unnoticed by the great unwashed?"*

"You are spot on, old chap. This restaurant was visited by many members of the bourgeoisie, such as Guy du Maupassant, Émile Zola, Alexandre Dumas and Victor Hugo, who spent the afternoons in the Salon Jean de la Fontaine. The Duke and Duchess of Windsor, Princess Margaret, the Aga Khan, and of course," my teacher acknowledged P's presence with a head bow, *"His Royal Highness are all distinguished guests at this infamous establishment."*

Our meals were as gourmet as the restaurant's distinguished guests list. By the time our three-hour dinner was over, Andy, Dubois, Didee, Elizabeth and I were ready to return to the Penthouse after a hectic day at the museums. The rest of our entourage, full of joie de vivre, headed for a night out on the town. His Highness, on the pretext of a difficult business day ahead, returned to our art nouveau lodging with us.

In the Rolls, my professor reminded me of my scheduled appointment at the prince's chamber that evening.

Zen in Motion

It was the prince's bodyguard who answered the door when I knocked. He waited outside P's chamber when Andy and I entered. His Highness was already seated comfortably on the sofa, dressed in a loose caftan. My teacher, in a smoking jacket, sat next to him. Andy was asked to stay.

My professor began, *"His Highness is joining in this evening's 'Zentology' session. He would like to witness your progress,"* he said before turning to address my Valet. *"You asked if my research is connected to Zen Buddhism; my answer is yes. Since you are new to the session, I'm giving you a little information on 'Zentology'."*

He continued, *"'Zen' is the Japanese pronunciation of the Chinese word Ch'an, which in turn is the Chinese pronunciation of the Sanskrit word Dhyana, which means meditation, more or less. You see, Andy, Zen Buddhism originated in China and mixed with Indian Mahayana Buddhism and Taoism before spreading to Korea and Japan. This form of Buddhism is relatively unknown in the West. I'm currently one of a handful of Zen practitioners in our culture."*

Andy chimed before Alain could continue. *"I recently read an article about Zen Buddhism in a periodical about this form of Eastern spirituality."*

Monsieur explained, *"It is often difficult for a westerner to come to 'Zen'. First and foremost, a practitioner needs to shake off the* intellectual and dualist ways of thinking that are so ingrained in our western culture.

"You see, Andy, Zen Masters often pay little attention to the Buddhist scriptures as a means of learning. They believed that they could reach enlightenment through direct transfer of knowledge from Master to pupil.

"In order to practice 'Zen', a student must aim at taking the rational and intellectual mind away from the mental equation; only after purifying his mind in this way can the pupil become aware and realize his or her own Buddha-nature. Sometimes, mild physical 'violence' is used to stop the student from intellectualizing or getting stuck on the path to enlightenment."

My Valet questioned, *"What kinds of 'mild' physical violence?"*

The Zentologist replied, *"The degree of physical violence will depend on each individual practitioner. For the moment, I will give you a few pointers that will help you better understand the nature of Zensuality and Zexuality practices."* He went on to speak for some time, but I have outlined his general thoughts for my readers.

- The essence of these practices is to achieve enlightenment by seeing one's original mind or nature directly and without the intervention of the intellect.
- These practices are based on intuitive understanding – on 'getting it,' not on philosophizing.

- Zentology is solicitous with what actually is rather than what we perceive or feel about what is.
- It is meticulous with things as they are, without trying to interpret them.
- It also points to the origin before thinking, before ideas were formed in the mind.
- The key to Buddhahood or enlightenment is self-knowledge.
- To be a human being is to be a Buddha. Buddha nature is true human nature.
- Zensuality and Zexuality are the practices of being completely alert and alive while also immersed in the meditation process.
- These forms of heightened meditations are referred to as 'Meditation in Motion', because they are neither a philosophy nor parts of a religious practice.
- Zentology frees the mind from the slavery of words and the constriction of logic.
- Its essence is in the experience of seeing one's nature through one's interpretation of the sensual and sexual acts, thus attaining freedom.

The prince pronounced animatedly, *"Zentologist practitioners, such as myself, aim to achieve enlightenment by the way they live. Through mental actions, we approach the truth without philosophical thoughts or intellectual endeavors."*

I was astonished to learn that His Highness was interested in Eastern meditative spirituality. In my limited adolescent mind, I thought that devotees of a chosen religion were bound to that faith for life, tuned into that religion's dogmas and doctrines only. I did not envision those people practicing other forms of spirituality outside the confines of that religion.

Dubois added, *"Some practitioners work to achieve sudden moments of enlightenment, while others prefer a gradual process.*

"In my research I have listed five basic types of meditation, which I'm going to introduce to you; Concentrative, Rejuvenative, Generative, Receptive, and Reflective. There are no hard-and-fast distinctions to this list; it derives from contemporary meditation teachers, from whom I drew my research, rather than from a single Buddhist tradition.

Like a well-mannered Bahriji student, I raised my hand to question, *"Didn't we practice the 'Concentrative Zensuality' and 'Rejuvenative Zexuality' the other evening, Sir?"*

"You are correct, Young; we did practice both of those meditations the evening before last. Tonight we are going to try something different; we will practice 'Generative Zensuality and Zexuality'. For this exercise I will require the active participation of your Valet and His Highness. Let me explain the procedures before we commence.

Metta Bhavana

*"An example of a 'generative' practice is the 'development of 'loving kindness' meditation (*metta bhavana*). This helps the practitioner develop an attitude of loving kindness using memory, imagination and awareness of bodily sensations.*

"In the initial stage, you have to feel metta *for yourself with the help of an image, such as a golden light, or phrases like, 'may I be well and happy,' and 'may I progress.'*

"As you progress to the second stage of the meditation, think of an image of an intimate friend or

confidant. Visualizing this image, a phrase, or the feeling of love, you develop metta toward this individual.

"As you dive deeper, direct 'loving kindness' towards somebody you are impartial to.

"Then, direct metta towards an adversary.

"Finally, feel metta for all four people at similar times: yourself, your friend, the neutral person and the enemy.

"Last but not least, extend the feeling of love to all living things in the universe.

"Throughout the 'Generative' practice, breathe in the suffering of others and breathe out a purifying white light, as if you are illuminating the universe with zensual compassion and zexual kindness.

"We will take turns working the magic of Zensuality and Zexuality on each other. There is no time constraint to an individual's experience. We have the entire night to practice. Free your mind and let your inner wisdom guide you to frontiers you've never visited before," my teacher advised.

I chimed **mischievously**, *"Ai, Ai Captain!"* I saluted Monsieur Dubois as if he were Captain Kirk, the head of Starship Enterprise.

My companions laughed at my playfulness before we stripped naked to begin our "Zerotic" meditation.

'Zerotism'

Since I was the youngest in the group, I was the first meditator, followed by the Prince and Andy; finally, we all worked our 'healing touch' on my teacher. Besides donning the leather harness, I was to stand upright with my hands tied above my head. My wrists were bound by a rope tied securely to a metal hook on the ceiling. My legs were spread apart as I stood firmly on the ground for mediators' easy access as they laid their hands on the surface of my skin. I felt vulnerable, exposed. In the beginning I had difficulty concentrating. Sensual and sexual scenarios played actively in my mind as Alain's soothing voice reminded me to relax and focus on my breathing. My imagination continued to wreak havoc. It seemed like hours before I finally calmed, and the tension in both mind and body slowly eased away. Under my professor's guiding voice, I drifted into a tranquil state and managed to focus on my breath. A homey coziness coursed through every cell of my physique as I gravitated towards the heated ardor that was drawing me towards the energy field. I felt caressed, but nothing was touching me. These affectionate sensations surged through my body.

Unlike the other night, where the energy had emanated from concentrated areas, this time around, these caressing sensual currents billowed around my person, and I was electrified. Suddenly, I shot out of my body, only to see 6 hands canoodling inches from my skin. I swirled around the men, longing for their touch. Their penises bounced beside my nakedness. My senses intensified as my vulnerability stirred them to lustful amorousness. Wings began to sprout on their backs. Two males had gigantic blood red wings, but the third grew a pair of iridescent white. Their illumination intensified, blinding my eyes. I could not decipher their faces or expressions, yet an enlightened knowingness kept my vigilance on the red-winged angels. I sensed malice within their magnanimous demeanors. The third angel was watchfully protecting me. The duo encircled me, waiting for me to lay down my guard.

I felt drawn to the malignant pair. Their pernicious intensity hypnotized my boyishness, yet I saw myself in the image of a female nineteenth-century courtesan, like those I had imagined frolicking in **Lapérouse**. I desired the red-winged angels' coveted lustfulness; my irreproachable naiveté sought to understand these malevolent beings. I was drawn into Lucifer's erotic web. I was harrowing my attention to their debaucherous game of unbridled Zensuality and licentious Zexuality. I yearned to experience their scandalous indulgence, longing to taste the forbidden fruits against which I, the virgin courtesan, had hitherto been guarded.

Past Life Regression

As much as I wished to be within the protective boundary of my benevolent **harbinger**, my soul was wrenched away by these two fantastical creatures. I was transported to their lair of **erogenous vassalage**, becoming an enslaved subservient hostage to their commands. Their colossal wings had wrapped me within the confines of their curling tongues as they titillated my youthfulness to trembling wetness. The duo coiled around me like rapturous serpents jabbing their salaciousness into my orifices. My adolescent resolve was too feeble to combat their persistent onslaught, yet my logical mind struggled for control. A distant voice coaxed me to surrender, to yield and to bare myself to this otherworldly force. I felt a twinge in my bosom, as if an electric current had surged through my body. I trembled at this sudden shock. It dissipated as quickly as it had arrived. The distant voice called again, *"Peregrinate, allow, and you will be released from this encumbrance."* I did not relent to the directive. Another electrifying tweak coursed through my erect nipples, sending ecstatic spasms through my being. I stubbornly refused to relinquish control to these sadistic creatures. In truth, I was secretly relishing the jabbing pain unleashed upon my heaving bosoms. My leaking vulva was quivering uncontrollably at each algolagnic affliction. I was unconsciously desiring their perverted attention, lusting to taste their concupiscent feed in my openings. These agent provocateurs held my young mind captive to their psychological manipulations. I longed for waves of orgasmic releases with each hurtful twang. Yet my liberation was kept intact. My Masters were successfully luring me into their devious techniques of Zensual and Zexual manipulations.

By the time I had finished my past-life regression session and returned to my physical form, I was begging for release. P and my teacher had specifically warranted that Andy and I refrain from any ejaculations. Both my Master and teacher wanted our emissions intact. Unbeknownst to me and my guardian, the two of them were controlling our psychological and physical well-beings with their sadomasochistic foreplay. We would be more than willing to do their bidding. We were pawns in their "Zentology" tournament to determine who would be the winner in their competitive mind sport.

30

Hôtel de Crillon

"I'm not homosexual. I'm not heterosexual. I am just sexual."
Michael Stipe

1967

On the King

Andy and I did not wake until ten A.M. the following Sunday, after our eight-hour Zensuality and Zexuality marathon. We were scheduled to meet Baron Pierre for a late brunch at Les Ambassadeurs in the famous Hôtel de Crillon at Place de la Concorde. While my lover and I were playfully lazing on the ginormous bed, he asked, *"What did you experience last night during the "Zentology" session?"*

"How about you? What did you experience?" I queried in return.

"You go first; I want to know your experience," my Valet tweeted roguishly.

I mischievously walloped my pillow over my lover's head, *"No, you go first. I want to know what deviant Zexuality you experienced."*

He trashed me with his pillow in retaliation. We started a rollicking pillow fight to see who would win the childish game. He tickled me relentlessly as I giggled, and we hit each other with pillows. Soon, a flurry of feathers came billowing over our heads and bodies; one of the pillows had torn. As my lover continued our puckishness, I squealed on top of my lungs, *"Stop! Stop tickling me! It's angels! It's angels I saw last night. Angels came to me!"*

He shouted playfully, *"What kind of angels did you see, you little devil? Tell me everything, or I'll continue tickling you."*

"Stop, stop, stop! I promise I'll tell you everything."

I lay on the bed, out of breath. I looked at my Valet adoringly. I wanted to make sure he wouldn't give me a surprise attack.

"Well?"

"I saw three winged angels: a benevolent white along with two red-winged beings."

"What did they do?" my lover asked curiously.

"We fucked!" I joked. Andy rained a pillow on my head, sending another flurry of loose feathers over us.

"Tell me what they did to you, you little devil! I'm going to tickle you, here it comes."

"Okay! Okay! I was a nineteenth-century virgin courtesan, and the red angels were titillating my libido to sensual ecstasies. They were mean and refused me orgasmic release," I cried. *"What did you experience?"*
"I saw you being tortured by your captors, and I came to your rescue," my lover joshed whimsically, *"I am the white angel who gets to fuck you before the other two."* He began tickling me pertinaciously. I was sexually aroused by Andy's sensual foreplay. He pinned me to the bed, arms outstretched, and planted a lingering French kiss on my mouth. He, too, was getting excited by our childish foreplay. As he moved his sensual kisses down my tender neck, I was more than ready to receive him. I loved him and desired to pleasure him in any way he wanted. My lover continued to work his oral magic. Out of the blue, I felt pinches of pain around my nipples. I did not realize the

tips of my sensitive nobs were swollen. Andy's tongue sent erotic twinges through me whenever it touched the tips. *"I felt electrifying pricks during my meditation session. What did they do to my nipples?"* I begged.

My sexy Valet looked at me wickedly without uttering a word. He snatched the handkerchief lying by the bedside table and tied it across my eyes. I felt his lips suckling my left nipple. Twitching pain coursed through my right nipple. I yelled, but my lover's mouth was on mine. The electrifying pain felt sensually erotic as he continued kissing me passionately. The twinge dissipated as quickly as it appeared, leaving a stinging afterglow on the nipple his lips had just left. Before I knew it, another stabbing pain emanated from my left nipple. As suddenly as it had come, the next moment it was gone.

"What are you doing to me? I'm more aroused than I've ever been," I whispered. Andy did not respond. Instead, he alternated the twitching pain between my perkiness, causing my erection to bounce uncontrollably. Precum oozed from my penis. My lover refused to allow me release. He warned, *"We are not to ejaculate; remember your promise to our Masters?"*

"Tell me, what instrument of torture are you using? These agonizing ecstasies are too covetous to forgo. Tell me what are you doing to my nipples?" I pleaded. Before I could finish my question there was a knock on our door.

My Valet shouted, *"Who is it?"*

"Monsieur Dubois requested that you be ready in an hour for your brunch appointment with Monsieur Baron Pierre." An Abd's voice syllabified from the other side.

I tore off the kerchief as Andy and I scrambled out of bed to the bathroom. Lying on the bed was a clothespin.

Les Ambassadeurs Restaurant

Pierre was already seated at the courtyard patio of Les Ambassadeurs when our entourage arrived. I was surprised to see him without Luc. He stood to greet us. After formal introductions, the Baron inquired of me, *"How are you doing, young man? You and your chaperone are looking as stunning as ever. I am delighted to meet your friends."* He turned to acknowledge His Highness, Elizabeth, Didee, Bryanna, Mario, Aziz, Alain, Ludovic, and Driss. *"I thought there were eleven of you? Where are your other friends?"*

Monsieur Dubois answered in French on our behalf, *"Ils sont tout seuls aujourd'hui." (They are on their own today).*

As brunch progressed, the Baron addressed the prince, *" J'aimerai inviter tous d'entre vous à me rejoindre pour une chasse de faisan à Aubigny-sur-Nere." (I'd like to invite all of you to join me for a pheasant hunt at Aubigny-sur-Nere).*

"We would love to visit the countryside," P replied.

"Your Highness is welcome to stay at Château Rouge, my country estate." The Baron added, *"I'll organize a hunt when you are at my château."*

"Thank you for the invitation. That will be wonderful," the prince nodded.

Gay France

As we continued our leisurely brunch, I had a chance to ask Pierre, *"Why did Luc not come today?"*

The baron responded amusingly, *"We are no longer together. He has moved to greener pastures, and so have I."*

I was surprised to hear the information, since they had seemed infatuated with one another the last time they were together. My teacher interjected, *"I take it that Luc is your ex-boyfriend?"*

The French aristocrat released a sigh before continuing, *"Luc was taking advantage of me when we were together. I introduced him to many influential friends. He ran off with one of them after robbing me blind."*

Alain responded while changing the subject, *"At least sodomy is no longer a capital crime these days, as it was before the French Revolution."*

The baron replied, *"Thanks to Cambacérès, who championed the decriminalization of homosexuality in this country."*

"Who is Cambacérès?" I asked.

My professor corrected the baron. *"Cambacérès was known to be a homosexual and made no effort to conceal it, and he kept to the company of bachelors during his lifetime. Napoleon is said to have made a number of jokes on the subject. In one of his speeches to the French National Assembly, during a debate on the reformation of the homosexual age of consent, Robert Badinter is known to have cited that Cambacérès was known in the gardens of the Palais-Royal as a lubricous pursuer of handsome young men."*

Monsieur Abriem supplemented, *"I know for a fact that Cambacérès had nothing to do with ending the legal prosecution of homosexuals. He did, however, play a key role in drafting the Code Napoléon, which was a civil law code and had nothing to do with the Penal Code of 1810, which covered sexual crimes.*

"I know for a fact that Cambacérès had no influence on this Code. However, Napoleonic officials did repress public expressions of homosexuality with other laws, such as those pertaining to 'offenses against public decency.'"

Dubois added, *"Despite police surveillance and harassment, the Revolutionary and Napoleonic period was a time of relative freedom. At least, it opened the modern era to legal toleration of homosexuality in Europe, although Napoleonic conquests did impose the principles of Napoleon's Penal Code (including the decriminalization of homosexuality) in many parts of Europe, such as Belgium, the Netherlands, the Rhineland, and Italy. Other states, such as Bavaria and Spain, soon followed the French example."*

"I didn't know our casual conversation had turned into a history lesson on gay France," Andy responded in jest.

Florence Sala Bianca

Bryanna interposed, *"Let's talk about a blither topic, such as fashion."*

"Yeah! My favorite subject," I exclaimed excitedly.

Mario, noticing my excitement, chimed in, *"The Florence Sala Bianca fashion show is happening next week. Did you guys receive invitations to the presentation?"* he asked, addressing Andy and me.

My Valet shrieked with astonishment, *"Thanks for reminding us. I did receive the invitations from the Roman designers. Daltonbury Hall forwarded the invites to me before we left Paris. I forgot to tell Young."* My guardian apologized. *"Thanks for the reminder, Monsieur Conti."*

"Bryanna and I will be leaving for Florence on Monday of next week. Do you want to travel with us?" Mario inquired.

I responded thoughtfully, *"We have to obtain permission from His Highness before we can attend the show."*

His Highness, overhearing our conversation, remarked, *"Young man, of course you have my permission. Maybe my girlfriend, Anastasie, would also like to go?"*

Mario added quickly, *"Of course, your Highness and Anastasie will be more than welcome to attend. I will arrange it with Giovanni Battista Giorgini, the Sala Bianca* chief organizer, and his team immediately, and I will inform them that your Highness and Anastasie will be coming.

"I wasn't aware that your Highness and Anastasie are interested in fashion?" The Count was as astonished by this piece of information as Andy and I were. Since arriving in Paris, none of us had heard of or met Anastasie. Her existence was news to our entourage, except Bryanna, who had introduced the couple and my professor who had acted as P's chaperone during the early days of their meeting. We pretended not to look aghast. After all, the prince was known for his eccentricity, and unexpected news was often announced at the last minute.

Bryanna declared, *"I'm modeling in the show."*

"Excellent! We can fly to Florence Monday while Aziz continues shooting with Elizabeth, Didee, Caroline, Christophe, and Driss with Ludovic's assistance," P spoke autocratically. Before anyone could comment, he finalized, *"Well, that's settled."*

Early October 2012

I continued answering Dr. Arius' other questions during the course of our regular correspondence. I wrote:

Hello, Dr. A.S.,

Your questions were:

- *What were your thoughts on Hadrah Hakim during your first encounter?*
- *Did he come onto you or any of the other Bahriji boys lecherously?*
- *I presume you were aware that you'd be summoned to have sexual liaisons with him and/or his household members. How did feel about the arrangements?*

My reply:

I was nervous when I first arrived on the Khayya'm. I had no idea how to behave or what was expected of me in the presence of the patriarch. But my anxiety soon dissipated, because I found him charming, polite and pleasant. He was not the lecherous man I had imagined him to be.

I've always preferred the company of mature gentlemen, both as companions and as lovers. Hadrah Hakim was my type: an amusing, pleasant-looking male fatherly figure whom I also desired sexually. I liked being pampered, looked after and showered with attention, especially by a worldly gentleman who could teach me the ways of the world. In short, I wanted a 'daddy' mentor.

My guess was that Professor Henderson and the other Bahriji authorities knew which student would best suit each household. They were like matchmakers for the students and the Household patriarchs and members.

Hadrah Hakim was a well-groomed and sophisticated gentleman. I secretly desired him to summon me to his chamber. I fantasized about what it would be like to make love to a man of his authoritative stature, power and wealth. These types of alpha males excite me tremendously. I presume my sentiments would be similar to those of a young female desiring a rich and powerful older man as her lover.

I've answered your questions as truthfully as possible.

Kind regards,
Young.

31

Église Saint-Sulpice

"If we were all like angels, the world would be a heavenly place."
Bernard Tristan Foong

1967

Angelic Visions

As soon as morning tutorial was over, our professor reminded his students, *"Don't forget! We have another Zentology session tomorrow evening at the prince's chamber. Be on time."*

Elizabeth and I replied simultaneously, *"Yes Sir. We'll be there."* With that confirmation, Elizabeth left me with Monsieur Dubois. Alain queried as soon as the door closed, *"I didn't have a chance to take note of your Generative Zensuality and Zexuality experiences from the other evening. Would you tell me what transpired, in detail?"*

Being a truthful student, I related my courtesan-and-angels experience to the Zentologist. I remarked, *"I told Andy what happened, and he made a few wisecracks."*

"Your Valet is not a Zentologist. He doesn't understand the importance of my work. Let me tell you something remarkable, young man. Visions of angels are not to be taken lightly. These otherworldly beings bring us messages from the unseen realms," Dubois counseled.

"People who have the ability to see angels or have angelic visions are a special breed. Your inner turmoil regarding the red-winged 'malevolent' angels informs me that these entities desire to show you secrets that have hitherto been locked away. It is their mission to guard the doorway to these by fighting. They do not disclose to those who are indolent and tepid – only to the ones who do not fear to do battle with them."

I questioned, *"What are the red-winged angels trying to show me?"*

Alain replied, *"Let me tell you a couple of stories. Have you heard of the French writer Jean Cocteau?"*

"Yes, I learned about Cocteau in our art and literature class at Daltonbury Hall," I answered.

"Good! You see, Young, after World War I, Cocteau met a fifteen-year-old up-and-coming poet and novelist, Raymond Radiguet, who advocated an aesthetic of simplicity and of classical clarity, qualities that eventually became characteristic of Cocteau's work. When the young man died at age twenty-one in 1923, the older man was bereft of a friendship that was based upon a constant exchange of ideas, encouragements, and enthusiasm."

"Was Monsieur Radiguet Cocteau's lover?" I asked.

"You are a clever boy. You figured it out. Cocteau's grief over his lover's death led him to an opium addiction, which eventually necessitated a period of cure. Through his friend Jacques Maritain, a French Thomist philosopher, the poet initiated a new period in his life. It was during this period that he produced some of his greatest works. In a lengthy poem called L'Ange Heurtebise, Cocteau describes an engagement in violent combat with an angel, who reappears continually in his work.

"If you win the battle with your combating angels, you'll be shown your life's destiny. So, my dear boy, don't

take your visions lightly, even though your Valet jokes about your otherworldly encounters."

I needed to know more. *"Do the angels have names?"*

"Of course they do. I'll give you an example: in 1925, Cocteau was in an elevator. He felt a sudden presence beside him of 'something both terrible and eternal'. This 'thing' identified itself, saying 'My name can be found on the plaque'. There was only one plaque in the enclosure, and it named the maker of the elevator: 'Heurtebise'.

"This entity, which for years had been sending its 'parliamentarians' to Cocteau, finally revealed itself. From then on, Heurtebise accompanied Cocteau in all his works. The angel showed him what road to take: the road that had originally been set out for him by the angel. Even though he was technically being helped by the forces of the invisible, he was not free to do as he pleased. He was no longer a man of this world. He was no longer in possession of free will; he became an automaton of the Otherworld. He was here to carry out their orders, as they do for the Almighty."

"Does that mean I have to wrestle with the 'malevolent' angels in order to win their trust, if and when I encounter them again in the next 'Zentology' session?" I queried.

My teacher answered, *"This is difficult to interpret. But let me return to Cocteau and Radiguet. Skeptics argued that Cocteau was taking drugs, and it could very well be true. The fifteen-year-old Radiguet's sudden death left the artist stunned. He did not attend his soul mate's funeral, and this marked the beginning of his long, deep exposure to opium; still, Cocteau felt that Raymond's demise did not initiate his opium dependency. The two events nevertheless did coincide.*

"He was addicted to drugs for most of his later life, but not as intensely as in the 1920s. His art did not suffer.

In fact, his most notable book, 'Les Enfants Terribles', was written within the week of a strenuous opium weaning."

"I, too, would be devastated if Andy dies on me. That would be a heart-wrenching experience. As I mentioned to you, I have a guardian angel but I don't know his name," I intervened before Alain could illuminate me further.

"Don't worry, boy, your guardian angel will reveal his name when the time is ripe, just like the angel Heurtebise, who made appearances under different guises in Cocteau's work – alternately a glazier, a driver, and a judge in his works about Orpheus. Heurtebise accused Cocteau of incessantly wishing to penetrate, fraudulently, a world that was not his. If the functions of a driver (a man who knows the road, who knows where to go) and then judge (the one who gives verdicts and makes sure the game is played according to the rules) convene well with a superior being, the profession of glazing may appear bizarre to the average person. For Cocteau, it is the glazier who makes mirrors, that all-important instrument that penetrates the other world. Therefore, is it any wonder that many of Cocteau's special effects rely on reversing the 'arrow of time' by playing back the film?" Monsieur Dubois blabbered. "This afternoon, when we do the photo-shoot at Église Saint-Sulpice, I will edify you further. I have much information to divulge to you." He continued, "Go get ready. We'll be leaving in an hour."

Saint-Sulpice

As soon as I entered this ancient mid-eighteenth-century Romanesque cathedral designed by the architect Jean-François-Thérèse Chalgrin, I was overwhelmed by the grandeur of the structure.

Behind me towered an enormous organ; its monumental organ case, also designed by Chalgrin, was admired by visitors daily. This organ is one the finest in the French kingdom, along with those of Saint-Martin de Tours and Notre-Dame de Paris. Thanks to Nicolas Sejan, the talented organist, this musical instrument became one of the most celebrated throughout Europe.

Chapelle des Anges (**Chapel of the Angels**)

While models and photographers were filming in the main areas of the church, Andy and I took to exploring the smaller chapels lining this massive structure, where the Marquis de Sade and Charles Baudelaire were baptized. Monsieur Dubois joined us while my Valet chatted with me. *"I've been told that Victor Hugo married Adèle Foucher in this very church,"* my Valet commented.

"There are several famous people buried within this sacred ground," the Frenchman chimed.

"Who?" I chirped.

"Louise Élisabeth de Bourbon-Condé, Louise Élisabeth d'Orléans – both were Louis XIV and Madame de Montespan's granddaughters. Louise de Lorraine and Duchesse de Bouillon are also buried here.

"Jules Massenet has set an act of Manon in this fashionable church," my teacher advised.

As we arrived at the Chapel of the Holy Angels, my professor suddenly turned serious. He was scrutinizing the murals of the sacred space.

"Professor, who painted these?" I asked.

He continued studying the murals without responding. He finally spoke, *"Young, the three most famous of these murals are 'Jacob Wrestling with the Ange', 'Saint Michael defeating the Devil', and 'Heliodorus Driven from the Temple'. These exquisite works were painted by one of France's most well-known Romantic painters, Ferdinand Victor Eugène Delacroix. I am fascinated by his work because Delacroix is believed to* be a vital link to a clandestine society known as the Angelic Society."

Spellbound by my teacher's declaration, I probed, *"What is the Angelic Society?"*

"The Angelic Society is a secret society that consists of artists, poets and visionaries who experience angelic visions. Visionaries such as yourself can be initiated," Dubois whispered into my ears as if he was passing on a secret. He continued, *"Delacroix, like Jean Cocteau, is a link to those great mysterious beings between heaven and earth."*

Just then, while Alain was mid-sentence, Ludovic and the prince came to join us. The gay Arab added as soon as my professor finished his sentence, *"It was on October 2nd, 1849, during the feast of the angels, that Delacroix began these three paintings. It took him twelve years to complete the series."*

Monsieur Dubois supplemented, *"According to Maurice Barrès, a political activist, in the 1920s, he managed to convince the French government to institute a national feast day for Joan of Arc – a woman who claimed to have communicated intensely with angels, including the Archangel Michael. According to Monsieur Barrès, who outlined the concepts of angelic communication, 'the greatest victory is indeed to conquer the angel, to wrestle from him his secret'. In short, to experience the divine, one has to be fearless, like Jacob."* He pointed at Jacob wrestling with the angel in the mural.

P interjected, "In our Islamic tradition, the Quran mentions angels, but they are not benevolent or malevolent. Satan or Lucifer to us is a jinn: a creation of Allah that is deemed parallel to human beings and angels. Therefore, there is no combat between good and evil angels. They are all one and the same."

I tweeted, *"Like Ying and Yang in Chinese astrology? Joined together, they become the 'Whole'."*

Monsieur Abriem nodded in agreement before asserting, *"Our Muslim tradition states that angels were created from light before humans came into existence. Although there are no 'good' or 'evil' angels, they do form different cosmic hierarchies and orders; they differ in size and status."*

His Highness proclaimed, *"The greatest of them is Gabriel. Our prophet Muhammad saw him in his original form. Our holy book states that different angels perform different tasks. Some are in charge of executing Allah's law in the physical world, while others have other duties. For example: Mika'eel (Michael) is responsible for directing rain and clouds according to the almighty's wishes. Israfeel is responsible for blowing the horn on judgment day. Malik guards over Hell, and his helpers are responsible for collecting the souls of the deceased at the time of death. Munkar and Nakeer, the 'honorable scribes' are in charge for testing souls in the grave."*

Ludovic surmounted, *"Then, there are guardian angels similar to those in Christianity, protecting and guarding believers throughout their life's journey. There are also angels responsible for breathing souls into fetuses and documenting their provisions, lifespans, and destinies. Some angels travel the world in search of multitudes where Allah is worshipped. Last but not least, some angels constitute the heavenly armies guarding and protecting the One and Only."*

I exclaimed, *"Good god! I didn't realize there are so many kinds of angels."*

The two Monsieurs answered in unison, *"Indeed, there are many unseen beings circumventing our realm to this day."*

On that remark, Andy and I were summoned to take our modeling positions for *'Sacred Sex in Sacred Places'*, leaving the prince, the gay Muslim Arab and the Frenchman to continue their discussion.

The Angelic Society

When it came time for a break, I was ready to go for a walk outside the grand cathedral with Andy, Driss, and Bryanna. My professor joined us in the gardens facing the prestigious cemetery, where well-known French aristocrats were buried.

Driss and Bryanna sat on a bench puffing away at their gauloise while Dubois, Andy and I went exploring the cemetery.

"As I was explaining earlier, Maurice Barrès is one of the few resources available that illuminates the enigma of the Angelic Society. Two French writers, Jean Cocteau and François-Anatole Thibault, famously known as Anatole France, revealed some pertinent information about this clandestine society. Jean Cocteau is alleged to have been a Grand Master of the Priory of Sion."

Andy questioned, *"What is the Priory of Sion?"*

"I'll get to that later. For now, let me tell you about Monsieur France. He wrote a profound novel, titled 'La Revolte des Anges' (The Revolt of the Angels). In it, he described the activities of the Angelic Society members. They believed that in the distant past, Lucifer had perverted the angelic realm, creating disastrous results for Mankind on earth. Although this information is not new and it came directly from Christianity, society members believed that with the guidance and assistance of angels, they could right this wrong and restore purity to the world. The mission of the Angelic Society is to return earth to a Golden Age, sometimes called Eden or the 'Time before Time'.

"In today's understanding, the equinoxes are the two times of the year when the Earth's axis is upright and the Earth is in the image of the 'Time Before Time'. Therefore, unsurprisingly, the equinoxes became extremely

important in the works of some of the Angelic Society's artists, including Botticelli's 'Primavera'. The original title of this painting was 'The Time Returns'. I believe that Botticelli knew of the Angelic Society's tradition. Botticelli played a vital part in the fifteenth century Italian Renaissance, which welcomed a revival of 'the Greek ways', and depicted angels prominently in art.

"Michelangelo, one of the greatest artists ever to live, was among Botticelli's friends. He was named after the Archangel Michael, a rare occurrence during that period in history. One could only surmise that the genius' hands were moved by the angels. There is much evidence to suggest that this was the case."

"Are you a member of the Angelic Society?" I asked curiously.

The Zentologist smiled wittily, *"Young, you must understand that the Angelic Society was never an organized secret society; it is unlike the Freemasons or the Rosicrucians. There are no membership lists. It's a society whose members share a common bond: their lives are guided by angels, and they fulfill a divine mission on Earth. Together with the denizens of the angelic realm, they work for the return of a Golden Age, a time before the 'Fall'. Their mission on earth is to right one of the most famous wrongs of all time: that of 'Lucifer's Rebellion.' Their endeavors are hardly known, but their art is the testimony to their angelic mission."*

Andy remarked, *"You didn't answer Young's question. Are you a member of this secret society?"*

The Frenchman went on to answer my Valet, *"The scope of research into the Angelic Society is vast, even for Monsieur France. I have touched upon only a few nineteenth and twentieth century artists. It is clear that the Angelic Society consisted of many famous artists. They excelled in their arts because of their angelic connection: their art truly was from another realm."*

"Are you working with the angels?" I insisted.

My teacher gave us a bewitching grin before returning to the rest of our entourage.

32

French Frivolities

*"There is always some frivolity in excellent minds;
they have wings to rise, but also stray."*
Joseph Joubert

1967

The Louvre

"This is one of the world's largest museums," Professor Dubois introduced as we entered the Louvre.

"This is a huge place! Where do we start, and how are we going to get through the buildings in a day?" I gawked at the tall ceiling and the massive number of pieces of art hanging on the walls.

Alain announced, *"There is a special exhibition of French Rococo aesthetics I'd like Young and Elizabeth or whoever would like to accompany us to see."*

As we walked quietly around the spacious halls, I couldn't help but notice an abundance of angels, cupids, fairies, nymphs, mythical creatures and nude figures depicted in the classical paintings. I remarked, *"There seem to be many artists who had visions of otherworldly beings. They must also be sexually charged, judging by the amount of nudity depicted in their art."*

My Valet grinned like a Cheshire cat as he stood, admiring *L'escarpolette (The Swing)* by Jean-Honoré

Fragonard. My teacher, with his hand on his chin, studied the work with intensity.

I expressed, *"This looks like a classic case of ludic flirtation."*

"Young, this is Rococo art at its best," the Frenchman explained.

Andy burst out in loud laugher. Dubois shushed him to be quiet. I continued, *"Most of the paintings are of people in sensual flirtation, sexual seduction, or provocative positions and erotic situations. It seems like these pictures were precursors to modern day pornographic romantic liaisons."*

My Valet couldn't contain himself. He burst forth, *"You mean like soft porn instead of hardcore sex?"*

"What's the difference between soft porn and hardcore sex?" I questioned. *"I thought there is only one kind of pornography; the kind that Rick Samuels taught me in his Art of Grooming class at the Bahriji School. He specifically advised that I should differentiate between artistic nudity and pornographic images. He made no references to soft, hardcore, or 'mid-core' pornography, for that matter."*

Andy found my statements funnier than before. He howled with laughter. Alain had to quiet him before speaking. *"I'm not going to explain the difference between soft, mid and hard-core pornography. I'll leave that to your 'enlightened' Valet; who seems to know the various kinds of pornography."* He announced sarcastically. Dubois continued, *"In order to understand each painting, one must understand the aesthetics of that particular period in the history of art. I am not referring to paintings only, but to all philosophical aspects of beauty.*

Rococo

"Since we are currently looking at Rococo art, please allow me to irradiate you with some useful insights into eighteenth-century French aesthetics. This artistic movement affected many aspects of the arts, including architecture, interior design, literature, music, theatre, sculpture, and, of course, painting.

"This style developed in the early part of the eighteenth century in Paris as a reaction to the grandeur, symmetry and strict regulation of the Baroque era, especially in the Palace of Versailles. Rococo artists opted for a more jocular, florid and graceful approach to art and architecture. This new form of art and architecture was ornate and full of creamy pastels, asymmetrical designs, and an abundance of curves and gold. Unlike the politically focused Baroque, Rococo emphasized playful and witty artistic themes. Rooms were designed as works of art with elegant and ornate furniture, miniature sculptures, ornamental mirrors, complementing tapestries, wall reliefs, and of course, paintings.

"In literature and theatre, it is often said that no other cultural period 'has produced a wittier, more elegant, and teasing dialogue, full of elusive and camouflaging language and gestures, refined feelings and subtle criticism' than Rococo theatre."

I quipped, *"What is the meaning of the word 'Rococo'?"*

Monsieur Abriem replied, *"According to the Dictionary of the French Academy, the word Rococo 'generally covers the kind of ornamental style and design associated with Louis XV's reign and the beginning of Louis XVI.' It also includes all kinds of French art produced around the mid-eighteenth century. The word Rococo is a combination of the French rocaille, meaning stone, and coquilles, meaning shell, because these objects served as means of decoration. In a similar vein, the term Rococo can also be interpreted as a combination of the*

Italian word 'barocco' (an irregularly shaped pearl, possibly the source of the word "baroque") and the French 'rocaille' (a popular form of garden or interior ornamentation using shells and pebbles). Owing to Rococo love of shell-like curves and the focus on the decorative arts, some critics have used the term derogatorily, implying that this style was frivolous or merely modish. When the term was first used in the English language, it was a colloquialism meaning 'old-fashioned'. As a matter of fact, the style received harsh criticism, and was seen by some to be superficial and of poor taste, especially when compared to neoclassicism, which has been praised for its aesthetic qualities. Since the mid-nineteenth century, the term Rococo has been accepted by art historians. While there are debates about the value of the style to art as a field, Rococo is now widely recognized as a major period in the development of European Art."

"Thank you for the detailed explanation, Ludovic." My professor patted the Muslim intellectual on the back.

As we continued down a hall chock-full of Rococo paintings, I remarked, *"I love Jean-Honoré Fragonard's works. They are so seductively romantic, with an abundance of chubby cupids shooting love arrows everywhere."*

Jean-Honoré Fragonard

My lover jested vivaciously, *"Of course you do! I bet you identify with these elaborately dressed maidens, enticing handsome beaus into their seductive bosoms."*

I slapped Andy's butt kittenishly. Before we knew it, we were chasing each other around the exhibition hall like mischievous children. Monsieur Dubois reprimanded, *"Boys! Stop this nonsense at once before the security guards kick us out."* He continued, *"You two lovebirds are just like those cupids in Fragonard's paintings; forever* chirping away at each other with your lovey-dovey child's play. Get back here and let me continue.

"Although Rococo originated in the decorative arts, the style showed clearly in these paintings. Artists used delicate colors on their canvases and included cherubs and other romantic mythological figures in carefree postures, suggesting that they behaved freely and recklessly, as you two are now." He stopped long enough to give us an objectionable stare. The professor resumed, *"Portraiture was also popular among Rococo painters. Some works emphasize the naughtiness or impurity of their subjects; this kind of display was unheard of in Baroque art. Landscapes were pastoral, often illustrating the leisurely outings of aristocratic couples."*

Elizabeth tweeted, *"The women in the paintings look as though they are conducting illicit affairs."* She was observing Fragonard's 'The Love Letter'. *"Are they mistresses of wealthy men?"* she added.

We all burst out laughing except for Alain, who remained composed. The teacher disclosed, *"As the fan was used in some of Fragonard's other paintings, the letter may be interpreted as a signal to another party, used in a game of seduction. Desire and seduction play an enormous part in the Rococo era.*

"In order to appreciate these paintings, one must also understand the rules and etiquette of the day. Despite widespread prostitution and general debauchery among the masses, aristocrats and the middle-classes had to follow strict protocols regarding courtship and the display of affection. Much of the seduction was circumlocutory. One never got to the point directly. As was so eloquently stated in Laurence Sterne's The Sentimental Journey, the eroticism was "suspended." Having mentioned that, Boucher and Fragonard did push the limits of propriety and incurred the wrath of art critics of their day."

François Boucher

Didee noted, *"I'm looking at two paintings by Francois Boucher: L'Odalisque (the brunette Odalisque) and his Blond Odalisque. I can see an aesthetic dialogue between and within the paintings. What do you think?"*

I asked, *"What is the meaning of Odalisque?"*

Monsieur Abriem jumped in to answer my question. *"The word 'odalisque' means a female slave or concubine in a harem."*

Andy elucidated, *"Neither of these paintings give me the impression that these women were female slaves or concubines within a harem. They look too sophisticated and refined."*

Driss answered grinningly, *"L'Odalisque is a painting of Boucher's wife. He deliberately emphasized the Oriental theme, but the pose is of an aristocrat lying on a luxurious sofa. The nude brunette looks like one of the young Turkish women about whom European men fantasized back then. Orientalism was in vogue at the time.*

"On the contrary, when I look at the Blond Odalisque, a commissioned painting of Marie-Louise O'Murphy, Louis XV's mistress; she is obviously European. The tones are flesh-coloured and is modulated to give form and feature to the body, whereas in the first painting, the blue gives a marble-like appearance. The model is much younger and more babyish-looking in the second decorative painting. I can feel the sensuous and tactile quality of the fabrics."

"Are you sure you are not feeling the tactile sensuality of the person instead of the fabrics?" Andy teased.

Bryanna chimed, *"Despite the 'princess' look of the brunette odalisque, her posture is one of availability. Her bottom is almost in the dead center of the lines of perspective!"*

The Frenchman resumed his educational stance, *"Indeed, this posture is one found in a number of important works of an erotic subgenre of the period: that of the woman awaiting an enema. In this subgenre, the nude rests on a bed; attended by a maid or a doctor who waits to deliver an enema using a telltale clyster or syringe held in the hand. This was an explicit pun on sexual intercourse, and perhaps even anal intercourse which was taboo. In both paintings, the artist is careful to have the woman not looking directly at us."* Before any one of us could respond, my professor continued, *"Rococo art was heavily influenced by the dramatic arts, particularly theatre. The two enjoyed a symbiotic relationship, since paintings required a plot and the theatre required decor and costumes. You see this painting? It is 'Venetian Pleasure' by Watteau; it is illustrative of this symbiosis. It shows the influence of the Italian dramatic forms which was also very much in vogue at the time."*

Didee declared, *"This painting does have an operatic feel to it. The setting is theatrical rather than natural. It shows the comic-theatrical world of the Venetian court, in which aristocrats played their parts to perfection. The Greco-Roman classical world is illustrated by the statuary in the background. This contrast indeed creates an aesthetic irony. Nearly everyone in the painting is courting; some are more successful than others. I see a couple in dialogue and a third party is looking at them with jealousy."*

Driss expressed, *"The statue of Venus overlooking all the various lovemaking activities seems to come alive with erotic potential. The goat's head on the large vase above the central woman's head is sculptural and in keeping with classical mythology. Isn't this a lustful symbolic function found in Renaissance paintings?"*

Dubois interrupted, *"Compare Watteau's painting, particularly the sculpture of the goat's head, with one by*

Fragonard, 'The Confession of Love.' The woman is placed on a pedestal, literally — she is the artwork, the tableau vivant. The confessor is taking more liberties in his affections than those in Watteau's painting. The painter has included sculptures of a putto (a cupid) and the Goddess Venus in the painting. Though they are not living beings in this painting, they are there for a reason. They both serve symbolic functions, much like the goat's head in Watteau's painting. The putto is in the form of a baby, and the Goddess is its mother; suggesting that at the end of courtship come marriage and children. However, the reaching for the apple connotes carnality as in the Adam and Eve story. The dog placed at their feet is a double emblem. It can signify both fidelity and lust.

"Fragonard's other painting, 'Young Woman with Dog', takes this latter element to the extreme. The dog becomes the object of lust. Bestiality was not uncommon among aristocratic women in those days. The landscape is also more 'real', aspiring to that of the Dutch landscape ideal, which you can find in the work of Jacob van Ruisdael."

"Is it fair to surmise that the Rococo period was filled with French sensual frivolities and sexual innuendos?" I interjected.

"I believe that is a correct observation," Ludovic acceded.

"Monsieur Dubois, you haven't answered Elizabeth's earlier question," I pressed.

"What question might that be, young man?"

"Are the women in the paintings mistresses of wealthy men?"

The Frenchman gave me a vulpine grin and advised, "This I will leave it to your own assessment."

33

Zensuality & Zexuality

"Is sex dirty? Only if it's done right."
Woody Allen

1967

The Prince Chamber

That evening's Zentology meditation was conducted differently from previous sessions. Andy's presence was not required. In his place were Elizabeth, Ludovic, P, and of course, the Zentologist himself, Monsieur Dubois.

We settled comfortably on the carpeted floor in lotus positions. Alain began, *"This evening's practice will be centered on Receptive Zensuality and Reflective Zexuality. As in previous sessions, I'd like you to get naked and position yourselves comfortably on the floor. Wear your eye harnesses so you'll be able to concentrate more effectively during the session. I will be monitoring your progress."*

Receptive Zensuality

My teacher continued as we disrobed to don our eye harnesses, *"Be mindful of your metta bhavana (breathing) meditation practice. Strike a balance between conscious attentions, and be receptive to whatever experience arises* within. This openness is the main focus of Receptive Zensuality practice.

"In 'zazen' (Japanese Zen - just sitting) practice, the meditator sits calmly, aware of what is happening in his or her experience without judging, fantasizing or trying to change things. This is similar to Tibetan 'dzogchen'. In both these cases, the meditator sits with his or her eyes open. But in your case, you can either close or open your eyes, since you'll be wearing an eye mask. You will not be experiencing any exterior interference or disturbance.

"You must understand, my friends: 'zazen' and 'dzogchen' practices can assist you to gain depth from the underlying belief of being in the present moment. Reflective Zensual meditation involves repeatedly turning your attention to a theme through open-mindedness and acceptance of experiences that passes through your mind and body. These practices include meditations on life's impermanence and interconnectedness to everything that are around you. They will also help you stay connected to your Buddha self."

"What is my 'Buddha self'?" I queried.

Alain laid a hand on my shoulder as he answered, "Your 'Buddha' self is what has gone before: that which is happening now and that which is to happen. You, along with every person, have the ability to choose your individual Buddha path if and when you allow yourself to listen and follow your calling. Some practitioners call it 'listening to your inner voice'; others term it 'listening to the voices of their guardian angels,' and still others label their Buddha experiences as 'hearing and taking heed to their higher calling.'"

"What am I supposed to experience during the session?" Elizabeth asked.

Dubois gave a sly laugh. "Relax, stay quiet and let your heart and mind do the walking. Don't control your thoughts. Release yourself to the flow of the universal *energy. Let 'God' be your guide; allow the experience to come to you."*

As the room went silent, my thoughts began to roam barbarously. Many scenarios whirled in my mind. As in previous Zentology sessions, I focused on my breath until I relaxed and calmed myself sufficiently.

I began floating above my body. Looking down at our group, I saw Ludovic's hands caressing the smoothness of my skin. Sitting in my lotus position, I was excited, and I gave in to his caressing touch. He was allowing his hands to guide his snogging fingers to my erect nipples. I felt my body tense involuntarily. Remembering the Zentologist's words, I released my thoughts to allow this sensuality to wash over my person. This enticing stimulation stirred me to throb involuntarily. Since I had refrained from ejaculation for a few days, these provocations only served to heighten my erotic senses. Jets of electric spasms surged across my physique. I welcomed his touch, not desiring him to stop. I detected the smell of his freshness as he leaned in to kiss my lips. We were propelled into fits of heaving titillation and quivering excitement as we kissed passionately. Neither of us desired our surreal foreplay to end. From the vertex of my 'zazen,' I saw P's erotic passion being played out with Elizabeth. She, like me, was tantalized to a state of intense arousal.

Amidst our amatory exhilaration, I suddenly experienced my life unfolding in a different dimension. As in the Rococo paintings I had witnessed earlier that day, I found myself in the arms of a handsome eighteenth-century Marquis. Our embroidered aristocratic fineries were discarded as we conducted our game of secrecy, similar to that which Ludovic and I were performing that very moment. I was flitting back and forth between two different realities at similar times. A beautiful adolescent courtesan, trained in the art of pleasuring, was in the midst of the Marquis and me. She suckled our loins with veneration, preparing our entry into her palpitating wetness while the aristocrat continued our lingering kisses.

While in the throes of passion with the Marquis, I suddenly felt my hardness encased in a warm tunnel of love, an aesthesis I had never experienced before. This fervor felt different from that of a boy's porta. I was in the viscid wetness of the female. She enveloped my length as she rode my palpitations with abandon. A tiny flickering organ within her opening pulsated against the head of my phallus, tickling me to orgasmic delight. As much as I desired to prolong this ecstasy, I was transported back to the now moment. Yet this otherworldly feeling did not dissipate; instead, it intensified as Elizabeth bounced on my manhood while P caressed her adolescent bosoms with the tip of his tongue. She was stimulated to mounts of rapturous transcendence. Ludovic wasted no time to enter me from behind as I pounded into the female. My double entry was inconceivably galvanizing. My thoughts faded to and fro between Abriem and the Marquis. At times, they merged into a single entity, but at others they were two persons in different realms, as Elizabeth was with the courtesan. I was pleasured by both and by one.

His Highness alternated his bulbous feed between Elizabeth and me. I could no longer hold off releasing into the cores of both the Courtesan and Elizabeth simultaneously, while the men compelled us to waves of orgasmic explosions. The silent requiters pleasured themselves; Ludovic and the Marquis deposited their satisfactions into my derrière while His Highness shared his emissions with me and my classmate.

The only voyeur among us was none other than the Zentologist, who recorded our Zensual and Zexual presentations with gusto. Our meditative performances were captured in his handheld camera while he masturbated to the meditative erotica before him. These photographs were later used for his PhD research presentation to the

Enlightened Royal Oracle Society's examination board.

Needless to say, Monsieur Alain Dubois obtained his doctorate with flying colours.

Reflective Zexuality

Our mediator gave us time to recuperate after our vigorous Zentology session, and we gathered our thoughts about our individual 'Receptive' and 'Reflective' experiences. As we sat in a circle, blindfolded and in meditative positions, Alain spoke, *"I'd like you to tell me your experiences during the session."* Before any one of us spoke, he continued, *"The practice of reflective or analytical meditative Zexuality is disciplined thinking: choosing a theme, question, or topic of contemplation when you focus on your reflection, or analysis, upon it. You must stay focused on your chosen topic and not wander to other thoughts.*

"Elizabeth, since you are the only female in our group, you be the first to tell us your experience."

The adolescent took her time to contemplate before responding, *"I had an out-of-body experience. I was mistress to two men from different time periods. In one, I was a woman like those in Fragonard's and Boucher's paintings. In the other, I was a geisha to a wealthy Japanese Samurai warlord."*

Dubois chimed before Elizabeth could continue, *"Through my scientific and philosophical Zentology analysis, I've arrive at a conclusion that Reflective Zexual meditation can be employed to gain insight into the meaning of one's life, death, interrelationships, social consciousness, or to come to an insight to some key ideas in one's past, present or future life. This will give rise to a strong sense of faith or conviction for an individual to make choices, to change, or to partake in one's current and future life."*

Alain pointed for me to speak. I did. *"Like Elizabeth, I found myself in two different realms simultaneously. I was a mid-eighteenth-century aristocrat and as I am in the present. I was having a three-way liaison with a handsome Marquis and a beautiful adolescent courtesan in that other realm; whereas in the Now Moment, I was in an orgiastic debauchery session with all of you here, except for you, Sir."* I waited for my teacher's response.

It took my professor a while before he answered, *"Young, in our day-to-day life and work, this kind of meditation provides us with a powerful and effective tool for focusing our attention upon personal or professional questions. The meditator can, through this work, discover a creative solution or breakthrough. Reflective Zexuality also helps us understand the issues or inner conflicts that may arise during our individual practices.*

"You and you alone have the ability to decipher your experience. I am not in a position to analyze or judge your experience. My advice is for you to search for the answer within your person. The answer will manifest to guide you along your life's journey. Come to me tomorrow after tutorial, and we will continue our discussion on your Receptive Zensuality and Reflective Zexuality experiences."

With that, the Zentologist recorded his findings about everyone in our group in his notebook. Our individual revelations were recorded on tape as his research findings.

34

La Sainte-Chapelle

"Angels can fly directly into the heart of the matter."
Bernard Tristan Foong

1967

The Holy Chapel

The last and final Paris destination for our *Sacred Sex in Scared Places* photo-shoot was none other than the famous La Sainte-Chapelle (The Holy Chapel), which stands at the heart of Paris. Hidden away within the Palace of Justice, a few steps away from Notre Dame, visitors climb a spiral staircase to a space that resembles paradise on earth. Everywhere I looked, I saw glittering stained glass, filtering magical colours into this place of weightless ecstasy. Tall, elegant windows separated by the slender pillars created the effect of total transparency, as if I was encased in a bejeweled crystal.

This gothic jewel box was erected six hundred years before the Crystal Palace that amazed Victorian London. The architect, Pierre de Montreuil, perforated the walls with huge areas of stained glass, and the supporting frame of stone vaulting was as airy as any steel frame of any modern glass building. Sainte-Chapelle challenges the 'medieval' cliché of darkness, heaviness, and primitiveness. In its place is a miracle of light, and it continues to reign as one of the most beautiful buildings on earth to this day.

The principle of the Gothic architectural revolution in thirteenth-century Europe was a stroke of brilliant practical engineering. The Romans had invented the arch, which distributes weight equally downwards onto its two ends. In early medieval architecture, round arches created aesthetic pleasure in buildings like the Great Mosque in Cordoba. But Gothic architecture took it further, making the arch pointed to increase its height and raising rib-like cages of vaulting that press the entire weight of the roof down through a system of arches on to a few columns. Although this structure is made of stone, it is actually a structure of arched scaffolding; the walls between carry no weight. A final touch of genius is the use of exterior flying buttresses, again using the principle of the arch, to permit even more daring extensions of height. This interior and exterior were where Aziz and Mario did the majority of the photography.

Haute Couture Fashion Shoot

On the pretext of shooting a haute couture fashion spread for Vogue Italia, models and camera crew were paraded out onto the pointy steeples and stone awnings high above ground. My acrophobia returned with a vengeance. If not for Andy and Monsieur Dubois's calming assurances, my diffidence would not have permitted me to step out onto the narrow balcony, let alone position myself at the highest point of the church's steeple.

Before my turn arrived to step outside from the cozy interior, my heart was already palpitating at one hundred and twenty miles per hour. My body had burst into a cold sweat, and my hands perspired copiously. I was close to being a nervous wreck when my Valet and teacher came to offer me courage and confidence.

Dubois inquired, *"Young, why are trembling as if you've seen a ghost?"*

"This fella is scared of heights, as you witnessed several days ago when we were filming at Notre Dame," my Valet answered on my behalf.

"There is nothing to fear except fear itself. I know that your guardian angel is on hand to assist you whenever troubles come your way. He will not abandon you, young man. Assure yourself with confidence, and others will see the dauntless you," my teacher deliberated. *"Remember your angelic experiences during your Zentology meditation sessions? They are here for you, so be fearless and put your best foot forward."* Both my mentors held my hands to their lips and kissed them affectionately, an adoring gesture on their part to help dissipate my phobia.

Visions

As I looked around the brilliantly lit stained-glass windows, I found myself facing a chorus of angelic hosts. They seemed to have leaped out from the coloured rayonnants to fly around the expansive ceiling, playing a variety of melodious instruments. Some strummed at their harps, others blew their trumpets and still others played their violins, making an abundance of joyful music. An angelic chorus sang triumphantly to the harmonious delight of these auditory sensations. I sat dumbfounded, charmed by this heavenly vision; my fears evaporated before my lover shook me back to reality. *"Young, are you alright? You were gasping in amazement at the gigantic rayonnant rose window as if you were in a trance. Did you have an otherworldly vision again?"*

I did not answer. Alain whispered in my ear as if he was afraid that Andy might hear his words, *"Young, are you having visions of angels?"*

'The Fog'

I nodded without uttering a syllable. He turned his attention to my guardian, continuing where he'd trailed off. *"Andy, have you heard of 'The Fog'?"* Andy shook his head. *"It is a secret alchemical society, also known under the Latin name of Voarchadumia, which means 'gold of two perfect cementations' or 'gold twice refined'. It is derived from a Chaldean word meaning 'gold' and a Hebrew expression that means 'on top of rubies'.*

"This society's members are practitioners of alchemy. Their mission is to create an ideal 'State' by using the principles of the Kaballah. This programme states that schools and academies should teach the Kaballah. Furthermore, the laws of this State should be adapted to base their knowledge on Wisdom and not on Power."

My teacher explained, *"In fifteenth-century Italy, such visions of a new State and a new age were not uncommon. An Italian painter by the name of Giorgione of the Venetian School, famous for his 'The Sleep of Venus' was believed to be a member of 'The Fog.' Around the same time, another Italian, a Dominican monk named Francesco Colonna, wrote the famous Hypnerotomachia Poliphilli, compounded from three Greek words: hypnos (sleep), eros (love) and mache (battle). It was published in Venice in the year 1499. This publication was like a bible to members of 'The Fog'."*

"What has this to do with Young's angelic visions?" Andy queried.

"Quite a fair amount, I must add. In the Hypnerotomachia of Poliphilo; it is shown that all human experiences are but a dream, and many other occurrences are worthy of knowledge and memory.

"This text is Renaissance prose. It is a piece of mysterious arcane allegory in which Poliphilo pursues his

love Polia through a dreamlike landscape. The sleep of the narrator and protagonist, Poliphilo, is the occasion for erotic dreams; his dreams comprise the entire Hypnertomachia. The 'battle' or 'strife' of the title refers not only to outward violence, but to the turmoil of his emotions and to his desperate efforts to gain the love of Polia. He was eventually victorious in his pursuits – but only in his dream. Poliphilo's name therefore, suggests that he is a 'poli-phile,' which undoubtedly means a lover of Polia, but could also mean a 'lover of many' in Greek, since his affection, as he ruefully admits, was set on many other things.

"For instance, Poliphilo adores architecture, gardens, sculptures, fashion and gold jewelries. He also had a passion for rich, colourful fabrics, especially when they were worn by nymphs; he reveled in music, pageantry, ritual, and other spectacles that induce a heightened state of consciousness. Most of all, Poliphilo is in love with antiquity; he was similar in personality and characteristics to your young charge here."

"What is the point you are making, Professor? Are you implying that Young is a member of 'The Fog'?"

Monsieur Dubois gave a knowing smile. Without answering, he continued, *"Hypnerotomachia is defined by this polymorphous eroticism that makes it intense and atmospheric, overflowing with the longing 'to gaze, to taste and to consume.' This polymorphic element dominates the book not only in terms of the narrative (which is filled with descriptions of places and objects), but it also expands to the language used and the book's physical appearance. The language is a mixture of Italian syntax and Latin vocabulary with additional phrases of Greek, Hebrew, Arabic and Chaldean origin. The book is also adorned with a great number of refined woodcut illustrations. It is a famous example of early Renaissance printing."*

Alain looked in my direction before expanding, *"This boy loves to paint and excels in fashion design and other artistic pursuits. Does he not possess similar qualities to Poliphilo?*

"One other piece of information, Andy; another name for 'The Fog' is 'The Angelic Society'." On that final note, the Zentologist departed, leaving my lover and me agape with his newly enlightened message of 'The Angelic Society.'

October 2012

Dr. Arius continued his questioning regarding my experiences at my first household, the Kosk:

- *Were any of the Kosk household members difficult to deal with?*

My response:

Although I was stationed at the Kosk for some time, I did not socialize with all the household members. Since most of them spoke only Arabic, it was difficult for me to communicate with them. The members I was in regular contact were my teacher, Ramiz, Aziz (the Hadrah's photographer son-in-law), Ubaid (the Hadrah's youngest son), Rizq (the Hadrah's grandson), Hadrah Hakim (the patriarch), his two daughters, Nasreen and Shiya, and the ladies whom I had the opportunity to style.

There were a few household men whom I was secretly called to service, but that was usually a one-time fling. I did not get to know them personally as I did others.

- *Did you have issues with any of them?*

As far as I'm aware, neither I nor my fellow students had any issues with any of the household members. There may have been occasions when they found our European ways odd or amusing. They would smile, speak to their companions in Arabic and move on with their lives. Sometimes we foreign students would find their

Arabian traditions strange; we too would smile pleasantly and sometimes discuss them among ourselves before continuing with our student exchange adventures. After all, we were there to learn and experience their way of life, not to impose judgments on their traditions and cultures. We were specially chosen by our boarding and Bahriji schools as ambassadors to their country; therefore, we were always cordial and respectful to the members of the households where we were stationed.

- *Was Aziz, the photographer an arduous person to work with?*

Like most creative artists, he had his eccentricities. But on the whole, I found him easygoing and willing to listen to his models and apprentices. Of course, he would do whatever he wanted to do anyway, heedless of our comments or suggestions. He and Mario made the final creative decisions when it came to filming *Sacred Sex in Sacred Places*.

We were models instructed to perform their bidding in order to capture the best and most picturesque "love-making" angle, as they saw through their camera lenses.

- *Did the Kosk women and men get along?*

On the whole, I would say yes. With many wealthy and the elite Middle Eastern and Asian families, they preferred to keep their 'dirty linens' under wraps, away from the prying eyes or malicious gossip of their neighbors or socialite friends. In this way, they were unlike westerners (especially Americans), who are often more outspoken. The Kosk household in the mid-60s possessed a sense of propitious decorum.

- *Were there power struggles, bickering, or quarrel between the Hadrah's wives or the other household members' wives/relatives living under the same compound?*

I'm positive that there were, but in a superficial capacity, they all seemed to get along. Maybe within their private culture, they existed in a different way. Since we did not speak Arabic fluently, we had no way of knowing what they said much of the time.

I could only speculate that there were power struggles, bickering and quarrels. Neither Andy nor I witnessed any acts of violence within the Kosk. On the surface, the wives seemed to get along harmoniously.

- *How did these big families cope with one another while living in such a "fish-bowl" environment?*

Maybe that's one reason the household men traveled frequently. Once out of their homeland, they behaved and acted differently. They were more open and unreserved when they were abroad. They were definitely more pompous and pretentious when in the United Arab Emirates; they'd to keep up with the Joneses, so to speak. They were judged constantly by their peers and clerics when in their own country.

As for the women, they did get to travel for pleasure (shopping and sight-seeing in foreign places), but they were always accompanied by one or more male chaperones. That is the nature of the Middle Eastern culture, although the younger, western-educated generations, of which Nasreen and Shiya were part, were certainly more unreserved than their mothers, aunties and older female relatives. They went around Europe unaccompanied or with their female friends as companions.

35

Hôtel Le Bristol Paris

"Style speaks a thousand words without uttering a syllable."
Bernard Tristan Foong

1967

Hôtel Le Bristol

This elegant hotel, located in the heart of the fashion design and art district at 112 rue de Faubourg Saint Honoré, is famous for its historic architecture and luxurious interior. Founded by Rudolf August Oetker, a member of one of Europe's richest families, this establishment opened its doors in 1925 (at the height of the roaring twenties). Starting in the 1960s, Hotel Le Bristol became a mecca for fashion photographers. This was the place where Mario and his film crew lodged while we were in Paris shooting *Sacred Sex in Sacred Places*.

Early that Friday evening, after our two-week photo shoot wrapped, the Count treated our entourage to a gala haute couture fashion event complete with a black-tie dinner affair at the Restaurant d'Hiver (the Restaurant of the Winter). During the warmer months, the dining scene was moved to the Restaurant d'Eté (the Restaurant of the Summer), which looked out onto the fountained, flower-filled garden of this opulent hotel.

Restaurant d'Hiver

It was a warm late autumn evening when we arrived at the Restaurant d'Hiver. Lavish dinner settings were already perfectly arranged at the *jardin*. The centerpiece on every table was decorated with an abundance of fresh gardenias and autumn berries, set against a cornucopia of golden orange leaves. It was a feast of floral fantasy for the eyes.

De l'Or à Blanc

The theme for the event was De l'Or à Blanc (from Gold to White). The prince had disappeared with Bryanna and Monsieur Dubois as soon as we were shown our VIP table. Mario, being Mario, seemed to know everyone who was anyone in the Parisian fashion world. Seated at the table next to us was a suavely dressed, good-looking man in his early forties. He was talking animatedly with a beautiful female seated next to him, separated by a scrumptiously upholstered red velvet stool, specially set in place to accommodate the woman's bejeweled clutch. The man's eyes would glance at Andy and me when he thought we were not looking. I caught his stare on several occasions. We smiled and nodded at one another from a distance.

As soon as the last entrée dishes were cleared, an emcee came on the garden's circular platform, where the live orchestra was serenading the guests with romantic French classical music. He announced the beginning of the Haute Couture fashion show. The orchestra began playing the theme song from the James Bond movie 'Goldfinger'. A raspy voice that belonged to none other than the famous Ms. Shirley Bassey resonated from behind the audience. The diva, dressed in gold from top to toe, slowly made her way around the tables to the stage as she serenaded the audience, which applauded with gusto. Models appeared from all directions, promenading the most delectable gold, cream and white ensembles I'd ever set eyes on. They floated like surreal beings from another realm. These tall, slim creatures drifted around the tables as their ethereal outfits swayed like floating wings behind their lithe physiques. Although I had attended several haute couture fashion presentations with the Kosk and Sekham women, those had showcased retail fashions for clients. They were not fashion for the sake of art as were these I now witnessed. I was agape and enthralled by this ostentatious display of mobile art. This theatrical presentation was my initiation into high fashion chorography.

As each model twirled by more opulently than the last, and as the presentation reached its crescendo, so did the stranger's stares. He became bolder and more obvious. I wanted to return his flirtatious glances, yet I felt strangely shy, my coyness only served to heighten his brazenness.

In the Washroom

The fashion show ended when desserts and beverages were served to the tables. During our after dinner conversations, I excused myself to the men's room. The washroom was as munificent as the rest of the hotel. High ceilings accommodating huge mirrors were set against the walls of the wash basins. Thick, lacquered doors of oak separated the toilet stalls, offering total privacy to the guests. There was no one in this spacious room when I entered.

No sooner had I positioned myself at a low marble-partitioned urinal, busily attending to my needs, when a person entered, unbeknownst to me. The man appeared mysteriously by the adjoining receptacle. Only then did I detect side glances from this stranger. He remarked in French, *"Je ne vous ai pas vus à Paris. Je ne vous ai pas vus auparavant."* (*You must be new to Paris. I haven't seen you before*). Before I could register his words, he continued, *"Mon nom est Mathieu. Qu'est-ce qui est le vôtre?"* (*My name is Matthew. What is yours?*)

I understood the last segment of his question, so I replied politely without looking up, *"Mon nom est Jeune (My name is Young.)"* Mathieu acted more valorously now that he knew my name; he stared unflinchingly at my pissing penis while I urinated. I stole a quick peek at the man; he was none other than the stranger who had been staring at me from across the dinner table. His throbbing erection was bobbing uncontrollably as he stood, watching me finish my business. As soon as I had dispensed the last tinkle, he caught my wrist and pulled me into an empty stall. I was staggered by this act of impropriety, yet I was also fascinated by his audacity. I did not resist his abduction. This the Frenchman took as my acceptance of his actions.

Mathieu locked the toilet door behind him; as he pulled me in, we kissed passionately. I was attracted by his irresistible manliness. I've always loved the 'take charge' kind of alpha males; Mathieu was definitely the type that took action without asking. I pretended to put up a struggle, which got him more aroused than he already was. His manhood pointed skyward, waiting for my attention. I took my time. I wanted to exercise my power – to tease, to play hard-to-get – as was taught to me by Professor Henderson at the Bahriji. I wanted to titillate the Frenchman so I could gain an upper hand. He would have to wait if he desired me. Like current E.R.O.S. members and those who came before, we knew how to manipulate the art of seduction to our advantage. Under the excellent tutelage of Monsieur Dubois, I had become a Zensual and Zexual sorcerer's apprentice. I would make this stranger go weak in his knees, begging to eat from my palms, if he desired my amore.

I reached to tantalize his manhood with my hands as he tore off my Tuxedo jacket, ripped away my bowtie, and unbuttoned my dress shirt. He reached his hairy arms into my chest to vellicate my boyish nipples. I was aroused by his virility, yet I kept my focus as I did during my Zentology meditation sessions. As much as I coveted him, I also craved to prolong our foreplay. I sought to know him better and to see what kind of a person he was. I desired for him to supplicate to my wishes before I would surrender myself to him. *"If I make him wait, he will desire me more,"* I reasoned. A well-trained 'Cicisbeo' will not give in to temptation so easily, whether to a married woman or a married man. This was a man of distinction. I had him, and I wanted to see if he was a big spender like the prince. Mathieu couldn't wait to pull down my pants. They fell to my ankles; he reached into my briefs to fondle my hardness while his other hand pried my buttocks apart. A couple of his fingers reached for my porta, which he so badly coveted. It wasn't easy for me to brush his fingers away, since I also yearned for him to be in me. By sheer willpower, I compelled myself to overcome my sexual urges. He slipped my hand to his hardness as I jerked it playfully. Before I could catch my breath from our lingering French kisses, he pushed my head onto his throbbing length. I suckled and teased him incessantly, bringing him close to orgasm before pulling back my oral stimulations. I watched him pulsate, its bulbous head leaking pre-ejaculation fluid onto the pristine marble floor. I waited for his hankering to subside before I resumed rubbing my thumb on his oozing passage, causing him to groan ecstatically.

    I consumed his phallus down my throat, releasing his length when he was near climax. I knew he desired to be in me, yet I refused him entry. I whispered in his ear in my most congenial disposition, *"Be patient, and you'll be rewarded. Patience, my dear fella, is a virtue."* I teased before pulling up my pants. I gathered my clothes and bolted out the toilet stall without turning around, in case I changed my mind. He was left dissatisfied.

As I dressed near the full-length mirror, the memory of his throbbing masculinity stirred in me a longing to return to complete the task I had left unfinished. He observed my wicked smile and my devilish wink in the looking glass. I knew I had him. True to my presentiment, he walked towards me, his pants swirling around his ankles, and planted a lingering kiss on my lips while his manhood bounced unceasingly against my dress pants. He whispered commandingly, *"I'm a determined person. I'll have you, and I will find you wherever you are."*

I smiled at the stranger enticingly before I disappeared from the men's room. Andy was about to enter to find me. I looked at my Valet adoringly and curled my hand around his arm as we proceeded to join our entourage while Mathieu observed my every move, his longing gaze reflecting in the antique mirrors that hung strategically around Hôtel Le Bristol Paris.

Like the courtly aristocrats depicted in the Rococo paintings I had studied only a few days ago, I was merging into the Parisian café society with ease and grace.

36

Château Rouge

"All men desire that which they cannot have."
Bernard Tristan Foong

1967

Château Rouge Parlour

As our three Rolls Royces drove down the long, tree-lined gravel driveway to Chateau Rouge, the gardeners, below-stairs maids, manservants, footmen, housekeeper and butler were already assembled outside the grand chateau waiting our arrival.

As soon as our black, silver and gold vehicles came to a halt, Baron Pierre, accompanied by his latest beau, Sébastien, came out to greet us. After the usual European kisses on our cheeks, we were ushered into the grand living parlour, while our luggage was transported to our various boudoirs by the footmen and menservants. Several of the Baron's guests were already sipping beverages from fine chinaware when we entered. One of the elegantly dressed ladies, Marquise Angélique, was the woman I recognized next to Mathieu, the Frenchman at Hôtel Le Bristol's fashion show from the previous evening. The other female, Anastasie, was P's latest model girlfriend, who had worn the creamy golden finale wedding dress at the fashion show. Last but not least, the third guest was none other than Marquis Mathieu, the husband of the Marquise, who in the hotel's men's room had sworn to find me soon enough. The Frenchman pretended we had never met when we were introduced. He inquired politely of me and Andy, *"Did I not see the both of you at the gala fashion show last evening?"*

My Valet replied on our behalf, *"I believe you were seated a couple of tables from us. We nodded in acknowledgement but were not formally introduced."*

Mathieu gave me an adoring look and smiled. I did not know how to respond to his false pretense, so I avoided his gaze, which he took as my acceptance of his unspoken flirtation. It was obvious that either Marquise Angélique had no concept of her husband's homosexual inclination or they, like Andy and me, had a mutual understanding of an open relationship. Throughout our polite salon conversation, the Marquise mentioned that she was a cousin of Marie-Laure de Noailles, who was more famously referred to as the Vicomtesse de Noailles; one of the most daring and influential patrons of the arts. She was noted for her associations with Salvador Dali, Balthus, Jean Cocteau, Man Ray, Luis Buñuel, Francis Poulenc, Jean Hugo, Jean-Michel Frank to name a few celebrity artists and filmmakers of her era.

"I must introduce you to Marie-Laure," Angélique addressed the Count and the prince. *"The three of you will have very much in common. She and Vicomte Charles financed Ray's film,* Les Mystères du Château de Dé, *Poulenc's* Aubade, *Buñuel and Dalí's film* L'Âge d'Or, *and Cocteau's* The Blood of a Poet.*"*

"I've heard of the celebrated Vicomtesse de Noailles but have not the opportunity to meet her in person," Mario replied politely.

"I, too, would like to meet the Vicomtesse," P interjected before continuing, *"Unfortunately, we'll be traveling to Florence the day after tomorrow before returning to my palace in Bahrain. Maybe the four of you*

can visit me in Bahrain. I can always send the 'Al-Fayoum' to pick you up whenever you are ready to pay me a visit."

"That will be splendid! It'll be fun for us to visit Bahrain. I've never been to your country. I'll speak to Marie-Laure and Charles Noailles before you leave for Florence on Monday," the Marquise responded cheerfully.

Les 120 Journées de Sodome

As our drawing-room conversation continued, Angélique commented, *"Marie-Laure is passionate about releasing the text of 'L'école du libertinage' (the School of Libertinism) that our great-great-great-grandfather the Marquis de Sade scripted."*

Monsieur Dubois supplemented enthrallingly, *"I heard that the Noailles family bought the original text of Les 120 Journées de Sodome (The 120 Days of Sodom), and Vicomtesse de Noailles has recently bequeathed it to her daughter Nathalie Valentine Marie for safe keeping."*

"What is Les 120 Journées de Sodome?" I queried.

Our entourage laughed at my naivety before my teacher, Alain could enlighten me on the subject; Monsieur Abriem exclaimed, *"Young man, I don't think you'll want to know the contents of this controversial manuscript."*

The very mention of the phrase 'controversial manuscript' perked my interest immediately. Young Elizabeth chimed, *"Enlighten us, Monsieur Ludovic. You seem very knowledgeable about its contents."*

"Allow me the honor of explaining Les 120 Journées de Sodome to these beautiful young people," Marquis Mathieu remarked ludicrously.

He gave Elizabeth and me a deceptive grin before he began, *"Brace yourselves, boys and girls. The text of the Marquis de Sade is one of the most violent and pornographic in the history of French literature. It was written in 1785, when Sade was imprisoned in the*

Bastille. It describes the days of four wealthy aristocratic men who gathered in a castle to torture, rape, and to humiliate young adolescents. Are you sure you want me to continue?"

I acted as if I wasn't afraid to hear of this polemical material. I was inquisitive to learn more. I replied, *"I've learned a little about the Marquis de Sade in school."*

Mathieu questioned amusingly, *"What school did you go to? Pray tell! As far as I'm aware, Sade's works are too pornographic and violent to be taught in any school. At least not in the French schools I know of."* There was a silence. Since no one spoke, he continued, *"Okay! I will elaborate as long as you guys are not squeamish about torture, blood, gore and murder. Some consider this text to have historical significance. You see, Sade wrote this in a short period of thirty seven days, on small pieces of paper that he kept hidden between the stones of his prison cell. When he died in 1814, he was convinced that the text had gone up in smoke during the 1789 burning of the Bastille. Unbeknownst to the author, an inmate had saved the manuscript.*

"The text disappeared for decades after the Revolution. Little is known of the ex-convict who retrieved the manuscript and later sold it to the Marquis de Villeneuve-Trans. The manuscript remained in the possession of this family for three generations before a German psychiatrist, Iwan Bloch bought the writings and published the text in 1904 as 'The Hundred Days of Sodom' under the pseudonym Eugen Dürhen. This early release was riddled with errors until the 1930s, when the Noailles got possession of it. Only then did the Marquis de Sade experience an incredible destiny: the Vicomtesse had it edited to what it is now known to us as Les 120 Journées de Sodome."

Mario queried, *"Am I able to read this text? I believe the French government is trying to get rid of this* sadistic publication. I, for one, would like to obtain a copy - for reference, of course."

The Marquise added, *"I'm sure Marie-Laure will have a copy made available for you. She is campaigning to have this transcript made public. She firmly believes that it is a French literary national treasure."*

I chirped, *"Based on the facts the Marquis has presented, I do not feel squeamish at all."*

The Marquis gave me a flirtatious wink, *"I'll be happy to show you what Sade performed on his minions."*

His remark made me coy with bashfulness. Andy, who stood next to me, extended his hand around my shoulders.

Château Rouge

Soon we were shown to our various lodgings by the baron's butler, the two footmen and the housekeeper. As was always the case, I shared a suite with my guardian. Our luxuriant boudoir was in keeping with the rest of the Art Nouveau architectural style of this early-twentieth-century château. The baron's industrialist grandfather had asked the Danish architect Viggo Petersen Dorph to design this imposing structure, complete with English landscaped gardens with water features, an interior swimming pool, a beautiful chapel, and an enormous conservatory linked together by three humongous glass domes; it reminded me of the glassed hothouse at Kew Gardens. The estate also consisted of a spacious lodge house, a fully functional stable and a considerable number of outbuildings, both for staff and visitors. Pyrenean marble was omnipresent within the castle's interior; from the entrance hall, the stairways, balustrades, and columns, ceiling roses to the numerous banisters, this was the material of choice.

The ground floor in the main building housed a billiard room, a gilded music room, an extravagant dining room, a lavish drawing room, a cozy living parlour, and the most impressive of all, an extensive private library that would make any French aristocrat proud. Our bedrooms were located on the first and second floors within the main house. The most opulent of the boudoir, decorated in honor of Bao Dai, the last emperor of Indo China, was reserved for none other than the prince.

Numerous well-known Parisian artists, the likes of Gervais and Henry Perrault of the Belle Époque era, graced the frescos in the entrance hall and the grand staircase and the first floor landing. I gawked at the stunning chandeliers that hung gleamingly above the main staircase and the music room.

Marquis de Sade

Our formal dinner conversation soon turned to the infamous Marquis de Sade again, since Ludovic was intrigued by the sexual libertine's literature. He declared, *"I'm fascinated by the story and the writings of the Marquis de Sade, especially his erotic works."* Seated opposite the marquise, he took the liberty to question Angélique about her great, great, great grand ancestor.

Before the marquise could answer, the baron remarked, *"Sade's works are a combination of philosophical discourse with pornography. He often depicts sexual fantasies with an emphasis on violence, criminality and blasphemy against the Catholic Church."*

The Marquis added, *"He was also a proponent of extreme sexual freedom, unrestrained by morality, religion or law. You do know that the words 'sadism' and 'sadist' are derived from his name."*

Angélique announced, *"For many years, our ancestral family regarded his life scandalous and not to be mentioned. It's only within the last twenty years that my cousin, Comte Xavier de Sade, reclaimed the marquis title along with Sade's writings. Many of our family members still consider the 'Divine Marquis' of legend unmentionable.*

"*Xavier only discovered Sade's papers in his family's Château de Condé when approached by a journalist in the late 1940s. He is working with scholars to enable their publication. My young nephew, Marquis Thibault de Sade, is assisting his father in the collaboration. Since then, his family has claimed copyright of Sade's name.*"

The Baron proclaimed, "*Come to think of it, you may find Sade's writings in my extensive library. I can hardly keep track of the numerous books and manuscripts in that room. Ludovic, if you are interested in Sade's works, or any other works for that matter, please feel free to use the premises anytime. I hardly use the library unless I have the need.*"

The Marquise resumed, "*One thing I know for sure: Sade lived a scandalous libertine existence, and he repeatedly procured young prostitutes as well as employees of both sexes. He was accused of blasphemy, a serious offense during his time. His bad behavior also included an affair with his wife's sister, Anne-Prospère, who lived with them at the castle.*

"*I'll be happy to introduce my cousin Xavier de Sade and my nephew, Thibault, to you, monsieur. I'm sure he will be able to shed more light on our great, great, great grandfather better than I can.*"

"*That will be superb! I'd love to meet Comte Xavier and his son, the Marquis Thibault de Sade.*"

"*I'll set up an introductory meeting as soon as possible. Are you travelling to Florence and Bahrain with your friends after Château Rouge?*" Angélique inquired.

"*I'll be stationed in Paris. If it's not inconvenient for the baron, I would like to stay a few days longer to peruse your well-stocked library for my literary research,"* the gay Muslim requested.

"*Of course you are welcome to stay. It'll be nice to have some company when all my lovely guests leave,"* Pierre responded with a seductive glint in his eyes. He was obviously smitten by the attractive and educated Turkish Frenchman.

The Billiard Room

While the women adjourned into the music room for their after-dinner titter-tatter, the men assembled in the comfortable billiards room to savor some exquisite French liqueurs manufactured directly from the Baron's estate and to taste Montecristo and Romeo y Julieta cigars, which Pierre had specially flown in from South America. The men were also discussing the logistics for tomorrow's la chasse à courre (hunt).

Although Andy and I wanted no part in the hunting expedition, which to me was an act of inhumane cruelty to wild life, I wanted to ride on horseback again. While the men were busy mapping their hunting strategy, my Valet and I gave billiards a try. I had no idea how to play the game, and neither did Andy. Monsieur Ludovic was busy giving pointers to my Valet. He leaned against Andy, both hands around him, showing my lover the techniques of shooting balls.

My first try at billiards was a disaster. I haphazardly hit the balls with my cue stick, sending a couple flying over the ledge of the table. Before I knew it, Mathieu leaned behind, wrapping his arms around mine. I could feel his excitement grow in his pants while he pretended to instruct me.

I was aroused by this turn of events, as I had not expected the Marquis to display such boldness in front of his peers. I had thought he was busy chatting with the prince, the baron, the count and Monsieur Dubois. I certainly did not expect him to glide his hidden erection against my derriere. I could feel his intoxicating breath against my neck as he bent his head against my shoulder. He announced to Andy, Ludovic and me, *"Let's play a game. Ludovic can assist Andy, and I will help Young."*

Before we could counter, he had already arranged the balls in a pyramid and was ready to begin. The persuasive Marquis was adamant that we try our hands at billiards. We had little choice, so we went along politely with his suggestion.

His hands were on mine throughout the game. When Abriem was busy advising my Valet, he whispered in my ear, *"I've got you now. I told you I would find you soon enough."* His persistence only served to heighten my coyness. I was unnerved by him, yet I was also drawn to this determined man.

I looked across at my Valet, who was listening attentively to Ludovic. I could detect Monsieur Abriem's arousal from his closeness to my lover, even though they assumed a fictitious friendliness in front of the cigar-smoking men.

I did not speak, nor did I resist Mathieu's advances as he discreetly gyrated his groin against my rear. His hardness was straining for release. I knew if I continued this dangerous liaison, I too would fall prey to this seasoned seducer. His aristocratic charisma would charm me beyond redemption, yet I was determined to hold my ground. I wanted him to be my victim. As much as I craved his deliriousness, I maintained a reserved, affectionate demeanor that seemed to fool the hedonist.

He was a married man, and that made it all the more exciting to exercise my allure, tantalizing and titillating him without relenting to his wishes. I was trained in the art of flirtation and seduction, but to him I seemed a naive young man who would eventually succumb to his desires if he continued his game of perseverance. Little did he know that I was also playing a similar game, which the aristocratic French are so excellent at. I played the role of the demure adolescent, like Cécile de Volanges in Dangerous Liaisons: at least for now.

37

La Chasse à Courre

> *"Fetishism, bisexuality, homosexuality, and bondage are all part of life, and our fiction and non-fiction should reflect that."*
>
> Bernard Tristan Foong

1967

Château Rouge Estate

The hunting horn sounded as soon as we were mounted on horseback. A pack of hunting dogs was running ahead to sniff out their prey. The male hunters, led by Baron Pierre, Count Mario, Marquis Mathieu, the Prince, and Aziz was followed by Monsieur Dubois, Sébastien, Ludovic, Andy, me and a group of huntsmen. A Russian friend of the baron, Felix, had arrived early that morning to join our entourage. Marquise Angélique, Anastasie, Bryanna, and Elizabeth, together with a few stable boys, followed behind. Dressed in our redingote chasse à courres (hunting coats) and pompous riding garb, we were ready for a hectic morning ride on the estate's expansive acreage.

Although Andy and I wanted no part in the hunt, I was delighted to be on Gabriel, a strong brown steed, and geared up for a cross-country run. I was ready for a vigorous workout. It had been several months since I had last ridden (and that was at Daltonbury Hall).

An Intruder

An hour into the hunt, I was ready to take Gabriel in a different direction, away from the maddening crowd. Andy rode by my side.

"Let's race! I'm dying for an invigorating gallop," I suggested.

Before the word 'gallop' could spring from my mouth, my Valet was cantering ahead. I gave Gabriel a tap with my whip, and off we flew to catch up with my competitor. We flew like the wind, speeding ahead with jubilation and jumping over wooden fences before slowing to a trot a few miles from our hunting companions. I commented, *"I'm thirsty. Let's stop by the stream to get a drink."*

We dismounted and led our horses to the edge of the water. I did not see my Valet behind me as I stooped down for a drink from the brook. Before I knew it, Andy had pushed me playfully into the brook, sending me tumbling into the water. He laughed and continued to splash water onto my already soaked person. I returned the favor, and we began a childish water fight. We were teenagers having fun; little did I know, a pair of eyes was hiding in a nearby bush, watching our every move.

Since there was no visible person around, we stripped bare and continued frolicking in the water before drying ourselves with the woolen blankets we bought with us. Andy wrapped his arms around me, whispering, *"You are such a silly boy. You're so easily capered."*

I hit my Valet's chest vivaciously as we continued our mischievous gaiety. I avoided his advances when he tried to kiss me roguishly. My puckishness stirred him to immense excitement below his waist, causing his groin to come alive. I escaped Andy's firm grip as he leaned forward to nibble my nipples, squirming impishly to avoid his tongue on my already hardening knobs. Our loving attraction never failed to excite our youthful libidos; still, I loved to engage him in a puerile game of foreplay, often arousing my lover to no end. I struggled free, running away naked and inducing a gigglish game of 'catch me if you can' with my ruttish lover.

Suddenly, the forest went quiet. I turned round, but Andy was nowhere in sight. Wondering where he was hiding, I tiptoed quietly to find my lover. There was no sound or movement.

Out of nowhere, a pair of hands reached for me from behind, cupping my mouth before dragging me to a nearby tree. I tried to wrestle free from his powerful grip. Before I had a chance to see the intruder, he had bound my eyes and tied my wrists spread eagle to a low-hanging branch. Believing him to be my lover, I pretended to grapple without any success. I hung on the branch, feeling more naked than I already was. During my struggle, I detected strong masculine pheromones, which I did not register as my lover's. Since I could not see or move, I wiggled helplessly, hoping to hear Andy's voice. All I could hear were the chirping birds and rustling of dried leaves on the ground, as if the invader was circling around my nakedness, admiring his handiwork.

Lingering kisses on my lips jerked me to reality. Those lips were not my Valet's, but those of a stranger I did not know. I panicked as his tongue pried open my mouth, forcing me to accept his lustful desires. Although I was afraid, my curiosity got the upper hand, and I responded to his passionate longing, yet my defenselessness struck fear within. I wanted to know who this stranger was.

My mind ran amuck. Tales of the diabolical Marquis de Sade came flooding into my mind. Would I be raped, tortured, mutilated and murdered? Where is my guardian when he's supposed to be protecting me? I was in a state of panic, when my lover's soothing hands held onto my slender waist from behind. His sweet breath was on my neck, inhaling my tenderness as he always did before his seductive vampire kisses forced me to surrender to his masculine intoxication. The stranger's erection rotated against my groin, his bulbous head pressing urgently against my hardness while his fingers caressed my inviting nipples, galvanizing me to lean to him. I could feel my Valet's phallus sliding against my opening, demanding entry. To him I would give myself compliantly, but who was this interloper I could not see? Andy whispered into my ear, *"Don't be afraid. No harm will befall you. Relax and play along."* My guardian's assurance relieved my mental tension. Heeding his words, I surrendered to the pleasure. My blindness and my bondage served only to heighten my other senses. Electric currents coursed through my being, stimulating my manhood to bounce uncontrollably as my lover's gliding length caressed my offering with expert precision. Andy, my Andy knew every part of my body. He was my teacher, my lover and most of all, he was the embodiment of my sensual and sexual fulfillment. I would gladly pleasure his desires as a skillful connoisseur. Now, our erotic hieros gamos had stirred our beholder to an intensified superlative ferocity. He had difficulty relinquishing his voyeuristic reverence. He watched me slide against my chaperone as we merged into an amatory entity.

My aphrodisiac thralldom served to inflame the stranger to suckle my hardness. He kneeled before me, worshipping my adolescence as his engorgement bounced in rhythmic ovation to his silent oral evocation. I could hold off no longer; both oral and anal galvanizations sent me spewing into the prowler's mouth. He gobbled my releases as if they were his last supper as he chafed his hardness against my leg; sending his life force gushing onto my thigh and feet. He knelt before me in supplication, lapping his own semen as if it was the blood of the crucified Christ.

My lover pounded into me. His final cry to the heavenly father was in and of itself an orgasmic sign of his imminent deliverance, which I received. Andy was my god and I his angel.

I could hear the stranger gulping down my lover's oozing length as it slid from my orifice. The man turned to devour my opening greedily, leaving no residue to the naked eye.

He plunged into the chilling brook leaving my Valet to release my bondage. Andy kissed me passionately; the affectionate gesture was his unspoken gratitude for my being an excellent sport in our game of unbridled sexuality. My lover untied my bonds from the hanging branch. The mystery man had long vanished by the time my guardian led me to the brook. We washed ourselves spunkily before he unfastened my blindfold. His loving beauty was sufficient assurance that he would always be my protector. No harm would befall me as long as my handsome Adonis was by my side. My Valet had promised the stranger not to divulge his identity as we rode merrily back to Château Rouge after our vigorous morning 'sexcitement'.

Graf Felix

We were back at Château Rouge before the hunters and huntresses returned from their energetic sport. By the time we assembled in the music room in the late afternoon, our formally attired friends were enjoying afternoon hors d'œuvres and aperitifs. Graf ('Count' in Russian) Felix took to the grand piano to perform Rachmaninoff.

The pianist had graduated with honors from the Paris Conservatory before making the city his permanent home, and as many dvoryanstvo (Russian nobility) did, he had the noble attitude but none of the family's money. He met Baron Pierre, an avid music appreciator, at a concert where Felix was performing before they became friends. Since then, the professional twenty-six-year-old concert pianist had become a regular at the château, often accompanying the baron and his ever-rotating number of lovers to social and intimate events such as the one we were at that evening.

After Dinner Conversation

Congratulatory compliments on Felix's excellent recital were in order, during and after a fresh-game dinner that I declined, having become a vegetarian for an evening. When the men retired to the billiards room for their ritualistic after-dinner discussions; Monsieur Ludovic, curious about the Graf's presence in France, inquired, *"Why are you in Paris?"*

"I am fascinated by the Parisian way of life. I can be who I want to be here. In Avignon, my family is constantly on my back. They want me to marry a wealthy heiress to save the family's financial misfortune but I'm not interested in marrying for money. I'm in Paris to reforge my life."

"Is Russia's sexual attitude conservative?" my Valet queried.

The baron jumped in with an answer. *"Homosexuality was decriminalized during the 1917 Russian Revolution, and same-sex marriage was legalized. This was a remarkable move for Russia, which was extremely backward, both economically and socially, at the time, and many conservative attitudes towards sexuality prevailed."*

"What brought on this liberal legalization of same-sex marriage?" Monsieur Abriem questioned.

Pierre continued, *"This move was part of a larger project of freeing sexual relationships and expanding women's rights; Russians legalized abortion, granted equal rights for women to divorce, and attempted to socialize housework."*

Before the baron could continue, Felix added, *"Unfortunately, when Stalin came into power, all these progressive measures were reverted: Stalin re-criminalized homosexuality, imprisoned gay men and banned abortion."*

The Victorian Era

Andy commented, *"Are you aware that throughout the nineteenth century, the English aristocracy viewed same-sex orientation and Greek love as a 'legitimating ideal'?*

"The prestige of Greece among educated middle-class Victorians was so massive that invocations of Hellenism could cast a veil of respectability over a hitherto unmentionable vice or crime. Thus, homosexuality emerged as a category of thought during the Victorian era. It was grouped with classical studies and 'manly' nationalism. However, the discourse on Greek love during this time often excluded women's sexuality."

Marquis Mathieu expressed, *"Late Victorian writers like Walter Pater, Oscar Wilde, and John Addington Symonds saw Greek love as a way to introduce individuality and diversity within their own civilization. Have any of you read Pater's short story 'Apollo in Picardy'? It is set at a fictional monastery where a pagan stranger named Apollyon causes the death of the young novice Hyacinth; it has been observed that this monastery maps Greek love as the site of a potential homoerotic community within Anglo Catholicism. There are others, such as Arthur Henry Hallem who addressed the subject of Greek love in letters, essays, and poetry."*

The prince, who had remained fairly quiet during our conversation, suddenly proclaimed, *"When I was at Cambridge, one of my professors taught that John Addington Symonds was influenced by Karl Otfried Müller's work on the Dorians; that included an 'unembarrassed' examination of the place of pederasty in Spartan pedagogy, military life, and society."*

He continued, *"Symonds distinguished 'heroic love', for which the ideal friendship of Achilles and Patroclus served as an ideal model, from 'Greek love', which combines social ideals with 'vulgar' reality. Symonds also envisioned a 'nationalist homosexuality' based on the model of Greek love, distanced from effeminacy and 'debasing' behaviors and viewed as 'in its origin and essence, military'."*

Mario stated emphatically, *"The part regarding distancing effeminacy and other 'debasing' behaviors I have difficulty grabbling. I believe all men should be equal and not discriminated.*

"Symonds tried to reconcile his presentation of Greek love with Christian and chivalrous values. In my understanding, his strategy for influencing social acceptance of homosexuality and legal reform in England often involved evoking an idealized Greek model that reflected Victorian moral values such as honor, devotion, and self-sacrifice."

Monsieur Dubois remarked, *"The efforts among aesthetes and intellectuals to legitimate various forms of homosexual behaviors and attitudes by virtue of a Hellenic model were not without opposition. In his essay 'The Greek Spirit in Modern Literature', Richard St. John Tyrwhitt warned against the perceived immorality of this agenda. Tyrwhitt, a vigorous supporter of Greek studies, characterized the Hellenism of his day as 'the total denial of any moral restraint on any human impulses'. He also* outlined what he saw as the proper scope of Greek influence on the education of young men.

"*He and other critics attacked several scholars and writers by name who tried to use Plato to support homosexual rights and whose careers were subsequently damaged by their association with Greek love. Of course, the trial of Oscar Wilde marked the end of the period when proponents of Greek love could hope to legitimate homosexuality by appeals to a classical model.*"

The learned gay Muslim disclosed, "*Did you know that since the 1870s, other countries have at times defended homosexuality, although their identities were kept secret? A certain secret British society called the Order of Chaeronea campaigned for the legalization of homosexuality and counted Oscar Wilde among its members in the last decades of the nineteenth century. Back in the 1890s, an English socialist poet, Edward Carpenter, and a Scottish anarchist, John Henry Mackey, wrote in defense of same-sex love and androgyny. Both Carpenter and Symonds contributed to the development of a groundbreaking book called 'Sexual Inversion', by Havelock Ellis. The book called for tolerance towards 'inverts', and it was suppressed when first published in England.*"

Graf Felix brought the discussion to an end when he propounded, "*In Europe and the United States, a broader movement of free love emerged in the 1860s among the first wave of feminists and radicals of the libertarian left. They openly criticized Victorian sexual morality and the traditional institutions of family and marriage, which were considered enslavement to women. In the early part of this century, advocates of free love such as the Russian anarchist and feminist Emma Goldman spoke in defense of same-sex love and challenged repressive legislation.*"

As the Russian was finishing his statement, a chilled breeze blew through the half-open windows, sending drifts of his manly pheromones my direction. Andy did not have to reveal his secret; I already knew who the stranger had been.

38

Museo delle Carrozze

"Of all the means I know to lead men, the most effectual is a concealed mystery."
Adam Weishaupt

1967

St. Regis Florence

The moment I walked into the St. Regis, I was greeted by the smell of cultural antiquities that was Florence. As with a great many European historical hotels, the spirit of opulence and grandeur lingered in this place, originally home to the noble Giuntini family. This former palace overlooking the Arno River was converted into the Grand Hotel Royal de la Paix in the second half of the eighteenth century before becoming the current St. Regis Florence. Located steps away from the Uffizi Gallery and Academia, this hotel is emblematic of the city's rich heritage, reflecting the crucial stages of social and architectural development in the Tuscan capital.

The splendor of this opulent hotel has drawn scores of renowned guests including Queen Victoria, the Marajà Chuttraputti di Kolapoor and his successor, Rajaram Chuttraputti, for whom the Indian Bridge or Ponte all'Indiano was named. Leland Stanford Jr., namesake of Stanford University, was also a visitor.

Throughout the 20th Century, many notable families and famous writers who resided north of the Alps sojourned to The St. Regis Florence for their celebrations. This dignified past is reflected in the elegant and elaborate décor of the hotel. The Art Deco-style Winter Garden was realized around 1922 in accordance with the designs of Enzio Giovannozzi together with The Sala delle Feste, a turn-of-the-century French-style ballroom that drew inspiration from the White Room in the nearby Pitti Palace. There, Count Mario threw a lavish celebration in honor of Franco Tancredi, who became the new president of Centro di Firenze per la Moda Italiana (CFMI) the year we attended Sala Bianca.

The Gifts

Bryanna and Anastasie wasted no time in rushing off to the upcoming fashion show rehearsals. Mario, forever the professional photographer and socialite, trotted off to photograph the backstage preparation for this important fashion event, leaving the prince, Monsieur Dubois, Andy and me to our own devices. Since the gala fashion presentation would not take place until the following evening, we were free to explore the city.
The moment Andy and I stepped into our hotel suite, two beautifully wrapped gifts sat on the king, waiting for us. Thinking they were complimentary gifts from the hotel, I left mine on the bed before I proceeded to soak myself in a luxurious bath prepared by one of the Abds who was traveling with our entourage. As I was enjoying my bath, Andy entered in great haste to show me a watch on his wrist. It was a handsome BVLGARI Tourbillon saphic white gold watch. I exclaimed, *"When did you purchase such an amazing timepiece? I haven't seen this on you before."*

He bent over to kiss me on my lips before presenting me with the gift I had left on the bed earlier. *"Open the package, my darling boy,"* he replied.

I tore off the wrapping impetuously. There, sitting on my hand, was an elegant pink gold box. Inside was a similar watch. The only difference was that this watch was crafted in awe-inspiring saphic pink gold. *"Who are these from?"* I cried.

My Valet did not answer. Instead, he leaned over and planted a kiss on my lips. After a few minutes of silence, he spoke, *"Aren't these babies gorgeous?"*

I stared at him, waiting for him to continue. He did not utter another word but admired his fantasy watch with a Cheshire grin on his face.

"Tell me who these gifts are from!" I demanded.

"Don't ask questions, pretty boy. Wear your watch when we meet the prince and Monsieur Dubois."

Before I could interrogate him further, Andy had lifted me up and was drying my body with a large fluffy towel. *"Get your butt moving; we are meeting His Highness and your teacher at the lobby. We are going to a museum."*

The Palazzo Pitti

The Pitti Palace is a vast Renaissance palace situated on the south side of the River Arno. This 1458 palazzo was originally the town residence of the ambitious Florentine banker Luca Pitti. In the year 1549, this grand palace was bought by the Medici family, and it was transformed into the main residence of the Grand Duchy of Tuscany. Over the generations, this property grew into a treasure trove of paintings, jewelry and numerous luxurious possessions.

By the late eighteenth century, the palazzo was occupied by Napoleon before it became the principal royal palace for the newly united Italy. In 1919, King Victor Emmanuel III donated the palace and its priceless contents to the citizens of Italy, thus throwing its doors open to the public as one of Florence's largest art and antiquities galleries. In addition to the Medici family's major collection, it also housed several other exhibits; one such display was an exquisite collection of ornate eighteenth- and nineteenth-century carriages used in the Lorraine and Savoy courts.

Royal Carriages

The prince, accompanied by Alain, Andy and me, had come to meet Signore Pietro di Alberto, the curator of this exquisite collection, for a private viewing of these rare carriages. Up until this juncture, I had no idea the prince was an aficionado of past and contemporary modes of transportation.

While Pietro was explaining the intricate decoration of each unique antique carriage to His Highness and Monsieur Dubois, Andy and I ventured off to view the other exhibits that were on display. My Valet inquired as soon as we were out of earshot, *"Did His Highness comment on the watch you are wearing?"* I stared at my guardian and shook my head.

"Did he comment on your new watch?" I asked.

"No," Andy responded before continuing, *"I thought these gifts were from His Highness. It's strange that he didn't seem to notice that we are wearing them."*

"You did not answer my question when I asked who these presents were from. Didn't a message accompany the gifts?" I questioned.

"There are no messages in either one of the packages. I automatically assumed it came from His Highness, since he has a generous habit of showering his entourage with unexpected presents," my Valet remarked.

Since I had no clue who our mysterious benefactor was, I shrugged my shoulders and kept quiet. I turned to inspect an elegantly decorated rocaille carriage before a voice spoke, *"The decorations on these barouches are so detailed and refined."* Surprised to find my teacher standing next to me, I was caught off guard.

"Oh! I thought you were with His Highness and Signore Alberto!" I blurted.

My teacher smiled as he turned in the direction of His Highness and my Valet, who were listening attentively to Pietro's every word.

"Do you like your new watch?" he asked.

I stared dumbfounded at Monsieur Dubois. *"Did you give us these watches?"* I questioned.

He smiled and continued observing the carriage's craftsmanship without replying. Now my curiosity was getting the better of me. I continued, *"Did these gifts come from you, Sir? If they are from you, Andy and I would like to thank you for your generosity. What did we do to deserve such princely presents?"*

Alain acted as if he hadn't heard what I said. He continued examining an antique sedan chair, which had been used to carry the grand Duchess Maria Luisa de Borbone, the wife of Ferdinando III of Lorraine. He finally remarked, *"Did you know, Young, that these impeccable moving works of art were once used by the refined gentlemen and sophisticated ladies of their day?"* Before I had a chance to comment, he added, *"It was not unheard for users to enjoy the occasional tryst within these equipages."* My professor gave me a wink and a nod before proceeding to examine the next exhibit. I followed behind.

"Ferdinando III of Lorraine was very fond of carriages, and upon his return from exile, he commissioned the construction of six luxurious berlins for himself and his court. This collection contains three of his carriages; among them is the most important of the six: this one," he

said, paused and pointed, *"being the Grand Duke's personal carriage, was built to be drawn by three pairs of horses.*

"Specialized artisans were employed to paint the triumphant quadrigas on the carriage's gilded box. The quadrigas depict Ferdinando III in glory, surrounded by cupids and bearing symbols of abundance, all of which was intended to signify not only the continuity between the two reigning Medici and Lorraine houses but also the enlightened nature and the patronage of the rulers of Tuscany."

He paused before adding, *"Did you also know that the secret affairs conducted within these carriages were often kept from polite society?"* I detected from his tone of voice that this comment was meant to be deciphered. I was beginning to realize the paradoxical conundrum my professor was spinning.

As I approached an excessively fastidious fairy-tale silver carriage, which had been gifted to the Savoys by Ferdinando II di Borbone, King of Naples, I remarked, *"I'm inquisitive to know the reason for such a lavish gift from the King of Naples. What could Ferdinando III desire from the Savoys that would merit such a present?"*

Dubois gave me a devilish pinch on my cheek before he whispered into my ear, *"I believe the generous benefactor wishes to spend an enchanted evening with the two handsome males with whom he is besotted from afar."*

"Who could this befuddled distant admirer be, I wonder?"

Before Professor Alain Dubois returned to join the prince and Signor Pietro, who was signaling to him from a short distance away, he said, *"The answer will be revealed to you if you observe closely the letters engraved at the back of your watch."*

I did not disclose to Andy my brief exchange with my professor by the silver carriage. I wanted to discover the secret for myself.

39

La Sala Bianca

"Strange how few, after all's said and done, things are of the moment."
Edna St. Vincent Millay

1967

At Palazzo Pitti

    The following evening, the prince, Count Mario, Monsieur Dubois, Elizabeth, Didee, Andy and I, dressed to the nines, arrived at a different section of the expansive Palazzo Pitti to attend the La Sala Bianca gala fashion extravaganza. Invited guests arrived in luxuriant vehicles at the red-carpeted grand entrance towards the fashion show hall. An abundance of Italian press photographers and fashion journalists were on hand to snap away and interview the elegantly dressed invitees of this annual talk-of-the-town fashion event. Movie stars including Ava Gardner, Bridget Bardot, and Audrey Hepburn ascended the opulent steps to numerous flashes of camera bulbs and disappeared into the lavish foyer before being guided to their front-row seats inside the gilded fashion show theatre.
    All eyes were on His Highness as soon as we stepped out of our golden Rolls Royce. Dressed from head to toe in formal Arabian garb, P and the Count smiled and posed for the paparazzi, which greeted us a few yards

away. Alain, Andy and I followed behind. As we proceeded up the grand entrance, my mind flashed back to my 'Countess Cornaro' gondola experience on the Grand Canal during the Venice Regata Storica's parade. I had felt like royalty while waving to the multitudes on the 'Countess Cornaro'; it was similar to what I was experiencing now. For this adolescent boy, the fleeting moment of being a glamorous celebrity fashionista was too enticing; I smiled and posed with Andy. I waved to the clicking photographers. This was my first red-carpet event, and moments like these would continue to appear sporadically throughout my fashion career.

Pre Fashion Show Conversation

Monsieur Dubois, Andy and I were seated two rows behind His Highness and the Count. Mario greeted everyone who was anyone in the high fashion world. He introduced the prince to countless Italian and international celebrities before and after the fashion presentation. I was mesmerized by the glitzy opulence of the Haute Couture fashion world. It wasn't long before my teacher turned to me. He commented, *"This is very much your kind of thing, isn't it?"*

"I'm grateful that my Valet agreed to accompany me to this once-in-a-lifetime event." I gave my lover an appreciative glance before continuing, *"Yes, professor, this indeed is my kind of thing."*

Andy, on the other hand, did not seem at ease with all the men and women staring in his direction. I asked, *"What's the matter? Don't you like the adoration showered in your direction? They are fascinated by your good looks!"*

"You know I don't care to be revered for my looks. I'd rather be venerated for my intellectual capabilities than for such superficiality," he responded.

"Andy, you may want to rethink that statement. There are very few who are blessed with both inner and outer beauty such as yourself and your charge. The pair of you should be grateful for that which has been bestowed upon you generically. Believe me, there are many who wish for the qualities the two of you possess," Alain remarked.

"Don't get me wrong, professor, I'm thankful for my natural genetics, and so is my young charge for his. I simply don't desire to be known as a pretty face without brains."

I chirped, *"You don't have to worry about that, Andy. I love you for all your attributes, both within and without. Even the times when you reprimand me, you are still my 'God'!"*

My teacher said humorously, *"You, Young, are such a lovey-dovey puppy dog. No wonder men and women fall for you, and E.R.O.S. recruited you into the society."*

"Why is that, professor?"

"Men love your innocence, and women adore your sweetness."

My Valet added, *"Even though he is quite the opposite, he has this childlike quality that fools many. This young man knows how to use his assets to get what he wants. He has a way with me that none of my previous charges have."*

"That's because you are in love with him," Dubois confirmed before adding jestingly, *"If he misbehaves, I'll spank him into shape. You should do the same, Andy."*

I looked at my lover adoringly. My guardian joked, *"I'm afraid he may like it too much. He'll want to be spanked all the time."*

"I know someone who will be more than happy to do the honors," Alain said amusingly. I could detect by the tone of his voice that he was beginning to spin a riddle for me to solve.

I questioned, *"Who may this person be?"*

Before I could continue, Andy chimed, *"Young, your professor is playing with you. He's not serious."*

I looked at my teacher. He gave me a sly wink, smiled and changed the topic. But I had a hunch that his jesting was more than just an amusing joke; could this person be the admirer who had engraved, *"I will find you at the appropriate time – M.M."* on my watch?

The Fashion Show

Under the sparkling opulent chandeliers, tall, lanky models paraded on the raised catwalk. Cordoned off at the far end of the room were throngs of fashion photographers who clicked away at the seemingly endless parade of models, each in an ensemble more glamorous than the last. Popular music blared out from loud speakers, signaling the mood for each designer's collection. I sat bewildered by this glittering display of lavish affluence before my eyes. I was mesmerized by the intricate co-ordination and detailing of each outfit: the hairstyles, make-up, and accessories that went with each ensemble blew me away. La Sala Bianca was the showcase of Italian haute fashion at its best.

An array of magnificent evening gowns accompanied by the crescendos of Italian baroque music brought the presentation to its grand finale. Gold and silver confetti rained down from the ornate ceiling as the designers and their accompanying muses came onstage to take their bows to a great fanfare of applauds and accolades showered upon them by their adoring fans and audience alike. I could not contain my excitement; I stood clapping and cheering until the last model disappeared off the runway. Although this would not be the last gala fashion event I would ever attend, it was my first, and it will forever remain etched in my mind. After all, wise men have cautioned throughout the ages, "The first impression is always the most unforgettable."

On The Al Fayoum

Finally, we were comfortably settled on P's plane, the Al Fayoum. We were zooming toward the Quwah, the prince's palatial home. I was filled with a sense of precariousness even though my protective Valet was by my side. I could not unravel the reason behind my apprehension, but it had begun the moment I stepped onto the Al Fayoum.

Andy queried, *"You look so wistful. What's the matter?"*

"I don't know. Maybe I'm having too much fun in Paris and Florence and don't want to leave so soon? The splendor of yesterday's fashion show, especially, blew me away. I'm more determined than ever to become a fashion designer, but I know my dad is going to convince me otherwise."

"Why do you think he's not going to agree to your career choice?" my Valet questioned.

"You don't know my father; he's very old school and wants his sons to be professionals."

Andy continued, *"Fashion designers are professionals."*

"Kuala Lumpur is not exactly a fashion capital of the world like Paris, Florence or London. My dad knows 'professionals' to be respectable doctors, accountants, and lawyers – the type of traditional careers that are supposed to generate a good and steady income with a respectable title behind a name. He has no knowledge of my experiences since entering E.R.O.S., and I know he will not support my studies in fashion. In his limited understanding, he sees fashion as a trivial subject, something women, housewives or 'sissy boys' do for a hobby. He has no clue about the size of the fashion industry." Tears began to stream down my face.

"Now, boy, don't cry. I'm here for you. I know the love you have for fashion. I'll always be here to support you," my lover affirmed.

"You are going to be an engineer, and that's a respectable career your father will approve of, even though you are not on speaking terms with him. I'm sure if I told my father I wanted to be an engineer, he'd have no problem with my career choice. But not as a fashion designer," I continued, weeping.

"Don't be silly, I'm sure Uncle James will be able to convince your dad to accept your choice of higher studies. I'm positive your mum will be supportive."

Just then, Monsieur Dubois came to sit by us. He extended a handkerchief for me to wipe my tears before inquiring, *"What's the matter with this little puppy?"*

Andy answered, *"He is overcome with pensiveness, worrying that his father will not allow him to pursue a fashion career."*

My teacher held my hand, looked me in the eyes and said, *"Young man, look at me."* I stared at his handsome face. He continued unblinkingly, *"Get a grip on yourself. You are worrying over an issue that hasn't happened and may not play out the way you have envisioned it in your mind. You are simply speculating about what your father will say, which holds no truth until he actually says it."* He paused for a moment before adding, *"There are always solutions to every issue. To me, you are imagining a problem that is not a problem. So, my dear boy, stop conjuring the worst; stay in the present. This is where you should be, not dwelling in the past or worrying about the future. Be in the now."*

He paused before speaking, *"Have you already forgotten what I taught you during our Zentology sessions? Stay focused in the present, and allow the universe to bring forth whatever is to unfold. Worrying about something that hasn't happened and may not happen is a waste of your productive energy. Now, hold my hands, close your eyes, and we'll have a private meditation session."*

I did as was told. Under the guidance of my teacher's soothing words, I soon glided into a peaceful and relaxed state. My anxiety dissipated and vanished by the time the air steward and stewardess asked us to fasten our seat beats for our imminent landing at Bahrain airport.

End of November 2012

It had been an entire month since I had last heard from Dr. Arius. He had mentioned in one of his earlier correspondences that he would be away in Switzerland for a psychiatric conference for several weeks. His email arrived after he was back in his regular routine. He wrote:

Hello Young,

It's been a while since we communicated. It was wonderful to reconnect with some of my ex-colleagues in the medical profession. I mentioned to a couple of doctors that I was doing research on your harem experiences. They were intrigued by your story. I believe they will be purchasing **A Harem Boy's Saga – I - Initiation.** *Is book two in the series published yet? I would like to obtain a copy when it is available.*

The good Doctor went on to inquire. *Here's the next set of questions for you.*

- *Did any of the Household members have abusive tendencies?*
- *What kind of personality was Ubaid, the Hadrah's third son? I know you mentioned he was a bisexual playboy and liked to behave in a controversial manner. How did his family and the Islamic community view his unconventional behaviors?*
- *Can you expand on your teacher, Ramiz? How did you find him as a person and teacher?*

- *Besides the few fashion-related meetings and stylings you did for the Kosk harem women, were there situations or occasions you found culturally different from those of western women?*
- *How did you and Andy feel when Aziz, the Hadrah's son-in-law, and his brother, Wazir Thabit, propose their controversial "Sacred Sex in Sacred Places" photography project to you?*

It is such a pleasure to communicate with you. I do enjoy reading your memoirs, and I can't wait to read book II. What is the title for the second volume?

Pepsi and Cola (my dogs) send their love. I look forward to hearing from you. Please send my regards to Walter and your 'daughter' Kali Durga, the kitty goddess.

All the best, my friend!
Dr. A.S.

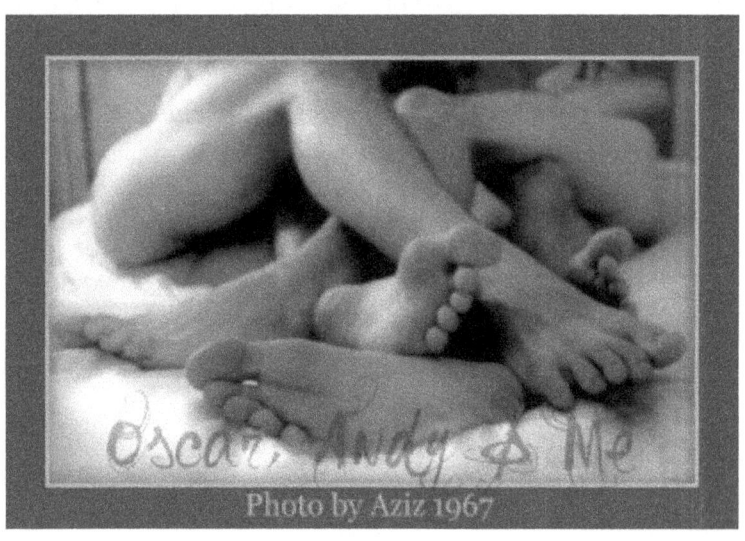

Part III

Bahrain – Manama.

Monaco – Monte Carlo.

France – Eze Village, Cannes.

40

Quwah

"Experience teaches only the teachable."
Aldous Huxley

1967

Bahrain

The moment the Al-Fayoum landed on a private airstrip at Bahrain airport, an emerald Rolls Royce was waiting for the prince. Several guards stood at attention at the bottom of the red-carpeted stairs, waiting for His Highness to disembark. The moment his feet landed on solid ground, the commander-in-chief of the guards shouted out an order, and they saluted His Highness as he proceeded toward the opened car door, accompanied by his bodyguards. As soon as His Highness drove away, Monsieur Dubois, Didee, Elizabeth, my Valet and I were ushered out of the plane without fanfare towards two waiting black Bentleys. Alain, Andy and I travelled in the first vehicle, followed by Didee and Elizabeth in the other.

A glass partition separated the passengers from the uniformed driver. Stretches of heat and sand loomed before us as our air-conditioned vehicles headed towards the Quwah, a forty-five minute journey from Bahrain airport.

My teacher gave me a briefing about Manama, the capital that stood on a seabed, parts of which had recently been reclaimed from the ocean.

Directing his gaze at my Valet, he said, *"Did you know that approximately four-fifths of Bahrain's population lives in Manama?"*

Before Andy could answer, my professor continued, *"As we go through the city, you'll notice that many modern buildings are under construction. The rebuilding has been going on for months."*

As our car wound through the dusty roads, I noticed workmen planting full-grown trees onto the wide boulevards. I asked, *"Why are the men planting full-grown palms and not baby plants along the sidewalks?"*

Dubois replied smilingly, *"Because the Emir wants the city to look lived-in, as if the trees have been here for generations. It's part of their 'quick growth' city planning. Did you notice when we arrived that the airport main terminals were under construction? News has been circulating that Bahrain will be one of Concorde's transatlantic landing routes. The authorities are anticipating the arrival of the supersonic jet age, when private planes will ferry super-rich vacationers to this desert city."*

Andy spoke. *"When is the Concorde scheduled to arrive in Bahrain?"*

"I believe it will be in a few years, but they have to get the airport and city ready for the influx of upcoming tourism."

"Is P involved in this project?" I blurted.

Alain gave me a cheeky grin, pinched my cheek lightly and said, *"Clever boy, you guessed correctly. He was in discussions with the British Aircraft Corporation and Aérospatiale while we were in Paris. That's why we hardly saw him during the day. He was planning the Concorde's flight to Bahrain."*

"I want to fly on the Concorde," I uttered impulsively.

"In due time, my boy! Maybe if you play your cards right, the prince will take you for a joyride. For now, I want to educate you a little about the city in which you'll be stationed during your Quwah service."

Just then, the Bentley turned a corner, and we found ourselves in the old section of the capital. Traditional Islamic architecture stood amidst modernized high–rise buildings. The houses had tall gates and shuttered windows, and most were designed around a central courtyard or garden. Some of them had wind towers, open on four sides at the top to direct passing breezes into the house.

As our vehicle drove out to the suburban villages, the houses looked more like sheds made from palm branches than homes. These old-fashioned structures were sprinkled among homes built with modern materials. My teacher commented, *"Young, these traditional houses are called barastis. They will soon be connected to electricity and running water from the city."*

"You mean they use candles to light up their surroundings at night? Does the Quwah have electricity and running water?" I exclaimed.

"Of course there is electricity and running water at the Quwah. You'll find that the powerful and the elite lead a very different life from the common folks. Wait till you see the Quwah; it's a world of its own."

"No wonder His Highness wants to live in Paris. I'd much prefer to live in Paris than in Bahrain," I chirped.

Both of my mentors laughed at my remark before Alain commented, *"Remember, Young: when you encounter a male member of P's family, ask about his health and the wellbeing of his children and family, but do not ask about his wife or wives -- it is impolite.*

"Another thing: remember to stand when someone enters any room you are in. That person will make rounds

to shake hands with everyone. After the handshake, make sure you touch your hand to your heart as an affectionate gesture. It is permissible for males and females to shake hands, but only when the woman initiates.

"A final word of caution, young man: when you visit someone, they will serve coffee or tea. This custom extends to visiting shops or offices. When given a beverage, you don't have to drink if you don't feel inclined to, but if you don't accept the offer, it is considered rude."

The Palaces

A few miles before we arrived at P's palatial home, our chauffeur tapped on the glass partition, reminding us to don our eye harnesses. The only passenger exempt from this was Monsieur Dubois, who was considered a member of the Quwah household staff.

When the Bentley came to a halt, Dubois guided Andy and me out of the vehicle. As soon as the masks were removed, acres and acres of well-groomed tropical landscape spread in front of me. I was surprised by the lushness of this expansive compound. A huge man-made lake separated five large buildings; each structure was as large as the other. One in particular stood out like a sore thumb from the rest. The mansions resembled a hodge-podge of Classical, Colonial and Moorish architecture. A single curved road linked the five properties that were some distance apart. Well-trimmed lawns and gardens separated each imposing structure. The largest and grandest of the palaces belonged to P's father, the King of Bahrain. The other four mansions were homes to his four sons. Each mansion had its own name, and P's home was the Quwah.

His Highness, the third in line to the throne, was by far the most beloved and respected prince in his country. All four brothers had been educated at the Manama Secondary School before completing their higher education abroad. P was, to me, the brightest of them and the most charismatic. Many thought he would be the heir apparent to the throne. Unfortunately, his father, Isa bin Salman Al Khalifa, bestowed that title to his youngest brother, Hamad, in the year 1964 at the tender age of sixteen. He would continue the centuries-old al-Khalifa dynasty. The heir apparent was three years my senior.

Hurt by this turn of events, the prince escaped to Paris, making France his second home. I spent much of my Quwah Household service in Paris and the coastal regions of Southern Mediterranean – the playground of the rich and famous.

The Quwah Household

Several manservants and Abds were at the ready to collect our luggage and to show us our lodgings. P had been chauffeured to greet his parents, since he had been away for two months. I was delighted to see Husni sleeping on our king when I entered the "Al-'iksīr" (Elixir), our suite.

My beautiful boy had grown fluffier and bigger in size since I left him at the Sekham. He had been looked after and groomed regularly by the household staff. We were overjoyed to be reunited. Husni stayed with me for the rest of my Quwah service in Bahrain and in Paris.

After a refreshing shower and rest, our Abds guided us to a huge downstairs living room. As soon as Elizabeth, Didee, Dubois, Andy and I were assembled, we were joined by four other foreign students, who had arrived the evening before. P, being the patriarch and following the traditional Arabian protocol, introduced us to his household members and staff.

I was surprised that His highness was not already married to a distant female cousin from the al-Khalifa clan or betrothed to a wealthy princess from a neighboring sheikdom.

His two sisters, Saffiya (the older of the two) and Ushna, plus a handful of female cousins from his mother's clan and an entourage of ladies in waiting and attendants to the royal females, lived in segregated quarters within the palace.

The men were Abdallah, Fiddha, and Ikram: P's unmarried cousins from his mother's family. The men occupied their own units within the twenty-room mansion. Abdallah and Fiddha were betrothed and soon to be married to daughters of wealthy Bahraini officials. Ikram was the only male who spoke some English, but he remained silent except when spoken to. He had an odd behavior that I couldn't quite put my finger on, until my teacher told me the truth about Ikram; only then did I understand the nature of a *kaneeth*.

November 2012

In response to Dr. Arius' questions, I wrote:
Hello Arius (I hope you don't mind me addressing you as Arius, without mentioning your title),
It is delightful to receive your news after a lengthy absence. Thank you for inquiring about Walter and Kali. They are well and send you their regards.
A Harem Boy's Saga – II - Unbridled *is close to completion. I'll be forwarding the manuscript to my editor for her review before publication. I hope to have* **Unbridled** *available sometime in March or April 2013.*
To answer your list of questions:
- *Did any of the Household members have abusive tendencies?*

It depends on which household you are referring to. A couple of the male Kosk members were eccentric, but I wouldn't classify them as having abusive tendencies.

With the abundance of wealth these folks possess, they are bound to do things that 'regular people' would find unusual. I'll cite an example:

Ramiz, my teacher, could have his erotic S&M fantasies played out by anyone he cared to pay to perform his services, yet he was educated and sensible, acting out his fantasies when away from his country. This was to honor and respect his and his family's social and political standing within the conservative Islamic community.

When you ask if any of the household members had abusive tendencies, it is difficult for me to provide you with a definitive black-and-white answer. I would say almost everyone has certain abusive tendencies, and it is okay as long as they are kept in check. I would prefer to use the term 'eccentric' rather than "abusive" when it comes to discussing the household members.

- *What kind of personality was Ubaid, the Hadrah's third son? You mentioned that he was a bisexual playboy and behaved in a controversial manner. How did his family and the Islamic community view his unconventional behavior?*

To some extent, I answered this question in my last paragraph. In my understanding, as long as they kept everything hush-hush, the household members could get away with their unconventional behaviors.

Unlike western societies, where leaving one's dirty linens out to dry is an act of individuality, Asian societies tend to be more reserved, and most individuals keep their personal and family secrets to themselves. I suppose I could generalize that Asian individuals have a more responsible attitude towards their family and peers; for westerners, individuality is the primary focus.

Returning to your question regarding Ubaid, he wanted to be free from the restraints of his Islamic community: that was the reason he acted the way he did. He was not rebellious in a malicious way. He was a happier and more content individual when he lived away from his homeland. When he was in a foreign country, nobody cared what he did, and he relished that freedom to be the man he wanted to be and do the things he wanted to do. His wealthy family would provide the means for him to do it as long as it wasn't under their noses.

- *Can you expand on your teacher, Ramiz? How did you find him as a person and teacher?*

Ramiz was a wonderful teacher and a considerate person. We got on well, and he was a great educator. In my opinion, all people possess positive and negative traits, which the Chinese call the yin and the yang energies. Without the negative (yin), one wouldn't understand the positive (yang) and vice-versa. It's the duality within a person that gives him or her character and personality.

Although all my teachers (I'm not just talking about Ramiz) had their quirks, each and every one of them had qualities that were uniquely theirs. Today, I am able to absorb and decipher for myself and be the person I choose to be with an open mind and an open heart. But without their guidance, I don't think I would be the non-judgmental and accepting person I am today.

- *Besides the few fashion-related meetings and styling you did for the Kosk harem women, were there other situations in which you noticed that the women you encountered were different from western women?*

Of course, there are major differences between easterners and westerners. As mentioned above, easterners tend to have a reserved outlook to life. To generalize, I would say that easterners (be they of any gender) have a Confucian, Buddhist or Islamic outlook to the cultivation of their lives.

Most westerners have an imprint of Christian core values, which are either consciously or unconsciously ingrained in them by their forebears (I'm including those who claim agnosticism or atheism.)

These cultural values are vastly different in their approach to life, therefore I'm glad I had the privilege to experience the eastern and western philosophies – now, I apply the best of both worlds to my daily life.

- How did you and Andy feel when Aziz, the Hadrah's son-in-law, and his brother, Wazir Thabit, proposed their controversial 'Sacred Sex in Sacred Places' photography project to you?

I felt privileged to be offered the opportunity to work on 'Sacred Sex in Sacred Places'. It was and still is one of the best projects I've ever worked on. Besides getting to travel and experience the world and to live life to the fullest, I also had wonderful sex with the handsomest of men. I believe Andy felt the same way; otherwise, we would have left the project before its completion. I think of Aldous Huxley and remember his words:

"The secret of genius is to carry the spirit of the child into old age, which means never losing your enthusiasm."

41

The Kaneeth

"A single prognostication can sometimes change your entire life"
Bernard Tristan Foong

1967

Within the Quwah

One day after we settled into the Quwah, my teacher requested that I stay behind after my tutorials; he wanted to have a word with me. After the students had departed, Dubois inquired, *"Are you settling into your new household?"*

"Everything is fine, sir. The Quwah is not quite as exciting as Europe," I answered.

"I'm glad you are settling in. Ikram asked me if he could meet with you and Andy this afternoon. I told him I would inform you before sending you to see him," Alain said with an amusing grin.

"Why can't he ask us himself?"

My teacher continued, *"It is impolite for him to approach the two of you."*

"Why is that? The men in the other households summoned us themselves or using their Abds. Why can't Ikram speak to us directly?" I questioned curiously.

It took my professor a while to think of an appropriate reply before he continued, *"He is unlike other*

Arab men you have encountered. He is a special type of man whom the Bahrainis call a kaneeth, kanith, xanith or a zenith."

"What's a kaneeth?" I queried.

"It is a difficult term to explain. Some refer to a kaneeth as the third sex, while others refer to them as male or female homosexuals, but it is a known fact that some kaneeths do get to marry, produce children and have a husband or wives."

"Are they transvestites or transsexuals?"

Dubois added, *"Quite the contrary; like a man, they wear thobes; instead of white, they wear colors. They also wear a belt, clinching in their waist like a woman. As you are aware, Arab men wear their hair short while the women keep theirs long. A kaneeth wears his hair in between men's and women's lengths. Some speak with a falsetto voice."*

Before Alain could continue, I remarked, *"No wonder I couldn't figure out Ikram when we met. He dresses like a man, but he has qualities that do not resemble a typical Arab male. Why does he want to see Andy and me?"*

"He did not tell me the reason. I'll leave that for you and Andy to figure out. My task is to set up an appointment for the three of you. I believe he is intrigued by your relationship with your Valet. He is also an avid artist and designer in his own right."

"Will you be our translator?" I questioned.

"If he requests my presence, I will stay; otherwise, I will leave you guys to your private discussion," my teacher concluded.

Ikram

Ikram was a shy twenty-three year old. He was already waiting for us when we entered the living room. He extended his hand to shake Andy's, holding it a little longer than was customary. As we had been instructed to do by my teacher, we were ready to touch our shaken hands to our hearts in a sign of politeness. Ikram, on the contrary, kissed his shaken hand he received from Andy. I gave Alain a puzzled look at this unconventional gesture.

When it was my turn to greet Ikram, instead of giving me a regular handshake, he caught hold of both my hands, closed his eyes and touched them to his heart. I wanted to pull away, but he was already in a trance-type state. He mumbled a series of foreign sentences, which none of us understood. I stood speechless, gazing at my professor and Valet for their guidance. Neither of them had any idea of what I was to do. They too seemed startled by this unfamiliar greeting.

Suddenly, our host went into an epileptic fit. He fell to the ground and trembled uncontrollably, his hand gripping mine tightly. I could not pull away and fell to the floor next to him. Dubois and Andy were in a panic, not knowing how to help the youth. Alain knelt beside the quivering man while spittle foamed around his mouth. Just then, a manservant carrying a tray of beverages entered. He came to our rescue. Picking up the shaking patient, he laid Ikram's convulsing head on his lap, cradling him gently until he returned to normal. Clutching my hands firmly to his, Ikram refused to let go. He continued his Arabic jibber-jabber. The rescuer soothed the splattering man to a relaxed state before he finally released my hands.

As suddenly as his seizure had come, he sat up as if nothing extraordinary had happened. He proceeded to ask after our wellbeing nonchalantly, inquiring about our stay at the Quwah. Monsieur Dubois, Andy and the manservant acted as if the ictus had never happened. I sat dumbfounded, staring at this astonishing person. Alain shot me a glance, implying that I should not ogle at Ikram.

After a lengthy greeting and small talk, Dubois turned to our host and remarked, *"I should leave the three of you to your discussion."*

The Arab replied in Arabic, *"You don't have to leave. Please stay, I'd like you to be my translator."*

He continued without waiting for Alain's response. *"There is something important I'd like to tell these two gentlemen."* He indicated Andy and me.

Andy and I looked at each other, wondering what on earth the Arab was about to divulge to us. He spoke to my teacher in Arabic. *"When I was introduced to these two men the other day, I was filled with a sense of foreboding. The moment I shook hands with you,"* he said, looking at Andy, *"I detected that you are an exceptional being.*

"I've been blessed with the ability to see into the past, present and the future for as long as I can remember.

"Andy, you are blessed with many lovers in your past, present and future life. You are love's devotee – love flows unceasingly to and from you. This young charge of yours is the greatest love of your life in this realm. Although you will have many affairs with other men, your heart is drawn to this boy alone. You will never forget him, and neither will he forget you. A few years from now, you'll both suffer heartbreak. Oceans will separate the two of you, and you may never get past this experience.

"You are stubborn beings. Be aware, and do not let your egos get in the way of a possible reconciliation in later years. Your individual careers will achieve many successes. But remember, there is a price for every successful accomplishment. My advice to you is to make your life choices with care and precision."

Andy and I looked at each other in astonishment. We had no idea how to respond to such prognostication; especially coming from someone we met less than an hour ago. We looked toward my professor for his counsel. He, too, was left speechless. We kept silent until Ikram finished speaking. He looked ill at ease and was embarrassed by what he had said. The words that came from his mouth were of divine providence, and it was obvious that he had no control over his delivery.

The kaneeth finally plucked up his courage to speak again. *"Please accept my apology if I have offended you. I have no control to my indecorous allocution. I'm Allah's messenger, and whatever he bids me deliver I have no say about. I often don't recollect what transpired during my conveyance,"* he said sadly.

Alain chimed in to dissipate the air of sobriety that had filled the massive living room. *"I'm sure the boys are grateful for your prescient messages."*

I couldn't help asking, *"Do all your clairvoyant predictions come true?"*

Ikram was surprised by my question. He took a while to respond. *"I am able to foresee some people's lives, but none have returned to tell if my divination did manifest in their lives. My calling is to channel Allah's divine messages to those who care to listen. It is up to the individual to take heed or to ignore my presages. I am not responsible for their life choices.*

"I felt affiliated with the both of you the moment you entered the Quwah. I can feel a strong bond between you two, and I want to see you lead happy and productive lives. That is the reason I requested to see you this afternoon."

Andy answered, *"We appreciate your kind words. We will take them to heart."*

"I have questions for you, Young. P mentioned that you are planning a career in fashion. I am also an artist and designer, although my interest is not in fashion but in interior design. I know we'll have a lot to talk about. Can we meet again tomorrow after your morning tutorials?

"You'll have to excuse me; I'm tired and have to take a rest now. I'll see you here tomorrow," the kaneeth

proclaimed without allowing Andy or me the opportunity to agree to the scheduled appointment.

The Arab rose to his feet, kissed his fingers, touched them to his heart and departed; leaving Dubois, Andy and me in a daze as we stood to watch his flowing thobe disappear through the ornate doorway.

Discussion with Monsieur Dubois

As soon as Ikram's manservant closed the door behind him, we looked at each other, dumbstruck. After a long silence, Monsieur Dubois spoke, *"Are you aware that some kaneeths are known for their cogent clairvoyance? In ancient times, they held esteem positions within their clans, often becoming healers and advisors to their tribes. I believe Ikram is one of these special beings, even though I've known him for less than a year.*

"When I was here as a Valet at the Quwah, he secretly told me that P would make France his second home. He also predicted disputes between the prince and his siblings, which manifested numerous times this year.

"If I were you, I will take his advice seriously. He's humble, and he means well."

My Valet questioned, *"All that he said of me is true, but I will never leave Young. In that part, I think, he is grossly mistaken. I love this boy too much to part ways with him."* He stared at me adoringly as he spoke.

I chirped, *"I love you very much, Andy. I'll never separate from you, ever!"*

Unfortunately, the kaneeth's prophecy did become reality, exactly three and half years to the day after our fateful meeting at the Quwah. True to the clairvoyant's words, Andy and I did make choices that sent us tumbling through lengthy devastation before our recent reconciliation, forty-five years later.

42

The Powers Behind the Throne

"When she raises her eyelids, it's as if arrows are piercing into your heart."

Bernard Tristan Foong

1967

The Dowager

    P's mother, Fatima, was a constant visitor to the Quwah. Although a governor was assigned to look after his palace, Fatima was the queen dowager of her son's household. When the prince and his entourage were away, his mother was the permanent resident of this lavish mansion. She made her appearance whenever she chose and without prior announcements. The household members and staff had to drop whatever they were doing when summoned by the matriarch. Behind the veiled face was a pair of piercing brown eyes that could cut through the toughest of steel. A stern look from her could either send shivers down the beholder's spine or could command a message so deadly that it would send the onlooker scrambling to perform the tasks she demanded. This was the innate strength and power of the queen. During the brief interludes when P was in residence, the household staff would heave a sigh of relief; their Master was much easier to please than his mother. They knew an impending storm would brew whenever their Master left for one of his numerous travels.

Besides being the queen regent of the Quwah, Fatima also wielded tremendous power in her husband's kingdom. Although she was his second wife, she was the king's favorite; a good word from her carried immense weight for those who wanted a favor from the king or the prince. Those who feared her, groveled, and those who loved her kowtowed to her demands. They knew that a whisper from her persuasive lips could either cement an influential liaison or ruin their chances of success in a country where the monarch had the final say.

Andy and I treated our encounters with Her Royal Highness with panache whenever we were around the iron lady. I had learned from my tutors never to ruffle any feathers but to mollify the fur of a potentially dangerous beast; she was one such animal. The Quwah was indeed an explosive minefield in which my lover and I trod with caution. During our services in this quivering household, I was enthralled by my Valet's composure; he was my guiding light.

The Bodyguards

The following day, at our appointed time with Ikram, Andy and I waited in the living room for the kaneeth to enter with one of his burly manservants, Makut, who was about thirty-five years of age. He was different from Khatum, who had revived his Master from his epileptic fit the day before. This aristocrat had three different bodyguards who took turns guarding him in case he fell unconscious, was injured or died during one of his many visionary moments. Besides Makut, there was Ebram, a strong, sinewy male in his early thirties. The three guards took turns chaperoning the prognosticator twenty-four seven. Although I have no solid evidence to suggest that these men were mere bodyguards, I had a strange suspicion they also acted as his occasional lovers and fuck buddies when desirous urges reared their yearning heads. This I had no way of confirming, since they acted politely when in the company of household members, foreign students and staff. It was difficult to decipher what went on behind those ornate closed doors, yet my gay-dar was seldom wrong, even then.

The Sidekick

The kaneeth held a prominent position in the Quwah household. Fatima consulted with him about almost everything, from decrypting mundane household chores to decoding a person's character. She sought him for daily, weekly, monthly and annual astronomical predictions. He was also consulted to analyze local and stately affairs. Last but not least, he was called upon to predict the kingdom's relationships with other nations. To me, Ikram was like Rasputin to Czarina Alexandra of Russia. The only difference between these two faith healers was that the former possessed good intentions, while the latter was a power-hungry fiend. Still, at times I saw that the kaneeth's positivity could easily turn the other way. This, I soon learned, was Allah's power of good and evil, of yin and yang, of positivity and negativity. These polar opposites are one and the same, residing together in every person. I was also becoming acutely aware of the real game of strategy within this massive palatial compound. Each of the five palaces had its own set of rules, and each differed vastly from the next.

The Foreign Students

The four foreign students that arrived a day earlier than Elizabeth, Didee, Andy and I, were a Norwegian named Alf, short for Adolf, his BB Gud, short for Gudrun, a manly Swede more mature in looks than his nineteen years of age, Matumi, a pretty petite girl, and her sassy BS Karina, from Japan and Poland respectively. The eight of us got on well, since we spoke English and were trained in the art of relationships, even though we had been educated in different Bahriji schools. We often found ourselves in heated discussions over the most trivial matters, although the debates were sharpest between our Valets and female guardians. We Juniors would chime in occasionally to pronounce our feeling about their confabulated topics.

It was usually the females in our group who unanimously agreed that the beloved Ikram was a spy sent by the dowager to appraise our characters.

One late afternoon during high tea, which we students normally took together, we began an emphatic discussion about whether the kaneeth had discussed us with the queen regent and household members.

Karina was the first to ask, *"What do you make of Ikram?"*

My Valet, the exhorter among us, advised, *"We shouldn't be discussing any member of the household we serve. You never know who is listening to our conversation. It's best to keep our opinions to ourselves."*

Didee, ignoring Andy's suggestion, commented, *"I find him to be a fascinating creature. He seems to know it all. Is there anything he doesn't poke his nose in?"*

"I agree with Andy. I don't think it's a good idea to discuss Ikram, even though there are no Abds or servants listening to our conversation," Gud affirmed.

"Even if they are, they have no idea what we are talking about, since they don't speak English," Karina chimed.

The Swede replied, *"Don't underestimate the servants; they often know more than we think they do. For all we know, they may be reporting our every word to P or*

Ms. Dowager as we speak." (We had nicknamed her Ms. Dowager.)

"I think you are being overzealous about the Abds. I'm sure they gossip about everyone in the Quwah. I don't think they'll report our conversation to anyone but each other," Karina quipped.

"If that is the case, I don't think we should discuss the household members' affairs. It's none of our business, and it's ill-mannered to do so," I added.

Andy, Gud and Elizabeth nodded in approval, but Karina continued, *"Oh, don't be a silly ninny. It's normal to want to understand the people we are in contact with. After all, we're here to learn their culture and way of life; are we not?"* She shot me a disagreeable look.

My Valet remarked in my defense, *"It is indeed true that we are here to learn about Middle Eastern culture and way of life, but to gossip about our host and his household members is quite a different matter. Learning through observation and appropriate questioning is one thing; scuttle-butting about household members is incongruous. Young is correct. We should stop our twaddle."*

"That's no fun. I like listening to gossips," Alf chirped.

"So do I," Matumi seconded.

I voiced, *"Ikram is a wonderful person, even if he behaves oddly at times. We shouldn't say nasty things about him."*

My pronouncement seemed to give Karina a reason to provoke me further. *"Well, well, well... what did the both of you do that makes you come to his defense so quickly? Do you guys..."* she paused a moment before continuing, *"or should I say, the three of you..."* she said and looked at Andy, *"have something going that we don't know about?"* she teased.

Before my Valet could respond, I said, *"We discussed artistic subjects when we met yesterday."* Andy jumped in before I could finish, saying, *"It's none of your business what we did or did not do when we were with Ikram. It's private and between us."*

His statement piqued the women's interest. Didee remarked, *"Come on, Andy, you don't have to be so prickly. We are being inquisitive to know what transpired. We are educated in similar arts; share with us so we can learn from your experiences."* She was obviously trying to coax my Valet into revealing more than what I already mentioned.

Just as she was completing her sentence, the conservatory door swung open, and in walked Professor Dubois. The room went quiet immediately; all we could hear were the chirping parakeets in their cage located next to an array of indoor plants.

Alain, seeing his students, inquired, *"What are you debating about? Don't let my presence interrupt your discussions."*

Gud quickly chimed, *"Oh! We are discussing Bahraini politics,"* he lied.

"Well then, do continue; I'd like to hear your various points of view. But before we start, I came in to inform Andy and Young to go to Ikram's chambers immediately. He wants to see the two of you as soon as possible."

"Why are we being summoned?" I asked my teacher.

"You can ask him when you see him. Go! Don't waste time chitter-chattering," our professor commanded.

Andy and I looked at each other and at the group before shooting out of our seats and heading towards the kaneeth's chambers.

Early December 2012

"*Another year is almost over,*" I wrote in response to Dr. A.S. "*It's been a hectic year. I'm finally getting close to publishing **Initiation**. I hope you've liked reading my manuscript thus far. This writing journey is indeed a lengthy process, and I'm busily working with CreateSpace, the self-publishing branch of amazon.com, on the layout and design of the book.*

"*A wonderful lady by the name of Christine Maynard manifested from Louisiana to edit **Initiation**. I found her through Craigslist classifieds when I advertised for an experienced copyeditor. She's now in Maui working with me. We work well together and have a lot of fun editing **Initiation** before it goes into print.*

"*Meanwhile, I'm also scouting for a publisher and have a couple of romance novel publishers interested in publishing the series. Anyway, I'm not going to bore you with my publication logistics.*

"*How are you, my friend? I hope the answers I've provided over the course of our correspondence have been helpful in your research. Please let me know if you require further information about my harem experiences. I'm always at your service.*

"*Until I hear from you again, stay well, be happy, and enjoy life to the fullest.*

Best Wishes!
Young."

43

The Carousel

> *With 'Carousel' I had an idea, and it all came out quickly.*
> George Murray

1967

Meeting with Ikram

Ikram's bodyguard, Khatum, was already waiting for my Valet and me outside the kaneeth's chambers. He ushered us into the sitting room. To our surprise, the brawny Arab spoke in perfect English, *"Gentlemen, please take a seat while I inform the Sahib (Master) of your arrival."*

When we looked surprised, he gave us a faint smile before disappearing into an adjoining room. I took the opportunity to ask my guardian, *"I didn't know he could speak English. The other day he conversed only in Arabic with Ikram during the seizure."*

"Neither did I. Maybe all three of his guards speak English," Andy replied.

Just then, Ikram entered, followed by Khatum. We stood to salute the Sahib with the customary nose rubs. I noticed him inhaling the scent of my Valet during their greeting. Obviously, the faith healer was attracted to my guardian, but Andy did not seem aware; he went on to inquire about the wellbeing of our host.

Khatum was our translator. We had difficulty understanding the kaneeth only when he moved back and forth from Arabic to English as if he couldn't find the correct words to describe his statements.

"Thank you for coming to see me on such short notice. I had difficulty sleeping last night while planning an important interior design project," declared the kaneeth.

Andy chimed in before the Arab could continue, *"Please feel free to ask for any of us anytime if you require our presence and assistance."*

Our host continued, *"I'll jump straight to the point. I'm working on the design of an exclusive and trendy nightclub for the local elite, visiting elite, and expatriates who live here. P and Aziz have told me that this boy,"* he said and paused, indicating me, *"is very artistic and has a head of good ideas. I'd like his input on my project."*

I stared at Andy, not knowing how to respond. *"I'm sure Young will be delighted to help. He does have a head of good ideas,"* my Valet answered on my behalf, giving me time to locate an appropriate answer to the keneeth's request. *"Please feel free to tell us what you require from us, we'll do our best to assist. We are humbled to be of service,"* Andy added.

A sudden flash transported me back to my Griffin Inn days, when I choreographed and designed my father's nightclub revues. Without thinking, the answer came to my lips: *"A couple years ago, I choreographed and designed my father's nightclub's song and dance revues. I had a lot of fun!"* I exclaimed.

"There you go. I love Young's exuberance. Let me show you the architectural plans and concepts I have developed for this space." Ikram snapped his fingers, and his bodyguard went to fetch the documents from the adjoining studio.

"We have much to discuss. I think I'll enjoy working with you. I've heard good things about your design

work from Hadrah Hakim, the Kosk and Sekham ladies. Last but not least, Wazir Thabit and Aziz speak highly of your work and your attention to detail.

"I want this nightclub to be the talk of the town for wealthy foreigners and celebrities visiting Manama. This is not a place for the local community unless they are of a certain caliber. This place is going to be a well-kept secret playground for the unconventional elite for whom money is no object. Do you understand what I mean?" He looked at Andy and me for our nods of approval.

I replied, "I have been to a couple of dance clubs that sound like the one you are planning. Our friend Ubaid took us to 'The CLUB' in Dubai, and we also went with Bryanna and her friends to 'The PANTHEON' in Athens, where we met the Aga Khan. Are these the kind of clubs you are referring to?"

The Sahib declared with an amusing grin on his face, "The project I'm planning is more than a dance club. It will combine dance, vaudeville theatre, burlesque, and 'anything goes'."

Andy asked, "Isn't this project a little ambitious for Bahrain? It sounds like something one would find in Paris or Berlin."

"Andy, you have a way of asking a question courteously. If you are wondering if our Islamic religious rules, regulations and government are a concern, let me say that I know many influential people in the right places who can give me the green light. Regarding that part of the equation, you don't have to be concerned; I'll handle the logistics. All I want from you and Young is your creative input." He looked at us wittingly.

I chirped, "What would you like me to do?"

"All I require of you are creative ideas from your imaginative mind. Tell me what you'd like to experience when you spend an evening at an unusual dance club?"

An idea suddenly flashed across my mind. I announced excitedly, *"I'd like to dance on a merry-go-round. It'd be fun to boogie amidst an array of circus animals – and I can jump on to ride when my dancing gets heated up. I would want to be on a revolving carousel covered with flashing disco lights. To me, that's the ultimate in dancing."*

My Valet chimed in quickly, *"Young, you are letting your imagination run a little too—"*

Ikram beamed energetically, *"What an excellent idea; that is exactly the kind of spirited effervescence I'd like Young to provide. Andy, you mustn't stop your young charge from expressing his creativity. All dazzling endeavors grow from an idea. Nurture the seed, and it'll grow into a healthy plant, but we must germinate that seed with the right ingredients and nurture it in the correct environment."*

"There are times I have to rein him in, otherwise he gets carried away and he becomes uncontrollable," my guardian advised.

The kaneeth came to my aid, *"This is the beauty of youth; his exuberance and ebullience is what I'm looking for.*

"I would never have thought of installing a rotating carousel in a dance club if not for his suggestion. Tell me more." He turned to me.

His encouragements gave me permission to continue, *"Apart from a rotating merry-go-round, I imagine operatic stage performances. The more unconventional the better; international performers can make appearances every so often to spruce up the nightly entertainments. That will draw celebrities to the club, which in turn will generate the buzz for this secret, difficult to get into, talk-of-the-town space. Create a 'must-have, must-see, must-go-to' venue, and you'll have your audience clamoring to get in the door.*

"I'm sure with your aristocratic stature and social standing you'll be able to draw the wealthy and the elite to be the first to experience this unparalleled adventure. Word of mouth is the best form of publicity. The jet-setting crowd will flock to this new place in less time than you expect, especially when they hear of its unprecedented escapade, and when the Concorde starts arriving to Bahrain, this night spot will be the in-place to visit."

The Sahib pronounced jubilantly, *"This is what I need from you, Young. We have a lot to discuss and brainstorm."*

Needless to say, Andy and I stayed with our host in his chambers until after dinner. That day, we became the kaneeth's kindred spirits. We vowed to our host not to reveal our discussions to anyone until the project came to fruition.

P's Visit

The following day after class, my teacher asked for me to wait privately in the drawing room. The moment he walked in with the prince, Andy and I stood to greet His Highness and the professor. We had not expected to see P. After formal greetings, the prince jumped straight to the point. *"I believe my cousin, Ikram is enamored of the both of you. I meet with him regularly. He mentioned you have good ideas for his new dance club. I'm one of his partners for this project, so tell me your ideas; I'd like to hear them before calling a meeting with the other partners."*

P and Dubois listened attentively while my Valet explained the conversation that transpired between us and the kaneeth. When he finished, His Highness said, *"This is a confidential and an unconventional project by Bahrain's standard. I want to make sure that neither of you reveal any of our discussions to anyone, not even to your fellow students, except those who are involved in this venture.*

"I have assigned Alain to work with you and Ikram. Your teacher will provide me with detailed reports on future meetings you have with my cousin.

"I'll summon a general meeting with our other investors when they arrive in a few days. Meanwhile, Monsieur Dubois and Andy will compile a business plan for our revue, which we will discuss at the board meeting.

"Andy, Alain will advise you about what is required at the meeting.

"One other thing: come to my chambers this evening after supper. I have something I'd like to see the two of you in private about."

With that remark, he got up, turned on his heel and left the room, followed by his bodyguard.

Conversation with Monsieur Dubois

My guardian and I looked to my teacher for his advice. *"As free-spirited and carefree as P is, he is also a resolute businessman. He doesn't take his investments lightly."* He addressed Andy: *"I suggest you and I put our heads together to draft a solid proposal, merging the creative with the facts and figures for this venture."*

"Didn't the Sahib say that it was already a work in progress? I thought he had been assigned to design and renovate the space?" my Valet queried.

"Yes and no. Ikram is a prolific interior designer, and he'll have the final say regarding the design of the club, but like most creative talents, he does not possess a mind for business as the prince does. A working budget has to be in place before work can begin; this has never been the Sahib's forte. That's the reason P has designated us to write a business plan," Dubois described.

"I thought money was no object, especially when the Al Khalifa family owns Bahrain," I mentioned, confused.

"It is true that P's family owns Bahrain, but this dance club is a joint venture between P and his cousin. It is not a consensual project among the other members of the Al Khalifa clan. That is one of the reasons His Highness asked you not to breathe a word to anyone," Alain reiterated.

It perked my curiosity. I asked, *"Is P's mother involved?"*

My professor took a while to answer, *"That's something I cannot divulge at this juncture. Just perform your task with love and precision, and leave the financial logistics to me and your Valet. We'll do our best to write a sound proposal to entice the foreign investors.*

"Meanwhile, rack your pretty little brain, and come up with plenty of phantasmagorical suggestions for us to incorporate into the proposition.

"P's venture capitalists are rich, worldly and well travelled. They are used to financing unconventional projects. I suggest you and Ikram woo them with the best of your creative talents; the more eccentric and outlandish they are, the better.

"Now, run along and start gearing up your imaginative engine. We'll meet with Ikram tomorrow and continue to brain storm." The professor guided Andy and me out the room.

Mid December 2012

Hi Young,

I'm sitting by my cozy fireplace to write to you. How fast the year has flown. Christmas will soon be upon us, and I haven't done any Christmas shopping. I'm hibernating in the warmth of my house, feeling alone but not lonely. Pepsi and Cola are lying by my feet as I write.

The more answers you provide me, the more questions I have for you.

- *Can you think of a moment in which you felt uncomfortable and did not desire to engage with any of the household members who summoned you?*
- *If so, how did you avoid such situations without offending your host or the household member?*
- *Did your Valet ever coerce you into performing sexual favors you didn't want to perform?*
- *Did jealousy ever rear its head between you and Andy during your separate liaisons with different people?*
- *If it did, how did you deal with it?*
- *Throughout your Kosk service, did you ever doubt your decision to enter E.R.O.S.?*

My dear friend, if I don't hear from you before the year is over, I wish you a very Merry Christmas and a successful New Year.

Regards to you and Walter.

A.S.

44

In the Altair

"Life is not governed by will or intention. Life is a question of nerves, and fibers, and slowly built-up cells in which thought hides itself, and passion has its dreams."

Oscar Wilde

1967

The Altair (The Flying Eagle)

Since my arrival at the Quwah, I had not been summoned by the prince until now. His lodgings were the most lavish I had seen among all the palatial homes I had been stationed at. The moment Andy and I entered, his bodyguard asked my Valet to wait in the living room as he guided me to the Master's private chamber. In the center of this opulently decorated boudoir sat a waterbed covered with inviting black silk sheets with contrasting emerald green satin pillows. Seated comfortably on a loveseat was Matumi. She, like me had been groomed by our personal Abds for this evening's rendezvous. She wore a loose pastel djellaba, and I wore a pale silk thobe. I asked, *"Have you been waiting for long? Where is your chaperone, Karina?"* I asked, guessing privately that she was waiting in the living room with Andy.

Before she could answer, His Highness entered through an antechamber, dressed in an emerald thobe, open to his navel that revealed his hairy chest as he proceeded toward the bed. He smiled at us without uttering a word. He motioned for us to join him on the bed. He smelt clean and fresh as I lay next to him. He had obviously had a relaxing spa treatment before coming into the chamber. Matumi lay on his other side. He gave the two of us an adoring squeeze before leaning toward the female to kiss her desirously. His organ throbbed beneath his robe as I reached to stroke his erection. I caressed his hardness between the smooth fabrics. The Arab's hand was fondling Matumi's girlish, androgynous breast, which aroused me immediately. With his other hand, he pushed my head toward his bobbing excitement. His hardness palpitated against my cheeks as I nuzzled him to euphoric exhilaration. I lifted his garment, exposing his genitalia before I nestled my nose to inhale the scent of his masculinity. His manliness intoxicated me. With a single gulp, I devoured all of him into my mouth. Teasing me, he grabbed my hair and pushed my face away, pretending not to permit my lips to suckle his engorgement. He pulled me towards him and we kissed as he had with Matumi. The girl had gotten between his legs, lapping and swaddling his swollen globes. From the corner of my eye, I could see his toes wriggling into her wet sex. He was also teasing, playing and tormenting her opening as we kissed passionately. I reached to massage his bristling nipples, set amidst a sea of jet-black chest hair. The three of us were in ecstasy. Before I knew it, my cock was thumping for attention, and a rapturous sensation washed over my being. Now, she was suckling my hardness and stroking his erection simultaneously. She took turns pleasuring our Master and me.

     P discarded both of our thobes, threw Matumi's djellaba on the floor and went to town jabbing his tongue into her wetness. They were sixty-nineing as I straddled above P's face so he could take turns alimenting our privates. I reached to fondle my classmate's bosoms, titillating her to ecstatic moans. P's fervent groans were a signal that he was ready for penetration. He took turns mounting her and entering me as I lay on top of Matsumi, swathing her tiny breasts with my tender lips. The arousal was too tantalizing for His Highness; he pulled his palpitating hardness out of the Japanese girl, and without losing a second, he entered me, spewing his masculinity deep into my yearning orifice. P convulsed as if in a trance. Jets of warmness flowed into my receiving openness. I turned to accept his adulating kisses before he released me from his encasement. Bending down, he lapped up the residue of his deposits from my twinkling orifice and pushed them into the female's vagina with his tongue, causing her to thrash uncontrollably with orgasmic rhapsodies.

This beguiling attraction was too enticing for me to withhold; I shot above Matumi's head. The prince wasted no time in suckling my oozing head, drinking the remainder of my elixir of love and imbricating that which had dripped from the side of the bed. He wasted none of its tastiness but shared his intake between us until our passions subsided. Only then did he lay us quietly beside him, as we had been before our ménage à trois had commenced.

A Talk with P

Matsumi was the first to be dismissed. P wanted me to stay. Laying naked next to his hairy chest, I couldn't help but run my fingers across his tuft of hairiness. He gave me an affectionate kiss, stroking my hair as if I were his pampered pet. He looked exhausted. From his closed eyes, I detected he had a lot on his mind. The sexual liaison was what he needed to relieve his tension. I inhaled his intoxicating masculinity. He was the first to speak as a gentle smile washed over his tired face. *"You are so cuddly and adorable."*

"Why shouldn't I be? You are a nice person to be with," I responded.

"I wish everyone I encountered would say the same. Unfortunately, most people I meet daily either want something from me or are difficult and unreasonable."

I did not have an answer, so I kept quiet. After a moment's silence he continued, "I wish I could relive my unencumbered childhood and not have to deal with all my current problems."

"Sir, you have everything in the world. Many are envious of your abundance. There are starving and less fortunate people who live in unsanitary conditions," I answered. Flashes of my Malayan fishing village visit came tumbling across my mind.

"You are right, Young. I'm surprised that a young man like you is concerned about humane issues. The majority of the students who pass through my Household are here for themselves. Few have compassion."

Before he could continue, I reciprocated, "You are a good and compassionate person. Your countrymen love you, and so do Andy and I."

Shaking his head, P burst out in laughter. He replied, "You sure have a way with words. To be honest, there are factions within my family who don't hold the views that you and your guardian do. They think I'm selfish, and I do everything for my own benefit."

"Your mother loves you," I chirped instantaneously.

That brought him further amusement. He riposted, "Ahh! My mother is a species of her own. Yes, that is true: she loves me, but she also wants me to further her own ascendancy in my father's kingdom. She has major plans for me. I am tired of my family's bunkum. I'd rather stay away from their power struggles." He seemed to be suddenly jolted back to reality, as if he had revealed more than he should. He changed the topic rapidly.

"I've assigned my accountant and lawyer to work with Alain and Andy in drafting a business proposal for the dance club. How are the design concepts coming along with my cousin?"

"I'm meeting the Sahib tomorrow to continue our brainstorming. He's excited to get going on this project," I declared.

"Several potential investors are arriving next week and will be staying at the Quwah. I would like you and Andy to 'entertain' them while they are here," P advised.

I promulgated, "Of course we will, Sir! We'll make sure they are well looked after."

"Excellent! I know I can depend on you and Andy. Dubois will be the official organizer. Answer to him if he requires you or your Valet's participation. You understand me?"

"Yes sir. We'll do our best," I promised.

Late December 2012

"I trust you had a Merry Christmas," I opened my email to Dr. Arius. "The New Year will soon be upon us. I hope 2013 will be a better year than 2012.

"It's been long drawn-out process working with the design team at CreateSpace. But with perseverance, **Initiation** will be published in no time.

"As I had mentioned previously, "Manuscripts to Books" is interested in partnering with me to publish **A Harem Boy's Saga** series. Although I'm in the process of self-publication, 'Manuscripts to Books' will work closely with me on the cover design, the interior layout, and the formatting of the books. Needless to say, I'm excited about this collaboration.

"I'll answer your questions in the order you gave them:

- *Can you think of a moment in which you felt uncomfortable and did not desire to engage with any of the household members who summoned you?*

Yes, there were occasions when I did not want to engage in sexual liaisons with certain household members, even if they had a liking for me. Andy would confer with me before dispatching my responses via polite notes or cards to the appropriate member.

On a few occasions, the rejected member or household guest would continue to pursue the issue. My Valet would then intervene on my behalf, and the patriarch usually settled the problem amicably during a private conversation with the family member or guest involved.

- *If so, how did you avoid such situations without offending your host or the household member?*

In the case that I (or any other student) did return a negative response to the recipient, the person would not lose face in front of his peers, as no spoken words were officially exchanged; after all, all solicitation was done in private. No one would know what had transpired between the summoned and the summoner. In the event that we encountered each other in passing, there would be no embarrassment.

- *Did your Valet ever coerce you into performing sexual favors you didn't want to perform?*

Andy was always respectful of my wishes and decisions. When I'd made up my mind, my Valet would never try to dissuade me.

- *Did jealousy ever rear its head between you and Andy during your separate liaisons with different people?*
- *If yes, how did you deal with it?*

Our relationship was built on trust and honesty. More often than not, it would be me who would be the *guilty party, keeping secrets from my lover. My guilt would manifest sooner or later, and I would confide my secrets to Andy. He would give me a lecture to remind me that honesty is usually the best policy. He would be disappointed in me for my dishonesty. Jealousy was never an issue in our relationship.*

Truthfully, the few times jealousy took hold of me, it was for a spilt second. It dissipated quickly, because I knew Andy's heart belonged to me and not to the person he'd had a casual fling with. That was the positivity of our relationship.

- *Throughout your Kosk service, did you ever doubt your decision to enter E.R.O.S.?*

Never. Although at times I missed my mother and some of my family members, it was for only a brief moment that I wanted to return home. The melancholy would soon pass. I was having too great of a time experiencing life to doubt my decision to enter E.R.O.S.

My dear friend, I hope I've answered your questions adequately and experientially.

I wish you a very prosperous and successful New Year. May 2013 bring in peace and goodwill to the world.

Best Wishes!

Young.

45

The Investors

*"Life is a song – sing it.
Life is a game – play it.
Life is a challenge – meet it.
Life is a dream – realize it.
Life is a sacrifice – offer it.
Life is love – enjoy it."*
Sai baba

1967

The Arrival

The week leading up to the arrival of the potential investors was as hectic as any other week at the Quwah. Most mornings, we had our regular tutorials with Monsieur Dubois; the afternoons were spent with Ikram on the designs of the Carousel. It was just about ready for presentation when the potential investors arrived for their week-long Bahrain visit.

The visitors received a similar welcome to the one we got when we drove up the main Quwah entrance. The household staff were out in full regalia, waiting to greet the guests as they alighted from the prince's two Rolls Royce sedans. We foreign students were waiting in the drawing room when the guests entered.

The Visitors

The first to enter was Anastasie, P's model girlfriend, on the arms of His Highness. Behind them were Marquise Angélique and her cousin, Vicomtesse de Noailles, the infamous Marie-Laure de Noailles. I knew immediately that Marquis Mathieu would be right behind the ladies. Accompanying Marquis Mathieu was another gentleman, whom I guessed to be the Vicomtesse's husband, Vicomte Charles. An elegant man in his forties, he was every inch as sophisticated as the Marquis. As Mathieu passed by, he gave me a sly wink, secretly informing me that he'd find me, wherever I was. The last trio to enter the building included our friends Baron Pierre, his boyfriend, Sébastien and Monsieur Abriem Ludovic. Andy and I were surprised to see them.

When it came time for me to be formally introduced to the Vicomte, his eyes were already checking out my person. I detected a subtle, flirtatious glance from beneath his polite demeanor when he thought I wasn't looking. He did the same to Andy, Gudrun and Adolf. I was getting a hunch that these aristocrats were birds of a feather. They obviously flocked together when it came to their secret trysts and business ventures.

These men's wives had either turned a blind eye to their husbands' homosexual inclinations, or they were completely oblivious to the secret amours that took place under their noses. I imagined that perhaps they may have had a prenuptial agreement: either party could conduct separate clandestine affairs as long as they were done discreetly and in private. I had no way of knowing.

As we settled into the opulent living room for tea and light beverages, Baron Pierre turned to the prince to express his gratitude, *"Thank you for this wonderful opportunity for us to visit the Quwah. This is my first trip to Bahrain."*

"The Concorde will be flying to Bahrain from Paris within a year or two. It's a stone's throw away. You'll have

to visit this part of the world more often. It will also give you reason to invest in my country. You'll be able to fly here in comfort to check on your investments," P commented light-heartedly.

"That is superb! I'm sure the jet-setting crowd will be heading this way in no time," Charles responded.

P continued, *"That is one good reason we plan to entertain the elite when they come to my country for business and for leisure. My cousin Ikram and I have been working on an entertainment business project to share with your good selves. Before we do that, I've assigned these beautiful young people to show you the city."*

"That is splendid!" Marie-Laure shrieked excitedly. *"I'd love to see the city with these young bright things."* She gave Gudrun a seductive glance before turning to address us.

"Why don't you all have a leisurely afternoon to enjoy the Quwah and its gardens? Tomorrow morning, I'll have my cousins, together with these young folks, show you Manama. Abdallah and Fiddha know the city better than I do, since I spend the majority of my time in your country," P remarked.

Alain chimed, *"The Abds will show you to your lodgings. Please feel free to explore the house and grounds. If you'd like any of us,"* he softened his tone, directing his gaze to us, the students, *"to give you a guided tour, we'll be happy to."*

After our light beverages, we bid the guests our temporary farewells before they headed in the directions of their various suites, guided by their assigned Abds.

The Summons

As soon as the visitors and entourage had retired, my teacher detained Andy and me for a while longer. He whispered, even though there was no one around to overhear our conversation.

"*The prince has given me specific instructions for you. Attend to the needs of the Marquis if and when he calls for you. He requested Young's presence, having taken a liking to this boy.*" My professor gave me a pat on the head before turning to my Valet, saying, "*You know what I mean?*"

My lover looked at me as if to ask if I was agreeable to this arrangement. "*Of course I'll be glad to be of assistance to the Marquis,*" I answered. At that, Alain bid us au revoir. His final words before he closed the door behind him: "*Thank you Young. You'll be well rewarded for this.*"

As soon as we entered the suite, a beautifully wrapped gift was already waiting for me. An Abd had left it on the coffee table in our living room. The attached card read, "*I would like to see you tomorrow evening. Meet me at the conservatory at ten P.M.*" It was signed, "*Your secret admirer.*"

In the box was an exquisitely crafted Van Cleef & Arpels sterling silver bracelet. Flabbergasted by such a present, I showed it to my Valet. "*Who is it from?*" he asked.

"*I've no idea,*" I replied, but my thought was of Marquis Mathieu. He had sworn to find me, wherever I was.

Dinner Conversation

That evening over formal dinner, our conversation turned to the Vicomtesse de Noailles and Vicomte Charles' philanthropies. Monsieur Dubois was the first to mention it. "*The Marquise mentioned that you and your husband are connoisseurs of the arts and have produced film projects for Man Ray and Jean Cocteau. Your salon must be a treasure trove of magnificent art objects."*

"Being an artist and a surrealist admirer, I'm indeed fond of the arts and assisting talented artists to better themselves in their craft. I love Picasso and Dali," the Vicomtesse crooned.

She continued, *"You know, no one who is content would ever conjure such violent beauty out of disparate works of art. Only an artist would, and a real artist is never happy, never finished. The simple pleasure of walking down the street in the sunshine is rarely an option for people with such temperaments."*

Mathieu chimed before Alain could respond, *"If you have the opportunity to visit the fabled hôtel particulier at 11 Place des États-Unis in Paris, you'll be amazed by the interior. Marie-Laure did such an astonishing job in their Paris mansion."*

Charles interjected, *"Besides being a phenomenal interior decorator, my dearest wife is also a patron of the arts. We love to entertain creative personalities."* Turning to His Highness, he continued, *"You and your entourage must visit us when you are in Paris. We'll introduce you to our artistic friends. You'll love them."*

"Yes! We'd love to have you visit us, your Highness. We will be honored to entertain you and your entourage at our mansion," the Vicomtesse supplemented.

"We would love to visit the two of you when we are in Paris in a few weeks, before I'm off to Monte Carlo for the upcoming Monaco Grand Prix," P announced.

"I didn't know Your Highness was into drag races," Baron Pierre propounded excitedly.

Monsieur Ludovic queried ebulliently, *"Are you personally racing, or are you sponsoring a formula-one driver to race your sports vehicle?"*

"I'm driving myself. I love the rush of adrenaline when I'm at the wheel. It gives me a buzz when I'm

competing in a race. I've been training for over a year for this major event. Will you come to the races to see me compete?"

"Of course we will be there to support Your Highness," several of us chirped.

Andy and I were secretly exhilarated that we would be experiencing another grand adventure in Europe, especially one we had not anticipated.

Drawing Room Conversation

I was glad for a chance to speak with Anastasie. She had remained quiet for the most part of the evening. As the women and men did most of the talking among themselves, I proceeded over to P's girlfriend who was looking out a large window. She was in deep contemplation as she gazed at the expansive gardens. I asked, *"Is this your first time to Bahrain?"*

When she saw me, she was taken aback. *"Oh! I didn't know you were next to me. I was marveling at the large expense of water in the middle of these grand palaces. This is my first time to Bahrain. I haven't known P for long."*

I probed, *"Was Bryanna the one who introduced you?"*

"She did. The prince and I met a month ago in Paris. I find him charming, so we started dating. He invited me to meet his family. That's why I came."

Since I had been trained to keep our E.R.O.S. activities private, I did not reveal any of our secret sexual rendezvous to the model. She asked, *"Have you met his family?"*

*"I've met those of his cousins who live in the Quwah and his biological mother, Fatima. I've not had the opportunity to be introduced to the king or the other members of the royal household. They live in the palaces

across the lake. When the time is ripe, I'm sure His Highness will introduce us. There is more than enough to keep me occupied in this household," I responded.

"Will Bryanna be coming to join you?" I questioned.

"She'll be here with the Aga Khan in a couple of days, in time for the business presentation. Are you and Andy assisting P with his projects?"

I was trying to find the correct correlative to her question, since P and my teacher had specifically advised that Andy and I do not divulge any Carousel information to anyone besides the investors. I wasn't sure if Anastasie was an investor, so I kept quiet. Andy and Gudrun came to join us – a good thing, as time was rapidly elapsing and I didn't know what to say.

"It's wonderful to see you in Bahrain. As always, you look stunning!" my Valet complimented the model.

Andy always seems to have a knack for turning an awkward situation around. This time, he did it again, making the female feel cherished.

Gud complemented, *"I hear you are an accomplished model. Are you stationed in Paris?"*

"I'm from New York. My agent sent me to Paris to work on a couple of runway shows. That's how I met Bryanna. She seems to know everyone who is anyone. She introduced me to His Highness."

I expressed to the men, *"Bryanna and the Aga Khan will be arriving in a couple of days. I look forward to seeing Bryanna again. She is fun to be with."*

As polite as Gudrun was to Anastasie, I detected hints of flirtatious innuendo between them. Andy gave me a subtle wink, informing me that the young man was treading on dangerous ground, especially since this particular female happened to be P's girlfriend. Andy and I were observers, watching the comings and goings of the intrigues within the confines of this aristocratic household. For now, everyone present was on his or her best behavior. What ensued behind closed doors was a very different story.

46

---•◆•---

Preying Wolves

"Seduction is always more singular and sublime than sex, and it commands the higher price."
Jean Baudrillard

1967

The City Tour

Early the following morning, our entourage, which consisted of the Marquis, the Marquise, the Vicomte, the Vicomtesse, the Baron, Sébastien, Ludovic, Dubois, Abdallah, Fiddha, Didee, Elizabeth, Karina, Matumi, Gudrun, Adolf, Andy and me, proceeded to visit various historical mosques and cultural places of interest.

We arrived at the Bab Al Bahrain, otherwise known as the Gateway of Bahrain (a historical building located in the Customs Square in Manama's central business district.) This entryway also marked the main entrance into the Manama souq, designed by Sir Charles Belgrave, adviser to the Emir (P's father) and completed in 1945.

Since most of our distinguished visitors had never been in a Middle Eastern souq, Monsieur Dubois suggested we split into smaller groups to explore this extensive outdoor market.

Andy and I were paired with none other than the Baron and his boyfriend, Sebastien. Alain and Abdallah accompanied the two aristocratic ladies, Marquise

Angélique and her cousin, Vicomtesse Marie-Laure de Noailles. Anastasie was chaperoned by Marquis Mathieu, Gudrun and Adolf. Vicomte Charles went with Karina, Matumi and Fiddha. The last of our four groups included Didee, Elizabeth and the gay Muslim scholar, Monsieur Abriem Ludovic. We agreed to return to the gateway in a couple of hours. We trotted off to explore this busy souq.

Conversations at the Souq

While Andy was helping Sébastien haggle, Pierre took the opportunity to ask me, *"Are you enjoying your stay at the Quwah?"*

"I am indeed. Thank you for asking. There are many intriguing experiences, and I'm learning and exploring every day," I answered.

"Are you assisting P and his cousin Ikram in their entertainment project?" the Baron continued.

Since I knew this visitor to be a potential investor, I was unafraid to reveal a little of the 'Carousel' to tantalize his curiosity. I replied, *"Yes, Sir, I am working closely with Ikram on the designs of the venue. It's going to be a spectacular space when it's completed. I'm sure it will draw many international visitors to Manama when it opens for business."*

"What's the space going to look like?" Pierre questioned.

"I'm afraid I cannot answer that, sir. You will find out at tomorrow's meeting. I'm sure the prince and his business associates will supply the investors with answers to all of the questions you have regarding your tentative investment. I'm sorry I cannot reveal this information to you."

I changed the topic by inquiring, *"How is it going between your good self and Sébastien?"*

Pierre smiled contemplatively before asking me, *"How is it going with you and Andy? Are the two of you happy together?"*

I was surprised by his dodge. I riposted, *"We are both very happy together. I can't ask for a better guardian and lover than Andy. He's the best lover a boy could ever have."*

"It's rare for homosexual relationships to work out so elegantly. It is difficult for an older man like me to love a younger person. In my experiences, my boyfriends have never loved me sincerely. All they want is to be supported financially and pampered incessantly, and when the initial attraction wears thin, they leave for greener pastures." He hesitated before continuing, *"It is rare to see a couple like you and Andy; you two have the looks, the brains, great education, and you're both financially secure. The two of you are together because you're in love with one another and want the best for each other. I am envious of your relationship."*

Surprised by this twist in our conversation, I managed to conjure a comforting response. *"I'm sure when the time is ripe, you'll find a wonderful person who will love you as much as you love him."*

"That's easier said than done. I wish I had all the God-given talents the two of you possess." The Baron shook his head humbly.

"Sir, you have everything you could ever want and desire in life. You are gifted in your own way, and I'm sure the right person will come along when you least expect him to."

Pierre gave me a pat on the head, smiled and said, *"You are such a compassionate boy. I wish you were my boyfriend."*

His comment caught me off guard. Eventually, I uttered, *"I'm sure Sébastien will prove to be different from your previous boyfriends. He seem like a genuine person."*

The Frenchman grinned, held my hand to his heart and said, *"I hope you are right, Young. I hope you are right."*

Andy and Sébastien joined us just as Pierre released my hand from his bosom. My Valet, not missing any details, gave me a wink as if to ask, *"What were the two of you up to while we were at the store?"* I smiled at my lover and said nothing as we continued exploring the souq.

Eavesdropping

As I was browsing the stalls, I noticed Anastasie and Gudrun chatting intimately a few stores ahead, and Alf and the Marquis were nowhere to be found. They were obviously bargaining for a purchase at one of the kiosks while Alf's Valet was busy making a move on P's girlfriend. I did not alarm Andy while he chatted animatedly with the Baron and his boyfriend.

I kept a watchful eye on the heterosexual couple. I was curious to find out what was transpiring between the two, so I eased myself nearer to eavesdrop on their conversation while pretending to look for items to purchase. The couple did not notice my presence. They were too absorbed in their flirtatious exchange to detect me.

In the course of their dialogue, Gud swooned, *"You are a beautiful lady. I'd like to see more of you."*

Flattered, the female replied shyly, *"You are too kind, Gudrun. I'm flattered by your compliment. You, too, are very handsome, my friend."* She smiled adoringly at the Valet.

"Let's take a stroll in the gardens this evening after dinner. I'd like to get to know you better," Gudrun suggested.

*"That would be lovely. It's too hot and humid to venture out of the mansion in the daytime. The evening will

be a perfect time to explore the palace's expansive grounds."

"It is indeed an enchanted romantic saunter in the evening, especially when the moon is out. I'll be delighted to show you a secret garden where few have ventured," the handsome Swede commented mischievously. "Meet me at the entrance of the Conservatory at ten thirty this evening, and we can explore the grounds."

"Lovely. I'll be there at our appointed time," the female agreed merrily before Alf joined them to continue their souq exploration.

While I was busy eavesdropping, a pair of hands reached for me from behind. They cupped my slender waist, spinning me around. I came face to face with Marquis Mathieu. I was shocked.

He leaned against me and whispered, *"Ahh! I told you I would find you wherever you are. Now that I've found you, I'm not letting you go,"* he smirked amusingly.

Before I could utter a response, Andy, the Baron and Sébastien were standing next to us. I was relieved to see my Valet, since I did not know how to react to the Marquis' sudden appearance. Pierre asked jokingly, *"Where is the rest of your group? I thought you'd be wiggling your way into young Alf's pants. Instead I find you seducing this lad here."*

Mathieu, embarrassed at being caught, went red in the face, even-though he knew his secret was safe with our group. He added quickly, *"I was just having some fun with this young chappy. He resembled an innocent mouse spying on Gudrun and Anastasie. I wanted to startle him. It's funny to watch him jump as if he has seen a ghost."* The man laughed at his own amusement.

While he was speaking, I eased myself quietly to Andy's side. He put his arm affectionately across my shoulder and held me close to him. *"This boy is easily frightened. He's like an inquisitive rabbit, hopping all over to find the next adventure."*

"That's correct. It is amusing to see him jump out of his wits. He's a funny character to watch," the Marquis remarked.

"Where is your group? Shouldn't you return to find them? They may be looking for you," the Baron inquired.

"I had better join them before they send out a search warrant for me."

The Marquis turned, gave me a devilish wink, and disappeared into the crowd.

As I walked hand in hand with my guardian, he said suddenly, *"You, my boy, better tread with caution. There are a lot of lustful wolves in this part of the wilderness. I'll make sure I'm by your side; I don't want you to get hurt."*

Within the Conservatory

My Valet entered the Quwah's conservatory with me at ten P.M. that evening. I heeded my summoner's call to be there at our appointed time. Dressed in a loose-fitting thobe, I stood by the parakeet's cage. Andy had camouflaged himself behind some large potted plants so he could observe my admirer and me without causing any unnecessary suspicion. He also wanted to make sure I was well protected if anything unsavory should befall me during this secret rendezvous.

At precisely five minutes past ten, I heard footsteps approaching from the rear entrance of the conservatory. My heart began pounding with excitement as I wondered who this admirer of mine could be. Although I had a fairly good idea who he could be, I wasn't entirely sure until I saw him. There were no lights from where I was standing. I could see a sinewy silhouette moving in my direction, but I could not make out who this person was. Anticipation rushed through me.

When he finally stood a few feet away, I noticed the man was in a hooded djellaba. The hood was pulled down low. I could not see his face. My heart was thumping furiously from the excitement of not knowing what was going to transpire. The parakeets must have had a similar premonition; they too were chirping and flapping away unrelentingly, creating a racket in their large cage. Before I had a chance to breathe, the intruder pulled me towards him and kissed me passionately. He pried my lips open to suckle at my tongue, as if savoring the nectar from the beak of a newborn bird. His demanding impropriety aroused me tremendously. In my young life, I had fantasized of such a man, exacting control over my person. Little did I imagine this formidable moment would happen in this Garden of Eden. I surrendered to the invader's dominance. Whiffs of Arabian Oudh intoxicated my person. I could feel his trim, lush beard brushing seductively against my smooth chin. His piercing brown eyes stared into mine, leaving me helpless in his arms. The interloper was none other than the one and only Abdallah, the prince's cousin, who had never showed the slightest sign of interest in me. Now, his huskiness was enveloping me in a swaddle of sexual potency. There were times I had mused over this Arab's masculinity and longed for his touch. Never did I allow myself to believe that my fantasy would come to pass.

His hardness was pressing against my thighs. It was obvious he wore no undergarment beneath his tunic. In the dimness of our surrounding, I could decipher his bulging manhood, straining for release from the confines of the thin material he wore. I reached down to caress his excitement. His pre-ejaculatory wetness had dampened the crotch area of the garment. I lowered myself to a squat and started nuzzling at the fabric's protrusion, causing the Arabian to moan ecstatically.

Suddenly, we heard voices at the Conservatory entrance. We suspended our passionate motions in mid-air, waiting and listening noiselessly to sense our night obtruders. Giggling sounds of merriment echoed from a male and female. I knew instantly it was Anastasie and Gudrun. I had overheard them speaking of meeting at the Conservatory. Abdallah took my hand and led me quietly to the furthest section of the glass enclosure, away from the secret lovers who had so abruptly invaded our privacy. I was at once cognizant that Andy was trailing behind us. I knew my lover, my Valet and my guardian would never abandon me. He was my shadow, and he was watching unobtrusively the eroticism that was occurring in this 'crystal palace'.

My admirer resumed our passion, French kissing me before sinking his pearly whiteness into my neck. His ferocity stirred a concupiscent lust I had never felt before. I was throbbing voraciously. I desired him and he me. I smothered my face against his hairy chest as he discarded our thobes. He lifted my legs onto his broad shoulders as he stood, firmly supporting me against him. I was ready for him when he entered my opening in a single stroke; impaling me onto his masculinity. I couldn't help but release an ebullient squeal.

Suddenly, a deadly silence fell around the glass structure. In case I started to squeal again, Abdallah kissed me fervidly. His length felt deliriously intoxicating as it pulsated within the core of my being. He knew he had conquered me, and I was at his mercy. The temporary silence was deafening until whispers were heard again at the far end of the echoing love chamber.

Ecstatic moans and groans continued from the opposite direction. The heterosexual couple had begun their coition. We were absorbed in our own reverberating throbs of passion. No sound could stop us from our sexual union as we rode hard and fast to our united palpitations. We quivered in unison to the rhythmic music of our love-making.

Abdallah cadenced me as I held tightly onto his powerful neck. He saddled my buttocks in his firm hands, riding me like a competitive stallion. He challenged me to gallop and canter to his masterly command. No longer able to withhold his impetuous emotions, his affection flowed unflaggingly into me. I kissed him to keep him from his frenzied orgasmic releases.

The unwearying onslaught of his fortitude sent me spewing onto my belly and toward our chins as we encircled our glowing auras in an illumination of sexual exuberance.

A short distance away, I heard a faint cry of ecstatic jubilation. I knew my Valet had released his excitement from watching the erotica that had eloquently unfolded before his voyeuristic observations. The truth is, my lover and I loved to witness each other's sexual trysts with another, be it openly or in secret. This was the nature of our unconditional love for one another.

As Abdallah's member was sliding away from his fill, we heard pleasurable groans emerging from the other side of the chamber. Judging from Gudrun's exalted groans, I could tell he was at the point of no return. He ejaculated his ruggedness to sounds of the female's rapturous moans. Their amorous music had engulfed the silence, and the raucous parakeets grew louder to drown out their sexual gratifications.

Before the Arab mysteriously disappeared, he gave me a lingering kiss, smiled and snuck out in the same direction from where he had arrived.

47

Solicitations

> *"Money was never a big motivation for me,*
> *Except as a way to keep score.*
> *The real excitement is playing the game."*
> Donald Trump

1967

The Presentation

    The moment finally arrived for His Highness, Ikram and their business advisors to commence the 'Carousel' presentation. Bryanna, the Aga Khan and a wealthy Japanese couple, Mr. and Mrs. Fujikawa had arrived the evening before, just in time for the presentation. The investors, together with Monsieur Dubois, Andy and me were ushered into a large room within the Quwah, set up especially as a conference room for that morning address.

    During the exposition, Vicomtesse de Noailles queried, *"This project seems more suited for Paris, the center of the arts. I believe 'Carousel' would do well in our city. Will you consider opening in Paris before Manama?"*

    P hesitated. Before he could reply, Vicomte Charles seconded his wife's opinion, *"I agree with Marie-Laure. From my observation, Paris is a more cosmopolitan city than Manama. Such a lavish entertainment project will be a progression of the existing dance clubs that are currently available in Paris."*

Marquis Mathieu added, *"Bahrain being an Islamic country; wouldn't your conservative clerics oppose to such a contentious project?"*

His Highness answered commandingly, *"This venture is created to entertain the local elite and well-to-do jet-setting visitors. It will not be flagrantly advertised to the average Bahrainis. You may have observed that there are substantial differences between the average Bahraini and the elites in my country.*

"This secret endeavor will not disrupt or alarm our Islamic community. It is a recreational benefit to attract the rich and famous to Bahrain when the supersonic jets begin to arrive in Manama."

"Are any members of your family involved in this venture?" Mr. Misaki Fujikawa asked. *"Or are you operating on your own?"*

P replied emphatically, *"This is a project devised by my cousin Ikram and me. My mother is a silent investor in this enterprise."*

Mrs. Fujikawa probed, *"Is the Emir involved? Or your brothers?"*

Diverting, the prince replied, *"This is a pet project of mine and Ikram's. We would like to entice foreign visitors to my country. This will contribute to the economic growth of our island."*

Mr. Fujikawa declared, *"I agree with the Vicomte and the Vicomtesse. This project will do well in Paris and in Tokyo. We Japanese are looking to modernize our country – to catch up with the twentith century. I'm intrigued with your proposal and would like to dispense your ideas to a group of wealthy entrepreneurs in Japan.*

"Are you and your entourage open to giving a presentation to our entrepreneurial organizations in Tokyo?"

The Aga Khan had kept silent during the disquisition. Now he opinioned, *"I agree with the Vicomte, the Vicomtesse and Mr. Fujikawa. As much as your Highness has the good intentions in furthering Bahrain's economy, it makes better investment sense to launch this venture in a larger and more cosmopolitan city. Maybe you may consider unveiling this in Paris and Tokyo before returning it to Bahrain.*

"*Once it proves successful in Paris and Tokyo, we can launch or franchise to other major capitals around the world.*"

Bryanna added, "*I'm a night owl and have been to many nightclubs and dance establishments around the globe. This project is the first of such a scale that I've witnessed in planning.*

"*Our world is changing. Young people like me are hanging out in droves to dance the night away. My prediction is that within a few years, top-notch discotheques will open in major fashion capitals. It does make sense to instigate the first of its kind in Paris. After all, Paris is the fashion capital of artistic expressions, and 'Carousel' is indeed a new form of social dance venue. In my opinion, Paris should be the place to inaugurate 'Carousel'.*"

Baron Pierre voiced, "*Maybe your Highness will reconsider our proposal before settling on Manama to initiate this venture. It may be worth our while to scout for possible venues in Europe, Japan or Asia before arriving at a conclusion.*

"*I suggest we commence a worldwide search for the right place for this unconventional project. We can then decide the most suitable location to instigate this venture, don't you agree?*"

The potential investors' votes were unanimous, so P relented. It was decided that the French representatives would start looking in Paris, while the Japanese husband and wife would set out to gather their entrepreneurial partners for a presentation meeting with His Highness and his business colleagues in Japan. Last but not least, Bryanna and the Aga Khan would begin scouting in Europe for other potential locations.

We, the assistant side-liners, would eventually form part of P's travelling entourage to visit viable international 'Carousel' venues. I, for one, was delighted at this arrangement.

Entertaining the Visitors

I wasn't surprised when Marquis Mathieu cornered me after the meeting, while I was catching up with Bryanna. I was glad to see the model and wanted to hear her latest news. She had just returned from a modelling assignment in Tokyo and had been introduced to Mr. and Mrs. Fujikawa. Besides owning a top-of-the-line jewelry business, they were also astute business impresarios, both in the Nipponese performing arts and the Japanese entertainment industry. Bryanna, with her power of persuasion, was able to convince the couple to attend the investors' presentation. She knew the Fujikawas were well connected and had an abundance of similar-minded business collaborators who might be interested in P's project.

I was the first to speak. *"Bryanna, you look fabulous. What beauty secrets do you keep? You always seem so fresh after a long journey."*

She ruffled my hair adoringly and said, *"You, young man, you do know how to flatter a woman. The beauty secret I keep is similar to yours."*

"And what's that?" I asked scrupulously.

"Lots of hot sex and men to love," she answered tantalizingly. We burst out in laughter when the Marquis came to join us.

"What's so humorous? Can I join the merriment?" the Frenchman quipped.

Bryanna chortled, *"We are discussing hot men and zesty sex."*

"An interesting subject. Enlighten me about hot men and zesty sex."

The model remarked, *"Ooh, you naughty devil, I'm sure you are more than experienced to enlighten us rather than the other way around."*

Before she could continue, Mathieu swanned, *"I do have a few stories to tell, but I don't want to alarm this young chap. He may think I'm a pervert."*

"What's a pervert?" I questioned innocently.

They burst out in hysterical conviviality. *"I'll tell you what a pervert is,"* said the baron, who overhearing our hilarity, had proceeded to join us. He explained, *"A pervert is someone who practices sexual perversion."* I stared at him unblinkingly; not grasping the meaning.

The three of them found my naiveté comical. *"Didn't they teach you in school what perverts or perversions are?"* Pierre chirped.

Suddenly, the meaning of perversion dawned on me. *"Ooh! You mean sadomasochism?"* I uttered.

They found me funnier than before. Bryanna said joyously, *"That's a nice way of putting it. Ask your Valet or your teacher, Alain, to explain the words to you. They will be able to edify you better than us.*

The Marquis joshed playfully, *"Meet me this evening, and I will teach you what perversion is."* He gave me an iniquitous wink as if he meant what he said.

Just then, His Highness waved Bryanna over to him, leaving me in the company of the two Frenchmen. Pierre took the opportunity to excuse himself on the pretext that he was going to locate Sébastien. I was left with the Marquis.

An Appointment

As much as I enjoyed flirting with the Marquis, I was also impervious to his advances. Although it was fun to play his superfluous game, when it came to a true-to-life sexual liaison, I wasn't sure if I was ready for this cunning 'wolf'. I needed my Valet's advice. My eyes were scouring for Andy. He was busy talking with the Japanese couple. I had little choice but to confront Mathieu alone.

"My boy, do you really not know the meaning of 'pervert', or are you playing a modesty stratagem?" the Frenchman asked.

I forced a fake smile, as if I was well aware of the meaning of 'pervert.' I replied, *"I deceived you for a moment, didn't I?"*

"You're an affable tempter; you sure know how to entice me to fall prey to you. Your boyish charm is too irresistible for a seasoned man like me. Meet me this evening at my chamber. I want to envelop and possess you."

"Your wife will be with you in your suite. Doesn't she mind you making love to a boy?" This line of questioning had suddenly flashed across my mind as a perfect excuse to dodge his advances.

"We stay in different suites. Mine is across the corridor from the Marquise. We haven't shared the same boudoir for a couple of years."

I probed inquisitively, *"She does her own thing, and you do yours?"*

"Something like that. You don't have to worry about Angélique finding out about my tryst, nor me about hers with others. We have an agreement that we can conduct affairs with others as long as we are discreet."

"If that's the case, why stay married?"

The Marquis said divertingly, *"We stay married for a number of reasons – financial benefit and respectability. Besides, we get on splendidly outside the bedroom. Why divorce when this arrangement is perfect for us?*

"*Flirtation is a recreational game among the French. It's part of our existence.*"

I commented, "*Much like the Italians.*" My mind flitted to Gabrielli and Mario. "*Flirtation and seduction to them are part of their genetic make-up.*"

"*That's correct, boy. That's why the French and the Italians are associated with Don Juan and Casanova. We are amorous lovers, romancers and seducers of both women and men.*"

I questioned attentively, "*Is that why the French and Italians are known for their sadomasochistic perversions?*"

He burst out in hysteria, causing some of the investors to turn our direction. "*You, Young, you say the funniest things!*"

"*What's so funny? You yourself said that you are a pervert,*" I restated his previous claim. "*And what sort of perversions are you into, if you don't mind me asking?*"

This stirred another frenzied round of laughter from the Frenchman. This time, he had difficulty speaking for some time. "*Come to my room this evening when the clock strikes twelve, and I will demonstrate the types of magical perversions I'm capable of performing.*"

"*You perform magic as well as sadomasochistic perversion?*" I quipped ludicrously.

Again, the man went into psychotic delirium. He was practically rolling on the floor with merriment, as he struggled over to a nearby sofa.

My Valet, hearing the commotion, came to my aid. "*What brought on this ebullience?*" he asked, looking at me as if I've played a prank on the Marquis. I shrugged my shoulders as if I'd had no part in this impolite effusion.

Andy queried forbiddingly, "*What did you say to Mathieu to rouse him to such a state?*"

I stared at my guardian and said, in all seriousness, "*All I asked was the kind of magical perversions he was* capable of performing, and he exploded into uncontrollable cachinnation thereafter. I don't know why he finds my question so comical."

My lover looked at the Marquis for an answer as he slowly recovered from his guffaw. *"I asked Young to come to my chambers at twelve midnight so I could demonstrate to him the various forms of magical perversions I'm capable of performing. He asked me, 'Do you perform magic as well as sadomasochistic perversion'?"*

My Valet, taking this as a serious summons by the aristocrat to his chambers, whispered in the Marquis' ear, *"Sir, I'll accompany Young to your chamber at the appointed hour. Your request is our command."*

"Thank you, Andy. You are truly a great Valet to your amusing charge. He is a very funny boy."

With that sentiment, the Frenchman rose from his seat to join his wife, who was chatting breezily with none other than our other Valet, Gudrun.

48

An Expedient Resolution

> *"The beauty of my unique education is that I was born, bred and schooled in the art of being a flirtatious seducer and an expedient tactician."*
> Bernard Tristan Foong

February 2013

I did not hear from Dr. A.S. until the end of January 2013. He wrote:

Hi Bernard,

The first month of the New Year is almost coming to a close. I'm sorry I haven't written for a while. I was diagnosed with early-stage prostate cancer shortly after our last correspondence, and I had to undergo a series of treatments. Luckily, I have recovered. Hopefully, it will not return. This ordeal left me weak, but I'm glad to report that I'm 80% back to my normal self.

*We have lots of catching up to do. Is **Initiation** up and running? Are book sales zooming through the roof? ☺ I'd like to purchase a paperback copy.*

I hope you had a good Christmas and a great start to the New Year.

I'm looking forward to your news.
Best Wishes!
A.S.

1967

A Gift

I was more than surprised to find another gift waiting for me in my chambers, ال ذه بي ال عجل (The Golden Calf). Sitting neatly on the mantelpiece was a gold envelope. Enclosed was a check made out to me for two thousand dollars. The gold notecard read: *"You are so beautiful. I want to see all of you. Meet me at the library tonight."* There was no signature on the card, and there was no hint as to who the sender was. I asked my Abd. He shrugged his shoulders, remained mute, and shook his head to inform me he had no idea how the envelope had gotten into my room.

I went looking for Andy, but he was nowhere to be found. As I rounded a corridor, I bumped into Monsieur Dubois.

He asked, *"Why are you walking aimlessly down the hall?"*

"I'm looking for Andy," I answered.

"Can I assist you?" my teacher inquired.

I decided to show him the mysterious note. He grinned amusingly before inviting me into his chamber. As soon as the door closed behind him, he jumped straight to the point. *"It is not unusual for you to receive an unsigned invitation. The sender doesn't want his identity revealed."*

"That is obvious, sir. But how am I to know who sent the note?"

Alain answered delectably, *"That's an easy question. All you have to do is turn up at the library at the appointed time. Whoever he or she is will be revealed."*

"What if I don't care to have a liaison with this mysterious person? How do I excuse myself from the situation politely without offending him or her?" I queried in puzzlement.

Dubois beamed cheekily, *"Your accompanying Valet will make some gracious excuse for you if you are not interested in having a dalliance with your admirer. Andy is there to protect you, and he will know what to say. Don't worry your pretty little head over such a trivial matter. My advice to you is to show up for the adventure."*

"But my suitor did not specify a time. When am I supposed to show myself? It's all too baffling for me to understand," I sighed.

My professor laughed and said, *"Whoever he or she is, is playing a cat-and-mouse game with you. This person is enticing you to play a coquettish game of libertine chess."*

I uttered wittingly, *"I guess this person must be Marquis Mathieu. He's been flirting with me ever since we met."*

Alain chimed, *"My dear fella, don't be so sure. You never know who's lurking around the periphery and is interested in bedding you, my handsome one."* He added, *"This evening the prince is having a formal function at one of his other palaces. The investors are invited to the reception, except for the other foreign students."* He paused before continuing, *"Did Your Valet inform you that the two of you are invited because you are assisting in the project?"*

Looking puzzled I asked, *"If I'm going to attend this ceremonious soiree, I will not be able to go to this mysterious meeting. What am I to do, sir?"*

My teacher replied composedly, *"Let me have a word with your Valet. I'll give him some advice so that the two of you do not jeopardize your standing in this household. Now, go and find your guardian; tell him to come to see me immediately."* On that note, he dispensed me to locate my guardian.

Bewilderment

For the rest of the day, I was in a state of befuddlement. I was at once enticed, intrigued and aflame with anticipation of this flirtatious game of sybarite "chess." I was fervent, because no one had secretly or openly played such a sexual cat-and-mouse game with me. I was beguiled by the possible outcomes to this upcoming tryst. My mind was set ablaze with all sorts of sexual innuendoes, and my fervent imagination had heightened me to shambolic sensual arousals; I could think of nothing else for the rest of that day.

"What's the matter with me?" I castigated myself. I've not felt this way since my early encounters with my 'big brother' Nikee and with Andy during our playful courtships. I'd thought I had learned the tricks of subduing my passionate obsessions, yet here I was, heaving with infatuation, desiring to know what lay ahead. I was at a loss.

I found Andy half an hour later. He was busy reading an engineering magazine in the otherwise solitudinous library. But that day, there were workmen installing hidden cameras around this extensive room. I tip-toed over to startle my BB by wrapping both palms over his eyes.

"What are you doing, you little devil?" Andy queried judiciously.

I answered, *"Professor Dubois wants to see you immediately. He asked me to tell you to meet him in his suite as soon as I could find you."*

"Why does he want to see me?" Andy asked.

"You'll find out when you talk to him."

"Are you coming with me to see your teacher?" Andy asked.

"Sure," I replied, and off we trooped to Monsieur's Dubois boudoir.

Discussion

My Valet was the first to speak after I opened the cheque and the card once again in Alain's chamber. He asked the same question I had inquired of my teacher: *"Young, do you have any idea whom this gift and card are from?"*

"I don't know. It's a mystery to me," I answered. *"Maybe it's from Abdallah or the Marquis. These are the only two I can think of."*

My professor declared before Andy had a chance to speak. *"Abdallah and Mathieu are attending this evening's formal event. I doubt it is either one of them."*

My lover asked, *"Do you want to go to this secret meeting?"*

His question caught me off guard. I stammered, *"I'm curious to find out who this mystery person is. If it's the Marquis, you've already promised to deliver me to his chamber at the stroke of twelve. Why, then, did he request to see me in the library? I don't think it is him."*

My guardian hypothesized, *"This cat-and-mouse recreation is too ambiguous. I'm not one to humor these kinds of arduous diversions. Either you meet your summoner or return the cheque politely to where it came."*

"But I have no idea who the cheque and the note are from; I don't know to whom to return these items."

"Besides, we have P's decorous occasion to attend; we can't decline this important invitation just to wait in the library," I answered.

Dubois remarked, *"Young, if you decide not to accept this gift and don't know who to return it to, I suggest you hold onto the present for now and not meet your summoner this evening. Maybe this mysterious admirer will show him or herself at a later date."*

"If I don't show, wouldn't I upset His Highness and the guest in question, since P specifically requested I entertain his guests?" I thought aloud.

My professor declared, *"This is a valid concern. We must come up with a viable solution to this unexpected occurrence."*

Andy suddenly leaped out of his seat as if an electric bulb had gone off above his head. He announced, *"I've a solution."* Before we knew what was happening, he was out of the suite, running to locate Alf and Gudrun.

A Stately Function

That evening's event was not without pomp and circumstance. This sententious affair was an unspoken informal introduction of Anastasie to P's family members, several of whom did not take too kindly to His Highness, the third in line to the throne, or to his selection of an American woman to be his potential wife (no matter how connected or wealthy her family was). They wanted her to play no part in their traditional and conservative Islamic institutions.

Superficially, as guests of the kingdom, they welcomed her with a gracious sense of decorum, but when Anastasie's back was turned, the guests who disapproved of the union whispered in their native tongue among themselves.

This tenacious escapade was P's way of defying his country's conventional protocol and asserting his defiance against his otherwise traditionalist peers and relatives. He wanted to advance his country folk's mentality to keep up with changes that were happening in the larger world. Unfortunately, old beliefs die hard. Not only did his rebellious duress bring on further disharmony between him and his family; it also backfired and caused an eventual distancing between P, his father and his brothers.

That evening, the cordiality I experienced within the palace walls made me realize that the rift between P and his father was similar to that between me and my dad. This age-old generational gap existed beyond international and cultural boundaries. That night, I felt happy that I was no longer operating within the confines of my father's jurisdiction. I was a free man, and so was P when he finally relinquished his Bahraini princely ascendancy to come into his own in his adopted country, France.

I was glad when we finally returned to the Quwah. I had forgone my mysterious suitor's summon and decided, as per my professor's advice, to be patient, waiting to see what would happen a day or two later.

The Clock Strikes Twelve

A boy tapped on the Marquis' chamber door at precisely twelve midnight. His guardian, standing next to him, observed and waited with bated breath for an answer from the opposite side.

The door slid ajar, and a voice beckoned them to enter the darkened chambers. A single candle illuminated the adjoining room. No sound was heard except that of the boy's thumping heartbeat, drumming audibly within the confines of his finely spun thobe. His Valet led him towards the authoritative voice. *"Come here!"*

Suddenly, darkness enveloped both chambers. The candle had been snuffed out. Unexpectedly, a hand grabbed the adolescent, pulling him into the adjoining room. He let out a whimpering sound from this abrupt incursion, as he was being pushed brusquely onto the king. The naked Marquis was atop the boy, while his guardian stood guard a few feet away. The Valet was ready to pounce if anything abhorrent was to happen to his charge.

Mathieu lifted the boy's hands above his head, pinning him onto the bed as he pried open his sensual lips to receive the man's passionate kisses. The lad feigned a series of wiggling movements, attempting to get free from his intruder. The Frenchman tied his wrists to a post before ripping away his thobe to reveal his flawless skin. The boy's hardness throbbed unflaggingly against his washboard stomach, stirring the man's erection to bounce frantically against his analog's excitement. Straddling the young man, they French kissed as their manhood oscillated in rhythmic synchronicity. The Marquis lifted himself to feed his bobbing length into the boy's oral orifice. The bound youth thrashed rousingly to this stimulating onslaught. He swallowed the bubulousness in gulps of ecstasy.

    Suddenly, a blindfold encased the aristocrat. Surprised by this unforeseen invasion, the Marquis was at a loss, but the oral stimulation was too enticing for him to forgo. He continued feeding his captive while he desperately tried to writhe free from the bondage that had now rendered him sightless. His hands were forced and roped tightly behind his back by a pair of muscular arms he had not seen in the dark. This precipitous turn of events served only to heighten his sexual anticipation. His attempted struggles soon transformed to rapturous exultations. Instead of being the dominant partner in this game of lustful eroticism, he was at the mercy of his surpriser, who had lubricated him sufficiently for the lad to slide his engorgement into the man's anal opening. The captive jounced jubilantly onto the hardness that encased him. He rode uncompromisingly onto the jabbing intrusion as if riding a wild stallion.

    The intruder had released the boy's hands. He clutched his captive's hips, impaling him onto the frantic assault of his impending release. Mathieu's exhilarations leaked a succession of stickiness onto his impaler's chest. The Valet scooped up the manliness before feeding his charge drips of gummy viscosity, to the lad's prodigious delight, as he groaned lustily, burying his abundance into the taut confines of his rider.

The provocative stimulation shoved Mathieu over the edge; his liberation shot onto his impaler's youthful face as they rode unyieldingly until his length receded from the man. The Marquis slumped onto the boy's torso as he extricated himself from the aristocrat. The Frenchman flumped onto the bed, waiting to be extradited from his bonded imprisonment. That act of clemency did not arrive until the Marquis wrestled himself free some hours later. By then, Gudrun and Adolf had left the sadomasochistic chambers that had been intended to entice my sagacious Andy and me at the stroke of midnight.

49

---◆---

Hickory, Dickory, Dock

"Some things are so unexpected that no one is prepared for them."
Leo Rosten

1967

An Unfortunate Predicament

The following day after regular tutorials with Monsieur Dubois, Andy and I pulled Gudrun and Adolf aside to ask what had transpired the night before at the Marquis' chambers. The Swede gave us an egregious smile, causing my Valet to raise an eyebrow. *"Tell us what happened, Gud,"* he insisted. *"What did you do to the Marquis?"*

The Valet took his time to respond as he flipped nonchalantly through the pages of a magazine. He was obviously keeping us in suspense. Alf couldn't wait. He blurted, *"Gud blindfolded and bound his hands behind his back while I f**ked him."*

"Did he realize it was the two of you and not Andy and me? How did he react?" I questioned.

Alf's guardian replied, *"I don't think he knew it was us. The rooms were dark. He probably thinks it was you and Andy. I think he was surprised by the turn of events. He probably wanted to play the sadist with you, but he ended up the passive party instead. He was still tied up when we left his chambers."* Gud laughed as if the Marquis deserved to be bound after their sexual assignation.

A look of alarm came over Andy's face. *"You did what? You tied him up and left him there, with him thinking it was me?! You hellion! Leaving me to get the blame for your actions!"* Andy exclaimed.

"Well, mate! You were the one who asked us to substitute for the two of you. You, mate, you should be thanking us instead of reprimanding me for leaving the sadomasochistic Mathieu in bondage. He probably loved the rough treatment," Gudrun chortled.

Just then, Monsieur Dubois passed by the corridor. He heard the effervescence and enquired, *"What's the ebullience, boys?"*

The Swede replied, *"Oh, it's something amusing Alf and I did last night. Andy is afraid that he may have to shoulder the blame."*

"You boys better not have played some prankish game with any of our guests. They are serious investors and are here for our Master's investment projects. You guys better tread with caution and respect the visitors. Your métier is to make their stay welcoming and entertaining. You understand me?" my teacher said authoritatively.

Gud and Alf quieted down, nodded their heads and promised the professor that they would behave in an edified manner before disappearing down the hall.

As soon as the duo was out of sight, Alain inquired, *"What was the real reason for the jubilant outburst?"*

My Valet explained anxiously what had transpired at Mathieu's chambers the previous evening. Dubois cried, *"It's too late to change this unfortunate outcome now. You'll have to wait to see what the Marquis will do. Meanwhile, I'll try and think of an elegant solution."*

He continued, *"Also, Ikram wants to see the both of you as soon as possible."*

"Why does he want to see us?" my Valet asked.

"I have no idea. I presume he wants to discuss the Carousel with Young," my teacher surmised.

An Unexpected Revelation

I could tell Ikram wasn't in the best disposition as soon as we entered. His usual effervescence had turned south. In its place was a tetchy Arab, slobbering precipitously over a table of design drafts.

Andy inquired, *"You asked to see us, sir?"*

The Arab did not speak, he stood by the desk as if seething with displeasure. He finally grasped demandingly, *"Where were the two of you last evening?"*

"Sir, we were attending His Highness' function. You were there; you saw us," my guardian replied.

"Why didn't you heed my summons to be in the library?" the interior designer demanded.

Andy and I looked at one another, amazed that we had finally discovered the true identity of the mystery admirer. I uttered, *"I'm sorry, Sir! I did not know the gift and request were from you. There weren't any indications of who it was or of an appointed time. When we met at the event, you gave us no indication of your summons."*

Ikram declared, *"It is not I that beckoned you, but somebody close to me is interested in the two of you."*

I stared at Andy for a response. He enunciated, *"May we know who this special person who desires to see us is?"*

"Go to the library this evening, and the answer will be waiting for you. Take heed, and be there at the appointed time. This person will not take too kindly to you if you miss the summons again. You understand me?"

"Yes sir! We will be there. May we know the name of this illustrious person, so that we can be better prepared to attend to his or her needs?" My guardian was trying to gain some insight into our summoner's identity.

"No!" The Arab stated abruptly. On that authoritative command, he dismissed Andy and me.

Back to Square One

Once again, we were at a loss. We had no idea who our mysterious admirer was. When we arrived back at the 'Golden Calf', two glossy black boxes embossed in gold with the words *L'hommes Provocateurs* sat waiting for us inside the entrance door. Within the larger container were the following:
- A black leather chest harness.
- A form-fitting pair of leather pants with the groin and derriere areas removed.
- A black leather half-mask with two holes for the eyes.
- A pair of black storm trooper boots that fitted Andy perfectly.
- A black leather horse whip.
- A pair of solid gold handcuffs.

These items were obviously meant for my Valet. In the smaller box was another set of artifacts that consisted of:
- A glossy black form-fitting rubberized pair of shorts with a Velcro front. On the trousers were two flaps that could be ripped away instantaneously, revealing the wearer's crotch and backside.
- A black Hermes silk kerchief printed in gold with images of saddles, horseshoes and riding crops. The scarf could be folded into a blindfold.
- A pair of rubberized thigh-high boots made to fit my foot size.

- A black and a gold candle laid neatly next to a solid gold cigarette lighter. Beside these tidily wrapped articles was an oversized black dildo and a jar of lubricant.
- There was also a pair of solid gold nipple clamps.
- And a rubberized half-mask that fitted snugly around the upper part of my face.

These articles were obviously meant for me.

Besides the list of sadomasochistic paraphernalia were two black finely woven hooded thobes with long slits that ran down the front to below the navel. These monk-like coverings were meant to be worn over the leather and rubberized clothing.

My lover and I turned the boxes inside out before we finally found a fancy black envelope trimmed with gold edges. Enclosed was a white note card. Embossed in gold lettering were the words: *"You are invited to a gathering of the 'Canterbury Tales of Bawdy Rhymes'. You'll be asked to recite this rhyme at the library:*

"Jack be nimble,
Jack be quick,
Jack sizzles while the candles drip."
See you at the bewitching hour."

Once again, no signature was scripted below the invitation. My lover and I scratched our heads in bafflement, wondering who could have sent such an unconventional invitation with these indecorous gifts. The only person we could think of was Marquis Mathieu. After all, he was the only person who had toyed and flirted with me about sadomasochism.

"Does that mean Mathieu was pleased with his evening's rendezvous with Gudrun and Alf?" I questioned Andy inquisitively.

"I presume so. Who would send such gifts besides the Marquis?" my lover continued with obfuscation.

"Does that mean he wants to see us this evening? He must desire an anomalous replay of his previous night's experience," I thought aloud.

Andy continued to scratch his head. *"I give up! I hate this cat-and-mouse game. I don't know what we should do."*

"Maybe we should consult Professor Dubois again?" I suggested.

Andy gave an anguished sigh, *"I hate having to consult Alain at every turn. I am old enough to figure out these games without having to run to your teacher for advice. I want to be able to protect you on my own. You, my precious, are my beloved and my charge. I'll make sure no harm comes to you, even if I have to protect you with my life."*

When I saw him in such a state, I felt a sudden surge of affection for my lover. *"Three minds are better than two. Besides, Alain has more experience than either of us. He completed E.R.O.S. and the harem programs and is also my learned teacher; he should be able to advise us on how best to proceed. Don't you agree?"*

After much persuasion, my guardian finally capitulated before we trotted off to consult Alain, who proved as perplexed as we were. My teacher's only advice: *"There are no classes tomorrow on Holy Friday. I'm sure all will be revealed to you when you go to the library at the bewitching hour of one A.M. There's nothing to lose! Go, experience the adventure."*

Hickory, Dickory, Dock,
The 'mice' ran up the clock.
The clock struck one,
The 'mice' ran down
Hickory, dickory, dock.

Dressed in the ludicrous garb beneath our black hooded thobes, Andy and I arrived at the large ornate library doors. Two unfamiliar-looking, burly Arabs stood guard on either side of the entrance. One of them opened the locked door to let us into a dimly candlelit room. A group of people in attire similar to ours were already scattered around the room. They seemed as flummoxed as we were. All of them were hooded and wearing leather half-masks that exposed only their eyes and the lower sections of their faces. I recognized them instantly. They were the four French aristocrats: Charles, Marie-Laure, Mathieu and Pierre. Next to the baron were Sébastien, Ludovic, Gudrun, and Adolf. At a corner of the expansive chamber, Didee, Elizabeth, Karina and Matumi were muttering amongst themselves in low voices. Last but not least, Alain stood next to the Marquis. Neither my Valet nor I had any idea that Dubois was part of this clandestine assembly. We were aghast at his presence, since he had given us no indication that he was an invitee to this unorthodox escapade.

    As we stood ruminating, several fully masked overseers entered through a side entrance. One of them, the premier, sat alone some distance away from us, guided by two of Ikram's handlers, Makut and Khatum. The other four principals came to join our entourage. They stood in the middle of our circle, which seemed to have opened up automatically.

    Under their full or half masks, I recognized them as Abdallah, Fiddha, Ikram and Ebram, the third of the kaneeth's handsome bodyguards. I couldn't help but wonder who the mystery person sitting at the far corner was. He sat motionless, as if a silent spectator of a pugnacious game.

    In perfect English, Ebram announced, *"I'll give each of you a sign to recite aloud the rhyme you've been assigned. Then, you are to step into the center of the circle to participate in a pleasurable game of sensual and sexual gratifications."*

My Valet and I looked at each other in astonishment; neither one of us or, for that matter, any of the visitors or foreign students, knew what would happen next.

The mysterious observer voiced decisively, *"Let the games begin."*

50

Let the Games Begin

"True debauchery is liberating because it creates no obligations. In it you possess only yourself; hence it remains the favorite pastime of the great lovers of their own person."
Albert Camus

1967

Within the Library

I was in suspense, not knowing what to expect. A tray of cocktails was passed around to the participants by Khatum, who had mixed the green elixir, while Ebram decreed the rules and regulations of *Canterbury Tales of Bawdy Rhymes*.

Afterwards, Ikram was the first to raise his glass to offer a toast. *"We are gathered here to partake in an evening of sensual and sexual liberation,"* he said. *"Let us raise our glasses to toast His Eminence, who is preceding over the games. We drink to celebrate the first Canterbury Tales of Bawdy Rhymes!"* The attendees raised our glasses towards the mystery man, who had thus far remained seated and unmoved on his throne, as we gulped down 'the green fairy', better known as Absinthe.

Before Andy had the opportunity to deter me from consuming the hallucinogenic alcohol, I had already guzzled the entire glass. Under the watchful eyes of the kaneeth's bodyguards, my Valet had little choice but to take a sip of his green elixir.

As soon as we had swigged down our drinks, Fiddha added, *"The winner of tonight's tournament will be rewarded heftily. He or she will be granted a private audience with His Royal Highness."*

Abdallah finished his cousin's sentence, *"Without further ado; let the games begin!"* he vociferated commandingly.

Mary Had a Little Lamb

Out of a bowl, the Emir picked a folded card. The first names to emerge belonged to Didee and her charge, Elizabeth. With paddles in hand, Khatum lead the two females to the center of the circle. Suddenly, a spotlight was shone on them, blinding their eyes for a second. It was as if they were about to perform.

Ebram announced, *"We need two volunteers."* The baron and his teenage boyfriend stepped forward voluntarily. Before we knew it, the handler had stripped off the couple's hooded thobes; hauling the half-naked, jock strapped Sébastien and the scuddy baron into the center of the circle. *"Kneel in supplication to your mistresses!"* the strapping bodyguard ordered. He shoved both men onto the floor with his rugged boots before securing two leather leashes onto their necks.

He commanded to Didee and Elizabeth, *"Now, recite aloud the rhyme you've been instructed to read."*

Didee began;
"Mary had a little lamb
His fleece was white as snow;
And everywhere that Mary went
The lamb was sure to go.
He followed her to school one day,

That was against the rule."

Elizabeth interjected before her chaperone could continue,

"It made Mary mad with anger
She paddled the lamb so hard,
He went howling for mercy
And scuttled to hide;
In case Mary wallop his backside
Again and again."

The women recited the rhyme as they push-pulled their human 'lambs' to do their bidding. Bread crumbs were handed to every one of us to scatter on the floor or feed the 'lambs' as we chose. If they disobeyed their mistresses or any of our orders, their naked bottoms were paddled, whipped or slapped unyieldingly by the instruments we had been given. The lambs were offered up for public humiliation. We could choose to do whatever we wanted with them.

Abdallah gesticulated for Elizabeth to bring Sébastien over. *"Come here, you little lamb. Come to daddy for your feed!"* the Arab dictated. Elizabeth dragged and pulled at the leash. The stubborn 'lamb' did not move. Wallop! Didee's paddle landed on the boy's naked buttocks. He let out a harrowing yelp, yet made no attempt to budge. Another blow hit the opposite side of his buttocks. He cried before relenting to his mistress' tug. He crawled at a snail's space towards the Master's direction. Some participants booed, jeered and threw crumbs to the lamb. If he was too slow to nab the crumbs thrown at him, his derriere got hit.

Ludovic came up from behind the boy as he desperately strived to catch the food with his mouth and tongue. The gay Arab lifted his toes to tickle the boy's anus, exposed between his jock straps. The adolescent lamb tilted his buttocks to receive the wriggling toes. He was obviously enjoying the sexual attention being bestowed upon his orifice. His mistress directed another blow on his backside, sending the lamb scrambling towards the commander.

The dazed Sébastien knelt in front of the Master as he shoved the boy's face towards his bulging crotch. The lamb was in seventh heaven as he sniffed to inhale his commander's masculinity. His hardness craned for release as it bobbed beneath the fabric of his rubberized jocks.

The commander's manhood, outlined against his tight leather pants, hankered for the youth's luscious lips. The 'lamb' lusted deliriously to wrap his mouth around the pulsating organ. He reached to unzip the leather covering. *Whack*! A slap landed on the boy's face. *"Did I tell you to unzip my pants?"* the Master roared. The youth continued to nuzzle at the man's throbbing hardness. *"Now! Unzip my pants, and do it quickly!"* his Master demanded. As soon as his zipper was undone, the lamb lapped eagerly at the bulging rod. He could not resist wrapping his succulent lips over his Master's manliness. A sudden blow rained down on the boy's cheek. *"I did not give you permission to suck my cock!"* the Arab hollered.

Although the lamb obeyed his Master's sanction, he was desirously longing for his feed. The boy was secretly relishing the humiliation. He was basking in his role as the obedient masochist.

The baron was being treated similarly. Pierre was also relishing this rare opportunity to be the submissive complement to his usual belligerent self. He surrendered to his punishments amicably when the mocking audience and his sadistic mistress mortified his person.

The Queen of Hearts

During the same time that *'Mary had a little Lamb'* was being played out, Fiddha directed his attention to the

Vicomtesse, Gudrun, Adolf and Matumi. He asked Marie-Laure to recite her rhyme. She delivered:

"The Queen of Hearts
She made some tarts,
All on a summer's day;
The Knaves of Hearts
They stole the tarts
And were punished all the way."

At Fiddha's injunction, the aristocrat lashed her bullwhip at Gudrun (a.k.a. one of the 'Knaves of Hearts'), sending the Valet scurrying for protection. The lashes landed on either side of the Knave. Vicomtesse de Noailles, 'The Queen of Hearts' mandated, *"Come here at once, you wretched thief. I'm going to teach you a lesson about stealing my tarts!"* She cracked her whip again. This time, the lash landed on Gud's buttocks, sending the Swede howling in agony.

Matumi wasted no time in slapping Knave Alf's backside, imitating the actions of the mature Queen. The boy yelped in distress. Both Queens yanked continuously at the thieves to facilitate their sexual demands.

"Crawl here, you rascal; I'll feed you my 'tarts,' you filthy burglar!" Marie-Laure commanded. She lifted off her hooded djellaba, revealing her naked voluptuous figure and beckoning the teenage Knave to sup at her breasts and the wetness between her craving thighs. The Vicomtesse desired him, and he knew it, yet he played her game; he did not move to pleasure his Queen. A blow landed on his rear as the other Queen thwacked his backside, sending the young Gud howling in anguish.

"Obey your Queen! You dirty criminal!" Matumi commanded while lifting her threatening hand.

The crowd, intoxicated by the hallucinogenic green alcohol, was aroused by the debauchery. They behaved wantonly as each rhyme was recited and played out in full spectacle.

Jack be Nimble

Andy's and my turn arrived when Ikram directed the Marquis to recite:

"Jack be Nimble,
Jack be quick,
Jack sizzles while the candles drip."

He had a wide Cheshire grin as he recited the rhyme. He could not wait to envelop me in his web of propensity. He had desired to possess me the moment he set eyes on me at Hôtel Le Bristol and I had cleverly avoided his seductive predilection. Now, I had no choice but to play his unscrupulous game of chess, which seemed to be in his favor. My quick-thinking mind hankered to outdo this aristocrat.

As Mathieu delineated the rhyme, I whispered into Andy's ear. He nodded before we were summoned to come face to face with the Marquis, my Master. The aristocrat pulled me forcibly to him and planted a French kiss in my mouth, prying me open to receive his dominance. My attempts to resist only served to heighten his desire to control me. In one fell swoop, he ripped away my thobe, revealing my nakedness for his covetous imposition. He could not wait to devour every part of me as I struggled to free myself from my captor.

Holding me tightly, he tore off the trouser flap that covered my modesty before pushing me onto the floor. He was at the ready to pounce on me when my Valet hindered him. Andy had lit the black candle he had brought with us.

"Monsieur, let me do the honor of making this young 'Jack' sizzle. Let's see if he is quick and nimble enough to get away from my scourge?" my guardian proclaimed.

"I'd like to do the honors, if you don't mind," the Marquis countered.

A crisp voice spoke from behind Mathieu, *"Let me make Jack seethe. I'll enjoy seeing him twinge his sexy body in pain."*

Startled by the sudden interruption, the French aristocrat turned around, only to find the hooded leather-masked man, who had thus far been quietly observing the lascivious orgy, standing behind him.

Khatum had lit a gold candle. I was instructed to lie on the floor. Makut bound my eyes with the Hermes scarf I had bought with me. My Valet whispered in my ear. *"Don't be afraid. I'll protect you if the situation gets out of hand. Give my wrist a tap if you can't take the pain."*

I lay on the floor, not knowing what to expect. Suddenly, I felt a seething pang near my left nipple. I let out an agonizing cry. Dripping hot wax had landed on my chest. Before I had time to recover, another prickling pain sizzled my abdomen. Drops after drops of molten wax rained down on my body as I wiggled and twisted in anguish. I struggled desperately to get free from this torturous infliction. But my hands were bound securely by my lover. I could smell his masculinity through my blindfold. I knew my protector would not abandon me. He would always be there for me.

As waves after waves of chafing afflictions spluttered over my body, I was at once overwhelmed by a sense of alleviation as my spirit lifted out from my person. I found myself looking down at my tormentors as drops of molten wax dribbled onto my body. I was simultaneously in searing discomfort and in sweltering ecstasy. Yet a sense of relief engulfed my suffering; I felt free from the drudgery of my earthly woes. My lightness transported me to a realm where adversities did not exist. There were no obligations within this enlightening liberation. In this dominion, I possessed no one but myself. For the first time, I saw myself as I was and am now. I was everything and the one thing that mattered. I was connected to all yet connected to none. In that surreal moment of knowingness, I became the OM, the Alpha, the Omega, the Aleph of consciousness and timelessness. The I AM.

When I woke, my tear-filled guardian was sitting by my side. He was wiping perspiration from my forehead, face and neck. In the darkness, a flickering candle burnt brightly by our bedside. The first light of dawn was making its dim appearance against the dissipating night sky. I tried sitting upright, but a throbbing headache pounded my head. *"Rest, my beautiful one, rest. I am here with you. You are safe,"* my chaperone whispered softly as he wiped tears from his tired eyes. He lay naked next to me as we both cuddled into a deep, peaceful slumber after an evening of unbridled debauchery.

51

Winners and Losers

"One thorn of experience is worth a whole wilderness of warning."
James Russell Lowell

1967

In the "Al-'iksīr"

It was Holy Friday. Andy and I woke up late, as there was no morning tutorials with Professor Alain Dubois. After an eventful evening of debaucherous wantonness, my lover and I lazed around on the palace grounds outside our suite. We were enjoying a leisurely brunch when our conversation drifted to the previous evening's happenings. I asked, *"Why were you crying when I awoke in the wee hours of the morning?"*

Andy took his time to answer. *"I was worried that you'd never wake. I was afraid you were traumatized."*

I leaned over to my guardian and gave him a kiss on the cheek. *"You are so sweet, my beloved. I purposely played a deceptive trick so I could outdo the Marquis in his cat-and-mouse game,"* I responded.

My lover looked at me with a puzzled look. I continued, *"I drank the entire glass of Absinthe because I knew I would black out. I knew you'd carry me to safety as soon as I lost consciousness. Isn't that an E.R.O.S. household rule?"*

"You quick-thinking devil! Here I was, worried sick that you could not endure the pain and you fainted from agony. As soon as you were out, they had no choice but to allow me to carry you to safety." Andy ruffled my hair and grinned.

I smiled and said, *"For a brief moment after drinking 'the green fairy', I had a hallucinogenic experience. I was one with my spirit and the universe. I saw Mathieu and His Eminence dripping wax on my torso, when I was floating above my body. What exactly happened after I fell unconscious?"*

"I wiped the wax off your chest after I carried you out of the library. Thank God your smooth skin was not scarred by the hot liquid. I was frightened you might be scarred for life," my lover remarked with great concern.

"Who is His Eminence?" I wondered aloud.

"I don't know, but I'm sure we'll find out soon enough," Andy rendered.

Monday's Child

Our group of foreign students together with Ludovic, Baron Pierre and Sébastien gathered for afternoon tea and snacks at the communal recreational room. We couldn't help but discuss the previous evening's proscenium. Gudrun, the mischievous rapscallion, was the first to speak. *"Let's play a game of guess who. I'll recite the 'Monday's Child' rhyme, and you guess the person I'm referring to."* He began, *"'Monday's child is fair of face.'"*

Karina chimed immediately, *"She must be Matumi. This fair child won a three thousand dollar consolation prize for her outstanding performance as the young 'Queen of Hearts'."* She teased, *"Alf, did you enjoy your 'Queen' whacking your pretty little bottom?"* Several of us howled with laughter, sending the coy Adolf to cover his bashful face. By the smile on his face, we knew the boy had enjoyed the spanking he received.

His Valet smirked, *"'Tuesday's child is full of daze.'"*

Didee chirped, *"If I'm not mistaken, this Tuesday child must be Sébastien. He was deliriously relishing the various organs being placed in him."*

The French teenager gave a playful curtsy, acknowledging his sexual prowess as a power bottom.

Pierre interjected, *"For his brilliant performances, he took the runner-up prize in the competition. He, my dear people, is one of three to be granted an audience with His Eminence."* We clapped and cheered to congratulate the boy.

Gud fleered, *"'Wednesday's child is full of woe.' I wonder who that is."* The group turned in my direction.

My lover jumped to my defense instantaneously. *"Young has his reasons for blacking out,"* he tallied, not wishing to give my secrets away. *"He is allergic to alcoholic beverages and is prone to falling unconscious. It is not fair to say he's full of woe."*

I pulled on Andy's trousers to hint at him not to play my defense. I smiled to pretend to take the Swede's sarcasm with a grain of salt. Of course, when all was said and done, I'd had the last laugh. In truth, if I had been conscious, Mathieu would already have had his way with me, yet I had cleverly avoided his sexual advances. He had yet to lay his hands on me, and I was determined to win this game of cat-and-mouse with the amorous French aristocrat. Little did I realize, I had attracted another aristocrat who was also secretly relishing my innocent pensiveness. My reticent shyness had made me an excellent philanderer. At the time, I was satisfied, knowing I would checkmate the Marquis in the end.

While I was deep in thoughts, Gudrun moved on. He recited, *"'Thursday's child has far to go'."* He was referring to Elizabeth, who had acted as the sadistic 'Mary' as well as she could, yet her natural acquiescence was insufficiently ruthless to wallop her 'lamb' – her big sister, Didee, had stepped in to assist.

With a wide Cheshire grin on his face, Pierre was undoubtedly reminiscing about the paddling he had received from the big sister. Similar to Sébastien, this French aristocrat had been in seventh heaven when he was sandwiched between his 'Masters', the mighty Makut and the sinewy Ebram. They had had their debaucherous ways, and he had screamed gleefully all the way.

The Swede proceeded to render the last few verses of the rhyme, *"'Friday's child is loving and giving. Who would that...'"*

Before he could continue, Ludovic announced, *"Ahh! That Friday's child must be the infamous Didee, who forcefully dominated you,"* he said and gestured to Gud, *"into indubitable submission. She, the winner of the grand prize, was awarded twenty grand and a private audience with His Eminence!"* Our group cheered and shouted in jubilation.

As soon as the ebullience subsided, Gudrun resumed, *"We still have Saturday's and Sunday's children."*

"'Saturday's child works hard for his provocation.' Now, who do you think this person is?"

Before the baron could speak, Karina exclaimed, *"I know him. He performed anilingus with meticulous precision on all the boys and men present. In fact, he performed the task so well, His Royal Highness awarded him a consolation prize of five thousand dollars."* All eyes turned to Monsieur Ludovic Makmud Albriem. The gay Muslim genuflected unashamedly to receive his accolades as we applauded.

"Last but not least, we come to the Sunday child; 'And the child who's born on the Sabbath day is fair and

wise and good and gay'." Alf's Valet stressed the last word. He directed his declaration to the man sitting next to me, my Valet. Andy did not respond to the Swede. We had not heard our teacher enter, and suddenly, Monsieur Dubois hollered at top of his lungs, "What's the elation? I'd like to partake in this. Will someone enlighten me, please?"

The room fell silent. We looked at the floor and at each other, not knowing how to respond. It was as if we had suddenly committed a serious crime. The only person who spoke was Baron Pierre.

Elucidation

"We were just finishing high tea with silly chitter-chatter about last evening's bacchanalian soiree," Pierre clarified lightheartedly before resuming. *"Professor, you did little to participate in our fun and games last evening. Do you not enjoy some harmless S & M play?"*

Alain took his time to reply. *"I was there as a witnessing percipient and to make sure nothing got out of hand."*

He turned to me with a concerned expression, before inquiring, *"Are you alright, Young?"*

"I'm fine, sir. I black out easily from alcoholic beverages," I answered.

By now, the group had dispersed while I spoke to my professor about my health. Alain, Andy and I were left alone in the chamber.

My Valet asked, *"Sir, do you know who His Eminence was?"*

Dubois shook his head as if he had been caught between a crossfire. He commented animatedly, *"I do know the person behind the mask."* Then, he changed the subject. *"It's been a nightmare this morning!"*

I tweeted, *"What happened?"*

"Unbeknownst to me, His Highness had no idea what transpired in the Quwah last evening. During our conversation, I asked why we did not see him at the Canterbury Tales of Bawdy Rhymes soiree. He looked surprised and probed me in earnest. I had little choice but to tell him what transpired at Canterbury Tales of Bawdy Rhymes."

"What did he say?" Andy queried.

"He became acrimoniously livid when I related the evening's sadomasochistic debauchery. He said he knew who had spearheaded the bacchanalian party in his mansion without his permission..."

Inquisitive and impatient, I jumped in to question, "Who organized the gathering?"

Andy chimed, "You overzealous chap, let your teacher finish."

Alain pronounced, "He guessed the person to be his younger brother, Hamad, the twenty-year-old heir apparent to the throne. He had just returned from his summer vacation from Germany. He had been known to exhibit sadomasochistic traits even when he was a young boy. P has never taken kindly to his brother's serious masochistic behaviors. He certainly does not condone this kind of conduct."

Andy declared, "I have known the prince to be rather perverse himself. How can he reprimand his brother for doing what he himself sometimes does?"

"P's casual play acting is harmless, but when his brother takes sadomasochism to a whole other level, there is cause for concern. That's the reason His Highness is infuriated. He knows if Hamad's actions are left unchecked, it will get worse, especially when His Eminence is eventually crowned king. He may likely commit atrocities against his own people and to others who refuse to obey his demands." He paused before continuing, "Andy, you must understand, Hamad is the Emir's favorite son, and he's a very spoiled child. He is used to getting away with everything. Within the Al-Khalifa, dynasty there are unspoken family dynamics that are too complicated to explain to you guys."*

I questioned, *"Is His Highness going to confront his brother?"*

"I'm sure P will report this incident to his father and to his older male siblings. Hopefully, they can curb this potentially perfidious young man and make sure his ego stays in check," my teacher sighed.

My Valet reasoned, *"Is Ikram a Hamad supporter? He was the spokesperson for His Eminence last evening, was he not?"*

Dubois shook his head again before commenting, *"Ikram will sway to support whichever faction is beneficial to him. He is known to be quite political within this royal household. He knows how to play his game of chess when it comes to diplomatic maneuvering."*

"What is going to happen now that His Highness is rancorous of his younger brother?" I questioned curiously.

Before my teacher could respond, my lover chirped, *"Why did Hamad use the Quwah's library for his debaucherous assemblage? Why doesn't he conduct the soiree at his own palace?"*

"That's a good question, Andy. Both brothers have had a rocky relationship since childhood. I surmise he wants to see how far he can push the envelope with His Highness by secretly organizing the gathering here. He knew P do not approve of his duplicitous behaviors." Alain riposted, *"We shall see what happens in the next couple of days."*

We did not have long to wait.

End February 2013

Several weeks passed before I responded to Dr. Arius' email.

Hi A.S.,

This month had been a roller coaster ride in regards to the publication of **Initiation.** My collaboration with the Romance Publisher, let's call it 'Manuscripts to Books', started smoothly. The owner, Mrs. W, assisted me in more ways than one. I had solicited CS, a self-publication paid services distributor, to work on the layout and formatting of ***A Harem Boy's Saga – I – Initiation*** for two months prior to the publication date. I surmised that CS would know the book's content, since their staff had been working on it diligently. The first week after **Initiation**'s publication, I was told by Mrs. W that my memoir had shot to number one (in the non-fiction category) on a couple of eBook retail sites. She was also monitoring the book's daily ranking on amazon.com, and the reports were excellent.

Ten days later, **Initiation** was pulled from amazon.com site without a reason. A day later, Mrs. W acquired a warning message from CS, stating that **Initiation** violated their publishing content guidelines. I also received a telephone call from a CS representative telling me that all characters in my book had to be over eighteen years of age during any sexual encounters. The CS representative advised me to delete any references to my young age – then **Initiation** would be deemed appropriate and would fall within their age-of-consent guideline.

Needless to say, it took me two days before the revised book was allowed back on sale on amazon.com. I followed their instructions and erased any references to my age, replacing the ages with the word 'adolescent.' This seemed to satisfy the CS censorship board.

It continues to baffle me that a non-fiction memoir, a true story about what actually happened during my adolescent years, could be deemed inappropriate and be *censored from readers. I can understand that this age-of-consent guideline is applicable to fictional novels. In short, I have to practically lie about my age in my memoirs.*

My dear friend, this was only the beginning of many events. I will relate that information to you in my next correspondence.

For now, I wish you well.
Stay healthy. I look forward to your latest news.
Aloha!
Young.

52

Loving Me, Loving You

> *"A boy is, of all wild beasts,*
> *The most difficult to manage.*
> *His love of himself,*
> *The most arduous to tame."*
>
> Bernard Tristan Foong

1967

Sibling Rivalries

A week before we were scheduled to depart for Monte Carlo to attend the Monaco Grand Prix, P was nowhere to be found. Our professor told us he was busy training for his upcoming drag race runs.

Although this was the truth, there were other, more pressing reasons for P's disappearance. Through Monsieur Dubois; Andy and I learned of His Highness meeting with his father and his older siblings regarding Hamad's contumacious behavior. He informed the Emir that his brother had held a rancorous *Canterbury Tale of Bawdy Rhymes* at the Quwah without his knowledge and had involved his guests, potential investors and the foreign students in this debaucherous soiree. P was not only despondent that his father had done nothing to reprimand his youngest (and instead had reproved the prince for being tight-ass about his brother's conduct). Both of his older brothers had remained reticent. They were playing a waiting game to see which faction they would eventually support – which best suited their political stance. It was better for them not to ruffle any feathers against their father or the crown prince, and even though deep within their hearts they knew Hamad could be treading on dangerous grounds if his sadomasochistic behaviors remained unchecked. Yet they did nothing.

In front of the Emir, they pretended to be unflustered by P's legitimate concerns, advising His Highness not to overreact. After all, Hamad was young, and he needed to sow his wild oats. Their excuse was that he would come round after a few years and move on to maturity when he reached his mid-to late twenties. Little did they know that turning a blind eye would cause an abhorrent upheaval when the man who was soon to be king assumed rule over the kingdom. In 1967, the heir to the throne was already exhibiting signs of contemptuousness. Hamad's excuse was that money could buy him and enable him to get away with everything he desired, no matter how disparaging his conduct. He was a selfish brat and difficult to tame.

P was aflame, desiring no part in his father's ignorance or his siblings' political maneuvering. He channeled his rage into one of his many passions, dissipating the anger he had for his family into his drag racing. He was more determined than ever to make France his adopted home.

Gifts

Two gold envelopes awaited me and Andy at Al-'iksīr on the morning before our entourage was to board the Al Fayoum to Monaco. All of P's guests had left a couple of days prior to our departure. When I returned to our suite after my tutorials with Alain, I was surprised to find the cards sitting neatly on our writing desk. Inside each of our packages was a personal note. The message addressed to me read:

"Jack was nimble,
Jack was quick,
Jack avoided the candles' drips.
But I will find you,
You little twink.
You'll be pinched till you cringe,
You crafty twirp.
No greater a punishment will your Master inflict;
Jack will be sorry if he conflicts.
His buttocks will surely be whipped,
Till they twinge, begging for more,
You saucy creep."

M.

My name was scripted on a three thousand dollar cheque sandwiched between the notecard.

I looked at my Valet as he read his message aloud:

"Bring 'Jack' to me when I see you in Monte Carlo."

M.

As my handler recited M's instructions, a fifteen hundred dollar cheque fell out of the envelope.

We stared at each other in astonishment. I asked, *"Who is M?"*

My lover shrugged his shoulders before I speculated, *"It must be the Marquis. He's determined to have his way with me, and he'll find me no matter where I am."*

"I'm not so sure that these gifts came from Mathieu."

"What makes you say that?" I questioned.

"I have a feeling they may be someone other than the Frenchman. My premonitions are seldom wrong." Andy scratched his head before he headed to the quiet

library. He needed to figure out an answer to this puzzling riddle while researching an engineering competition he was planning to enter when we returned to Daltonbury Hall.

Sensual Blossoming

I disappeared into our chamber's living room on the pretext that I needed to complete an assignment for my professor. Like my guardian's, my head was churning for a mystery name for this mystery M.

A little more than an hour had passed when an Abd handed me a small parcel wrapped in silver paper. A royal blue velvet box materialized on the palm of my hand. Inside the luxuriant container was a tiny antique sapphire earring. Encased within the elegant box was a folded note. It read:

"I'll always be with you when you wear this close to your bosom."

I held the earring up to the filtering sunlight that streamed through our large French window. The greenish-blue jewel sparkled like my lover's dazzling eyes. Déjà vu immediately overwhelmed my person, and euphoria encompassed my mind; this piece of precious jewelry had been given me in a bygone era by a good-looking, titled gentleman. It was his token of affection, given to me prior to a perpetual separation. We had endured many trials and tribulations, yet our hearts continued to beat as one; in death, we reunited.

Tears welled in my eyes. My irresistible desire to don this piece of jewelry close to my bosom stirred me to strip naked. I stood, preening in front of the full-length mirror as I pinned this bewitching gem through my one pierced nipple. The solitary jewel glistened in the afternoon sun. I felt my lover's piercing third eye watching over me as I stared, admiring my nakedness. The sapphire dazzled at me. My organ began to harden at the sight of my private sensual delight. I was at once in love with myself and my beloved Andy. Over the course of these eight months, my lover had become my Yang and I his Yin. I could not disparage the two; our amatory bond had unconsciously united us into a single entity.

Sexual Correlation

Suddenly, I felt a pair of hands reaching to embrace my waist as I revered my reflection in the looking glass. My lover's beatified scent excited my quivering body while my hardness trembled irresistibly surrounded by his nimble fingers. His manliness never failed to inebriate my person. He held firmly onto my pulsating shaft as he rotated his thumb around my bubulousness, sending me into fits of sensual contractions. I gyrated against his furore, tantalizing his hardness as it strained against his denim constrictions. The blue stone glowed on my indurated knob as his hand twitched rousingly at my unadorned nipple, causing me to whimper deliriously. I leaned against his muscular chest to kiss him sideways. I stared longingly into his radiant eyes as he pried my mouth open, and I received him into the fathomless recesses of my soul. My Valet loved me unceasingly, and I in return adored his affectionate precipitation.

I reached behind to unzip his jeans. They fell to the ground. I wasted no time in relishing his bulging manhood into my accepting oral orifice. I encased his throbbing length into my bobbing throat as he stood spread eagle, pressing my head forcibly onto his intoxicating groin. I knelt in supplication, worshipping my handsome Apollo with abandonment. We glanced ardently into the mirror at our stimulating oral copulation. Andy lifted me off the floor to quench my fiery soul. Our passionate lovemaking never ceased to enamor our quelling adoration, my Phoebus and his Adonis.

I bent over to receive my demigod, cherishing his rhythmic gyrations as we perforated our love dance. Our eyes ogled at our every move, at times metaphorically slow, at others rapturously fast. We copulated in every conceivable carnal position we had learned through our Bahriji and E.R.O.S. experiences. We could no longer withhold our cohesive sensual amorousness. The harmonizing images of our sexual sodomy seduced us to the point of no return. Straddling above my lover's solicitous strokes, streams of my prurient nectar shot onto our heaving chests, just as my lover deposited his gratuitous affection into my welcoming crevice. We French kissed deliriously, not yearning for our radiant infatuation to disentangle so rapidly. I loved my beloved in me, and he did not desire to relinquish his affection but to stay buried within for eternity. The tantric bond we shared was our infinite salvation.

I lay on Andy's chest, savoring the afterglow of our fervid intercourse as the jewel glittered in the last rays of the setting sun. A sudden flash of simmering blue sparkled on my lover's left nipple. He had on his bosom the other half of our connecting link, a venerated gift bestowed upon my lover by his great-grandmother for when he found the right girl's hand for marriage. This pair of precious gems was to be her engagement present from granny. This piece of antiquity had been given to her as a token of affection from her fiancé when they parted ways. He went to war and she to refuge in Vaduz, Liechtenstein.

One half of this priceless gift was now bestowed to me by none other than my 'big brother', my mentor, my guardian, my friend, my Valet and most importantly, my lover. He had given me a slice of his treasured heart.

53

One Enchanted Evening

"Pleasure is the only thing to live for. Nothing ages like happiness."
Oscar Wilde

1967

Monte Carlo

The few months I have been acquainted with His Highness had been a whirlwind of social activities. A true 'Playboy of the Eastern World', P had his hands full with numerous exciting projects. The *Carousel* was just one of his many entrepreneurial investments – he took to business like fish to water. He, like the Aga Khan, was a larger-than-life lover of all things glamorous, from his jet-setting life to the people he chose to bed. Now that I'm older and wiser, I feel privileged to have been part of his entourage, if only for a three-month interlude in the year 1967.

Our party of a dozen checked into the elegantly refined historical Belle Époque hotel, *Hermitage,* steps away from the Casino de Monte-Carlo, made famous by David Niven as the 007 British secret agent James Bond in the 1967 *Casino Royale* movie.

His Highness had reserved the penthouse for himself and the floor below for his harem of minions, Andy and me included. P's handlers and bodyguards made sure that both floors were out of bounds to other hotel guests, even when the hotel was fully occupied by the up-coming grand prix revelers, spectators, and competitors during this important annual Monaco event.

Casino Royale

Our entourage arrived three days prior to the race. The evening of our arrival, we were treated by the prince to an evening at the casino. P had disappeared into a private gambling room with other high-rollers for an evening of stud poker, while Andy and I hung around the casino taking in the sights and sounds of gamblers taking their turns at the roulette tables and the slot machines. Monsieur Dubois handed us a bag of change for some fun at the machines. While we were enjoying nudging each other on the slot, a gentleman in a tuxedo tapped my shoulder.

The man remarked. *"I've been observing you and your friend from a distance. The two of you are very handsome."*

I struggled to find words. Andy jumped in with a witty response, saying, *"You don't look bad yourself."* My Valet extended his hand to shake the man's. *"I am Andy and this is my companion, Young. How do we address you, sir?"*

"Call me Miyaz." He shook our hands. He continued, *"Are you here for the grand prix?"*

"Yes! We are here with our host and competitor, Prince P. Are you also here for the race?" Andy inquired.

The stranger smiled but made no attempt to respond. Instead he queried, *"Are you staying in the hotel?"*

"No, we are staying at the Hermitage," I replied.

"Good! Can I have the pleasure of buying the two of you drinks?"

"This boy doesn't drink. If he does, he'll fall flat on his face," my mentor commented. *"I, on the other hand, would love a glass of wine."*

"Come, let's go to a quieter area where I can have a chance to better acquaint myself with you."

He led us towards the casino's entrance where he signaled the valet for his gold sports car, a racer that Andy and I had never set eyes on before. As soon as we packed ourselves into the vehicle, Miyaz exclaimed, *"Isn't she a beauty? She is my love and joy!"*

"What make is this unusual machine?" I inquired.

"It's my latest design; I named it Mercedes McLaren. Do you like the name?"

Both my Valet and my jaws dropped in amazement. *"Are you a competitor in the grand prix?"* we queried in unison.

"What makes you think that?" he asked.

Andy rejoined, *"That's a no-brainer. You drive a top-of-the-line sports car of your own creation, and you are here for the race. What else can you be but a fellow competitor, like our host? Are you acquainted with His Highness?"*

"Of course I know P! I don't just know him; I'm also a relative of his through marriage, and I've been to a few of his soirees at the Quwah."

"You have?" we burst out simultaneously.

"I haven't seen you before," I declared.

The man gave us a sly smile before speaking, *"Ahh! I keep myself very well hidden, so the both of you wouldn't know I was there, until the appropriate time came for me to reveal myself."*

"Why?" I blazoned.

"I want to get to know the two of you intimately, and I've no desire to share my intimacies with others such as Hamad or Abdallah or any other."

I chirped before my guardian had a chance to respond. *"I'm sure you are aware that we are under the auspices of Prince P."*

"Oh yes! That, my boy, I'm well aware of." The New Zealander remained silent after this last sentence.

He drove aimlessly through the winding streets away from the city. I blurted. *"Are you the mysterious M?"*

Andy gave me a stupefied glance, not knowing what to make of my utterance. The man smiled but continued to say nothing. By now, we were zooming along the winding cliffside towards Eze village.

Chateau Eza

The car finally came to a complete stop. Miyaz opened the passage door for us to alight. *"Welcome to Chateau Eza,"* he announced.

This mesmerizing baroque structure mounted outside of Nice had been constructed within the nineth century Eze village. Chateau Eza was once the residence of Prince William of Sweden and Norway. He, a passionate enthusiast for French art and culture, left his royal duties and found asylum at this undisturbed village, where its serene and tranquil atmosphere proved to inspire many of his publications. In 1953, three years before the famous actress Grace Kelly married Prince Rainier of Monaco, the Swedish Norwegian prince received news of his lover's passing, and he returned to Sweden to attend to his royal duties at once. Since then this 'Prince of Sweden's Castle' (as it was nicknamed) was on the market for sale. Several interested parties had their eyes on this historical site. Among them were our newly acquainted friends, Miyaz and his relative Prince P. It seemed that this racing driver, besides competing with His Highness at the wheel, was also vying for this picturesque property.

At my tender age, I was beginning to understand the meaning of powerful family rivalries, even among distant relatives who were partially related, if only through marriage.

On the surface, Miyaz and P got on eloquently, yet beneath their superficial showmanship lay layers of unspoken antipathies. Little did I know that my service at the next Household had already been forged into motion through our 'chance' meeting with Miyaz.

A Night to Remember

The moment the New Zealander opened the passenger door of his racer at Chateau Eza's entrance, I had the astonishment of my life. He reached for me over my Valet's lap, grabbed hold of my slender person and threw me over his shoulder. With a free hand, he gripped Andy's wrist and pulled him out of the Mercedes McLaren.

Amazed by such an unexpected welcome, I was dazzled by this aggressive gesture, and so was my guardian, who was left speechless, but he allowed the man to continue. Miyaz carried me across the threshold. He headed straight into the bedroom before throwing me onto the king. Before I could adjust my mind to this unexpected reality, he was French kissing me passionately, his masculine physique atop me, pinning me to the softness of the large eiderdown. Miyaz jostled my Valet next to me, demanding his lips join us in a three-way kiss. His intrepid forcefulness left us compliant to his imperious game.

It was also a game His Highness won through divine intervention when, four years later, Miyaz met his untimely demise. His racer's bodywork came adrift at speed, hitting a bunker before crashing at Goodwood Circuit, England in the summer of 1970. He was testing his latest M8D, ready to compete in that year's Monaco Grand Prix. He had obviously wanted his very own 'Batmobile' to be more superior to P's. He killed himself in the process.

The debonair's outback ruggedness captivated my senses. As long as I could remember, I had looked up to masculine males such as my Valet and now Miyaz – a man who took control of the situation and tamed it to his stance. I could surmise for once that my lover, too, was fascinated by this New Zealander. His sturdiness stirred in me an involuntary longing for him to take charge. He had known he had me in the palms of his hands ever since he first saw me in the video clips captured by the hidden cameras within the walls of the Quwah library, during Hamad's *Canterbury Tales of Bawdy Rhythms*. He had been there without being present.

My prognostication was indeed correct; he was the one, the mysterious M, who had given me a three thousand dollar cheque sandwiched inside a note that read:

"Jack was nimble,
Jack was quick,
Jack avoided the candles' drips.
But I will find you,
You little twink.
You'll be pinched till you cringe,
You crafty twirp.
No greater a punishment will your Master inflict;
Jack will be sorry if he conflicts.
His buttocks will surely be whipped,
Till they twinge, begging for more,
You saucy creep."
M.

I was at once sensually electrified and yet emotionally recalcitrant in anticipation to what lay ahead. I desired his lasciviousness but was petrified of the pain he had promised in his bawdy rhyme. I was grateful that Andy was by my side. I knew he would never permit harm to come my way unless I willingly subjected myself to what was unleashed upon me. My Valet, my Angel of Protection, was always there to save the day – or in this case, the night.

Miyaz's passionate caresses moved from my luscious lips to my neck as I forcefully shared my oral passion with my lover. We stimulated our growing longings for one another to heights of sensual delights, and our organs throbbed in anticipation for release within the confines of our tuxedo pants. The stranger's virility filled my being as if I were intoxicated. He reached into my unbuttoned dress shirt, pinching, twitching and gratifying his playful fingers on my nubile nipples, provoking my arching spine to receive his electrifying waves of sensual stimulations. His lingering kisses on my lover's lips stirred a submissive yearning I had not hitherto witnessed in my guardian. He, like I, was under the bewitching spell of this sybaritic wizard as they kissed with abandonment, tonguing each other in throes of manly passion, their souls united in an ancient ritual of masculine love. The beauty of their feverous embrace aroused in me an uncontrollable craving to engulf both bobbing manhoods in my hankering mouth. Heady muskiness permeated through their unzipped pants, driving me insane with bewilderment. I needed them, I desired them and I craved for their bubulousness to fill my person; pleasuring every crevice of my body with ferocious intensity. I would willingly be their serendipitous boy toy, their plaything they could possess anytime and in any way their whims, fancies and desires propelled them to. I lusted for them and they for me.

Pulling their trousers to their ankles, I savored their deliciousness like a child in need of nourishment. Their pulsating engorgements sent me into a feeding frenzy, at times enveloping their hardness in a single gulp and at others immersing on each individual with cherished admiration. Signs of their wetness, combined with my drooling dribbles, told of their imminent discharges. No longer able to hold off their exhilaration, Miyaz released his manliness deep into my receiving throat, pushing my head onto his life force in an ecstatic act of sexual liberation. He held my head firmly on his groin until Andy was ready to deliver his masculinity; only then did he repudiate my orifice to my lover's ejaculatory onslaught, feeding my mouth and face with his gustatory virility. This lubricious carnality triggered me to jerks of orgasmic transcendence, and I exploded my youthfulness onto my lover's groins and pelvises before my dripping abundance trickled onto the king from their dangling jewels. We were not ready to relinquish our blissful jubilations. The men knelt above me as I suckled and lapped at their succulence. I relished every drop of their uncharted delivery in this spontaneous act of erotic coitus. They wasted no time in basking in the glory of my boyhood, licking and nursing me to life for round two of our unbridled copulation.

54

The Artist & His Protégé

> *"Lust is to the other passions what the nervous fluid is to life; it supports them all, lends strength to them all. Ambition, cruelty, avarice, revenge, are all founded on lust."*
> Marquis de Sade

1967

Where Have You Been?

That was the question that came out of Gudrun's mouth as soon as Andy and I stepped out of the lift on our way to our suite. Gudrun, Adolf, Matumi and Karina were waiting to descend to the ground floor to go for a shopping spree.

"Professor Dubois has been searching high and low for the two of you. We hadn't a clue where you guys disappeared to. He wants to see you," Karina stated.

I asked, *"Where is the professor?"*

"The last I saw him, he was in the lobby talking with the concierge. He's probably looking for you," Adolf answered.

My Valet promulgated, *"If you see him, please tell him we'll be right down, as soon as we have a change of clothing."*

"Judging by the way you look, you didn't return to the hotel last evening, did you?" Alf queried inquisitively.

Andy held my hand as we ran towards our chamber without answering. As soon as he shut the door behind us, he advised, *"Don't tell any of the others where we were last evening. You know how they love to gossip. Now, get ready quickly so we can meet your teacher as soon as possible."*

Just as we were about to leave our suite, the doorbell rang. Standing opposite us was my professor. He looked at us inquiringly, *"Where were the two of you? The prince and Mathieu asked for you at breakfast. They want to see you immediately."*

Andy remarked, *"I thought His Highness had race practices this morning? Why does he want to see us?"*

I chimed before Alain could respond, *"I didn't know the Marquis had arrived. I thought he and the Marquise wouldn't be here until the afternoon. Why the urgency?"*

"P has already left for his trial runs, but Mathieu is waiting for you in his chamber. Go to him at once and find out what he requires of you," my professor advised. *"Where have the two of you been?"* he queried.

"We'll tell you later," Andy bellowed as he held my hand and we proceeded towards the Marquis' chamber.

Within the Marquis' Chamber

As soon as we entered the Marquis' living room, I was surprised to see Baron Pierre and Mathieu chatting animatedly. Marquise Angélique and Sébastien were nowhere to be found. The two French men had their 'freedom' to themselves. Mathieu commanded immediately as soon as he saw us, *"I am going to take you boys shopping."*

"Why?" I queried.

"We are going to a Piano Club this evening. I don't want you boys to look like paupers at the club."

"What's a Piano Club?" I asked excitedly.

Pierre smiled at my ignorance. He explained, *"My boy, a Piano Club is where we have drinks and listen to pianists."*

"Oh! You mean we're going to a concert," I uttered.

"Not quite. You'll understand when we get there. But before we do, we must spiff you up so you are not underdressed," Pierre blazoned.

"It's a private club, you must be well groomed to enter," Mathieu declared.

I asked, *"Will the other students be joining us on this outing?"*

"They will be spending the evening with the prince's entourage. I have specially requested both your company from His Highness. He has given his approval. You are on loan to me for the evening," the Marquis announced pompously.

"Let's go, before we waste any more time," the baron beckoned.

'Cercle d'Or' (Golden Circle)

I was awestruck and bewildered by the elegance of the stylish 'Cercle d'Or' district, otherwise known as 'The Golden Circle'. Many of the shops displayed a single unique item in their expansive windows. I had never in my young life seen so many empty display spaces. It proved to be a fashion marketing lesson in and of itself, though I did not consciously think about it at the time. The first boutique we entered that day was to suit Andy and me up in a bespoke 'un complet trois pieces' (a three-piece ensemble). Unlike the Savile Row, Gieves & Hawkes tailor to whom Uncle James had taken me a year and half ago in London, where the attendant was as snobby and snotty as the shop, this shop steward was friendly and welcoming. He knew that those who came through its revolving doors would not hesitate to make purchases. Those who stopped to admire the window display would not be their intended clients; they did not have bottomless pockets. Only big spenders would have the audacity to enter.

My selection was a finely crafted three-piece ensemble with their signature silhouette: a three-button front, side vents and soft shoulders from the well-known Czech menswear company, Knize, which the baron described as a "rounded-off shape." I was delighted with my selection, paid for by the Marquis.

After numerous comments and suggestions from Pierre and Mathieu, my Valet settled on an Anderson & Sheppard ensemble from their legendary 'drape cut' silhouette. It combined a small armhole and fitted waist with a generous chest and soft construction. The result was a comfortable suit that was easy to wear but nonetheless emphasized the masculinity of the wearer. The Baron settled the bill.

Next stop: shirt boutique. It was there that my lover selected a dress shirt by Turnbull & Asser, the shirt specialist that had made shirts for Prince Charles since he was a boy. I, on the other hand, had picked a shirt by Cluett, Peabody, & Co., the parent company of Arrow, which is now synonymous with 'sanforizing', a process that keeps our shirts and jeans from shrinking.

Our final shopping destination was none other than Ferragamo. To bottom off our couture outfits, we needed stylish, sleek, and distinctive footwear. Who better to complete our looks than the Italian shoemaker, Salvatore Ferragamo? Although the man had died seven years before we made our purchases, his legacy lived on, and his company remained the go-to shoemaker back in 1967.

Last but not least, the Marquis marched us to the **'Prince de la coiffure', Monsieur Alexandre,** whose clients included the Duchess of Windsor, Princess Grace of

Monaco, Audrey Hepburn, Lauren Bacall, King Hassan II, the Shah of Iran Mohammad Reza Pahlavi to name a few. Under the hairstylist's magical touch, Andy and I were coiffured to look as if we had just stepped out from the pages of L'Uomo Vogue.

Le Piano Club (The Piano Club)

After Pierre and Mathieu gave my Valet and me a thorough look-over to make sure we were spiffily attired and groomed, we departed the Hermitage in a Rolls Royce, complimentary for the hotel's VIP guests. Our chauffeur drove through the winding Monte Carlo streets. Before long, we were on our way to Nice.

We arrived at the city's old town and flower market district, forty minutes later. We came to a complete stop at a discreet historical building located at the end of a narrow side street. From the outside, the structure looked like a three-storied government administrative office. Marquis Mathieu rang the doorbell, situated beneath a gold placard that read *Privé: ne sonne pas si vous n'êtes pas un membre (Private: do not ring if you are not a member)*. After a few minutes of silence, footsteps were heard coming towards the large oak doors. A pair of brilliant blue eyes stared at us behind the door. The only thing that separated us was the security chain.

"Bonne soirée, monsieur!" The man greeted us politely. *"Comment puis-je vous être utile, monsieur (How can I be of assistance to you, Mr.)?* he inquired.

The Marquis handed the man a calling card. Within seconds, we were inside the stately establishment. A good-looking footman in his mid-twenties guided us upstairs to a richly decorated salon. A grand Steingraeber & Söhne sat tastefully in the middle beneath a magnificent chandelier that hung in the center of a high ceiling chamber. Understated upholstered chairs, velvet love seats, and a couple of comfortable chesterfields accompanied with matching low tables decorated this opulent room. Large blooms of pink Madonna Lilies filled the oversized Lalique vases, above the fireplace.

Several modish gentlemen sat chatting by the well-stocked bar in an adjoining chamber. I recognized two of them instantly. They were none other than Aziz's former school chums, whom we had met in Makkah. Seated next to Najib and Ismile was a French ethnographer and art critic, whom the Arabs introduced to our group as Monsieur Michel Leiris. Standing next to him was Lawrence Gowing, a professor of Fine Arts at an English university. The last two gentlemen were Francis Bacon, an artist whom Monsieur Leiris was actively championing, and his lover, George Dyer, the artist's handsome protégé. After formal introductions the conversation drifted to the topic of art.

The Marquis remarked, *"What brings you gentlemen to this part of the world?"*

"We are advocating Bacon's paintings to art connoisseurs in Monte Carlo, Nice and Cannes," the Fine Arts professor replied.

"Our friends Najib and Ismile are interested in purchasing a Francis Bacon for their Riyadh home. They have invited us to join them for the Monte Carlo grand prix tomorrow," Mr. Gowing added.

Ismile supplemented excitedly, *"We're here to support Prince P and our relative, Miyaz. Why are you in Nice?"*

Baron Pierre replied, *"Similar reasons. We are guests of His Highness, Prince P. The Marquis suggested we be his guests at the Piano Club."* He gave the Marquis a devilish grin.

As our conversation continued, I detected duplicitous glances between Mathieu and George, while Francis was trifling with my Valet, who was not in the least bit interested in the man. Andy, being a polite gentleman, carried on a civil conversation until Mr. Bacon turned to my guardian with a request: *"I'd like to paint you in the nude."*

Andy answered courteously, *"I'm flattered by your offer. Unfortunately, Young and I will be leaving the Riviera in a few days. Maybe, if the opportunity arises in the future, I will consider your generous offer again."*

"I can take some photos of you this evening and work from those," the artist said uncompromisingly as he continued consuming glass upon glass of alcoholic beverages (as did his protégé, George, who was already tipsy).

My Valet made another gracious excuse, yet Francis was determined to see how far he could get with his seduction before the baron stepped in to dissipate the awkward situation.

"I'm going into the piano room to listen to my favorite bit of repertoire, which will soon be played. Does anyone care to join me?" Pierre announced.

Andy and I jumped to our feet, leaving the three Brits, the two Arabs and the couple of Frenchmen to continue their flirtatious tête-à-tête.

As soon as we found a quiet corner to relocate, the baron commented, *"Les deux sont des nombres à virgule flottante dans le jus! (They're both flies in the ointment!)"* He resumed, *"I wouldn't go with those two. They smell of trouble."*

"What makes you say that?" I questioned.

"Young man, you don't know what I know about Bacon and Dyer. Their notorious reputation precedes them."

I was curious to know more. I decided to probe. *"What's so disreputable about Mr. Bacon and Mr. Dyer?"*

"First, I'm not a fan of Bacon's art. To me, his paintings are vile and his portraitures are frightful to the

eye. I'm glad you, Andy, didn't agree to have your portrait painted by him. I, for one, will not purchase any of his art. I prefer to see handsome men depicted as they truly are, not in some grotesque fashion."

Andy expressed, *"Art is a matter of personal taste. Although I don't recall having seen his paintings, I'm sure there are critics who would see it otherwise."*

"Besides his abhorrent artworks, their opprobrious lifestyles are legendary," Pierre said contemptuously.

"How so?" I queried with great curiosity.

"I'm glad the two of you are not like them. For a start, Francis met George when he was a petty thief, breaking into Bacon's flat. He was in and out of juvenile detention centers and had done time in jail. The artist must have seen his own reflection in the young man. They became lovers. Francis' history is as sordid as Dyer's." The Frenchman could not wait to tell us the verminous gossip he had heard through the art world. He proclaimed, *"Bacon loves to be abused physically by those he beds. In return, he inflicts psychological misery as revenge on them. His sexual relationships are built on mutual cruelty. Those two are also alcoholics. Look at the way they drink. I wouldn't be surprised if, before we leave the club, they are in drunken stupors."*

Just as the baron was becoming more inflamed with exasperated evaluations of both men, whiffs of soothing music drifted through our ears. Very soon, the Frenchman's fiery assessments dissipated. Chopin, Prelude No. 15, 'Raindrops', had performed its magic.

55

The Laws of Attraction

"A bright boy is far more intelligent and far better company than the average adult."

John B. S. Haldane

1967

The Assault

As our entourage gathered at the VIP Grand Prix grand stand, dressed in our fineries and waiting for the races to begin, who should walk into the VIP enclosure but my former 'Master', Thabit, and his brother, Aziz. They were in the company of Najib, Ismile and our photographer marvel, Mario, who (not surprisingly) had a gorgeous beau by his side. Needless to say, this young Dutch model, introduced as Padraic, was the Italian's latest lover. The two had met at a fashion shoot for an Italian menswear magazine.

While the racers took their positions below the Grand Stand, the marquis conducted an exuberant French conversation with the baron and my teacher. I walked over to join them while Andy inquired after the well-being of our ex-'Master' and his brother.

"What dark secrets are you men discussing?" Ludovic inquired before I could say anything. Like me, the

gay Muslim had gravitated towards the Frenchmen's adrenalized dialogue.

The Marquis responded, *"I was relating my evening's appalling experience to Pierre and Alain."*

Last night, when we had bid our friends at the Piano Club au revoir, Bacon and Dryer had already been talking balderdash. My Valet, the baron and I had left the club without the marquis. What transpired thereafter Andy and I had no idea.

"Do you mind sharing?" Abriem asked.

"Not at all. We consider you and Young a part of our inner circle," the aristocrat answered resolutely. He continued, *"I spent a diabolical night with a couple of deviant Brits. They're infinitely more fiendish, even than Hamad."*

The last remark perked up our prickling ears. Ludovic raised an eyebrow and bent closer to the circle, as if he didn't want to miss any detail of Mathieu's confessions. The marquis paused. When all eyes were upon him, he began, *"When we came out of the club at midnight, the artist, Francis, his friend George and I decided to go for a walk. The others retired to their hotels, leaving us to wander the streets of Nice. The further we walked, the more idiotic we became. We were full of liquor and other drugs. We were flying!*

"George challenged us to strip naked and walk around in the nude. We betted to see who could strip the quickest. Before we knew it, our clothes were strewn all over the place. We paraded around naked, acting like fiendish vampires."

Alain chirped in astonishment, *"Didn't the police or passersby see you naked?"*

"Several pedestrians did as we streaked past. Francis and George flashed their penises at them. They were consternated with disbelief. At one juncture, Bacon

started peeing in front of a heterosexual couple. They were aghast."

The gay Arab chimed in disbelief, *"Did they call the police?"*

"Not that I was aware. Before I knew, we were inside colline du chateau. While we were cavorting in the waterfall, George flipped me onto my belly and began pelting my buttocks with his belt. I struggled to get away, but Bacon pinned me down, pushing my head under the water. I was choking, desperately scuffling for air. Those two were relentless. They took turns beating me until my derriere was bruised. Francis kept throttling me with his erect phallus and strangling my throat while Dyer penetrated me. I grappled to get free, but they chastened me with brutal force."

I remarked entrancedly, *"Why didn't you holler for help?"*

"No one could have heard me even if I had. The noise of the cascading water was so loud, it would have drowned out my cries. There was no one there at that hour of the morning."

Alain asked anxiously, *"How did you escape?"*

"I couldn't. I had to endure their brutality until Dyer shot his load inside my ass and Bacon ejaculated in my mouth. After their sexual releases, they continued to hold me captive. I begged for liberation before their inebriation took over. They puked all over me. Thank God I could clean myself in the waterfall." Mathieu relived his tale in anguish.

I questioned inquisitively, *"What happened to the culprits?"*

"They passed out by the edge of the pond. I left them there as I scrambled out of the park."

"Naked? You left the park naked?" I cried.

The Marquis looked embarrassed. *"Yes, naked. I flagged down the police who were patrolling the area on* the main road. They drove me to the station for questioning."

Before Mathieu could continue, Dubois posed, *"Did they arrest the two scumbags?"*

"Yes, they did. The police interrogated me before they finally released me and drove me back to the Hermitage. It was a nightmare. I didn't get into bed until four A.M. this morning."

Abriem baffled, *"Are you pressing charges against Bacon and Dyer?"*

Just as the aristocrat was about to respond, an announcement came through the loud speaker, informing the spectators to gather by the large glassed-in balcony to witness the start of the races. My teacher gripped my hand as I got up. He whispered, *"Keep this information to yourself. Discretion is prudent."* With his counsel, I proceeded to watch the formula-one drivers gear up their engines, ready to zoom toward the finish line.

As I observed the racers whizzing by, a serendipitous euphoria blurred my senses. I couldn't help but glance affectionately at my lover, whose adoration for me would never degenerate to the level of assault. Andy must have detected my reverence for him from a few feet away. He gave me a coup d'oeil and smiled amorously before returning to behold the fervor speeding past on the tracks. At that very moment, I felt like a blessed boy, held in veneration by my revered 'angel' in human form. Yet within the recesses of my mind, I was curious to experience the demonic conflagration that had possessed Bacon, Dyer and all those infused with malignant propensities. Little did I suspect that within a few years, I would descend into a similar fiery abyss upon my separation from Andy. Human beings are capable of propitious dispositions and chthonic proclivities at the drop of a hat.

A Mile A Minute

Neither the prince nor Miyaz were the three finalists in that year's Monaco Grand Prix, but they both came in at seventh and fifth places respectively. That evening at the celebratory dinner hosted by Wazir Thabit, I was curious to know more about the marquis' vituperative incident. As our entourage sat confabulating over the day's racing event, I needed a breath of fresh air. I discreetly removed myself from my fellow retinue.

As I stood contemplating the setting sun and the expanse of the Mediterranean, I was again transfixed by the fortunate events playing out in my life. *"How could I be so lucky as to be loved by a handsome, educated and Godly man and living the most lavish lifestyle that money could buy?"* I questioned in my mind.

My hands, spread against the balustrade, were suddenly warmed by a pair of strong hands. I could feel his warm breath on my neck. I knew instinctively that he was not the Godly man in my life but the formidable race car driver who had competed with my 'Master' that day. This time, it was me racing a mile a minute – my heart drummed loudly, and I could hear it thundering. It was the sound of African warriors preparing for a war dance. I was intimidated by this alpha male, yet I longed for his masculinity to overpower my being. My knees felt weak, as if they were crumbling. On the surface, I stood calm and collected. Inside, I struggled for equilibrium. I pretended to be impervious to his advances. Finally, I plucked up my courage and muttered, *"Aren't you concerned, being so unfurled with your affections towards a boy?"*

I could hear his unflustered laughter behind me. *"Why should I be concerned? Your 'Masters' are used to attesting to man-boy love. I am a man and you are a boy. Shouldn't I have the right to love you?"*

I blurted, *"You are not in love with me; you're in lust with me."*

The New Zealander found my proclamation amusing and belted out a laugh. He spun me around and planted a kiss on my lips. My head was swimming with ambivalence. I longed for his sweet lips lingering on mine, yet I vacillated, concerned about his intentions. Was he using me to trump my 'Master'? Or was he genuinely interested in me as a person? I was torn within my being. I desired him to love me for who I was, yet my harem and E.R.O.S. experiences told me otherwise. Don't trust this charismatic playboy. He's toying with your emotions. As soon as you allow him into the depths of your soul, you're history. He'll be on to the next person. To him, you are a toy, a plaything to exploit and discard. Before I could stabilize myself, he pulled away precipitously. I was left dazzled and speechless. He whispered in my ear, *"Meet me alone at eleven P.M. tonight at the lobby. Don't tell Andy."* With that, he vanished to join the recreational jubilations that was happening indoors. I was dumbstruck. I slumped onto the deckchair. I tried desperately to decipher what had just transpired. I was at a loss.

Why?

Not only was my heart racing ahead of me, I was also perspiring profusely after having gone from serene contemplation to an electrifying upheaval. What excuse will I give my guardian if I follow Miyaz's order? If I don't meet him at the appointed hour, will I miss a chance of a lifetime to discover if his motives were fraudulent or genuine? And most significantly, why am I feeling so disconcerted? Am I unconsciously falling in love with this man? I ruminated.

Suddenly, I was rustled back to reality by a question from my professor, *"Young, are you alright? You seem miles away."*

I answered tepidly, *"I'm fine, sir."*

He continued probing, *"You seem deep in thought. What is perplexing you?"*

I redirected the subject to the marquis' recent incident. *"Oh, I was wondering, whatever happened to Bacon and Dyer? Were they charged with assault?"*

"I think not. I don't believe Mathieu wishes to bring notoriety upon himself. If he presses charges, the paparazzi will be after him for blood. This type of misconduct will only bring abhorrent headlines to his otherwise discreet homosexual lifestyle. It's not conducive to his or the marquise's social standing. They will be shamed beyond redemption." Dubois explained.

I exclaimed, *"Then Francis and George will get away?"*

"I'm afraid so," my teacher replied.

I declared, *"Wouldn't they do these kinds of despicable acts again if not made to pay for their misconduct?"*

"The best answer I can give you, young man, is to be careful of the company you associate with. Contempt breeds contemptuousness. Likewise, esteem cultivates reverence. Therefore, choose wisely, my boy. Take the high road instead of the downtrodden alleyways. One never know the dangers that lurk behind those dark corridors," my teacher advised.

I supplemented, *"From my personal observations, Mathieu himself is quite affixed to sadomasochism. I reckon he would not hesitate to inflict pain on me if I were with him and my Valet were not present."*

"Your assessments are not incorrect, my boy. We humans are indeed capable of propitious dispositions and chthonic proclivities. Both these qualities co-exist within our DNA. That is what makes us human," my professor mused.

"How, then, do I balance the scale so it doesn't topple to one or to the other?" I questioned yearningly.

Alain deliberated, *"Regarding that, my dear boy, you will have to listen attentively to your heart. Always be true to yourself, and your inner voice will guide you to choose rightly."*

"Come, let's go inside. It's getting dark," the Frenchman remarked. As we proceeded towards the open doorway, he turned and uttered, *"Seek and you will find. Ask and you will receive. Those, Young, are the Laws of Attraction."*

56

---◆---

The Dissipated Mr. 'M'

"I loved the idea of seeing the world through a boy's eyes."
Martin Scorsese

End March 2013

After weeks of absence I finally received word from Dr. Arius. He wrote:

Hi Young,

I've been in and out of the hospital since our last correspondence. I am currently involved in a clinical trial treatment of a drug called NX-1207. Luckily, my prostate cancer was diagnosed in its infancy, and the treatment seems to be working. Now that I'm feeling better, I am catching up with my correspondences.

In your last email, you mentioned that you made revisions to your age in **Initiation***. I'm curious to know what happened after your revision of the manuscript with CS and your working relationship with your publisher, 'Manuscripts to Books.'*

I look forward to resuming our regular correspondence.

Sincerely yours,
A.S.

1967

What Am I To Do?

Throughout the remainder of the celebration, I was beside myself. Everything around me seemed wrong. Andy asked, *"What's up, Young? You've been behaving anomalously since you came in from the terrace. What happened out there?"*

"Nothing," I lied.

My Valet looked at me puzzled, *"Are you lying to me again? I can always detect when you keep secrets from me."*

I prevaricated, *"I'm abhorred that Bacon and Dryer got away free after what they did to the marquis."* Although I spoke the truth, my actual flummox was that I didn't know what to make of Miyaz or of myself for feeling so bedeviled by this charismatic formula-one driver. Monsieur Dubois' advice rang in my head. *"Be careful of the company you associate with. Contempt breeds contemptuousness. Likewise, esteem cultivates reverence. Therefore, choose wisely, my boy. Take the high road instead of the downtrodden alleyways. One never know the dangers that lurk behind those dark corridors,"* he had said. Why, then, I wondered to myself, do I not heed my inner voice when it tells me not to meet the New Zealander? Why am I lying to my beloved, the one who will always protect me? I struggled to reason with myself.

I did not hear Andy speak until he tapped my shoulder. *"Did you hear what I said?"* he questioned. I stared at him blankly. *"Tell me what's disquieting you? You are obviously keeping something from me,"* my guardian refuted.

"I don't know how to begin!" I blurted.

Andy held my hand and guided me to a quiet corner. He said, *"Yes, you do. Sit down and tell me the truth. Nothing but the truth. Don't lie to me. I can tell when you're lying."*

I had little choice but to repeat what Miyaz had asked of me. My Valet thought for a couple of seconds before he spoke. *"Do you want to see Miyaz alone?"*

Surprised by his question, I stared at him, speechless. I kept silent before muttering, *"I don't know what I want to do. I'm at a loss."*

"Are you infatuated with the man?" my guardian inquired.

I stalled before I answered, *"I'm confused. I am well aware that I should not fall in love but play the field while I'm in service. Andy, you know I'm in love with you, yet I'm fascinated by Miyaz's charm. His magnetism has drawn me to a crossroads – I don't know how to proceed."*

My Valet *ran his fingers through my hair and looked into my eyes. "I'm not mad at you for feeling this way. I've been down this road, and I understand your emotional turmoil."* He hesitated before continuing, *"I'm asking you again; do you want to see him alone? I know this is a tough decision for you, because I've made most of your decisions since I became your Valet. But you are growing up, young man; sooner or later, you'll have to make your own decisions. Maybe this is a good opportunity for you to take the bull by the horns, confront your emotional feelings and put yourself to the test. Perhaps this exercise will be the first of several that transform you from a boy to a man."*

Astounded by my mentor's remark, I was dumbstruck. I did not know how to respond. I had not expected a reply like this. My expectation had been that Andy would insist on chaperoning me to the meeting. I certainly did not envision him giving me free rein to go on my own.

I uttered, *"What if he abuses me when I'm left on my own?"*

"You'll have to brave the consequences of your decision," my Valet stated. *"That's a choice you'll have to*

make. On the other hand, he may treat you with genuine respect. It's a risk you'll have to take in any situation as an adult."

"I'm torn; I don't know what to do!" I cried.

My emotional distress caused Andy to hesitate for a moment, as if he wanted to retract his statement. The baron came to my aid. *"Young man, you look distraught,"* he stated. He wrapped his arms around me to shush me from bursting into tears. *"Andy, what did you do to the poor boy?"* he questioned.

My lover declared, *"I didn't do anything. I gave him the opportunity to make a decision for himself and he started crying."*

Pierre comforted, *"Whatever it is; it's alright. There is nothing to fear except fear itself. Wipe your tears. Tell me what's troubling you."* He handed me his handkerchief.

I glanced to my Valet for an appropriate answer. He read my mind and answered on my behalf, *"He's tired after a full day. I'll escort him to our suite and put him to bed. He'll be fine after a good night's rest."*

"Are you sure you'll be alright, young man?" The baron turned to me for confirmation.

I nodded in agreement as my guardian escorted me to our chamber.

The Roadrunner

Miyaz greeted me with kisses on both cheeks before escorting me to his racing machine. I was surprised to find a sleek and stylish Honda RC181 motorcycle parked in front of the Hermitage porte de cochere. The New Zealander snapped his fingers, and the parking valet brought over two highly polished racing motorcycle helmets. As soon as I was seated securely behind my host, we zoomed into the winding streets of Monaco. I had never been on a fancy motorcycle, so I held tightly onto Miyaz's athletic waist in case I fell off the bike. The closeness of our bodies intoxicated my senses as we sped into the night. I couldn't help but lean against his muscular back. His black leather jacket and my cagoule separated us. My manhood between my loins grew, as the racer accelerated towards our destination. The uncharted territory of what could happen stirred me to an unbridled eroticism I had not experienced before. I inched my fingers toward the driver's crotch. He did not move away but he stayed focused on the road ahead. I got bolder. I slipped my fingers inside his leather pants, caressing his weighty pouch in the palm of my hand. I stroked his bulging protuberance with my other. Entranced by this unexpected inhibition, its engorged head peeked above his tight trousers. I seized the moment to massage his percolating excitement, sending his capricious masculinity into fits of amorous palpitations.

I reached under his shirt, nuzzling his distended nipples that lay amidst his hairy chest. He pretended to pay no attention to my stimulation, yet his body seemed to listen to me, gravitating to my every move. Aroused by my titillation, he had no desire for me to stop my foreplay. He wanted more. His muscular back glided against my torso as he oscillated his buttocks seductively against the denim confines concealing my throbbing hardness. He careened ahead faster than lightning, eager to reach our destination and to continue our sensual sojourn I had circumstantially started. I lusted after this roadrunner as much as he after me.

Villa Domergue

Instead of arriving at chateau Eza, the formula-one driver stopped at a large Italian villa. Miyaz lifted me off the seat and planted a lingering kiss on my lips, prying my mouth open to receive his yearning passion. He couldn't wait to get us inside the elegantly decorated Art Deco-style *'Villa Fiesole'*, otherwise known as Villa Domergue. In 1967, this lavish mansion belonged to Miyaz's friend, Odette Maudrange-Domergue (wife of the deceased painter Jean-Gabriel Domergue). The New Zealander had full use of her property while she was away in Paris.

The moment we entered the main hall, the Eurasian pulled me towards himself in a perfervid embrace. He ripped off my clothes – and his own – frantically. His pulsating manhood demanded attention. He pushed me onto the sofa and straddled my slender physique before lowering his palpitations onto my lips for my oral deliberation. Holding my head firmly, he thrust his pelvis into my face. The heady scent of his bulging sac drove me wild with insanity.

Holding my mouth open, he rammed his erection down my throat, and I choked at this sudden onslaught. I tried to jostle away, but his sturdiness pinned me to the sofa. He continued to stuff his hardness down my oral orifice as I gagged on its invasion. I thrashed wildly, to get away from his powerful grip. A slap landed on my face. I was dazzled for a brief second before another blow landed on my other cheek. The further I struggled, the more enlivened he became. Straddling my torso, he pulled my hands roughly above my head. He tied my wrists with a necktie that sat on the side table. He yanked me onto the floor, pulling me toward a nearby room. I kicked and screamed for him to stop, but my cries fell on deaf ears. He yelled, *"You little cunt, I've got you now. You'll understand the meaning of punishment when I'm through with you! You twirp!"*

M's message flashed through my mind as he dragged me mercilessly down the corridor. His note had said;

"Jack was nimble,
Jack was quick,

> *Jack avoided the candles' drips.*
> *But I will find you,*
> *You little twink.*
> *You'll be pinched till you cringe,*
> *You crafty twirp.*
> *No greater a punishment will your Master inflict;*
> *Jack will be sorry if he conflicts.*
> *His buttocks will surely be whipped,*
> *Till they twinge, begging for more,*
> *You saucy creep."*

I panicked, wishing Andy were with me. He would never allow this kind barbarous behavior to befall me. I grappled to get free, and he became more ferocious. He trawled me like a fish caught in a net and hauled me into the exercise room before tying me securely to the barre in the front of a huge mirror. The Eurasian yanked off my underpants as I wrestled and shrilled hysterically. As terrified as I was, I was also sexually aroused by the man's belligerence. My quivering penis throbbed uncontrollably as he became more pugnacious. Bewildered by my innervation, I unconsciously relished playing the role of a victim. Raunchy thoughts of debaucherous molestations flashed through my mind. Had I subconsciously invited this plight into my life? I wondered. Before I had time to excogitate my masochistic sentiment, Miyaz was above me, jamming his swollen manhood into my mouth. He wrenched my head backwards for me to swallow his cock. Tears welled in my eyes from this brutality, yet the Eurasian found my vulnerability tantalizing. Looking directly at me, he spat driblets of spittle into my mouth before jabbing his tongue perversely into my orifice. He lapped at his own saliva to share with mine, claiming ownership of my whole person.

Before I had a chance to catch my breath, he lifted my legs above his shoulders, delving his mouth onto my twitching anal opening. His mouth plowed fiercely into my farrow, only to emerge for air. Gobs of his drivels trickled out from my shuddering hollow. I cried for him to stop as he slapped my buttocks viciously. The more I shrieked, the more antagonistic he became. *"You pampered little twink! You were indeed nimble and quick, but now your flawless backside will be smacked and defiled by none other than me,"* he roared.

"Please, sir!" I pleaded relentlessly, *"Release me! I'll do whatever you ask of me."*

I trembled when he lifted his hand to wallop my derriere again. *"I enjoy seeing you cringe, you saucy creep!"* he thundered.

"Let me go, sir! Please, let me go!" I begged.

Before the race car driver could land another blow on my ass, the lights in the house suddenly came on, blinding my eyes. A familiar voice echoed loudly in the chamber. Miyaz's hand froze in mid-air. He, like me, was astonished to see my Valet and Monsieur Dubois standing at the entrance to the room.

Before the Eurasian could hit me again, Alain had gripped Miyaz's hand. My guardian rushed over to my side. He held onto me compassionately as he untied my bondage. Tears of despondency formed in his eyes. He cradled me as if protecting a baby. The bright overhead lights dissipated the menacing energy that had grown not so long ago in darkness. My professor escorted the formula-one driver to the living room. He was obviously giving a staunch talking-to to my maltreater. Andy stayed to comfort me, reprimanding himself for allowing this to get out of hand. I assuaged my lover that it was my fault for venturing out on my own, and I told him he shouldn't blame himself. I solemnly promised my guardian that I would tread with circumspection in the future.

Andy's final promulgation before he escorted me into the hotel Rolls Royce: *"You, young man, will not be left unaccompanied. I will make sure I'm with you at all times."*

My teacher was already waiting in the car. He instructed the chauffeur to transport us back to the Hermitage, and we left the New Zealander on his own.

Part IV

Japan – Tokyo, Kyoto.

United States of America – Pennsylvania.

France – Paris.

United Kingdom – Isle of Wight

57

Learning from the Best

"I'm not just a toy. I have feelings and dreams like anybody else."

Bernard Tristan Foong

1967

What Transpired?

The rest of the foreign students, Monsieur Dubois, and several members of the prince's entourage returned to the Quwah on the Al Fayoum the morning after my incident with Miyaz. The private jet would carry Ikram and his bodyguards to Tokyo after dropping its other passengers in Bahrain. His Highness decided to bring Andy and me to Japan with him, along with Aziz, Thabit, Mario, Ludovic, Karina, Matumi and Padraic. Mr. and Mrs. Fujikawa had secured a meeting with a group of Japanese investors for Carousel. Their real estate agent had found several possible sites for the project. We would meet them in the *Land of The Rising Sun* as soon as P could get away after his race. Being the Wazir's business advisor, my ex-professor Gabrielli would met us in Tokio. It was arranged that he would also be our temporary tutor during the course of our stay in Nippon.

The evening prior, when we had been heading back to Monte Carlo from Nice, I'd had a chance to talk to my professor in the Rolls Royce. He had gathered my clothing after his 'talk' with the New Zealander. As I dressed in the car, my Valet apologized to me, disheartened: *"I shouldn't have allowed you to be alone with Miyaz. I'm sorry I put you in harm's way."*

Dubois consoled, *"Andy, you mustn't be too hard on yourself. You did the right thing to allow Young to make his own decision. I'm proud of you for your cautious ingenuity in following them. I'm glad I accompanied you. You wouldn't have managed it alone."*

I couldn't help but ask, *"We were zooming along fast; how did you manage to follow us?"*

My teacher replied, *"We lost you a short distance from Villa Domergue. We drove around several blocks before we spotted the motorcycle parked in the front entrance of the villa.*

"There weren't any lights in the mansion. We quietly crept in through the front door. Your Valet was thunderstruck when he heard Miyaz cussing at you as you begged for release."

I exclaimed gratefully, *"Thank you for coming to my rescue. I'm deeply indebted to both of you!"*

My lover blazoned, *"From now on, you are not leaving my side. I will not permit it!"*

My professor reasoned, *"I know it's difficult for you to have witnessed Young in such a dilemma, but this is part of growing up. You can't protect him all the time. Sooner or later, he'll have to learn to take care of himself."* He paused before adding, *"Did you know that the word crisis, when written in Chinese, is composed of two characters? One represents danger and the other represents opportunity. JFK once said that."*

Andy was about to contradict, but he remained silent. He knew Alain's advice was true, yet he kept his promise, never leaving my side until we were in the fifth household. Only then did he gradually allow me alone time during my sexual services.

I seized this opportunity to ask Monsieur Dubois the question that had been boggling me, *"What transpired in the living room?"*

My teacher beamed artfully. He did not utter a word as if he didn't hear my question. It was my lover who dittoed, *"What did you say to the New Zealander?"*

"My dear pupil and guardian, I have my way with men like Miyaz. I learned certain techniques during my harem service." He gave us a conniving grin.

My Valet coerced, *"Share, so we can learn from The Grand Master!"*

The Frenchman cooed, *"Are you sure you're interested in learning my gambit?"*

We nodded in unison.

"Feed the dog his own medicine and he'll eventually come to his senses."

I quavered incomprehensibly, *"I don't understand."*

Andy stared at Alain in amazement, *"You bound him and left him in the villa? How did you overpower him?"*

Dubois laughed stridently, *"I gave a stern warning that if he disclosed the truth of his bondage to the police, I would not hesitate to reveal his sadomasochistic secrets to the press. If he wants his privacy intact, he'd better make up some story about a break-in."*

I asked in bewilderment, *"How will the police know he's tied up in the villa?"*

"An anonymous caller will be reporting the incident when we reach the Hermitage." He smirked at his own craftiness.

My Valet exclaimed, *"My, oh my! That trick would never have entered my mind."*

True to his word, by the time the police found the formula-one driver, my professor was above the clouds and on his way to Bahrain, while Andy and I were chirping excitedly on board the SAQR, heading towards *The Land of The Raising Sun.*

Tokio

Three vintage Jaguars were waiting for our entourage as soon as we touched down at Haneda airport. His Highness and the Wazir were escorted by Mr. and Mrs. Fujikawa and several handlers to the green MK IX.

Aziz, Mario, Abriem, Andy, Padraic and I travelled in a highly polished red vehicle. The rest of our group was ushered into a white luxury sedan. I was excited to see a country I'd never been before. The scenery to the Tokyo Hilton was as exhilarating as the conversation.

Mario, always exuberant, commented as soon as we were in the vehicle, *"I love Japan. It's one of my favorite countries to visit."* He bent forward as if divulging a secret. *"The Japanese boys are scrumptious to eat."* He gave me a devilish wink, as if I were of Nipponese descent and would understand his sentiment.

Padraic didn't take his boyfriend's bon mot too blithely. He wanted the count for himself, like someone I had known intimately in Italy some months ago. I couldn't help empathizing with the Dutch model, who was infatuated with the playboy. Fortunately, I had recovered speedily from my obsession with the help of my guardian. Andy had helped me overcome my emotional fixation with the manizer through his inundated love.

As the Italian carried on about nothing, I ruminated over the count's philandering before I heard Mario mention the name Twiggy. My attention turned. *"Twiggy! Did you just mention Twiggy?"* I vociferated buoyantly.

"I said, Twiggy is in town. She is here on several modelling assignments, and I'll be photographing her for Vogue Italia," the playboy announced.

I exclaimed, "Twiggy! The famous Twiggy! You are photographing Twiggy?"

The count laughed gaily. "Yes, I'll be meeting the 'famous' Twiggy tomorrow for an interview and a photo session."

My mouth gaped open. I chirped deliriously, "Can I tag along? She has been my fashion icon for as long as I can remember. To meet her in person would be a great honor."

The photographer laughed at my childlike exuberance. "You and Andy can be my apprentices. You, my boy, can meet your favorite fashion idol and assist me at the same time." He pecked me on the cheek.

"Yes, sir! Yes, yes!" I exclaimed appreciatively.

"Where are you conducting the interview and the shoot?" Andy inquired.

Mario responded instantly, "She is staying at the Hilton with her manager and boyfriend, Justin de Villeneuve. I'll do the interview at our hotel and schedule a shoot a couple of days later at an outdoor venue."

Changing the subject, Ludovic asked, "Do any of you know how long are we staying in Nihon?"

Aziz answered, "For as long as it takes to complete our 'Sacred Sex in Sacred Places' photo-shoot. We are filming at the sacred shines and temples in this mystical country."

The gay Muslim promulgated, "That could take weeks!"

Mario interposed, "Or months."

Andy chimed apprehensively, "Our service at the prince's household terminates in two weeks. Are we on loan to the two of you when we are assigned to our next household after our school break?"

Aziz interrupted, *"We are well aware that you guys have to be home for your holidays. Do you know which household you're assigned to?"*

I answered, *"I don't know."* I looked at my guardian for a response.

"I have not been informed by our school authorities," my Valet stated.

Aziz smiled as if he knew something. We looked at the Arab for edification. He looked out the window. We suspected that he knew which household we would be assigned to next.

The Italian voiced jestingly, *"Wherever you are, I'll find you. I'm a genius at extracting information about peoples' whereabouts."*

The Tokyo Hilton

Three pretty Japanese ladies in traditional kimonos lined up in a row to greet our entourage with welcome bows as we entered the hotel entrance. They reminded me of Yum-Yum, Pitti Sing and Peep-Bo (the three little maids) from the Mikado, a comic operetta by Gilbert and Sullivan.

Travelling with His Highness has its perks. We did not have to check in at the front desk, neither did we have to lift a finger to do anything except be escorted to our suites by the uniformed bell boys who were assigned to take care of us individually. Much like the Household Abds, who wore loose lightweight thobes and were of Middle Eastern ancestry, these boys were of Japanese descent and wore fitted white uniforms. There was a tremendous amount of bowing wherever we went. To me this customary gesture appeared a nullity, performed out of habit, but Matumi insisted that this was a polite, proprietary custom and an etiquette not to be sneered at. Once, she caught me snickering when the mannerly parking valet opened our car door and bowed to us. She gave me a flinty glare, as if I had done an unforgivable deed. She rebuked me for being a disrespectful guest in her patrimonial motherland. From that moment forward, I performed a reciprocal kowtow in acknowledgement of their civic manners.

The front desk had assigned Andy and me a suite with two single beds and a nightstand permanently fixed in between. Since we disliked sleeping apart, Andy called the reception to request a change to a king bedchamber. A long silence followed at the other end of the telephone. We heard a male and a female muttering in the background. They spoke sardonically in Japanese, *"*私はこれらの2が「nanshokus」であると思います．（彼‐それ）らは一緒に国王ベッドで眠ることを望みます．*(I think these two are 'nanshokus' (sodomites or pederasts). They want to sleep together on a king bed)."* Finally a man's voice came on the line. He lied, *"I'm sorry sir, we do not have a king bedchamber available."*

Andy must have known, but being a well-bred gentleman, he thanked the receptionist courteously. As soon as he hung up the line, he dialed Count Mario. After the usual pleasantries, my Valet queried, *"Did the front desk allocate you and Padraic a king-size bed chamber?"*

After a brief dialogue, Andy told me to stay while he hurriedly descended to meet the count at the check-in counter. He returned fifteen minutes later with our personal bell boys, who informed me that we were moving to a different suite on the same floor. In the new chamber was a king-size bed, neatly spruced and waiting for its next occupants. I queried as soon as the boys had unpacked our belongings and stored them tidily into the closet drawers, *"How did you get this room? I thought they didn't have a king bedchamber available?"*

"Just like your teacher, Dubois, I have a few wiles up my sleeves," my mentor smirked.

"What happened downstairs?" I pealed.

"Don't worry your cute little head over such trivial matters. Leave this heavy-duty stuff to the big-boys. We'll make things right for pretty boys like you!" He preened before the looking glass.

"Tell me what happened. I want to know," I begged for an explanation.

My lover plumed like a peacock. He began, *"The count created a huge pother, saying he'd report this kind of homosexual prejudice to 'the' Mr. Conrad Hilton, whom he had interviewed for an Italian economic magazine. The staff at the front desk also got wind that we are part of the prince's entourage.*

"They apologized profusely, blaming the mishap on their computer system and saying they would rectify the matter immediately. Within seconds, we were upgraded to this premium suite."

"You are getting to be like Monsieur Alain Dubious!"

My tease flew over his head. My lover was too absorbed with himself to bother with me.

58

Japanese Homosexuality

"Homosexuality is like the weather. It just is."
Andrew Sullivan

Early April 2013

Hello Dr. Arius,
Sorry to hear of your illness. I'm glad you are feeling better and back in the swing of things. My prayers are with you for your full recovery.
Back to your questions:
After **Initiation** *was reinstated by CS and on sale on amazon.com again, 'Manuscripts to Books' stopped communicating with me. Mrs. Wright would correspond only with my partner, Walter, bypassing me altogether. I had requested a written book sales report from her after the bo-ha-ha with CS, and she gave me some ridiculous sales figure that did not correspond with her previous email reports. After two weeks of anomalous aberrance, Walter and I decided to terminate our working relationship with 'Manuscripts to Books'.*
After re-reading the contract, we found a small clause that states: if the author chooses to terminate with 'Manuscripts to Books' prior to their quarterly royalty compensation, the publisher is eligible to keep the entirety of the pecuniary profits generated from the book sales. We suspect the reason for Mrs. W's aberrant deportment was

she wanted to keep all the profits rather than give me my dues. We terminated our contract with 'Manuscripts to Books' immediately so we could regain our book rights, even if we had to lose two months of royalty dues. It was in my best interest to discontinue this pernicious relationship with a scammer, Walter advised.

It took me another month to fully regain the sales rights to **Initiation**. In the process of self-publishing, I had already learned a lot. I reloaded **Initiation** onto amazon.com and other e-book sales sites. Since our last correspondence, **A Harem Boy's Saga – I - Initiation** and **II – Unbridled** are back on the shelves again.

I'm currently writing book **III – Debauchery**. The previous month's headaches are behind me. I'm now proceeding full steam ahead with my writing.

My dear friend, stay healthy and be positive, as always.

Blessings!
Young.

1967

Yuri

I was delighted to see Gabrielli after a few months' absence, and he was pleased to see me as well. After formal pleasantries, my teacher said amusingly, *"Mario told me about the 'king bed' episode at the hotel's front desk yesterday. I'm glad Andy and the count created a tizzy. They have every right to be angry at such prejudice."*

I looked at my professor, not knowing how to respond. He added, *"Japan, in its speediness to wallow in westernization, also enveloped the negativities of Judeo-Christian morals. The country seems to have forgotten its Buddhist roots."* The Italian shook his head.

The puzzled look on my face roused him to resume, *"Much like the ancient Greeks and Spartans, Japan has a long history of pederasty. It's a lesson unto itself. Maybe I will use this tutorial to educate you and Matumi on Japan's history of homosexuality."*

Matumi and I nodded in agreement. *"I'd like to learn more about my country's 'Yuri' history."*

"What's 'Yuri'?" I questioned.

Our teacher gave her a knowing smile before answering, *"The word yuri literally means 'lily', and it is a relatively common Japanese feminine name."* He continued, *"Yuri is also known by the wasei-eigo (Japanese-made English, English words coined in Japan) - Girls' Love gāruzu rabu). The Japanese use the word in reference to a genre of art and literature involving love between women, especially in anime. This phenomenon is currently taking shape as we speak. Yuri focuses on the sexual and also emotional aspects of the relationship, the latter of which is sometimes referred to as shōjo-ai by westerners."*

Matumi announced proudly, *"I've read Nobuko Yoshiya's - Onna no yujo, 'Women's Friendship', and kugawa no fujintachi, 'Tokugawa Women', the author's latest novel about romantic adolescent girls' love for each other."*

Our teacher gave her a hearty smile before commenting, *"Yes, Nobuko Yoshiya is a prolific writer, and she is unafraid of revealing details of her personal life through photographs, personal essays and magazine interviews. Her lover, Monma Chiyo, was a mathematics teacher at a girls' school in Tokyo when they met. She adopted Monma as her daughter in 1957. That was the only legitimate way for lesbians to share property and make medical decisions for each other. They are both well-travelled women. They have been to Manchuria, the Soviet*

Union, Netherlands, Dutch East Indies, French Indochina and, of course, Paris and the United States."

"How did you know so much about her personal life?" Matumi asked.

"Like you, I've also read her works. Her life is well publicized. She wrote Hana monogatari, 'Flower Tales', which is a series of fifty-two tales of romantic friendships that are very popular among female students like yourself," Gabrielli teased. "I've also read a few of her other works, such as Yaneura no nishojo, 'Two Virgins in the Attic', which is semi-autobiographical. She describes a female-female love experience with her dorm roommate. In the final scene of the book, the two girls decide to live together as a couple. Then there is Chi no hate made, 'To the Ends of the Earth,' which won a literary prize from the Osaka Asahi Shimbun."

I queried inquisitively, "How do you know so much about Japanese gay culture and literature?"

He laughed lightheartedly, "Don't forget, boy, I'm a well-travelled man, and I make it a point to learn as much as possible about different cultures and their histories."

"I want to be like you, sir!" I exclaimed.

He replied, "Aren't you already doing that? You little rascal!" He ruffled my hair affectionately.

"Enlighten us, professor, about nanshoku and wakashudo," the Japanese student pressured.

Gabrielli asked, "How did you know these two words?"

"My sex-education teacher at the Oasis School taught me a little about Japan's homosexual history. I'm curious to know more about my culture."

The learned Italian began, "It is widely known that the Japanese term nanshoku, which can also be read 'danshoku,' means 'male colors.' The second character," he paused and drew a symbol in his notepad that looked like this: 色, "is the word for color. 色 connotes sexual *pleasure in China and Japan. This term was widely used to refer to male–male sex in pre-modern era Japan. The term shudō, abbreviated from wakashudō, means the 'way of adolescent boys' and also has the same connotation. The Japanese danshoku tradition is heavily influenced by China's same-sex love tradition."*

I chimed before my teacher could express, *"I've also been taught by Dr. Henderson that some Chinese emperors have had homosexual relations with handsome adolescent boys."*

My professor declared, *"It is similar to the Arabian tradition in which the two of you are currently involved."* Our educator iterated, *"There are several kinds of same-sex love in historical Japan. I'll go through them one at a time since we have a couple weeks together."*

Monastic Homosexuality

*"Let's begin with the Japanese Buddhist institutions. There is a tradition of open bisexuality and homosexuality among Buddhist monks. Nanshoku relationships inside the monasteries were typically pederastic, somewhat similar to the Greek relationship between the eraste and eromenos (an older mentor and a younger acolyte). The older partner, or nenja (which means 'lover' or 'admirer'), would be a monk, a priest or an abbot. The younger partner, a chigo (*稚児*. 'Acolyte' or 'student'), would be a prepubescent or adolescent boy. Their erotic relationship would dissolve once the boy reached adulthood or left the monastery. Both parties were often encouraged to treat the relationship seriously and conduct the affair honorably. In some cases, the nenja were required to write a formal vow of fidelity. As is often the case, outside the monasteries, monks were considered to have a particular predilection for male prostitutes, and that inspired much ribald humor.*

"Traditionally, there was no religious opposition to homosexuality in Japan in non-Buddhist kami tradition. During the Tokugawa period, some of the Shinto gods, especially those of Hachiman, Myoshin, Shinmei and Tenjin, were known to be the guardian deities of nanshoku (male–male love). One Tokugawa-era writer, Ihara Saikaku, joked that since there are no women for the first three generations in the genealogy of the gods found in the Nihon Shoki, the gods must have enjoyed homosexual relationships — which Saikaku argued was the real origin of nanshoku. Very often, Tokugawa commentators felt free to illustrate the kami engaging in anal sex with one another," Gabrielli explained.

Matumi queried, "Why do the monks still prefer males instead of female prostitutes from outside the monasteries?"

"That's a good question, Matumi." Our teacher expressed, "You must understand that in pre-modern Japan, the Buddhist priesthood and the samurai military caste constructed a vision of the female body as being unattractive, whereas the youthful male body was displayed as a fitting object of aesthetic and sensual appreciation for other men."

I questioned, "Why is homosexuality frowned upon today if Japan has such a long history of man-boy love?"

My professor shook his head. "With the advent of Western influence, Christian explorers, merchants and missionaries from Europe bristled at the ancient Japanese Buddhist traditions, thinking them 'loose' or depraved. They degraded the Japanese for their 'lack of morality' and disapproved of their practices.

"Japan opened to the western world under the threat of American guns during the Meiji restoration of 1867. Western Christian morality dominated Japanese thoughts, and wakashudo and danshoku went into their final eclipse. It was a sad time for this island empire, which *was then filled with open-mindedness towards many different aspects of sexuality,"* he sighed.

I queried, *"What are the differences between Greek pederasty and Japanese nanshuko?"*

My teacher explained, *"Nanshuko is very similar to Greek pederasty. Besides being a sexual relationship between and an adult male and an adolescent male, it is also a relationship based on mentorship. When a young man comes of age, the relationship transforms into a platonic friendship or terminates. This type of relationship does not exclude the love of women. Although a monk does not marry, a Samurai in later years may marry, just as Greek warriors could."*

Matumi and I vociferated in amazement, *"I didn't know Samurai warriors took boys as lovers!"*

Gabrielli shushed us to keep our voices down. He replied, *"That lesson, my young ones, will be for tomorrow's tutorial. For now, your homework, boy, is to write an essay on Buddhism and sex in Japan. You, Matumi, may write about the role of women in Japanese Buddhism."*

On that note, our professor dismissed us. Our morning tutorial was over.

59

Naked Japan

"The old believe everything; the middle-aged suspect everything; the young know everything."

Oscar Wilde

1967

Ginza

Mr. Takashi, Mrs. Misaki Fujikawa and their business associates had been most courteous. True to Japanese tradition, they had arranged a week of non-stop banqueting and entertainment during our stay in the cosmopolitan metropolis.

On our first afternoon, our entourage was spirited away for a fancy French luncheon soiree at a Japanese-French bistro cafe in the heart of the fashionable Ginza district. The difference between a traditional French bistro and a Japanese café is the nationality of the clientele. The majority of customers were fashionably dressed Japanese people in their twenties and thirties. Mrs. Fujikawa referred to them as *'mobos'* and *'mogas'* (short for *modan boi* and *modan garu,* or 'modern boy' and 'modern girl'). Over our delicious French-inspired Japanese cuisine, Misaki and Takashi gave us a summary of traditional and contemporary Japan.

Mr. Fujikawa said to His Highness, *"Ginza is one of the fastest growing commercial districts in Tokyo. It is both a meeting place and a melting pot for wealthy socialites, a place for 'modan boi' and 'modan garu' to socialize, shop, eat and entertain themselves. Our realtor found a couple of strategic venues within the vicinity. We think Carousel will do well here.*

"I've set up a meeting with our venture capitalist group after lunch to discuss the project with your Highness."

Misaki added, *"The streetcars you see outside will be eliminated by year's end, making room for cars and pedestrians only. This area is the hub of all things contemporary, fashionable and arousing in Tokyo."*

Mario proclaimed, *"All the high-end stores and brands are opening in Ginza. This is a boomtown."* He continued, *"The Beatles performed here last year to thousands of overzealous teenagers. An army of Japanese security forces had to keep the peace."*

Gabrielli seconded, *"Not only that, but the Japanese economy is booming, and this new economic growth is unparalleled in the recent history of the West."*

Mr. Fujikawa responded, *"That's because after WWII, we Japanese concentrated our efforts in building our economy to what it is now. The world is buying Japanese-made products, from cars to luxury items. We are redefining consumerism. As a nation, we are also the fastest-growing group of consumers of all things western. My wife and I believe that now is the perfect time to launch Carousel in our cosmopolitan city."*

The prince, the Wazir and Aziz listened attentively to the heated discussion.

The count directed his gaze towards Matumi. *"Tell me, young lady, will you and your teenage friends go to Carousel if we open here?"*

Surprised to be asked her opinion, the Japanese teenager replied after thinking for a brief moment, *"Definitely. I love to dance, and so do my friends. We are always looking for trendy and fashionable venues to spread our wings. We love to dress up and go dancing. It's one of my magical pastimes! And we love all things British and French."*

My professor gave a lighthearted smile before commenting, *"I believe the young know everything. We, middle-aged folks, analyze everything, while the old believe everything. The young have the power to change the world. The Beatles, The Who, The Rolling Stones, Peter, Paul and Mary – they are excellent examples of who have been or are on their way here to perform to maniacal crowds. Japan is the 'Flower Power' of the East."* He lifted his fingers in a *'Make Love not War'* sign.

We laughed at his joviality.

Tamotsu Yato

While P and his business associates and advisors went to their after-lunch Carousel meeting, Mario, Ludovic, Karina, Matumi, Andy and I went a different direction. We headed back to Shinjuku to our hotel. In the Jaguar, Ludovic said, *"There is an exhibition of Tamotsu Yato's photography I'd like to see. The gallery is in the vicinity of our hotel."*

Mario chirped, *"I'd like to go, too."*

"In that case, let's go now," I announced.

Karina asked curiously, *"Who is Tamotsu Yato? What genre of photography is he known for?"*

The gay Muslim answered excitedly, *"He is one of Japan's contemporary gay photographers. His images of macho Japanese men evoke a homoeroticism that is rare in this culture."*

"Even more reason to see his work -- professor Gabrielli has assigned Young and me to write an essay about homosexuality in Japan," Matumi declared.

Mario jumped in, *"Although his work is homoerotic, it is not about Japanese homosexuality. He likes to photograph Japanese bodybuilders in competitions, cultural festivals such as the Hadaka Masuri, and young muscular men masquerading as nude or near-naked Samurais."*

Andy proclaimed, *"Well, let's go see Tamotsu Yato's exhibition now."*

At the Gallery

A crowd of Tamotsu Yato's photography enthusiasts and supporters were crowding the gallery. Most were gay men who came to admire the machismo pictures. Among the throngs of attendees, Mario was the first to spot a group of good-looking male adolescents chatting among themselves. Two were of Japanese nationality, one was Eurasian and the other Caucasian. The Count immediately gravitated towards the group, introducing himself as an admirer of Yato's work and a fashion photographer. He wasted no time in striking up a conversation with them. He inquired, *"Tamotsu's works are exquisite, aren't they?"*

The boys giggled shyly, except for the blond Caucasian, who turned out to be an American exchange student from New Jersey. They were obviously not used to an outgoing, hot-blooded Italian man of the world barging into their private circle.

"Do you like the photographs?" Mario asked.

The blond answered bashfully, *"The men are very masculine and seductive."*

"What men are you referring to? The ones in the photographs or the ones viewing the exhibition?" the Eurasian chimed awkwardly. The group giggled.

The count extended his hand to introduce himself. *"I'm Mario, and these are my friends,"* he said, indicating the entourage standing nearby.

The Caucasian introduced himself as Guy before introducing each of his friends. *"This is Keiko (the Eurasian), Ikio and Edaki (the two Japanese)."*

Andy stared at Keiko as we introduced ourselves to the adolescents. I had a presage that my Valet was attracted to the cute Eurasian. The count took the opportunity to be the group's commentator as we perused the exhibition.

Hadaki Matsuri (Naked Festival)

While we viewed a series of photographs of a crowd of loincloth-covered Japanese men climbing on top of each other, Ludovic commented, *"Japanese men are definitely comfortable being naked in public, judging from these highly energetic pictures."*

Ikio remarked, *"When I was a young lad, my family bathed naked in onsens."* (These were communal indoor bath houses and/or outdoor hot springs). *"During Hadaki Matsuri, we wore only loincloths. Sometimes we were in the nude to compete for rice cakes and treasured trinkets. We are very comfortable in our skin."*

Guy commented, *"My parents had me and my brothers covered up when we were a few years old. It's a taboo to show our nakedness to anybody, especially in public, in our land of the free."*

Keiko added, *"I'm glad my parents live in Japan instead of America. I'm accustomed to the Japanese culture."*

Before I had a chance to speak, my Valet asked, *"What part of you is Japanese?"*

"My mother is Japanese, and dad is from Alabama. I was born here," the boy answered.

"You'll have to show us naked Japan, since you are from this liberal part of the world," Andy flirted.

The Eurasian darted a coy glance at my handsome Valet, obviously loving the attention from this six foot three inch gentleman. *"I'd love to show you more of my liberal country. A good place to start will be at the upcoming Hadaki Matsuri,"* he said as he gave my lover a devilish grin.

"What's a Hadaki Matsuri?" I chirped.

Edaki jumped in with the answer, *"It is a Naked Festival where thousands of men wearing loincloths compete fiercely with one another over sacred sticks, thrown into the crowd by the priest from a window above the temple ground. Anyone who is lucky enough to get hold of the 'shingis' (amulets/talismans) and can thrust them upright into a 'masu' (a wooden measuring box) heaped with rice will be blessed with a year of happiness."*

Ikio added, *"The other lucky charms are bundles of willow strips, and only a hundred of these are thrown to the crowd. It is not easy to catch them. Everyone rushes to snatch a handful. Only the blessed ones are lucky enough to* catch them."

Ludovic asked, *"Where and when is the festival? I'll love to attend and participate. It'll be fun to be in close proximity to all these naked men."*

"The winter festival is next week, and it's held at the Saidaiji Temple in Okayama," the Japanese boy answered.

Ludovic and Mario responded almost simultaneously, *"Fabulous! Will we get a chance to photograph you lads in your full glory? Will you be our guides at the festival?"*

The boys looked abashed by this remark, especially the Japanese in their group. They were not used to such flirtatious forwardness from towering foreigners.

Kanamara Matsuri (Penis Festival)

Karina asked curiously, *"Are there naked females in this festival?"*

Her charge responded, *"For that, you'll have to attend the Kanamara Matsuri."*

Surprised, her big-sister looked at Matumi. *"What's Kanamara Matsuri? When and where is it held?"*

Guy said amusingly, *"It's the 'Penis Festival'. It's held at the Kanamara Shrine in Kawasaki, Kanagawa. You'll have to be here in April for it."*

"What happens at the festival?" Ludovic queried inquisitively.

Edaki explained, *"This is a phallic worshipping festival centered on a penis-venerating shrine. It was once popular among prostitutes who wished to pray for protection against sexually transmitted diseases."*

Ikio venerated, *"It is said that there are other divine protections among their clan – business prosperity, easy delivery, marriage, and married couples' harmony."*

"What happens at the festival?" I questioned.

Guy tweeted excitedly, *"There are hundreds of women running around naked, except for their loincloths. They carry a mikoshi (portable shine) with a humungous phallus on top."*

He furthered, *"If that doesn't make you blush, the spectacle of grandmas and grandpas sucking on carnal candy and sweetmeat replicas of the stupendous phalluses is more than likely to."*

Keiko added with a **mischievous grin,** *"Other attractions include locals carving penises and vaginas out of daikon (radishes), children and young women sitting astride penis-shaped see-saws for good luck and fertility blessings, and a seated banquet in the compound of Kanamara Jinja (aka Wakamiya Hachiman-gu shrine), where the phallic radishes are then auctioned."*

Andy seized the opportunity to dally with the Eurasian: *"You can suck on my daikon anytime or sit on my 'see-saw' for your fertility blessing."*

The months I'd been with my Valet, I had never known him to be so wanton with another. Jealousy crept into my person. I stared at my lover, not knowing what to make of his coquettishness.

Mario, Ludovic and Karina laughed at the comment. The count teased, *"I'll show you boys some 'good-luck' techniques on auctioning off and suckling this daddy's radish."*

The boys' faces turned various shades of red at the suggestive invitations. Mario was sufficiently experienced to vaticinate about the boys' secret desires, even though they professed embarrassment.

As we progressed to the other photo exhibits, I overheard my Valet whispering amorously to Keiko, *"I'd like to get to know you better. Can I meet you alone…?"*

60

A Sacred Path to Enlightenment

"You can be the moon and still be jealous of the stars."

Gary Allan

1967

Jealousy

I wasn't quite myself at tutorials the following morning. Although I did not confront Andy about the twinkie Keiko, I had a nagging feeling of jealousy that wouldn't leave, no matter how hard I reasoned with myself. I kept telling myself that my beloved Andy would never consciously hurt my feelings. He was a gentleman and he loved me. He would never betray my trust, yet I had tossed and turned throughout the night. I was unable to sleep. My Valet slept soundly, as if dreaming of Allah's paradise - *'Round about him will serve boys as handsome as pearls well-guarded' (Koran 52:24).*

My teacher detected something amiss in me. He asked, *"What's the matter, boy? You look so mopey. Are you not well?"*

I lied, *"I'm fine sir. I slept peacefully last night."*

He commented before he began the lesson. *"You're lying. I can detect a liar before he opens his mouth to speak,"* he adulated wryly before starting our lesson on homosexuality in Japan and the love of the samurai.

"As I had mentioned in my previous lesson on the topic of nanshoku and wakashudo, the samurai's erotic life in modern Japan sank below the level of the untouchable to the level of the unmentionable; it was truly 'the love that dared not speak its name.' The fact remains that one of the fundamental aspects of samurai life was the emotional and sexual bond cultivated between an older warrior and a younger apprentice." He turned to me and remarked, *"Much like your relationship with your Valet, their love was founded in education, mentorship and a stalwart code of honor that flourished from the time of the grand master Kobo Daishi.*

"In the world of the nobles and warriors, and in the abbeys of Kyoto and Kamakura, lovers swore perfect and eternal love on their mutual goodwill. Whether they were of noble birth or common, wealthy or poor, their commitments to each other were moved by their spirits, which were never permitted to disappear during this period of Japanese history."

As Gabrielli spoke, I looked into space. Memories of Andy and me came rushing into my mind. My eyes teared up as droplets trickled down my face.

"Why are you crying, young man?" My professor's voice jolted me back to reality.

I blurted. *"I love Andy terribly."*

"I know you do, and he loves you dearly!" the Italian affirmed. *"Why, then, are you crying?"*

"Because, because I'm a stupid, jealous boy!" I declared.

"Now, don't be a silly ninny. Tell me why and what you're jealous of."

Bi-Do (The Beautiful Way)

I did not know how to respond. I didn't want to appear immature, especially when Andy had taught me that immaturity is a weakness. He had reminded me that he loved me because he needed me. I continued to stare at my teacher while tears streamed down my face. He handed me a handkerchief to wipe my face before he continued, *"The bi-do, 'the beautiful way', is the way of the samurai. You, my beautiful boy must remember the basic principle of nanshoku: 'To lay down one's life for another. If it is not so, it becomes a matter of shame.' I know that Andy will follow this samurai principle to a 'T'. Your Valet is a man of honor, and he will not disgrace you in any way. Therefore, my little lost puppy, stop feeling sorry for yourself as if you've been abandoned like Cio-Cio San in Madam Butterfly,"* my professor teased.

"The ancient Japanese, like the ancient Greeks, equated the love between a man and a beardless youth with all that was best in human nature. They saw it as the ideal path and a goal in itself." Gabrielli looked directly at me and voiced, *"Therefore, I assure you, your Valet will not abandon or degrade you in any way. His love for you is unconditional. As Erich Fromm write on his book The Art of Loving, 'He needs you because he loves you.'"*

His words rang true, and he made me feel better. I wondered if I was over-reacting to my lover's flirtation with Keiko. After all, Andy had been gentlemanly enough to allow me to love Oscar. Could I not do the same for him and invite Keiko into our midst? My lover has always desired happiness for me, and this was my opportunity to do the same for him. As soon as this notion entered my head, I felt at ease. My selfish, egotistical 'love' had magically transformed from self-pity to happiness for another. I stood to gain from this mature love, I reasoned. The very moment my thoughts transmuted, I felt grown-up. A smile shone in my soul as I wiped my tears away. Once again, I had driven the green-eyed-monster back into its deceitful lair.

My wise professor gave me a friendly peck before commenting, *"See how easy it is to change your thoughts? The moment you allow unselfish love into your heart, the way you view the world changes. That, my boy, Ihara Saikaku calls 'bi-do', the beautiful way, as was written in his collection of forty short homoerotic stories, 'The Great Mirror of Male Love.'"*

The Flowering

Matumi questioned, *"How did this ancient custom disappear altogether?"*

"A good question, Matumi," our teacher announced. *"I'll give you a little history."* He added, *"Samurai shudo had its early beginnings in the Kamakura period around 1200 AD. It reached its apogee at the beginning of the Tokugawa shogunate in 1603. The history of Japanese male love predated and outlasted the last of the samurai, when Japan became unified and the importance of the warrior class diminished.*

"The Heian (Peace and Tranquility) period (794-1185) was a time of enlightened rule. This era marked the founding of the great imperial capital, Kyoto. It was also the flowering of culture and civic life.

"As Genji Monogatari, the great poet, who lived during this period wrote in the Tale of Genji:

'Well, you, at least, must not abandon me. Genji pulled the boy down beside him. The boy was delighted; such were Genji's youthful charms. Genji, for his part, found the boy more attractive than his chilly sister.'

"My dear students, this prose contains one of the first known allusions to male love, in which a spurned suitor consoles himself with the younger brother of his betrothed."

I questioned, *"Sir, you mentioned in the previous class that Japanese nanshoku practice derived from Chinese homoerotic traditions. Can you expand on that?"*

"Of course, my boy," Gabrielli patted my head before answering, *"In the 1100s, Kukai was mentioned as the father of nanshoku. He was known after his death as Kobo Daishi, 'the great master from Kobo'. He was also the founder of Japanese Vajrayana Buddhism, the esoteric Shingon School, in the year 816 at Mount Koya. He had travelled extensively in China, and upon his return, he received the teachings and dissemination from the Sixth Patriarch, Dàjiàn Huìnéng of Chán (Zen) Buddhism. Apart from his religious and linguistic achievements, Kobo Daishi also translated the sacred texts from Chinese into Japanese. He was the first to devise the Japanese alphabet.*

"Although historians have no basis to credit him with the introduction of male love, legend has it that he learned about the joys of nanshoku in China.

"You see, boy and girl, in ancient times, China was universally renowned for its rich homoerotic tradition. It ranged from the Chinese court's imperial favorites to sanctioned boy-marriages for the commoners. Kukai is known to have brought the practice to Japan. Therefore, Mount Koya became synonymous with shudo, as documented in the poetry and prose of medieval Japan."

I remarked, *"In one of Dr. Henderson's 'China's Homosexuality' classes, he mentioned that boys played female roles in classical Chinese operas, among them Dieyi and Xiaolou of the famous Peking Opera. Did the Japanese also borrow this tradition from the Chinese?"*

"Ahh Hah! A clever question. In traditional Kabuki and Noh plays, boys are also known to play female roles. As in Chinese opera, the bond between the dominant male actor and the boy who plays the feminine role often becomes inseparable. Therefore, wakashudo relationships thrived in the theatre." He continued, *"Young, you must*

understand that the history of Japan through the end of the sixteenth century was one of warring feudal lords. With the ascendance of the Tokugawa Teyasu to the shogunate in 1003, the fighting came to an end. Then, the country entered a period of peace and tranquility that lasted for two hundred and fifty years. One of the effects of this pacification was the decline in the power and influence of the warrior class; in other words, the samurai class evaporated. The bourgeoisie flourished under this new stability. They adopted many customs and practices that were once the exclusive domain of the samurai. Fighting techniques were transformed into martial arts like judo, karate, kyudo and kendo, to name a few.

"Shudo gave way to a culture of travelling boy actors whose favors were vied for, or, in many cases, bought by hordes of admiring dandies. The public display of wakashudo fans caused such a commotion that laws were passed to restrict the haircuts and costumes of the boy actors so as not to over-inflame the passions of the audience. It was during this period that boy brothels became common features in pleasure districts within the larger towns and cities. Sadly, the currency of nanshoku morphed from honor and 'giri' (duty) to gold and silver. Towards the end of the eighteenth century, the 'kegema' (boy actors) dressed themselves as girls, while in the Genroku period they had dressed and presented themselves as beautifully graceful young men. This transmutation indicated the serious degeneration of the wakashuko tradition."

The Italian shook his head before continuing, "Unfortunately, this dispositional shift brought about the decline and disappearance of the age-old socially sanctioned male love in this great empire." He pronounced, "This turn of events mirrors the decline and eventual fall of Greco-Roman pederasty. Male love lost its identification with the warrior ethic and pedagogic ideals. With it, the *fiber of moral foundations crumpled under the weight of commercialized decadence and abuses. The reaction to those excesses solidified an anti-erotic, utilitarian view of nanshoku sexuality."*

The Decline

The Japanese female queried, *"Sir, you mentioned in our last class that the advent of western influence played a role as well. Can you enlighten us?"*

"Of course I will, my dear," Gabrielli stated. *"From the very first contact of European explorers and western merchants with this remote island empire, the foreigners had lambasted their host's country's 'immorality' and 'depravity'. With the influx of Christian missionaries came more support of those who disapproved of male love practices. The straw that broke the camel's back was that of the Meiji restoration. As a result, Japan threw its doors wide open to the West and Western influence. Western Christian morals rapidly dominated Japanese thought. That was the final eclipse of wakashudo."* With a glimmer of hope, our teacher acknowledged, *"Since the dawn of the Age of Aquarius, a new generation of Japanese are embracing the freedom of speech and action. I hope that freedom and tolerance will revive what has been degraded and restore a once-honorable and revered ancient form of noble love as one of many sacred paths to enlightenment."*

With that closing statement, our professor inquired about the progress of our individual homework assignments.

Mentorship

When it was my turn, my learned teacher clasped both my hands. He said, *"Young man, remember, you are a bright shining moon among many twinkling stars. The most beautiful moon can still be jealous of the sparkling stars.*

"Jealousy is the fear of comparison. Who are you comparing yourself to? It should be no one except yourself, because you are intelligent, smart and a cut above the rest. For that reason, you were selected to be in E.R.O.S. No one can take away that self-assurance except you. My handsome boy, jealousy is clawing away at who you truly are. Trust, believe and have faith in your Valet; he's in your life because he loves you. Never confuse lust with love. If you allow yourself to be belittled, your integrity will topple like the great civilization I've just mentioned."

61

Lusting After Love

"Keep love in your heart. A life without it is like a sunless garden when the flowers are dead."

Oscar Wilde

1967

At Budokan

This imposing octagonal structure located in the center of Tokyo was built for the 1964 Summer Olympics judo competition. At any given event, it holds up to 14,200 people. That afternoon, thousands of Japanese fashionistas, international fashion journalists, photographers, buyers, models, fashion trade personals and fans turned out en masse to witness one of Britain's first ever 'supermodels' (though the word supermodel had not even been invented) gracing the Tokyo catwalk. She was none other than 'the' Lesley Hornby, better known throughout the world as Twiggy.

Earlier that afternoon, her manager and boyfriend, Justin Villeneuve, who was previously her hairdresser and known as Nigel Davies, had organized a press conference for his now-famous muse. Hundreds of hysterical fans lined the main Budokan entrance, hoping to catch the petite five foot six inch fashion celebrity for a personal autograph and possibly a handshake.

The count, Andy and I were already stationed inside the conference room where the press interview was being conducted. Mario, being a prominent photographer, had a front-row seat while Andy and I sat behind the Italian Count.

As the gamine model discussed her role as England's fashion ambassador to Japan and promoted her latest fashion line to Japanese consumers, I noticed Andy's side glances at me. Before long, he whispered, *"We need to talk. You've been behaving very strangely since we left Tamotsu Yato's exhibition yesterday. Tell me what is bothering you."*

"Nothing is bothering me. I just want you to be happy," I murmured.

"You're definitely hiding something. That last comment of yours gave you away," my Valet countered.

"What comment?" I pretended not to know what he was talking about.

He gripped my wrist and led us out of the conference room. Startled, I followed. I had no idea where he was ushering me. He sat me down by a quiet corridor as soon as we were out of the meeting room. He demanded, *"You, young man better be honest with me and confess what's eating at you. I know you sufficiently to detect that something is not right. Time to confess, boy!"*

I stared adoringly at my lover before bursting into tears. *"I'm a silly, vacuous person. I don't deserve your love,"* I cried.

Andy pulled me to him and patted my head. I leaned against his musculature. *"Shush! Don't be a nincompoop. Tell me who's been bullying you or what is eating at you,"* he urged.

"Nobody is bullying me. I'm jealous of Keiko," I burbled.

He stared at me, *"Why on earth are you jealous of Keiko? You don't know the boy. We've met him for an hour and half, and you are jealous? Why?"*

Andy held me tightly against his chest as I continued to weep. My Valet didn't take long to figure out the reason. *"You are truly a doltish little puppy!"* He reprimanded skittishly before he continued, *"You think I'm going to leave you for Keiko because I flirted with him?"* he questioned amusedly.

I nodded. I dared not look at my lover. He lifted my chin to his face. He said as he wiped the tears from my face, *"You, my beloved angel, must have faith in me. I love you and I need you."* He paused before he added, *"I do find the Eurasian attractive and would like to bed him, if the opportunity arises. That doesn't mean I don't love you. In fact, I have every intention to involve you in the equation. If I'm to do anything with Keiko, you will be the first to know."*

Before I could utter a word, my lover questioned, *"Do you like Keiko?"*

I nodded guiltily. *"Would you like us to have a three-way with him?"* he asked.

I did not reply but gave Andy a mischievous grin. My lover bent down to kiss me. My groin began to stir from the attention he was showering upon me. We continued to kiss affectionately. I felt his manhood growing beneath his pants. After an extension of time, my Valet finally released his grasp. He held my hand and directed us towards the men's room. As soon as we entered, he locked the door and pulled me to him. He kissed me urgently as I surrendered to his control. Prying my mouth open, he drove his alluring tongue into my mouth. His pressing imperativeness drove us wild with desire. We couldn't wait to unfasten each other's trousers, letting them drop to our ankles as we continued to French kiss. Andy reached behind my backside and tore apart the cotton fabric of my underwear. With his strong hands, he cupped my tantalizing smoothness before spreading my butt cheeks apart. My inamorato stuck a couple of his fingers into my mouth to suckle. I coated them with my saliva. Teasing my opening with my wetness, he thrust them into my quivering orifice while his tongue continued to probe my longing oral crevice. We tore at each other's shirts, discarding them as fast as we could. We had only our trousers, straggling at our ankles, left.

    I was more than ready to receive his masculinity when my chaperone turned me around to spit into my tunnel. His hardness throbbed uncontrollably between his heaving pelvis. Bending me against the stucco, he jabbed his tongue ferociously at my bulls-eye. Droplets of saliva dripped from my slit. I longed for his pounding thickness as I relished his lapping tongue around the gateway to my paradise. Andy's love-making never ceased to taunt my person. No man aroused me as much as my guardian.

    I basked in his amorous anilingus as he plunged his tongue deep into my hollow. I heaved in joyous anticipation as his stiffness bobbed vigorously against my derriere. I turned to suckle his bubulousness down my yearning throat, inhaling the scent of his pubic masculinity with treasured affection. I nursed his pulsating manliness to heights of tempestuous ecstasy. Soon, his precum trickled down the side of my lips. He could no longer starve off his excitement. Lifting me to a standing position, he flipped me around, and with a single stroke, he plunged his stiffness into my core. We kissed furiously as if this were our last moment of oneness. I surrendered to my Andy, my Valet, my mentor, my chaperone and my cherished lover. Our unified wholeness served only to elevate our emotional bond as our gyrating motions propelled us to the inevitable. So too did our spiritual correlations shackle us to our mutual destiny in this lifetime. I felt like the earth, he the seed; together, we co-created the tree of life. Together, we flourished and grew as my lover poured his deposits into the depths of my being. His abundance gave nourishment for me to thrive as a man of substance, but most ardently, his germination transformed me from a mere lad to a man of unconditional love.

Before long his savage exertions gave way to precipitous moans and subsiding groans. I, filled with dexterity, was ready to savor the residue of his sentiments. I suckled his receding organ like a baby needing feed as I jerked my member furiously. Like a connoisseur of fine liqueur, I scooped his delicious remains into my mouth, drinking the remnants of his precious delivery. I savored the last drop of his superiority from my overflowing pit while relinquishing my priceless emissions into Andy's adoring mouth. Unwilling to abandon our passionate embrace we pleasured every crevice of our precious amorousness. We were rooted in love and at one with the universe. Unless we unanimously allowed another into our circle of equanimity, no one could come between me and my lover, we vowed.

Where Were You?

By the time we returned to the conference hall, Twiggy's entourage had departed. Mario was packing his equipment when he saw us enter. *"Where in the world have you been? I was looking for assistance, but the two of you were nowhere to be found,"* he demanded.

We look flustered and apologized profusely. The count looked at us smugly. *"Where were you when I needed your help? You audacious brutes!"* he questioned sarcastically, giving us a nefarious smirk.

I stared at the floor, embarrassed, when Andy replied, *"We had some urgent business to take care of in the men's room."*

The photographer gave us a sly Cheshire grin. *"What kind of urgent business did the two of you have to take care of in the men's room?"* he asked. *"You should have informed me so I could also lend a helping hand,"* he quipped teasingly before adding, *"We'd better hurry into the stadium before the show starts."*

I jumped in with a question, *"When are you scheduled to shoot Twiggy? I didn't have a chance to get her autograph."*

Mario responded, *"She is fully booked with appearances to promote her fashion line. I've scheduled with Justin to photograph her at the Meiji-jingu in the next couple of days. You boys will have to get up at the crack of dawn so we can start the shoot at first light, before the tourists descend to the famous shrine. If they discover I'm doing a fashion shoot with Twiggy, a riot of fans will descend on the venue. We do not want that to happen, do we?"*

"Yes, sir! I will be up at the crack of dawn and ready at your beck and call," I announced. Andy did not look too happy. He did not like the idea of waking up early to assist in a fashion shoot. He said nothing as we proceeded into the martial arts stadium to watch the gamine model parade in her latest mini-garb and embroidered kimonos in front of a hall filled with screaming fans.

At Ukai Toriyama

It was six P.M. by the time we returned to the Hilton. A message was waiting for me at our suite. Gabrielli had left a note for me on behalf of His Highness. It read:

Be at the hotel lobby at seven thirty P.M. sharp.
P

After a quick shower and a fresh change of clothes, Andy and I rushed to the lobby, only to find Matumi,

Karina, Ikram, his three handlers, Ludovic, Gabrielli, Thabit and Aziz. They were waiting for the prince, his girlfriend Anastasie, Bryanna and a mystery guest to join us.

Six glimmering vehicles dropped our entourage at a Japanese traditional *gasshokuzukuri*-style building located in a valley behind Mount Takao. This historic restaurant and teahouse boasted an extensive garden and separate *sukiyazukuri* (private dining rooms). That evening, Mr. and Mrs. Fujikawa hosted a lavish *kaiseki* (Japanese banquet) in honor of prince P and his entourage at Ukai Toriyama. The Japanese couple had brought along their good-looking son, Takioko, who had recently graduated from Harvard Law School. He had just returned from New York City after working in the metropolis for a year. Now, under his father's guidance, he was ready to join his parents' venture capitalist business as a junior law and business advisor.

Over the extensive meal, Takioko, seated next to Andy and me, commented, *"During the summer, this tea house is 'the' place to visit. Every year, Ukai Toriyama organizes a firefly hunt."*

I inquired curiously, *"What happens at a firefly hunt?"*

The Japanese man, similar in age to His Highness, answered, *"The restaurant switches off all the lights so customers can watch the abundance of graceful fireflies dance within the vicinity of this garden sanctuary while savoring the restaurant's gourmet cuisine. A special menu is prepared by their chefs for this once-in-a-lifetime experience. The sparkling view is breathtaking, like a magical painting come to life."*

My Valet chimed, *"When does firefly season begin and end?"*

The lawyer replied, *"It starts in May and can last until mid-August. You guys should come back for this spectacular experience. I'll be happy to show you my captivating country. Besides, when Carousel opens in Tokyo, I'm sure I'll see more of you and the prince."*

Andy remarked, *"We'll be with His Highness for another week and half before we leave for our winter holiday. Young and I are foreign exchange students sent by our school to experience life in the Middle East. We may return to help with Carousel if the prince requests Young's assistance. I am his chaperone and 'big brother'. I make sure he stays out of trouble."*

"What kind of trouble is he staying out of?" Takioko jested before he added, *"Naughty trouble?"*

Andy responded, *"Boy oh boy! You have no idea what this boy can get himself into."*

"I was naughty when I was his age," Takioko said as he gave my chaperone and me a crafty smile. *"I still like to be naughty at times. What kind of naughty things is he capable of?"* he commented flirtatiously.

My guardian gave him a devilish wink and smiled, saying nothing.

Meanwhile, seated between Anastasie and Bryanna at the far end of the table, P's mysterious guest shot me the occasional glance when he thought I wasn't looking.

62

The Tea Room

"When he raises his eyelids, it's as if he is taking off all my clothes."

Bernard Tristan Foong

1967

Carousel Venues

For the next day or two, our entourage trooped off to visit potential Carousel sites that Mr. and Mrs. Fujikawa's realtors had arranged for us to view. The area that impressed the count, Ikram, Ludovic and me was then known as Jingu-mae. It included Harajuku Station to Aoyama Street, as well as Takeshita-machi, Onden blocks 1 to 3, and Harajuku blocks 1 to 3. These were within the larger area of Shibuya Ward. Back in 1964, the Tokyo Olympics had been held in the neighboring Yoyogi National Gymnasium.

Towards the end of the 1960s, the fashion-obsessed youth culture was beginning to transition from Shinjuku to Harajuku before moving to Shibuya. New shopping malls and boutiques popped up constantly. These shops sold quirky clothing, accessories, household furniture and trendy interior decorating items. 'Palais France' was being constructed on Meiji Street towards the exit of Takeshita Street. A few years later, Togo Shrine was established as the au courant must-visit store, on a par with London's modish Biba department store on Kensington High Street. Harajuku was fast gaining a reputation as the center of unconventional fashion as well as innovation. When the realtor took us to a spacious old warehouse, Mario, Ikram, Bryanna and I had already made our space selection. Gabrielli, being the prince's financial consultant liked the idea of the property and its price. It was less costly and larger than the Ginza commercial venues. This facility was set in the midst of Tokyo's up-and-coming commercial sector. The shrewd Italian businessman was convinced that the financial investment was justifiable for Carousel. *"It is a perfect venue for a dance club set to attract the international party for wild nights on the town,"* Mario declared.

It was also close to Yoyogi Park, where voguish teenagers were already making this recreational park into a Sunday rock-and-roll dance thoroughfare. This was their regular open-air Sunday dance club, soon to be a tourist attraction where the energetic youth culture would explode. *"A place where everyone can dance the day away, as long as their exhaustion has not already overtaken them from the night before at Carousel,"* said the transsexual Bryanna.

Preparation for the Tea Ceremony

On Mr. Takashi and Mrs. Misaki's suggestion, our entourage headed to a traditional Japanese Tea House. Our six-car convoy arrived at a charming *sukiya (*sukiya is a classical form of Japanese architecture that blends with nature) style *chashitsu* (Tea Room) or *chaseki* (place for tea).

These free-standing structures were designed exclusively for private tea ceremonies and commercial tea gatherings. The series of wooden *chashitsu* were located within a beautiful landscaped garden, where visitors could stroll on the *roji* (garden pathway) that led to tranquil gardens. Tatami mats covered the indoor areas. A *furo* (sunken hearth) was situated within the *chaseki* for the host to sit in front of to prepare tea.

Our entourage arrived a little before the appointed time for the autumn *chaji* (season). Upon entering the waiting room, we were ushered in gracefully by several beautiful geishas clad in elaborate kimonos who asked us to leave our coats, jackets, shoes and other personal belongings for safe keeping, before proceeding into the main tea ceremonial area. Each of us was allocated a set of comfortable silk kimono, a *hakama* (a long divided or undivided skirt worn over the long-sleeved kimono), an *obi* (sash), a *kaishi* (small piece of silk cloth to be tucked into the breast of the kimono), a pair of white *tabi* (divided-toe socks) and a fan (to be tucked into the obi).

During the ceremony, certain motions are intended to move the long kimono sleeves out of the way to prevent them from soiling when serving or partaking of tea. The kimono sleeves also function as hidden pockets where used kaishi are folded and placed. The women did not wear hakamas. Our kimonos and hakamas were later gifted to us as mementoes by the proprietor of the chashitsu. The wearing of kimonos is very much a part of the tea ceremony.

Our host and hostess donned *montsuki kimonos,* specially embroidered with their family crests on the sleeves and at the back of each garment.

Two elegant Japanese calligraphy scrolls hung above a *tokonoma* (an alcove), describing the autumn *chaji*. We were each served a cup of hot water, kombu tea and *sakurayu* (roasted barley tea) while waiting on wooden benches in the roji until summoned by our hosts to enter the chaseki.

Tea Ceremony Etiquettes

When the geishas invited us to enter, we exchanged silent bows with the Fujikawas (our hosts) before proceeding in an orderly fashion to wash our hands and rinse our mouths with water in a stone basin. This was a traditional purifying ritual before the tea ceremony was to begin. When Andy and I arrived to bow to Takioko, the Japanese gave us a seductive wink. He was obviously playing a flirtatious game to see how we would respond to his advances.

As we removed our footwear to enter the chaseki by 'crawling-in' through a *nijiri-guchi* (small door), Takioko held out his hand to assist me through. When no one was looking, he held my hand to his lips and kissed my fingers before letting go, in case somebody noticed. He did the same to Andy.

Once we were *seiza* (kneeling) comfortably in the cozy chamber, I was sandwiched between Takioko on my left and the mystery guest on my right – the one who had joined our entourage the day before. His Highness had not introduced the Arab to either one of us. My guardian, situated next to Takioko, extended his hand to introduce us to the Arabian stranger.

The Fall

Before any of us had a chance to speak, Mr. Takashi voiced, *"We are delighted to share tea with all of you. As is Japanese custom, before we begin the tea ceremony, let me explain my country's tea ceremonial etiquette. The calligraphy scrolls above the tokonoma and the other items are part of our tea ceremony."*

Mrs. Masaki added, *"These scrolls were written by a famous Japanese calligrapher and a renowned Buddhist monk. The one on the left speaks of the beauty of two lovers strolling under the golden orange maple trees set within these very chashitsu gardens during the autumnal season.*

"The scroll on the right is a famous Buddhist poem describing the glorious beauty of this chaseki autumn landscape."

As the couple continued to explain the *wakeiseijaku* (harmony, respect, purity and tranquility) of the calligraphy, a hand brushed against the right side of my kimonoed thigh. Tantalized by a whiff of lemony patchouli, I drew closer to the handsome Arab. Our proximity stirred in me a newfound eroticism, too irresistible to ignore. His occasional glances and his roguish grin sent goosebumps over my skin. I felt like he was lustfully disrobing me every time he raised his eyelids to steal secret glimpses at me. My loins stirred to this mysterious attention. He continued to rest his palm by the side of my thigh as he slyly exerted pressure to see if I would move away; I didn't dare move a muscle. I behaved as if nothing unusual was happening, when in truth, my organ was throbbing excitedly beneath my *hakama* to his stimulation. I pretended to listen attentively to Mrs. Fujikawa but did not hear her.

She soon turned towards the elegant floral arrangement placed in the middle of the low table. She elucidated, *"Chabana (tea flower) is a simple floral arrangement style used in many tea ceremonies. This type of 'free-form' floral arrangement was used by early tea masters. Chabana is said to have been championed by Sen no Rikyū. According to his teachings, 'Chabana gives the viewer an impression of flowers growing naturally outdoors.' Therefore, artificial hanaire (vases/containers) are never used in this kind of arrangement."* As she continued her commentary, another hand inched against my derriere from my left. I was sure that both the hands were testing my reaction. Arousing shivers ran up and down my spine from these erotic evocations, yet I knelt immobile, as if nothing extraordinary was happening. My mind played havoc on my person.

Suddenly, I flashed back to my childhood, remembering when my father enrolled me in Mr. Chen's karate class at the Kuala Lumpur's Chin Woo stadium. Philip, the handsome Caucasian teaching assistant, was leaning against my quivering body, holding my boyish hand to his. He was demonstrating a karate chop to me. I could smell his masculinity. As much as I longed for him to kiss me passionately, I was afraid. He backed away suddenly, as if frightened of his own emotions. He quickly released his grip on my adolescent hands. My heart pounded then like it was pounding now. I wanted Philip to embrace me, to love me and to make love to me. He did not.

From that moment forward, the scent of his virility lingered in me. I craved for his closeness, yet he avoided eye contact. I knew in my heart he secretly desired me. I felt his lustful eyes boring at my nakedness beneath my karate garb when he thought I wasn't paying attention. It was happening all over again with this mystery man and Takioko.

The hands had inched closer from either side while I was lost in reverie. I had to excuse myself to the men's room to recover from this psychological incursion. I needed to lock myself in a toilet stall to wait for my bobbing hardness to subside.

Placing my closed fist on the tatami I pushed myself backwards, rising from my kneeling seiza position. I shuffled quietly out of the chashitsu so I wouldn't cause any unnecessary disturbance to the attendees who were absorbed in Mrs. Masaki's commentary. Suddenly, a loud bang was heard by everyone. I had slipped and landed excruciatingly backwards. My soleless socks and my constricted garb had restricted my stride on the slippery floor. All eyes were on me, as if a clumsy meteorite had plummeted into the room.

When Andy, Mario, Gabrielli and the mystery man rushed to my rescue, my head was spinning round and round with stars and circling moons. It took me sometime to regain my bearing. Mario laid me on my back. A sharp pain ran up and down my spine, and my body was hurting badly from the fall.

The mysterious person who until then had teased my person turned out to be a highly qualified doctor. He said pressingly, *"Don't sit up. I'll roll you on your stomach to examine your spine."*

The physician undressed me carefully for examination. After tapping and pressing his nimble fingers on my back, he announced, *"Thank goodness, nothing is broken. Is there a mattress I can lay the boy on?"* he queried.

"Yes, in the adjoining building. There are private rooms where he can lie comfortably," the chashitsu's proprietor replied.

Mario, Gabrielli, my Valet and the physician carried me on an emergency stretcher to a private chamber across the garden. As soon as I was on the mattress, Andy held my hand while the doctor continued to examine me. Mario and Gabrielli had returned to the chaseki to inform the others that apart from suffering a minor concussion and a few bruises, I was otherwise all right. The tea ceremony should continue.

The Doctor

My guardian and I were left with the handsome physician. We were finally able to get to know him better. Doctor Fahrib was a longtime friend and ally of the prince. They had been pals since they were students at Islamic

School and had kept in touch through their university years. Whenever they could get away from their busy schedules, they would visit each other to rekindle their friendship. He, being his father's favorite son, was bestowed the title of Sheik Abdul Mutmud bin Fahrib by his father, Sheik Mustafar, in the event of the elder sheik's demise. The MD would then become the leader of his tribe.

Sharjah was once an important trade route to India. The British sovereignty had bestowed the title of a 'salute state' on this settlement. With the discovery of oil, this thriving port had continued to prosper, allowing Fahrib's ancestral family to garner more wealth than they could spend. Many of Sheik Fahrib's twelve male and six female siblings from his father's wives had gone on to higher education abroad. Several of his sisters had married into wealthy and influential families, and so had a few of his brothers. They had strong marital ties with royalties from neighboring principalities and ruling families.

The intelligent Arab doctor had applied his learned skills to improve his homeland's medical facilities, creating hospitals and health care provisions for its citizens. Under family pressure, he had married a girl from a prominent family in Yemen, producing two heirs before taking a second wife. He had thought a second wife would make his life more bearable, as the first marriage was an unhappy union. Unfortunately, the two women did not often see eye to eye. Their jealously of their attractive husband caused much uneasiness in the Fahrib household. In order to avoid his wives' bickering and family squabbles, he poured all of his energy into his medical projects.

Unlike his father and some of his male siblings, who had accumulated their individual harems, this honorable doctor could not allow himself to amass his own. Throughout our conversation, I detected the sheik's loneliness. Most importantly, I felt that he was running from himself, from a sexuality he had not come to terms with. He desired to be loved by someone who would reciprocate his benevolent generosity – that special someone who would hold similar beliefs to his.

P had persuaded him to join our Carousel entourage in hope that he would invest. So the sheik had formulated an excuse to travel to Japan to attend some medical seminar. In reality, he had enjoyed P's company since childhood, and today, little did His Highness suspect, his handsome pal was secretly in love with him. The well-traveled surgeon desired a male companion as worldly and sophisticated as he.

A few months later, I learned that he prayed diligently to Allah five times per day for the opportunity to forge a unified man-to-man relationship and friendship that would last many lifetimes. I thought of Alexander the Great and his and long-time companion, Hephaestion.

63

From Kenzo, Yogji, Kansei to Hanae

"If you have zest and enthusiasm, you attract zest and enthusiasm. Life does give back in kind."

Norman Vincent Peale

Beginning May 2013

It had been a while since I last heard from Dr. Arius. I sent him an email.
Hello Dr. A.S.,
It's been a month since I wrote. I hope you are doing well and recovering speedily from your cancer treatment. Are you back to your regular routine and catching up with your many projects? When you have a chance, drop me a line. I miss our regular correspondence, and I look forward to hearing from you soon.
Best Wishes!
Young.

1967

Tokyo Hilton

After our regular tutorial with Professor Gabrielli, I handed him the paper I had written on *Buddhism and Sex in*

Japan. He replied, *"Judging from this stack of paper, I believe you've outdone yourself again. I hope you've included your personal perspective on the subject. I like my students to form their own frame of reference instead of giving me an essay based solely on historical citations."*

I answered smilingly, *"I hope you like my comments, sir."*

He ruffled my hair, *"You've always been a crafty little devil. I don't expect anything less from students who are handpicked by E.R.O.S. I'm sure Matumi has her own viewpoint on Women in Japanese Buddhism, too."* He gave her an eloquent glance. She nodded cheerfully.

Our teacher continued, *"I'll have these essays back to you in a day or two. Then, we'll have an open discussion of the topics.*

"For now, the two of you had better run along to see the Count. He wants to take you on a field trip to visit several Japanese fashion designers and the Bunka Fukuso Gakuin."

I burst out in jubilation, *"We are visiting the Bunka Fukuso Gakuin? It's been one of my childhood dreams. That's amazing!"*

"You, young man, are so spirited. Your passion is so contagious, it's difficult not to be stirred by your exuberance." He gave my cheek a peck. *"Now go, before I give you a writing assignment on the Bunka Fukuso Gakuin."*

"That would be right up my alley, professor!" I chimed before disappearing from his chamber to meet Count Mario, while Matumi scratched her head, wondering what in the world Bunka Fukuso Gakuin was.

A Brief Japanese Fashion History

On our way to Bunka Fukuso Gakuin, Mario, the fashion wizard, asked Karina, Matumi, Andy and me, *"Do you know what Bunka Fukuso Gakuin means?"*

I couldn't wait to answer that question. *"Everybody knows what Bunka Fukuso Gakuin is,"* I declared.

The three passengers sitting beside Mario stared at me as if I'd gone bonkers. Karina chimed, *"I have no idea what Bunka Fukuso Gakuin is!"* Andy and Matumi nodded.

I cried emphatically, *"How can you not know Bunka Fukuso Gakuin? It's the most famous fashion college in Japan, otherwise known as the Bunka Fashion College."*

The Italian gave me a thumbs-up, nudging me to continue. *"Besides being a famous fashion institution, it also produced So-en, the first Japanese fashion magazine to be launched in this country.*

"I fell in love with So-en when assisting my cousin and aunty in their sewing and garment-making projects when I was six years old. I translated some of the magazine's designs to my own creations. So-en was my fashion bible until I went to England."

The group laughed at my animated gusto. Andy curbed me as I bobbed up and down from my seat. He uttered gleefully, *"Calm down, boy! You get yourself so worked up whenever we have a conversation about fashion. I've seen pictures of you dressed in your self-designed garb at age 12. You look like a fairy in those head-to-toe matching outfits."*

"What do you expect from a future fashion designer? He has to dress the part, don't you boy?" the Count teased before he added, *"Since we are visiting the new wave of Japanese fashion designers, I'd better fill you in with a brief fashion history of this exotic country."*

"Yes, please!" I tweeted exuberantly. The rest of our group had little choice but to listen, especially Andy, who came along because he was my guardian.

The photographer began, *"After World War II, starting in the late 1940s through to the 1950s, the Japanese copied Parisian and American styles of dress. When Christian Dior debuted Dior's New Look in 1947, Japanese women caught onto the trend.*

"Back in those days, when overseas travel was still out of the question for the average Japanese, Western movies became a major fashion inspiration. Films made popular by Audrey Hepburn, such as 'Sabrina' and 'Roman Holiday', solidified American and European styles of dress in the eyes of young Japanese females. Not to mention, Elvis Presley in 'Blue Hawaii' and a host of other American productions had Japanese males donning Hawaiian Aloha print shirts, goofy printed T-shirts, dark sunglasses and slicked-back Teddy boy hairdos. Japanese women were seen wearing colorfully patterned short pants, flip-flops and espadrilles in the summer."

I couldn't wait to add my commentary before the fashion arbiter could continue. *"In the early 1960s, ready-to-wear changed the way we dress."*

Mario remarked, *"'Puretaporute' was the term Japanese consumers used to refer to the French 'prêt-à-porter', which ushered in the era of casual dress."*

I poured the little fashion knowledge I knew out to my fellow compatriots. *"The queen of miniskirts, Mary Quant, created a must-have trend. Need I even mention the famous Twiggy, who just yesterday caused such a hysteria at Budokan Hall. That is the effect that ready-to-wear has on young people like us."* I preened at my fashion knowledge before announcing, *"Andy and I are assisting the famous photographer in our midst (I looked at Mario) when he photographs Twiggy tomorrow."*

My Valet didn't seem too excited to be reminded that he had to get up at the crack of dawn to assist in a fashion shoot. If Andy had his way, he'd sleep in. Unfortunately, my beloved was responsible for his charge.

He had no choice but to tag along with the Count and me to Meiji Jingū.

Bunka Fukuso Gakuin

We were met by the school's dean and a senior staff member, Ms. Mariko. After formal introductions, the dean handed us to Ms. Mariko for a tour of the campus. She introduced our group to some of their current and former students' work.

During the tour, she gave us a brief history of this renowned fashion establishment. *"Bunka Fashion College was founded in 1919 as a dressmaking school for girls. It was then known as the Namiki Dressmaking School. Our school became Bunka Fashion College in 1936 as we began publishing Japan's first fashion magazine, So-en."*

I couldn't wait to declare that many of my early fashion designs were influenced by So-en magazines. She looked at me smilingly, *"Young man, you must apply to our college. One of our outstanding male alumni is currently working in Paris."*

Mario asked, *"Who is he? Maybe when I'm in Pari, I can interview him."*

Ms. Mariko answered, *"His name is Kenzo Takada. Have you heard of him? He was one of our first male graduates after men were allowed entry in 1957. In 1960, he won the school's prestigious So-en prize and began working for Sanai department store as their girl's clothing designer. He moved to Paris in 1964. He did not speak French and had little money, but he managed to do some sketches for Courreges and also for Louis Feraud. He is currently working for the Pisanti Textile Group and Relations Textile."*

The Count added, *"So it's the story of the struggling artist. I'd definitely like to see his work and possibly interview him in the future."*

The senior professor stated, *"Although several of our graduates have displayed their work in the Paris Collections, it's not easy for outsiders to enter the Parisian haute couture world.*

"The latest news I have of Kenzo is that he's planning to open 'Jungle Jap'' a new boutique at Gallerie Vivienne, in a former antique clothing shop."

"I'll call on him when I'm next in Paris," Mario replied.

Mariko asserted, *"I'm sure he'll love to hear from you. Meanwhile, there are a couple of outstanding students I'll like to introduce you to. Let's proceed to the design studio."*

The Design Studio

A group of fashion students were already hard at work in the studio. Several were doing flat pattern construction while others were draping and pinning toiles onto dress forms.

The fashion professor approached a student whom she introduced as Mr. Yogji Yamamoto. I, never having been inside a fashion school, was hypnotized by all the inner workings of the design studio. I was fascinated by the students' fantastic creations. I stared spellbound as Mr. Yamamoto pinned and draped a large piece of black fabric around and away from the dummy, chopping and cutting away what seemed like holes and openings, here and there. I had never seen anything resembling such pattern construction. This kind of innovative draping was completely foreign to me. My young mind absorbed every detail of the workroom that day. Andy brought me back to reality when he tapped my shoulder and said, *"Young, you seem to have gone to another world. You've been staring at Mr. Yamamoto's draping and snipping as if you've witnessed a ghostly apparition."*

Before I could fully return to my senses, Ms. Mariko was at our side, introducing Mr. Yamamoto's work to us. Since the designer did not speak English, his teacher did all the talking. *"Yogji is one of our outstanding students. He has a knack for taking a piece of fabric and twisting and turning it into wearable art. He joined us after graduating from Keio University in law. Since he's been at Bunka, he has practically transformed the way we think of pattern construction. His is an avant-garde approach to draping."*

Mario exclaimed, *"I'd love to photograph his work. I'm doing a fashion shoot tomorrow at Meiji Jingū. Will he have a mini collection available for me to photograph by tomorrow?"*

The teacher replied, *"That's splendid! I'll have a few pieces from his collection sent to your hotel before tomorrow."*

As we moved to watch another student at work, Ms. Mariko voiced, *"This is Mr. Kansai Yamamoto. He designs amazing embroidery, often translating his designs onto casual zipper jackets and anoraks. Isn't his work stunning?"* The fashion professor reiterated, *"He's another one of our outstanding students who, after studying civil engineering and English at Nippon University, enrolled at Bunka. This is his final year at the school. We are sad to see him leave, but I know he'll do well in Paris."* Kansai turned and gave us a smile. He did not utter a word but allowed his teacher to continue her introduction of his work.

I was spellbound by the creativity in the room. I assured myself that I would definitely attend fashion school to study all aspects of fashion when I left Daltonbury Hall. My destiny was presented in front of me, and nothing would come between me and fashion. I vowed to myself that I would live and breathe fashion in my lifetime.

By the time we left Bunka Fukuso Gakuin, the Count had already made arrangements for the school to deliver several racks of garments for our shoot tomorrow. I was awe-struck as I visited the various Japanese fashion establishments and learned firsthand the inner workings of the international fashion industry.

Hanae Mori

As soon as we got into the white Jaguar, the Count asked, *"Have any of you heard of Hanae Mori?"*

I nodded and said, *"Of course I have. I have seen some of her designs in French fashion magazines. She is very famous in Japan."*

Mario joked, *"You, you gay boy, you're definitely a little fashionista, aren't you?"*

Karina supplemented, *"Doesn't she have several retail stores in Tokyo? I believe we passed one a couple of blocks back. Judging from what's displayed in the window, her designs seems to cater to mature society women. It's not something I would wear."*

"That's right, Karina. In 1965, she was the first designer to show her collection outside of Japan. We are going to her haute couture salon to view her latest collection. I'd like to borrow some of her gowns for our photography session tomorrow. Unfortunately for you, girl, you may have to wear some of her creations at the photo-shoot," the Italian smirked.

The big sister didn't seem too happy. She responded, *"Hopefully, she'll have something more modish available for me. I don't feel comfortable wearing clothes that are made for the older generation. I prefer minis and A-line dresses. Maybe Bryanna and Anastasie can be photographed in her creations."*

The Count continued, *"As much as you dislike her work, Hanae is very prolific. Besides having boutiques in*

Tokyo, she also has branch stores throughout Japan, where local factories manufacture her ready-to-wear line. Not to mention, she writes a weekly fashion column for a major newspaper and appears regularly on local television shows."

Matumi chimed, *"I'm not a fan of her designs. It's too conservative for me. I saw her creations in Japanese films before I left this country for boarding school abroad."*

"Although I'm not a Mori fan, I do appreciate her straight, simple silhouettes, executed in beautifully printed silks, and her combination of the traditional Japanese elements with Western garment forms. I do like her Japanese calligraphy, stylized kimono evening gowns of embroidered satins, and especially her dresses with long furi-sode (swinging) sleeves," I declared.

The photographer concluded, *"Her success comes from merging Eastern and Western clothing traditions. This is the hallmark of Mori's aesthetic."*

We had arrived at Hanae Mori's Ginza haute couture salon.

64

The Chigo's Way

"Zest is the secret of all beauty. There is no beauty that is attractive without zest."
Christian Dior

1967

Meiji Jingū

We arrived at Meiji Jingu Shrine at four thirty A.M., when the morning sky was still shrouded in darkness. One of Mr. Fujikawa's colleagues, Mr. Hikaru, a board member from the Association of Shinto Shrines, had made arrangements with the Meiji Jingū High Priest for us to conduct our fashion shoot within the historical building and its extensive gardens.

Alongside us were the female models, Anastasie, Bryanna, Karen, Matumi, and of course, the famous Twiggy. Justin de Villeneuve, together with a couple of Japanese hairdressers and make-up artists, were there as well. The styling team was sponsored by Shiseido, the famous Japanese cosmetic company. Takioko acted as our guide and translator. Since Fahrib and Ikram had never witnessed a fashion shoot, they tagged along with our entourage.

Enchanting sounds from the temple monks echoed within the walls of the ancient temple. They gave Meiji

Jingū a tranquility I found calming and serene. I busied myself helping Mario set up his photography equipment. A sense of inner peace befell my person as the first light of dawn peeked through the autumnal landscape. It created a surrealist magnetism that belonged solely to the Land of the Rising Sun. I felt one with the universe as I stood gazing into space. I was returned to the present by a voice from behind.

Takioko cooed, *"The glow of light against your hair created a halo around your flawless face. You looked like an angelic cherub descended to earth. I can't take my eyes off your beauty."*

Surprised by his unexpected compliment, I was at a loss for words. I smiled at him self-consciously. He stared at me without averting his gaze. I felt like I was being scrutinized like an alien from outer space. After a long silence, I finally uttered, *"Thank you sir. You are very kind to flatter me with such a salute."*

Changing the subject, he asked, *"Have you handed your essay in to your professor? Did he like it? How did you score?"*

I gave the Japanese a thank-you nod before I replied, *"Thank you, sir, for writing the essay on my behalf. I am deeply grateful for your help. I handed your pile of papers to my teacher yesterday. He was impressed with the abundance of information. We are going to have an open discussion when we meet for our next tutorial."*

"You were very devious to have me do your assignment for you when you were supposed to do the research on your own," Takioko attested. *"I have a soft spot for pretty boys like you,"* he muttered. *"I like to help twinks, especially when they stare at me with their large puppy eyes."*

I did not respond but continued my task. *"You're so cute,"* he remarked. *"I'd like to cuddle you like a teddy bear. Is that the reason your chaperone adores you? He's a *lot like me; he likes adolescent dandies, to shelter their innocence for as long as he can,"* he continued murmuring to himself in English and Japanese.

If only he knew I'm not as innocent as I look, I thought to myself. The man would surely be staggered by my E.R.O.S. experiences. For now, I will continue to play him with my childlike façade, to give him the impression that I'm a toy boy who needs an alpha male for protection. Surely, he'll pamper me like my other suitors, whose fundamental concern was to get into my pants, I reasoned to myself.

I gave Takioko a bewitching grin. He came to my aid. I didn't lift a finger while he went about setting up the photographers' equipment. When he finished, I leaned over and gave him an unexpected peck on the cheek. He gaped at me fixatedly when I effused winsomely, *"Thank you for your kind assistance, sir. I'm indebted to you forever."* I had already hypnotized the Japanese with my art of seduction, much like I had Marquis Mathieu.

An Adjacent Photo-shoot

The fashion shoot was smoothly on its way at a little past six. Mario, like the professional I had first encountered aboard the 'Countess Cornara' during the Venice Vogue fashion shoot, was once again the man with the magic camera. He clicked away, twisting upward, downward and every which way to capture the perfect shot.

Unbeknownst to me, at one of the other temples, Aziz was conducting his own *'Sacred Sex in Sacred Places'* photo-shoot with Ludovic, Ikram, his three handlers and several Japanese geishas from an *ochaya* ('Tea House' - an establishment where patrons are entertained by geishas) in the Toyko geisha district.

Mr. Hikaru had paid a secret visit to the president of the Shinto Shrine Association to request permission – i.e., inform the president that Prince P and Wazir Thabit had made a large donation towards the upkeep of the shrines and another, larger donation, to the introducer, the president and the temple officials. No outsider was to be informed of this creative project except those involved. The only others who knew were the Count and the junior lawyer, Takioko (who had acted as the Japanese interpreter between the Arabian contingent and the temple's chief abbot). Mario and Takioko had kept mum throughout our fashion shoot. During our session, the Japanese lawyer mysteriously disappeared and reappeared every now and again. I, absorbed in assisting the Count and helping the models change, did not pay any attention to the appearance, disappearance or reappearance of the Harvard graduate.

Conversation with Twiggy

During one of Twiggy's breaks, while I was priming and readying her next outfit, the model said to me, *"You are passionate about fashion, aren't you, young man?"*

Unaware that she was addressing me, I continued my task. *"Hey, boy, my girlfriend is talking to you,"* Justin de Villeneuve vociferated loudly. He gave the back of my head a light slap as if I was a servant.

I turned around to find her manager snickering at me. *"Did you hear what she said?"* he demanded crassly.

I took an instant dislike to this unrefined Brit. I turned to the model and ignored her boyfriend. *"Did you ask me a question, mademoiselle?"* I queried politely.

"You are so diligent at sorting out our outfits. Are you planning to be a fashion photographer or a stylist?" she inquired in a friendly voice.

"No, Miss. I'm planning to attend fashion school when I graduate from Daltonbury Hall," I answered.

Upon hearing the phrase 'Daltonbury Hall,' Mr. Villeneuve's tone of voice changed, as he questioned further, *"What are you doing assisting the Count if you are a student at Daltonbury Hall? Aren't you supposed to be in school?"*

"I'm in a Middle Eastern student exchange program. My Valet and I are stationed at Prince P's household. Andy (I pointed to my chaperone, who was busy running around with a large silver foil and directing the right amount of light for the photographer's camera) and I are assisting Count Mario, our friend." I looked at Twiggy, ignoring her brash boyfriend.

Her manager continued, *"It must cost your parents a pretty penny to send you to Daltonbury Hall!"*

I did not respond. Twiggy asked, *"Which fashion school are you planning to attend?"*

I reciprocated, *"I'm not sure, Miss. I have three and half years before I graduate. I'm currently learning the ropes of the fashion trade under the count's tutelage."*

The celebrity model declared, *"Saint Martin's School of Art has a great fashion department. I've modeled for a few of their graduates, one of them being Jeff Banks, and the other, a designer I love, Bill Gibb."*

I chimed exuberantly, *"I love Bill Gibb's designs – Ossie Clark's chiffon dresses and Gina Fratini's romantic outfits."*

"I suggest you enroll at Saint Martin's School of Art. Another excellent fashion school is the Royal College of Art. Both these colleges have excellent fashion departments. When you are ready to apply, inform the head of the fashion department that I recommended you. I like your work ethic and your fashion sensibilities," Twiggy opined.

"Your advice means a great deal to me. Thank you, Miss," I replied gratefully.

Just then, she was called to change into her next outfit to begin her session with the Italian photographer.

At the Café

By the time we finished the shoot, it was time for Meiji Jingū to open its gates to the day's tourists. Twiggy and her manager had departed as soon as she changed out of her final garment. Since our entourage had been hard at work and needed strong cups of coffee to unwind, Takioko herded us to a nearby French-Japanese bakery. The scrumptious aroma of French coffee, together with an enticing array of Japanese delicacies, drew us to the counter. I was ready to devour the entire display, or rather, as much as I could fit in my hungry stomach. Andy looked at me as if I'd gone kooky. *"Young, you can't eat all that sugary stuff. You'll get sick and throw up like you did in Italy."*

Takioko came to my defense. *"Andy, the boy is hungry. Let him eat what he wants."*

"This boy doesn't know how to curb his appetite. I had to nurse him back to health after he threw up the sweets he consumed in Venice. His eyes are bigger than his stomach," my Valet weened.

I gave the Japanese a kittenish look. He winked at me before he retorted, *"Oh, Andy! Let the boy have what he wants. He's a growing lad."*

"Don't let his doe-eyed allure cloud your judgment. Trust me, this one is a master of disguise. He knows how to get his way," my Valet warned.

As soon as Andy's back was turned, I tested my flirtation skills on my admirer. *"Sir, what are you having?"*

Takioko answered, *"I'm having a cappuccino and a chocolate croissant."*

Can I tack on a piece of that appetizing blackberry cake and a fruit tart? To go?" I asked.

"Your guardian will not be pleased if he knows I gave in to your request," the Japanese advised.

"Sir, you can have it boxed. Andy will think it's for you. You can hand the bag to me when we part ways. I can sneak it up to my suite and eat them when he's not around."

"You are a devious lad. If I collaborate with you, what will I get in return?" the lawyer bargained.

I hadn't expected him to request a favor in return. A quick response rushed through my mind. *"Ooouu! Sir, you strike a hard bargain. I assure you, you'll be pleasantly rewarded."*

He gave me a seductive grin as I continued, *"Surprises come to those that least expect them. You'll have to wait to see what coup de theatre is installed for you,"* I teased.

"You little twink, you're an irresistible charmer. You know exactly what to say to get what you want," he remarked devilishly. I gave him a guileless grin.

Our entourage was already seated at several small tables. I proceeded to join the Count, who was on his own. Takioko joined us.

The photographer asked the moment I sat down, *"Did you manage to get Twiggy's autograph?"*

I tweeted ruefully, *"Oh, no! I was too busy with the shoot and forgot to ask for her autograph."*

The Italian smiled but said nothing. Takioko chirped, *"This boy is crazy about fashion. The intensity he puts into his work is very inspiring."*

Mario said wittily, *"Young is not intense only in fashion; his love-making is fanatically passionate."*

"Really..." The lawyer urged. *"Tell me more!"*

"You'll have to give him a try. I don't want to let on too much," the Count jested.

Embarrassed by the attention, my face went red. My infatuation with the Count loomed in my head. It hadn't been long since I'd gotten over the Italian's sexual charisma. Now, he was telling others about my lovemaking skills. I kept quiet and looked towards Andy, seated next to Bryanna and Anastasie. My Valet saw me across the room and smiled. I felt empowered by his distant encouragement. Andy's love gave me the strength to respond to the situation at hand.

"My skills are a far cry from that of the distinguished Count within our midst," I scintillated.

They laughed before the photographer turned me to him. In full view of everyone in the café he planted a lingering kiss on my tender lips. This unexpected turn of events caught me off guard.

Takioko's Experience

Takioko aired cheerfully, *"Let's go to an Onsen later today. I know a resplendent ryokan in Minakami that you'll enjoy."*

I asked, *"What's a ryokan?"*

Mario answered, *"My boy, a ryokan is a Japanese inn."*

Before Mario could continue, Takioko explained, *"An onsen ryokan has natural hot springs and baths where we can rest and relax in comfort. The particular all-male ryokan I'd like to take you guys to, was built during the Edo period. I went there with my Shinto master when I was a lad."*

"Why were you with a Shinto master?" the playboy asked.

"I studied Shintoism and Buddhism when I was a young boy. He was my Master teacher. I was his acolyte – I followed him everywhere."

"Is that how you know so much about Buddhism and Sex in Japan?" I queried.

Takioko smiled shyly before he declared, *"My Master taught me the ethics of being a good chigo."*

"What's a chigo?" I asked.

Mario answered on the lawyer's behalf, *"It means an acolyte or boy attendant to a monk."*

"My parents sent me to Master Gorou when I was twelve, I left the monastery when I turned sixteen. Master Gorou taught me to be graceful, noble and cultured, particularly in the arts of music, dance and poetry. He encouraged me to use my physical attributes to entice the brother monks," Takioko recalled.

I questioned before he could proceed, *"So you were taught the arts of seduction and flirtation at the temple?"*

He replied, *"I suppose you can call it that."*

Although I made no mention of my education in the arts of seduction and flirtation, I couldn't help thinking how similar my education was to his.

Takioko continued, *"Master Gorou's advice to me, 'The acolyte who speaks quietly is sensitive to love. He must be somewhat shy. You've always shown a great liking to me,' he'd said. He summoned me into his chamber one day and asked me to remove my robes. He explained that he was teaching me the way of love and that I shouldn't be afraid. I was to remain calm, and I did as was told.*

"He massaged my chest, which stimulated my nipples tremendously. He proceeded to stroke my penis to erection. Before I knew it, he had flipped me onto my stomach. He lifted my bottom to his face, licking and delving his tongue into my ass."

"Did you like it?" I interrupted.

The Count butted in, *"Young, let him continue."*

I stared at Takioko as he spoke. *"Master Gorou was persistent. He tried to work his engorgement inside me. Since I wasn't used to taking such a thick rod, it hurt. It wasn't until our third encounter that I was able to receive him all the way. The first couple of times, he used his fingers to loosen me. I kept clamming up. He told me erotic tales until I was aroused, and I desired to experience the pleasure he recounted to me."*

I reiterated, *"Did he penetrate you?"*

The lawyer replied impishly, *"Let me put it this way. I prefer to penetrate."*

I blurted without thinking, *"You're a TOP!"*

Mario exclaimed, *"Young! Where are your manners?"* He shushed to keep my voice down. Luckily, my proclamation flew past the crowd. The café bustled too loudly for its guests to overhear our discussion.

He coaxed, *"Was there sadomasochism in the monastery?"*

The Japanese laughed, *"You, sir, will find that out when we go to the ryokan onsan at Minakami."*

65

To the City of Brotherly Love

"Whatever else can be said about sex, it cannot be called a dignified performance."

Helen Lawrenson

1967

The Summon

The moment we stepped into the hotel foyer, the concierge handed me an envelope. The note, addressed to me, read:

Young,
Get ready as soon as possible. We are leaving for Pennsylvania.
Gabrielli
(On Behalf of Prince P)

Andy hurried us to our room to start packing. I asked, *"Why are we going to Pennsylvania? Where is it?"*

My Valet replied while stuffing our belongings into our suitcases, *"I don't know why we're going to America. I'm sure your teacher will inform us as soon as we see him. Get ready and don't ask so many questions,"* my lover commanded.

"Is everyone leaving, or just us?" I continued.

"*Stop talking. You'll know soon enough. Just get your ass moving and pack,*" he commanded.

The phone rang as I was stuffing my toiletries into my suitcase. Andy informed the caller that we'd be in the lobby as soon as possible. The bell boys were already knocking at our door to collect our luggage. My professor, Wazir Thabit, Dr. Fahrib, Ikram, and his handlers were already in the lobby. The last to arrive was His Highness. The nine of us departed in the Jaguars we had arrived in, and my Valet and I shared the red vehicle with Gabrielli.

As soon as we were seated comfortably and zooming towards Haneda airport, I asked my professor, "*Why are we going to Pennsylvania in such a hurry?*"

He replied, "*We are going to visit a merry-go-round manufacturer in Philadelphia.*"

I chirped before he could continue, "*I thought the best caousel makers were in Germany.*"

"*What makes you think that?*" he queried.

"*Aren't Rottenburg Am Necker and Nuremberg famous toy-producing towns?*" I queried.

"*They are indeed famous for toy manufacturing. Carousels are not toys; they are mechanical merry-go-rounds that demand skilled craftsmanship to produce. Although some of the world's renowned carousel craftsmen are of German descent, they and their families migrated to the United States at the turn of the twentieth century,*" the Italian declared.

My chaperone posed, "*Who are we visiting in The City of Brotherly Love?*"

My educator responded, "*We are paying a visit to the Dentzel Company and the Philadelphia Toboggan Company in Germantown. They are famous for their finely handcrafted carousel animals.*"

"*How did you locate these company?*" I tweeted curiously.

"It was Vicomtesse de Noailles who found them through her artist friends. She recommended to His Highness a master craftsman by the name of Salvatore Cernigliaro. He works for the Dentzel Company."

Andy inquired, "Will the French investors be joining us?"

"I believe we'll be meeting Marquis Mathieu, Vicomte Charles and the baron."

"So it's an all-male contingent? Why aren't any of the women joining us?" I asked.

Gabrielli proclaimed, "The final artistic decision rests on Ikram and you, since the two of you are the creative instigators of this project."

Surprised by the pronouncement, I voiced, *"I'm only an assistant to Ikram. Shouldn't Ikram and the Prince be the ones to make the final decision?"*

"Prince P and the investors will have the final say in regards to the financial and business decisions. The creative and artistic input falls on you and Ikram," my teacher stated.

I was puzzled. *"As you are aware, professor, I'll be leaving P's service in a week. How will I continue on Carousel?"*

"My dear boy, you don't have to concern yourself with that. It's a minor issue. We'll find you if His Highness requires your service."

Andy questioned, *"Are we back with the Prince for Young's next household assignment?"*

My professor smiled before reiterating, *"As I said, when the prince requires your service, we'll find the two of you. For now, relax and go with the flow."*

Andy changed the subject. *"We didn't say goodbye to the rest of our group in Tokyo."*

"Don't worry, Valet, you'll be back in Japan in no time. The count, Aziz, and the Sacred Sex in Sacred Places *entourage will be waiting for us in Kyoto. They'll begin shooting while we're in Philadelphia,"* Gabrielli advised.

"Takioko had plans to take us to an onsen this evening," I declared.

"In Kyoto, there'll be other onsens. For now, concentrate on the task at hand," he counseled as we readied ourselves to board the emerald plane.

Medical Examination

As we zoomed across the time zones, Dr. Fahrib inquired about my health. He asked attentively, *"How are you doing, young man? Have you recovered from your fall?"*

"I feel fine, sir," I answered.

"Take off your shirt and let me take a look at your back," he beckoned.

Sensual vibrations pulsated through my body as his gentle fingers tapped my slender back. My throbbing excitement awoke to the touch of his fingers on my spine. The doctor straddled against my behind and leaned close for inspection. His masculinity permeated my nostrils, arousing every fiber of my body. I remained frozen as his stethoscope reached to listen to my thumping heart. I leaned against his muscular chest. I felt his drumming palpitations. I knew we were attracted to each other, but I dared not initiate. I wasn't sure how to segue with this sexy orthodox Arabian physician. Fahrib was of a different breed. He was unlike any of the other Middle Easterners, who were eager to have their way with me. I didn't know how to react to the man's conservative charm. His electrifying sensuality was melting the auras that separated us. He whispered in my ear, *"Come to my chambers tomorrow night. I want to be with you alone."*

He released his firm grip before pronouncing, *"You, my boy, have a clean bill of health. The minor bruises on your arms will disappear in a couple days."* He gave me a seductive wink when no one was paying any attention, reminding me of our upcoming rendezvous.

Dinner

The Al Fayoum landed at a private airstrip in the late afternoon. A couple of Lincoln limousines were waiting to ferry us to a luxury townhouse in Germantown. We were joined by the French delegation, consisting of Baron Pierre, Marquis Mathieu, Vicomte Charles and a husband-and-wife team Andy and I had not met before. Although the aristocratic couple, Margrave Alexander and Markgräfin Aliciä were from the Comté de Montbéliard, they were Germans from the House of Württemberg.

Sheik Fahrib sat next to me during dinner. *"P told me he recruited the two of you from the Enlightened Royal Oracle Society,"* he said. *"What is the nature of this fraternity?"*

I looked to my Valet for an answer. My guardian responded assiduously, *"I'm sure His Highness has filled you in with the details."*

The doctor gave us a swotty grin before adding, *"He did mention that he's a member, and so are the Wazir and his brother Habibi Aziz, plus a selection of high-ranking officials and aristocrats from our various kingdoms."*

My chaperone replied, *"In that case, I don't have to explain further. I'm sure they'll provide you with adequate information if you intend on becoming a member."*

"P said the membership selection is a stringent process and is granted only to people with integrity," the Arab emphasized.

"I'm afraid I can't shed any light on this matter. It is best to consult the E.R.O.S. authorities and with their other fellow members. I believe a new associate must be

nominated and recommended by three participating comrades who can attest to his character. This is also to safeguard the foreign exchange students that are assigned to the households," my guardian explained.

"Are you planning to join E.R.O.S.?" I asked.

"I find the program intriguing. After meeting Karina, Matumi and the two of you, I'm enthralled by the intelligence, magnetism and charisma you possess. Do all E.R.O.S. students have alluring personalities like the four of you?"

Andy replied, "Our admission process is as demanding as that of the household members' recruitment. We have to pass a series of tests and attend a special training programme before we are assigned to be of service."

Marquis Mathieu overheard our conversation. He interposed, "I wish I could enroll to be an E.R.O.S. member. I'd enjoy you boys at my household. Unfortunately, my wife would never let me garner an entourage like our Arabian friends."

The baron chimed vivaciously, "That has never deterred you from having fun with the E.R.O.S. recruits."

Mathieu said amusingly, "Pierre, you know my darkest secrets. I hope you are not letting the cat out of the bag to my beloved Marquise. She'll have a fit and will surely threaten divorce if she finds out what I'm up to behind her back."

Pierre answered playfully, "Don't worry, my friend, your secrets are safe with me." The two bantered back and forth as if in a private parlor game.

Dr. Fahrib smiled to himself. He found their exchange doltish. He reminded me when Andy was out of ear shot, "Don't forget our appointment tomorrow evening. I've questions I need answered."

Before I could utter a response, he was conducting a conversation with the French German aristocrats.

An Unexpected Present

During the course of dinner, a hand crawled up my lap from under the table. I had no idea whose arm it belonged to. I reached down to cup the appendage before a tiny container was placed onto my palm. I slipped it into my pocket. The hand continued to stroke my inner thighs before stroking the base of my crotch. I held a polite comportment above table. The hand began playing with my scrotum.

Prowling fingers soon reached into my underwear, fondling my growing erection. The mysterious appendage could belong to one of two people: the baron on my left or the doctor on my right. The fingers released my organ from its confines, stroking my hardness to debaucherous ecstasy. Yet I remained resolute, carrying on polite dinner conversations as if nothing extraordinary were happening below the waist. The hand rubbed playfully around the head of my cock, arousing streams of dripping wetness onto its thumb. The mysterious fingers continued stimulating my excitement while I strained to control my release. Just as I was close to ejaculation, the hand stopped until my fervent enthusiasm eased and then began the amatory stroking again. I struggled to maintain composure against the onslaught of passionate stimulation to my lower abdomen. It was an acute test of equanimity. I was enraptured by this erotic bondage. I yearned for the inevitable, yet I coveted the sensual delight that was protracting my sexuality. This electrifying galvanization was beyond my comprehension. I longed for this lascivious carnality to continue, yet I desired release. My uncontrollable erection was throbbing against the administering fingers. I had become enslaved to this enigmatic admirer. He had trounced his dominance over my adolescence – I was literally in the palm of his hand. I could do little but permit its tantalizing invasion.

When dinner was over, I was left ungratified. I had fallen prey to the mystery intruder. Whoever he was, I was already his toy boy.

66

The Vivacious Vicious Vixen

"Love is a perky vixen dancing a merry little jig and then suddenly she turns on you with a machine gun."

German Proverb

1967

Germantown

    The morning started off splendidly. Our appointment with the Philadelphia Toboggan Company was scheduled after a hearty German breakfast at a German café in Germantown.
    As soon as I had retired to my chamber the previous evening, I had opened the mysterious gift tucked in my pocket. Inside a *Mauboussin* blue velvet container was a magnificent mother-of-pearl ring, edged with pure gold and topped with a large sparkling sapphire. I wore the glimmering sparkle on my middle finger when I showed it to my guardian.
    "Where did you get this extraordinary piece of jewelry?" my lover questioned.
    I ignored his query as I posed my hand this way and that, admiring the shimmering sparkler. My lover caught

my wrist. *"Who gave you this ring?"* he demanded roguishly.

I said nothing. He gripped my hand and pulled the gemstone off my finger, holding it high above his head. *"I won't give it back until you tell me who gave it to you!"* he commanded.

"An admirer!" I cried merrily, trying to snatch the ring from my Valet.

"You won't get it until you tell me!" he challenged.

The truth was, I did not know who my admirer was. I screamed as I chased Andy around the room. *"Give it back! I'll tell you."*

"I don't trust you. Tell me now!" he ordered as we pranced around the room.

I had no choice but explain that I hadn't a clue who had given me the opulent gift. He continued to keep the gem from me. *"Show me the box so I can try to find verification clues,"* my chaperone ordered.

"Okay, okay! The box is lying on the bed. Look all you want," I exclaimed.

"You mischievous rascal! You'd better confess everything. I want to know every little secret you are keeping from me," he mandated.

"Give me my ring, and I'll confess," I lied.

He donned the sparkler on his finger and pushed me onto the bed, pinning my wrists above my head. I wrestled to get free, but his athletic musculature was already pinned against my slender physique. His dominance kindled my arousal. Leaning close to my face, my lover planted a devilish bite on my neck. I squirmed from its tickling sensation. The more I wiggled, the harder he bit. His stiffness pressed against my hardening groin as we scuffled spiritedly. We tore at our clothes as we French kissed passionately. My lover couldn't wait to throw my legs above his shoulders. He uttered, *"You little slut, tell me who gave you the ring!"*

I responded spunkily, *"I don't know, Sir! Let me go, Master!"* I begged, *"I promise I'll let you know when I find out."* I twisted around boisterously to avoid his probing erection.

My lover gave my buttocks a slap. *"Keep still, you bitch in heat. Let me in,"* my Master ordered.

"No!" I yelled waggishly.

Knocks on our bedroom door hushed us back to reality. *"Is everything okay?"* a voice hollered.

"We're fine, sir. Just mucking around," Andy pronounced.

"Boys, keep your voices down. You don't have to wake the entire neighborhood," Gabrielli enunciated.

"Yes, sir!" Andy answered apologetically.

As soon as we heard the footsteps depart, we giggled like mischievous children who had been discovered by their parents.

My chaperone peered at me adoringly. He planted an amorous kiss on my lips, languorously delving his tongue into my receiving orifice. I opened to my Valet. He knew I loved him unconditionally and would perform anything he desired of me – and he would do the same for me. We were lovers united in a joint quest; our mission was to pleasure those we had agreed to serve.

Andy, my beloved guardian, never failed to fill my soul with rapturous exultations as we rocked back and forth in our rhythmic motions. His ardor pried open every crevice of my being. In return, I clawed at his sinewy back like an oestrus feline as he plowed furiously into my yielding hollow. Andy's powerful exhilaration stirred in me emotions I had not felt with any of my other admirers. Tears trickled from my eyes as waves of euphoric spirituality gushed forth from the unfathomable recesses of my spirit, fusing our souls into electrifying currents of eudemonia. Our expiatory devotions were ours from now to eternity. Little did we realize our vows of loyalty would lead to propitiatory redemptions decades later.

We were young and in love; our throes of amorous intercourse were the envy of our gentry. Men coveted the opportunity to propagate our savoir faire, and women desired to penetrate our inner sanctum, lusting for the sacred shackles that fettered our godliness.

Lapping at my divine jubilations, Andy fed me my salty teardrops as his affectionate gyrations bored deep into my core. His fervid enthusiasm mixed with my eager avidity hurled us into bouts of orgasmic gratification. I spilled my erotic enchantments onto my face while he deposited his fill into my tunnel. He glided his wetness inside me as we shared my seed between us. He had no wish to relinquish his prowess but continued his onslaught. My sprightly countenance needed no repose. I was ready to match my chaperone's resilience. Neither of us aspired to end our congress anytime soon. I twitch my sphincter over his bobbing rigidity and felt his thickness throb within. This act of sensual provocation had rejuvenated his manhood again. Goosebumps formed on his perspiring physique. Laying me sideways, he lifted my leg above my waist and penetrated me. The floor-to-ceiling mirror bore witness to our erotic intensity, propelling me to sporadic contractions. Gobs of amatory deposits flowed onto my lover's hand, which he wiped on his palpitating manhood before sliding his masculinity into my being once more.

His tender gyrations grinded emphatically against my quivering receptacle. Blissful flurries coursed through my 'city of jewels'. I was in nirvana and had little wish to surrender my sacred Manipura back to this earthly existence. Andy's groaning agility notified me of his imminent delivery. I was ready for another seething transmission to swirl deliriously within the depths of my hallowed cavity. My beloved finally poured his frenzied eruptions into my intoxicated sacrosanctum. Rivers of overflowing venerations filled my profundity. My Apollo slumped against my back, gripping me as he retrieved his breath. He held me tightly, as if afraid I might disintegrate if he ever released his clutch. We lay motionless. We had merged into a cognitive state of perfection as we drifted into pleasurable slumber, my beloved still buried within.

I awoke to whiffs of his potent masculinity. His erection stirred as I backed against his loins. Andy was ready, and so was I. His gentle oscillations triggered me to life as he whispered into my ear, *"I know who your secret wooer is."* I did not answer. His puissant intoxication was too invigorating. We needed no dialogue. I eased into his stroking revivification as he readied us for the next round of our copulation. That night, my quest for gratuitous gratification was filled many times over.

My Secret Wooer

Loud knocking on our chamber door woke us. My teacher bellowed, *"Guys, are you up? Be ready in fifteen minutes, or we'll be leaving without you!"*

We jumped out of bed and readied ourselves hastily. We ran downstairs to join our entourage as they were walking out the front door. A couple of senior executives from the Philadelphia Toboggan Company had arrived to accompany us to breakfast before journeying to tour their headquarters.

Over breakfast, the executives, Klaus and Dominik, gave us a briefing of their company's history. *"Welcome to The City of Brotherly Love,"* Dominik announced. *"I hope your accommodations are to your liking?"* Prince P gave the man a suboptimal nod but did not respond. Klaus added, *"We've been informed by your representative, Herr Gabrielli Marciano Castrogiovanni, that you may be interested in engaging our company to manufacture a custom merry-go-round for a discotheque project."* We nodded in unison but did not answer. He continued, *"Our Company has an extensive history of carousel manufacturing. Herr Henry Auchy and Chester Albright founded our company in 1904. Since then, we have come a long way in the production of premium carousels. The Philadelphia Toboggan Company bought the rights to Dentzel Company after Mr. William Dentzel's demise. We work closely with the Dentzel's descendant, Mr. William Dentzel II, who is a genius carver of carousel animals."*

Dominik commented, *"I believe you'd like to meet with Herr Salvatore Cernigliaro. He was a former carver for Gustav and William Dentzel I and II. Salvatore is an excellent craftsman."*

"We would also like to introduce you to another prolific carver, Mr. Barney Illions. Our artisans are the few remaining craftsmen still working today after the passing of the Golden Age of merry-go-round manufacturing.

"Cernigliaro and Illions love the art of creating carousel rides. I'm sure they will embrace your project wholeheartedly," Klaus declared excitedly.

As the duo continued dispatching their firm's history, my Valet whispered, *"Did you hear what I said last night? I know who gave you the sparkler."*

"Who?" I muttered.

"Have a guess," Andy murmured.

I looked across the table at the Marquis. Sensing my glimpse, he turned and gave me a devilish wink. The Baron caught me gazing and smiled portentously. The only person who didn't notice me peering was the doctor. His attention was focused on the Toboggan Company briefing.

I rustled, *"My guess is, it's Sheik Fahrib."*

My chaperone grinned foxily. He did not give me a definitive answer. He remarked, *"You are required in his chamber this evening."*

I thought to myself, it must be the doctor, because he reminded me several times that he wanted to see me in his room tonight without my guardian. I asked, *"Whose chamber? How did you find out I'm expected in 'his' chamber tonight?"*

Our private whispers came to a screeching halt when His Highness and the rest of our entourage got up to leave. We were heading to tour the Toboggan factory.

The Tour

Markgräfin Aliciä asked many questions during the tour. She wanted information on every aspect of carousel manufacturing, from creative designs to the mechanical operational details of each and every carousel the company was manufacturing. My Valet and I had a feeling that this tiny, vivacious woman was not easy to handle. Maybe her overbearing confidence was restitution for her smallish frame. This I would never know. Her dictatorial attitude could come across as annoying. Superficially, neither the prince nor the rest of the investors expressed any vexation, but when her back was turned, Andy and I detected apprehension within our entourage.

Falling several steps behind, I murmured to my Valet, *"You haven't answered my question."*

"What question, my lovely one?" He pretended he didn't understand my query.

"How did you find out who summoned me this evening?" I tweeted.

"I have the mind of the Sherlock. I can decipher anything and everything. It's elementary!" he quipped.

I hit my Valet's bottom puckishly. Before we could continue our frivolity, a pandemonium began a short distance away.

The Markgräfin screamed licentious profanities at the kaneeth. Her husband, Alexander, had wrapped his hands protectively around her. He tried to calm her explosive verbal assault on our Arab companion. Our entourage was stupefied by such displays of vulgarity. Yet none of us had a clue to what had triggered this unexpected uproar. The kaneeth's handlers stood in a row, arms on hips, protecting their gaffer in case the woman turned violent on the fragile Ikram. She continued screaming abuses at the Arab, accusing him of sexual harassment.

Suddenly, Ikram went into an epileptic fit. He convulsed riotously on the floor. The doctor and his handlers rushed to the man's aid. Fahrib ordered Makut, Ebram and Khatum to carry him to a quieter place. Klaus led them to the company's recreational room.

Bewildered, our mouths gapped open as we watched the unfolding drama as if at a circus.

Mr. Barney Illions, who until then had been explaining the procedures of his creative artistry to His Highness, the Sheik and the French aristocrats, barged in. He tore the Margrave and the Markgräfin from the furor and quickly escorted the couple into a secluded office.

Stunned, we were urgently ushered into a conference room at the opposite side of the building by the infamous Herr Salvatore Cernigliaro.

As soon as our entourage had quiesced, Gabrielli inquired, *"Can anyone shed some light on this mayhem?"*

Dominik spoke, *"Fräulein Aliciä's authoritarian mannerisms did not sit well with Mr. Ikram."*

"What happened?" P interrogated.

"I believe Fräulein Aliciä had made up her mind about which animals she wanted on the carousel, leaving Mr. Ikram's decision out of the equation," the executive relayed.

I reasoned to myself; that must not have sat well with our Arab decorator.

"For as long as I've known Aliciä, she has never been the easiest person to get along with. Many don't take kindly to her dominating comportment. I'm unsure of how she got wind of this project," the Marquis voiced.

Vicomte Charles chimed apologetically, *"It was my wife's doing. At a Paris social function, she unintentionally let this project slip off her tongue to the Margrave. From that moment forward, the Markgräfin had been pestering Marie-Laure to introduce them to His Highness.*

"It's my fault, and I should have warned your eminence of her injudiciousness. I didn't want to ruin her reputation before you even met."

Baron Pierre soothed his friend, *"Charles, you are not to be blamed for this mishap. She brought this on herself. You gave Aliciä a chance, and she ruined it."*

Mathieu admonished, *"I hope this vicious vixen won't sue Ikram. She can be ruthless and turn on the harmless."*

The prince had remained silent thus far. He spoke: *"I'll see to it that that will not be the case. For now, I had better check on my cousin to make sure he's all right. The last thing I want is him dying on me."*

67

Lone Rangers

*"A table, a chair, a glass of wine and a violin –
what else does a man need to be happy?"*
Albert Einstein

1967

Befuddlement

The unfortunate contretemps threw everyone off balance. Doctor Fahrib called 911 and the ambulance carted Ikram to the nearest hospital. His Highness, the three handlers and the physician followed.

Without remonstrance to the prince or any member of our entourage, the husband-and-wife team departed posthaste to France, leaving Gabrielli, Ludovic, the three French aristocrats, my Valet and me dumbfounded. Instead of wasting a work day, my assiduous professor took the reins and put me in charge of the creative aspects of the project. Andy was to chronicle every detail that transpired at our meetings. The documents and blueprints could then be presented to the epileptic decorator later for his final approval. Gabrielli, the shrewd business administrator, made sure that my decisions did not exceed the allocated budget.

For me, this accidental annexation was a dream come true. Under the professional advice of Herr

Cernigliaro and Mr. Illions, I was able to incorporate the racing Arabians, the dazzling animals, the anomalous sea creatures, and an array of outlandish sailboats, racing cars and dashing chariots into the circling menagerie. I had a hunch that His Highness and Ikram would approve of my selections.

I surmised that an excellent designer-decorator has the ability to incorporate the client's aspirations with the artisan's cultivated fastidiousness. It is from this collective consciousness that magical innovations emerged.

I thought back to the Markgräfin and the way she had demanded complete creative control from Ikram over the project. In the process, her uncompromising, power-grabbing disposition had left the creator vexed and dissatisfied. The kaneeth came from a wealthy, powerful and privileged patriarchal society. He could not bear to lose face to a domineering female. It was of little wonder that our Arab contingent did not take kindly to the irrepressibly spoiled Aliciä. To them, she was a boorish farm girl from Boulogne who had tricked the Margrave into marriage, by threatening to publicly announce her pregnancy after a roll in the hay with the wealthy aristocrat.

Vicomte Charles made known to us that Marie-Laure de Noailles had had no intention of introducing the couple to His Highness, but the Markgräfin held a secret over the Vicomtesse and left her no choice but to execute the introduction. Marie-Laure knew from the inception that this liaison would be unfruitful but had decided that it was better than having Aliciä reveal her clandestine affair, publicly. She did not want to fend off the invasive paparazzi and scandalmongers, always at the ready to persecute and humiliate their next victim, especially a socialite such as herself.

The Entourage

While Ludovic and the three Frenchmen left to explore the City of Brotherly Love, Gabrielli, Andy and I busied ourselves with the merry-go-round artisans and business executives. By the time we completed our day's work, Gabrielli suggested we pay the kaneeth a visit. Off we trotted to the hospital. The epileptic patient had regained consciousness after a temporary black-out that had unnerved His Highness and the Sheik. Fortunately, Ikram's three beloved handlers were on hand to whisper consolations to their honcho. What more lucrative job could an average man have but to service and be serviced by their employer? Most remunerative of all, they were compensated excellently when 'extracurricular duties' were called for by their boss.

Since the kaneeth's condition had remained stable and he was in good hands, Fahrib, P and his two bodyguards decided to go through with their original plan to attend the Philadelphia Spartans soccer match.

The only working people that day were my teacher, my Valet and me. When we arrived at the hospital, Ikram was his normal self. The decorator was notified of the carousel design developments, after which he professed, *"I knew the two of you would make good assistants and would organize the project to my liking. If that bitch had snatched the reins, Carousel would have become a tawdry mess."* He added, *"That cunt is one of the worst I've met. I'm glad we've gotten rid of her. She fancies herself as an excellent designer-decorator, but that vulgar weasel is nothing but a wolf..."*

He blurted out a string of loathsome remarks about his nemesis, which I care not to repeat. Gabrielli, Andy and I listened but said nothing. The sympathetic professor did his best to console Ikram, assuring the decorator that everything was under control and running according to plan.

Flummoxed

That evening, our entourage had dinner separately. Left in the company of my educator and my guardian, I couldn't help but ask, *"Now that we have worked out the design details with the Toboggan Company, when are we returning to Japan?"*

"That will depend on His Highness. I just received word from the Aga Khan that there are a couple of potential Carousel locations to view in Paris," P's business partner answered.

I queried inquisitively, *"Are we flying from here to Paris?"*

Andy admonished, *"Your teacher already told you that it'll depend on His Highness. Stop questioning everything, and just go with the programme. Besides, why are you so eager to return to Japan?"*

"I'd like to see Kyoto," I trilled.

"Kyoto will always be there. If you don't see it this trip, you'll see it on the next," my mentor chided.

Gabrielli responded fondly, *"Don't be too hard on the boy, Andy. He's eager to experience the world. I'm sure you were like him when you first joined E.R.O.S."*

That remark quieted my Valet. My teacher queried, *"Young, why are so keen to be in Kyoto?"*

Before I could answer, he resumed, *"Let me guess, you can't wait to be involved in the Sacred Sex in Sacred Places photo sessions, right? You provocative devil!"*

I smiled sheepishly but did not answer. My lover replied jokingly, *"This lad is a sex fiend. He's ready to copulate at the drop of a hat."*

"And you are not?" my professor challenged.

My guardian quickly changed the subject. *"The baron has summoned him this evening."*

"The baron!" I detonated.

"Yes, the baron," my lover stated.

Surprised by Andy's statement, I stared at my chaperone. *"Where did you come up with the notion that Baron Pierre wants to see me?"*

"I told you last night and this morning that you've been summoned. Did you not hear what I said?" he reiterated.

I replied, *"You asked me to guess and I said Sheik Fahrib. He told me to see him alone at his chamber this evening."*

"What! You didn't tell me that the doctor had asked to see you tonight. You should have told me," my Valet rebuked. *"You are not supposed to pay visits without me."*

I changed the topic quickly, knowing that I should have informed my chaperone of Sheik Fahrib's summon. *"How do you know the baron wants to see me?"* I questioned.

"A folded note was tucked into the bottom of the jewelry box from Baron Pierre," Andy proclaimed.

Finally, my mystery wooer was revealed. I exclaimed, *"I promised to meet the Sheik in his chamber this evening. I can't be in two places at the same time."*

"You'll have to cancel one of the appointments, won't you?" my lover chastised.

My professor came to my rescue. *"Boys, stop squabbling. I have a suggestion that could solve the problem."*

We looked at Gabrielli.

That Evening

Primed, showered and groomed, I trotted to the doctor's chamber while my Valet headed the opposite direction towards the baron's room. After much razzmatazz, my teacher had finally convinced my chaperone that he should allow me another chance to venture to an appointment alone. He promised Andy he'd keep vigilant watch outside the doctor's chamber while my Valet took my place to call on the baron. My Valet would make an excuse to the French aristocrat that I was under the weather and would pay him a visit at a later date. He was also to thank my admirer for the generous gift he had conferred on me.

The Sheik was already seated comfortably on a lone chair when I entered his room. A glass of red wine stood on a pedestal beside him. Below the stand was a violin lying inside an open case. He motioned me to sit on the sofa opposite him. Without uttering a word, he took a sip of the wine. I took a couple sips and settled onto the chair. Gentle sounds of melancholic violin melodies drifted through the room. I sat spellbound by his skill. His eyes teared as he played Schumann's lugubrious Violin Concerto.

I had no idea how to respond to such an emotional surge. I observed the man until he could no longer continue; I wanted to reach out to the violinist but did not know how. We sat in silence. I could no longer hold off my empathy. I went over and laid my hands on his shoulders.

For the first time in my life, I took the initiative to whisper in his ear, *"I'm here for you."* I did not know why I said it. It came out of my mouth as if from some unseen force. I wrapped my arms around his broad shoulders and hugged him affectionately. He smiled as if I had performed a charitable act.

He began another tune. This time, the strings resounded blithely. My compassionate touch seemed to have transformed his disconsolation. He circled around me buoyantly, gesturing me to keep in step with his fiddling and dancing. We danced around cheerfully, and our merriment soon gave way to exhaustion before we plummeted laughingly onto the settee. He leaned his masculinity against my physique and laid his head on my chest. I wrapped my arms around his heaving torso as we sank onto the cushions to catch our breath. No word had been exchanged since I entered. There was no reason. I lifted my hand to soothe his perspiring forehead. He looked up and gave me a gratifying smile. He lay on my chest as I continued mollifying his temple with my handkerchief. I ran my palms against his sideburns and stubbly chin, feeling his sensual facial hair. I was turned on by this brawny man of no words, although his light-hearted gaiety did nothing to hide his unhappiness. Enlightened Royal Oracle Society recruits pledged never to ask intrusive questions unless esoteric information was disclosed willingly by those we served. My sensitivity had always been my guiding light, and this instance was no exception to the rule.

I gently reached my hand inside his velvet smoking jacket. His thumping heart pulsated against his hairy chest. Fahrib's ruggedness electrified me as I inched unhurriedly towards his loins. I hankered to languish my face against his pubic hair, his length and his sack, to inhale his masculinity as naturally as breathing l'air du printemps. The man gripped my wrist just as I was about to twirl my fingers around his pubes. My hand remained unmoved on his lower torso.

For the first time that evening, he spoke. *"I have many questions for you."*

Startled, I replied, *"Yes, sir. I'll do my best to answer your questions."*

He queried, *"What kind of services are E.R.O.S. recruits expected to perform in their allocated households?"*

I was caught off guard as a speedy response came to mind: *"Whatever is required of us we will execute."*

"Is it okay if I tell you what's on my mind?" he asked.

"Of course, sir. Whatever you wish to divulge to me will be kept confidential," I invited.

He began, *"It has always been difficult for me to confide to anyone, let alone to someone as young as you. Yet my presentiment tells me that I can trust you. Will you promise to keep my secrets?"*

"Certainly sir! I swear with a gentleman's honor that I will keep your secrets to myself."

Fahrib signed deplorably, *"I don't love my wives as I vowed to Allah that I should."* After a brief silence, he continued, *"I married because of filial duty to my family and religion. I have never loved my wives, nor can I ever love them."*

I listened but did not speak. He resumed. *"It's a heavy burden for me to live a life of secrecy. I have no one to tell my unhappiness to. You're the one person to whom I am disclosing this."*

I held him tenderly and comforted, *"Could you not talk to His Highness? Isn't he your bosom pal?"*

"The more reason I cannot expose my feelings to him. In truth, I'm in love with P. He doesn't know it. It would be disastrous if he found out. He could terminate our friendship and reject me altogether."

"Why do you think His Highness will not reciprocate your love? He is an intelligent and worldly man, like your good self. Surely he'll not jeopardize your friendship because you professed your sentiments to him," I reasoned.

Fahrib shook his head, *"Young, you don't understand my culture. It is perfectly acceptable for a mature man to take an adolescent lover, as long as the boy's body is smooth and hairless, like your own. Once the young man becomes an adult, a role reversal occurs. Adult males are to marry, bear heirs and be responsible patriarchs to our families. Although many wealthy and influential families have harems, the procured adolescents are like you, Matumi and the other E.R.O.S. initiates. They are with the harem for a brief period.*

"Our culture does not take kindly to adult same-sex love. It is frowned upon. We could be persecuted or, in certain instances, executed. I envy the love you and your chaperone share – I had yearned for years for that kind of divine sacredness between P and me. Unfortunately, my prayers have fallen on deaf ears. Allah has not heard my invocations," the Arab declared sadly.

I listened attentively as the Sheik poured out his heart to me. I couldn't help but commiserate with him. We spoke at length until he had no more tears to dry.

From that evening forward, I swore to myself that I would do my best to assist the doctor in his quest. Hopefully, one day, his affection will be requited. The prince and the sheik would enjoy the divine union that was our sacred birthright.

68

Matchmaker, Make Me a Match

"A man is already halfway in love with any person who listens to him."
Brendan Francis

End May 2013

I finally received a reply from Dr. Arius. It was difficult for me to make sense of what he had written – his message oscillated from understandable sentences to jibber-jabber. I understood that the retired psychiatrist was losing the battle against cancer, and I feared his time on earth would be short.

I shed drops of tears for this compassionate man I had never met but had the fortuitous serendipity to cross paths with. For the rest of that day, I went about my business with a heavy heart. I did not respond until I was ready.

1967

Above the Clouds

On our journey back to Japan, I had the opportunity to talk with my Valet. When we had a quiet moment together, I queried, *"How did it go last evening with the baron?"*

Andy gave me a conniving smile. *"Fine,"* he answered.

"Fine? That's not a good enough answer," I prodded his side. *"Tell me everything that happened,"* I demanded.

"Why don't you tell me everything that happened between you and the doctor?" my lover retaliated.

I answered, *"There's nothing to tell."*

"I've nothing much to say either," he countered.

"Yes, you have! I can tell by the covert grin on your face," I carped.

He bargained, *"If you tell me what transpired, I'll do the same."*

I thought for a moment before answering, *"I promised the sheik not to tell anyone what occurred last evening. I cannot break my oath of confidentiality."*

"I cannot break my pledge of allegiance to the baron either," my lover chaffed.

As Andy and I bantered back and forth, the baron joined us. *"What are the two of you carrying on about?"* he asked.

My Valet quipped, *"This inquisitive lad wants to know what transpired last evening when I was with you."*

Embarrassed by my guardian's straightforwardness, I dared not look at the baron. *"Boy oh boy, you missed a delightful show,"* Pierre teased.

"Show? He didn't tell me he performed," I chirped.

"Sorry you couldn't join us. We had a sublime ménage à trois. It would have been a ménage à quatre if you had been with us," the Frenchman razzed.

"Who was the third person?" I twittered curiously.

"We found Josh and a couple of others at a tavern in Germantown," the baron rejoined.

"Who are we, Josh and the others?" I probed.

The aristocrat laughed at my cheekiness. *"We, my cutie, is Charles, Mathieu, Abriem and I. We found Josh and his companions in the pub. We were hoping you would turn up, but your Valet came in your place."*

Before he could continue, I asked, *"You guys had an orgy?"*

Pierre found my comment amusing. *"I've no doubt that you'd enjoy an orgy with these strapping dudes."*

"Tell me everything!" I quipped feistily.

"When the time is ripe, I'm sure your guardian will tell you everything. For now, I have a question for both of you."

Andy and I listened. The baron inquired, *"Would you boys like to ring in Christmas at Chateau Rouge? Yuletide is a merry time to be festive and gay!"* He gave us a salacious wink.

A voice spoke behind me. *"Pierre's Christmas soirees are to die for. You'll have the time of your life,"* the marquis affirmed.

My Valet remarked, *"Thank you for the invitation. We'll do our best to come. Young and I have been invited to visit our friends Alfonzo and Oscar in Spain the week before Christmas."*

I chimed before my chaperone could resume, *"Yes, but that's before Christmas. Can we go to Chateau Rouge for Christmas? It'll be fun!"* I pleaded.

I could feel my lover's resistance melt at my coquettish grin. *"Please?"* I implored. My beloved gave me an affectionate peck on my cheek and gave his approval. I always knew my Valet was a romantic at heart, and he wasn't alone in our entourage.

Confidant

In the few days we spent in Kyoto, I had become Dr. Fahrib's confidant. After our private conversation, I had been summoned to his chamber nightly. Many times, he needed an understanding and compassionate ear; at others, he simply required companionship. The moments we spent together were largely platonic. On a few occasions, we exchanged sensual caresses. As charming as he was, the Arab was not a man who opened up easily to intimate conversations. I was a rare specimen with whom he felt sufficiently comfortable to confide his deepest emotions and darkest fears. One evening, when we had stretched out on the settee with his head resting on my lap, he declared, *"P mentioned that you are passionate about fashion and you intend to attend fashion school when you graduate from Daltonbury Hall. Is he correct?"*

"Yes, sir," I replied.

He added, *"My wives' favorite pastime is shopping. They love to beautify themselves in the hope of gaining my affection. Unfortunately, my interests are not invested in them, no matter how beautiful they look."*

I listened without commenting. *"There is so much unrest in my family. I have problems of my own, and I don't want to deal with their insecurities as well."* The Arab sighed. *"Yet for the sake of my parents, I have to produce heirs to continue the family tree."*

After listening for some time, a thought flashed through my mind. I asked, *"Sir, how often do you make love to your wives, and when you do, do you have the lights on or off?"*

He stared at me, not knowing how to respond to my unexpected query. A brief silence ensued before he answered, *"To be honest with you, our lovemaking is far between, unless my sexual urges are working overtime and I hanker for release – then, will I bed one of my wives in darkness.*

"I can fantasize making love to the man I love and imagine the intimacy we would enjoy together. It is during these infrequent circumstances I bed my wives."

I gave the sheik a devious smile but said nothing until he queried, *"What's on your mind, young man?"*

"What I'm about to suggest may be aberrantly deviant and you may consider dishonorable." I paused to observe the man's reaction.

A hint of curiosity shown on the doctor's face. He gazed at me inquisitively before conveying, *"What disreputable notoriety are you proposing?"*

I gave him a devilish grin. *"If I tell you, will you promise not to breathe a word to any one? Not even to my chaperone?"*

The man, intrigued by my incongruous impropriety, urged, *"I'll give you my word of honor. Tell me what's on your indecorous mind."*

I slowly divulged my minatory plan to my friend. Although he rebuked my suggestions that evening, we did discuss the possibilities my suggestion could work if it were executed with caution. The following evening, while relaxing at a sumptuous onsen, Fahrib changed his tune.

At Kiyomizu-dera

Mario and the *Sacred Sex in Sacred Places* gang now consisted of Takioko, a couple of Japanese female models (whom the two photographers had acquired through a Japanese modelling agency), and last but not least, the three boys we had encountered at the Tamotsu Yato exhibition plus their friend Yuri (whom the Italian had charmed). They, like many young men would be, were pleased to be selected by an accomplished fashion photographer to have their portraitures immortalized, whether the poses were provocative or otherwise.

Their entourage had been photographing for the past three days. The day we arrived in Kyoto, the photographers and models were already assembled at Kiyomizu-dera, an ancient Buddhist temple the east of the city. The place of worship was built in 798 in the early Heian period. The present building was constructed in 1633 by the Tokugawa Iemitsu (the third shogan of the Tugugawa Dynasty). The structure took its name from the Otowa waterfall, which runs beneath the main hall. There, three separate channels of water from nearby hills fall into a pond. Kiyomizu means clear water or pure water. Visitors can catch and drink the water, which is believed to have wish-granting powers.

The temple complex also included several other shrines, among them the Jishu Shrine, dedicated to the deity Okuninushi, a god of love and 'good matches'. Jishu Shrine possesses a pair of 'love stones' placed twenty feet apart, where lonely visitors can walk in between with their eyes closed or blindfolded. Success in reaching the other stone without seeing implies that the pilgrim will eventually find his or her true love. Although one can be assisted in the crossing, it is taken to mean that a matchmaker or go-between would be required. It was also possible that the person's romantic interest could also assist them in the crossing without their knowledge.

This information fascinated the Arab doctor tremendously. He pulled me aside and pronounced excitedly, *"I'm going to walk between the 'love stones' blindfolded. If I stumble, will you come to my rescue?"*

"Of course I will," I replied without hesitation.

The Arab took out his handkerchief and had me blindfold his eyes before reaching out to feel his way across the pebbly gravel. Mario and Aziz hollered to me as I watched the doctor's progress with interest. The impatient photographers wanted my immediate presence for a three-way pairing with Keiko and Guy. Before I could respond, Sheik Fahrib had stumbled headfirst onto the stony ground. His Highness rushed to assist his friend, helping him back on his feet. Not only that, he aided the blindfolded man to the opposite stone before he sat him down to check his bleeding knees. The physician was flabbergasted by this unanticipated turn of events. Like the sheik, I too had a weird feeling that maybe Okuninushi had had heard the Arab's prayers, and this was an omen that would bring these two childhood companions together in love.

As I posed lightheartedly for the cameras, I knew I would hear the details of this incident at my next session with the physician.

At the Onsen

After our fevered photography session, Takioko shepherded the men in our entourage to an all-male onsen for some limpid rest and relaxation. It was magnificent to soak naked in a sizeable *rotemburo* (outdoor hot-spring). I found a quiet corner for some alone time. The view of a gentle flowing stream against a golden orange mountainous landscape set against the chilly autumnal air brought back memories of my time at Chalet Marmont in Lucerne. My washcloth as my pillow, I soon drifted into a dream-like state of semi-unconsciousness as the steamy water rose to soothe my tender skin.

A nebulous voice whispered into my ear, *"Don't stir, stay as you are; I want to enjoy the beauty of your stillness,"* as a pair of hands grazed my body under water. The voice was neither that of my Valet nor of the doctor. It was His Highness, the prince. As per his instructions, I did not move. His gentle fingers continued to caress my youthfulness. I throbbed with enthusiasm. The further he progressed, the more excited I became. I wanted to tell him that I should be the one pleasuring him, not the other way round. He had laid a finger on my lips to supress my speech.

"You beautiful boy, you are a feast to behold," he murmured.

I wanted to tell him that it was not to me that he should whisper this to but the Sheik, yet I remained silent.

His fondling hands continued to play with my insouciant physique. *"I know what you're up to, you mischievous sprite. You raffish rapscallion, you need to be punished. I want you alone in my chambers in fifteen minutes. Be prompt; otherwise you'll suffer my wrath,"* he ordered.

Before I had a chance to ask him where his chambers were, he disappeared. Flustered, I reached for my kimono wrap and scrambled out of the hot spring to locate my chaperone. On the one hand, I needed to tell him I had been summoned, but on the other, I was instructed to be in P's chambers alone. What should I do? My scheduled time ticked away quickly as I searched for my Valet. When I needed Andy, I could never find him, and when I didn't, he would appear out of thin air.

I did manage to find my teacher, who could pass on the message and also told me where I would find P. Even though I scuffled as fast as my slippered feet could carry me, I was several minutes late for my appointment. I had no intension of falling flat on my face like I had at the tea house.

In the Ryokan

I knelt to quell my exhilaration before tapping on the sliding door to His Highness' chamber. *"Enter!"* a voice authorized.

Nobody was inside the chamber. I saw an open doorway into a beautifully landscaped Japanese garden. Not sure how to proceed, I waited before entering. The voice behest from an adjoining chamber, *"In here!"*

I knocked lightly at the closed door. No sound was heard. I rapped again. Nothing. I slid the door slowly ajar, when a hand reached out to grab the back of my kimono collar. I was dragged into the unilluminated chamber. Ropes bound my hands behind my back. I did not know what had hit me. A cloth gagged my mouth and another blinded my eyes. I couldn't scream or see. Images of the roguish Miyaz at Villa Domergue flashed through my mind. I was frightened and aroused all at once. I panicked!

69

Andy, Where are You?

"Life is not complex. We are complex. Life is simple, and the simple thing is the right thing."
Oscar Wilde

1967

In P's Chambers

It was close to dinnertime when I left the prince's chambers. The experience would leave a lasting impression throughout my life. Although the good doctor had iterated that it was perfectly acceptable in their culture for mature men to take adolescent boys or girls as lovers; never did he mention that at certain occasions, he and P were involved in orgies or ménage à trois with adolescent playmates. The notion that the sheik and the prince played together had never entered my mind. I finally surmised that it was during these trysts that Fahrib had the opportunity to be intimate with His Highness. Although fellatio, sodomy and anilingus did not enter their equation of shared activities, they did exchange passionate kisses and sensual caresses – as long as the other parties involved were the center of attention. That was precisely what transpired at P's chamber that evening.

Bondage

The mystery master knotter who tied me to the pole worked with precision and swiftness. My legs were strung securely over a bamboo pole, and I was hoisted upside down like a naked sacrificial lamb. With my hands tied behind my back and my head and shoulders slumped lightly on the floor, my heart palpitated with fear and vulnerability. Uncertain of what was to happen, I struggled to get free. P's voice echoed in the noiseless chamber, *"Hmm! Nice! You are truly a beautiful boy now, especially when you are so* defenseless. *It is indeed a beautiful sight to behold."* He circled the room admiring his henchman's handiwork. He sneered, *"No harm will befall you if you obey my commands. If you don't..."* he paused for drama, *"Your smooth little backside will be whacked raw. You understand me, you little twerp?"* he lifted my head and barked at my face. *"If you do my bidding, I will release your blindfold."*

I nodded timorously. He ordered his accomplice to untie my blindfold. It took me several seconds to get my bearings within the dimly light room. P wore a jockstrap and held a paddle in hand. His musky masculinity intoxicated me as he knelt in front and pushed my nose to sniff his engorgement. He gave my face a slap before pulling away. He hollered, *"You like that, boy?"* he sniggered. *"You'll have to work for it if you want it down your throat."* He gestured to his Japanese accomplice to take his stance. Takioko stood in front of me, his throbbing erection beating against my gagged mouth. He lowered his heaving sack to tantalize my nostrils before pushing my face to inhale his dangling manliness. My oral constraints restricted me from suckling its roundness.

"Whack!" The sound of P's paddle landed on my backside. I twitched in pain. *"You rascal! I didn't tell you to inhale his scent!"* my master commanded as he pulled

my hair backwards. *"If you want your gag released, you stay silent! Understand, imp?"*

I concurred apprehensively. A third man stepped forward to untie the kerchief. It took me a moment to recognize the doctor. During the times we were together, he was cordial and intangible. Never was there a moment when he showed signs of erotic interest in my person. I had never seen him completely naked, let alone sprouting a pulsating erection against my face. His sexiness aroused my length to hardness. Without uttering a word, he forced my head onto his groin and plunged his stiffness into my oral orifice. I choked from the onslaught, yet I longed to savor his curvaceousness, to relish the object of my lustful affection. He relinquished his length from my mouth as rapidly as he had inserted it, leaving me pining for more. Holding my face to his, he spat into my mouth before planting a passionate kiss in my receiving orifice. The scent of Old Spice whiffed through my nostrils, stirring my hardness to quiver.

I **secretly** reveled in this inevasible Masters-and-Slave game. This enticing sexuality was at once **deplorable and laudable**. Before I could luxuriate in my thoughts, a luscious mouth was suckling my engorgement. A blow hit my derriere, propelling my palpitating organ into Takioko's oral orifice. The Japanese straddled the front of my hanging physique. He pried my buttocks apart for P's exploring fingers while I swallowed deliriously the doctor's feed, tasting his manhood as he alternated between French kissing and shoving his thrusts into my mouth. These rapturous barrages threw me into fits of perspicacious dexterity. I was pleasuring my domineering Masters as much as they were gratifying my prurience. My vulnerability thrilled their alpha manliness to states of heightened enthusiasm as His Highness chastised me with verbal castigations. His fingers continued jabbing into my anal opening. His other hand paddled my bottom. *"Open* *up!"* he roared. The pricking pain from the paddling had become sensual revelations to sexual gratifications of great expectations. I yearned to be filled with my Master's virility. P's prodding gave way to Takioko's rimming. His ramming tongue electrified my trembling body to rhapsody.

Fahrib's bouncing tumescence was soon replaced by the prince's intensified desires. I knew P was ready to deposit his brawniness into my mouth as his leaking pre-emissions flowed capriciously down my receiving throat. The sheik's ravenous **fellatio**, together with the lawyer's enthralling anilingus, triggered multiple orgasmic contractions in my being. I wiggled ebulliently on the hanging pole as I exploded blasts of creamy lava into the Arab's oral cavity.

Before I had a chance to catch my breath, the Japanese had lowered my depleted body onto the futon. Releasing my bondage, he threw my legs over his shoulders and plowed into me with abandon.

The doctor shared my bounty with His Highness as I suckled provocatively on his drumming organ and tumid pouch. Takioko's amatory yowling coursed through my reverberating anatomy. Streams of nourishing nectar douched into my core to overflowing capacity. My tightness engulfed his shuddering member as he slumped onto my heaving chest. Only when his heavy breathing subsided and with the remains of his pollination seeded deep within me, did he relinquish his authority only to be supervened by none other than my beloved, the very person I had been searching for before I had come to His Highness. In the semi-darkness, my lover had camouflaged himself to keep vigilance over the entire proceeding. If the precession had gotten too belligerent, he would have appeared sooner to rescue me. Now, the salubrious erotism had aroused his libido. He had to partake in this intrepid revelry, especially when witnessing his amore in an unhinged euphoric delirium. Like the others in the party, he too was entranced by my unbridled defenselessness. Their tempestuous aroma of unrestrained copulation had besotted Andy's infatuation for me. He needed to lay claim to my person, to acknowledge that I was his, no matter who had asserted himself over me. I handed my spirit to his dexterity, warranting subliminal sexual transcendence that only lovers of unified intellect could share. He eased into my wetness, oscillating us into an enchanted field of lucidity where young lovers dwell in magical silence amidst the envious eyes observing from the periphery. My lover made love to me without haste or immediacy. His **scrupulous** organ glided in and out, sending electrifying reveries throughout my being. I could not sustain this sexual arousal any further; I climaxed onto our heaving torsos just as my chaperone erupted his bounteousness into my core, sending quavering goose bumps all through our perspiring tenderness.

Our magnetism had also hypnotized the handsome doctor. He lowered his head and lapped at the oozing residues that were leaking out of my orifice. As soon as my guardian withdrew from my twitching hollow, the ruttish Arab jerked his stiffness and unleashed his libations onto Andy's rigidity. My Valet's erection responded to the man's bawdiness, he plunged his liberation back into the furthest recesses of my being, burying his firmness into my well lubricated tunnel. This time around, his pumping was hard and fast. I clawed at his muscular back, afraid to lose grip of his potency. He relinquished another abundance into my core. Our passionate kisses lingered as if time had stood still.

By the time we unfettered our spiritual bond, the men had disappeared to the onsen to cleanse away the telltale signs of our debacherous union.

A Feast for the Gods

When Andy and I entered a private dining room at the Ryokan, the rest of our entourage had already gathered. I did not know that the sheik had arranged this special dinner. The prince was the first to speak, *"I'd like to thank all of you for the hard work you've put into the Japan segment of Sacred Sex in Sacred Places. As you are aware, my good friend, Sheik Fahrib, has taken time from his busy schedule to join us on this trip. Without further ado, I'll have him take over the evening's proceedings."*

The doctor raised his glass to thank His Highness. We too toasted to the prince's generosity. *"Thank you for giving me the opportunity to be a part of Sacred Sex in Sacred Places,"* he announced. *"I'm deeply indebted to His Highness and my longtime friend, Prince P, whom I've known since Islamic School. He's a capable leader to his people. I'm glad to renew our friendship whenever I can get away from my medical schedule, and I'm sure I'll see more of His Highness in the near future when we work together on different projects,"* he added as the restaurant staff brought out trays of raw food and fired up the fondue hotpots, readying the scrumptious feast for us to partake. *"Besides having a chance to meet all you wonderful people, there is a special young man I'm very honored to be acquainted with."* We looked around to see who the Arab was referring.

I was astonished when Fahrib stared at me and announced, *"Although we met a little more than a week ago, through this boy's exculpatory eyes, I've come to know and to understand myself better. It is refreshing to view the world in his childlike light. I would very much like to see more of him in the future."* He continued, *"Once, he quoted me a saying from Oscar Wilde. He said, 'Life is not complex. We are complex. Life is simple, and the simple thing is the right thing.'"* P was the first to applaud, followed by the rest us.

The prince congratulated Fahrib, *"Well said, my friend, well said. Let us toast to this young chap, whoever he is."*

We mumbled among ourselves as we raised our glasses to toast this mystery boy.

70

The Golden Pavillion

"When you are in harmony with yourself everything unfolds with grace and ease."
Panache Desai

1967

In Kinkaku-ji

This Zen Buddhist temple, the Temple of the Golden Pavilion, was located in the heart of Kyoto. It is an excellent example of Muromachi design; a minimalistic approach, recreating a larger landscape around a single opulent gold-leafed structure. Kinkaku-ji (the Temple of the Golden Pavilion) or Rokuon-ji (Deer Garden Temple) is an ancient Japanese architectural wonder. However, the present pavilion dates only from 1955: it was rebuilt after a schizophrenic monk, Hayashi Yoken, burned the original structure down. Yoken's story and Kinkaku-ji were made famous in 1958 by the renowned twentith century Japanese author and revolutionary, Mishima, who was nominated for the literary Nobel Prize three times during his life. Mishima's death was as dramatic as the temple's arson – he and his private militia took over a government building, where he gave a speech on a balcony before proceeding indoors to commit *Seppuku,* a Japanese form of ritualistic **suicide by disembowelment.**

It was at this tranquil Deer Garden Temple that our final segment of *Sacred Sex in Sacred Places* was filmed. As was our photographers' ritual, our entourage assembled at the Kinkaku-ji in the wee hours of dawn, before the tourists arrived en mass to view this ancient monument.

At the first glow of an autumnal morning, when the rising sun was just peeping its golden head over the horizon, Andy and Keiko were called to position by our photographers. When it came time for my Valet to simulate a love-making scene with Keiko, their rapport was one of true lovers rather than models or actors playing an intimate scene. Andy's enthusiasm and the Eurasian's avidity sparked an ineffable jealousy within me. An overwhelming invidiousness washed over my person. I hated myself for this negativity, yet my covetousness also inflamed a sexual curiosity I had never felt before. I watched the two paramours with incongruous intensity as the tantalizing eroticism was enacted. Like Mario and Aziz's camera lenses, I, too, was enthralled by their vehemence. Their arousing prelude seemed to defy rationality. They glided with serenity and grace like a pair of flittering dragonflies who were to merge into an inseparable pulsating organism. Magnetized by their intrinsic quiddity, I envisaged Andy's and my love-making. Insurmountable questions whirled in my swirling mind:

- Was this the same kind of alluring magnificence that captivated our *Sacred Sex in Sacred Places* photographers when Andy and I made love?
- Is this that certain chemistry that transforms the mundane into magic when the lovers are unperturbed, relaxed and self-possessed?
- Is this the 'look of love' that Shakespearean sonnets and Byronic heroes so wordily described throughout the ages?
- Am I witnessing the love between my Valet and me being played out by Andy and Keiko?

Thrown off by my preoccupation, I did not detect the sheik standing next to me. He whispered in my ear, *"This is art in motion. It is like watching you and your chaperone copulate."* He continued as he directed his gaze towards the copulating couple, *"Sex is indeed wholly satisfying when two affectionate people emerge unanxious, rewarded, and ready for more."*

I was caught off guard and did not know how to respond to his observations. Seeing my cheerlessness, he inquired, *"Do I detect traces of jealousy in your spirit, my boy?"*

"I'm not the jealous type," I lied.

"Ahh Hah! I don't believe you. I think you are not being truthful," the Arab declared.

I turned away sheepishly.

"Don't forget I'm a doctor; I've taken psychiatric seminars to know when a person is not jocund. I can tell when my patient is unhappy.

"Tell me what's bothering you, young man," he pressed.

Subduing Jealousy

Finally, I turned to face my friend, my eyes about to burst into tears. Fahrib took my hand and guided me to the terrace overlooking the glistening lake and tranquil gardens. He began, *"My beautiful boy, allow me to give you some suggestions to overcome jealousy."*

"How?" I blurted as tears of sadness streamed down my face.

He put my hand in his, said, *"In order to conquer jealousy, you have to know that the person whom you are jealous of has done something good in the past, and now he is reaping the fruit. Therefore, if you release your ego-driven self to the wind, you, too, will one day receive good kismet in return. That my boy, is rule number one.*

"Rule number two: take your jealousy as inspiration to gain merit from Allah.

"Rule number three: create a sense of belonging with the person you are jealous of, and visualize him as an extension of you.

"Rule number four: be grateful for all that you have that he doesn't have. In your case, an example would be your unique education, which only a few have the privilege to experience. You also have a Valet, mentor and chaperone who loves you unconditionally and unceasingly.

"The fifth rule may be difficult, but if you can become friends with your adversary, you'll find that you have a lot more in common than not.

"The sixth rule is to be aware that in the current of time, everything will perish and cease to exist, and this grievous affliction will also pass."

I listened attentively to the physician's sound advice. He promulgated, "This brings me to rule number seven: remind yourself that at one time or another, he, too, had jealous feelings similar to your own, and understand that all that envy of you has not brought fulfillment in the long haul.

"Rule number eight is to praise the person you are jealous of superlatively. Remember: what goes around will return to you.

"Always remind yourself that feelings of elation or rejection are temporary; these emotions will soon pass to nothingness. That is rule number nine.

"Rule number ten may be difficult, but one of the best ways to overcome jealousy is not to recognize this negative emotion. If you view this negative feeling as your reality, it will energize your ignorance to grow. Sooner or later it will expand to become the monster that you visualize it to be. This negative emotion will dissipate if you do not give it power.

"The final rule is to see your opponent as a passing phase in your mind's eye. Our physical bodies will return to dust sooner or later, and he too will perish. Therefore, don't waste your positive energy by giving strength to the negative forces.

"Last, but not least, is a rule of thumb. If none of the above suggestions work, go for a stroll or sleep it off," my advisor jested flippantly.

My Guardian Angel

While the sheik dished out his rules of subduing the green-eyed-monster, the golden exterior of Kinkaku-ji was lit by the morning sun. The sparkling reflection of the temple on the shimmering pond blinded my eyes. Beams of flaxen rays glistened as if an angelic host had descended from the cloudless sky. My guardian angel had once again manifested in my presence. He beckoned me to his side with outstretched arms before wrapping his gigantic wings around my person. He embraced my spirit, warming my disillusionment with his cozy, feathery down. My disenchantment evaporated. My heart enveloped the purity of his ethos, as he had done a year ago when I had dreamed of him before joining the Enlightened Royal Oracle Society. He whispered now as he did before, *"When you call my name, I will be by your side. I will never abandon you. Do not be afraid. No harm will befall you. Now go and be on your way."*

The angel evanesced as quickly as he had appeared, leaving me in the company of the doctor and the Marquis. Mathieu queried as soon as I had snapped out of my euphoria, *"What's with this boy?"*

Before I could get my bearings, Fahrib had replied on my behalf, *"He is suffering from a case of 'jalousie'."*

Amused by the doctor's diagnosis, Mathieu queried, *"De qui est-il jaloux (who is he jealous of)?"* The sheik indicated the copulating couple, now passionately weaving around the icon of Bodhisattva Kannon within The Tower of Sound Waves.

The French aristocrat mused, *"I see."*

The Arab dispensed, *"Young, a walk in these serene gardens will brighten your spirit and cheer up your soul."*

"What an excellent idea! I'll be delighted to keep him company while his chaperone is busy at it," the marquis championed.

I was afraid to be alone with the Frenchman in case he used this opportunity to accost me. I commented importunately, *"I'm not allowed to be out of Andy's sight. He is very strict about this."*

"I'll come with you. I, too, would like to see the grounds of this majestic property," Fahrib remarked.

I was indeed glad that the doctor accompanied us. It was not that I disliked the marquis – it had more to do with my desire to gain the upper hand with this man by holding off his sexual advances for as long as I possibly could. At that young age, I already knew the rules of cat and mouse. The further I could stave him off, the more he would covet my affection and the more lavish gifts I would receive from this wealthy aristocrat. This was a secret I did not reveal to anyone, not even to my beloved Andy. His forthrightness would have censured my iniquitous scheme. I was sure my noble Valet would never approve my repugnant stratagem. I was also fully aware that my outward innocence could charm many, and this asset was my weapon for achieving my goals and aspirations. I had yet to conceive that what I put out would eventually return to haunt me.

Ginkaku-ji

This sister pavilion never attained the glory of the Temple of the Golden Pavilion. The creator, Ashikaga Yoshimasa, of Ginkaku-ji (the Silver Pavilion) had planned his retirement villa and gardens as early as 1460. It was after his passing that this extensive property was converted into a Zen temple. The Silver Pavilion sought to emulate the golden **Kinkaku-ji**, built by Yoshimasa's grandfather, Ashikaga Yoshimitsu. Yoshimasa's initial plan was to cover the exterior with a distinctive silver foil, but due to the onset of the Ōnin War, construction halted.

Similar to Kinkaku-ji, Ginkaku-ji was originally built to serve as a place of rest and solitude for the Shogun. During his reign, Shogun Ashikaga Yoshimasa inspired a new outpouring of traditional culture, which came to be known as **Higashiyama Bunka** (the Culture of the Eastern Mountain). Having retired to the villa, it was rumored that Yoshimasa sat in the pavilion, contemplating the serenity and beauty of the gardens as the war worsened and Kyoto burned to the ground.

It was here that the three of us sat to contemplate the eternal beauty of the unfinished Temple of the Silver Pavilion, officially known as Jishō-ji, the Temple of Shining Mercy. The abundance of varieties of mosses and the 'Mount Fuji' sand garden within the inner courtyard garnered an emotional poignancy within me.

Tears filled my eyes once again. This time, they were droplets of joy. I was weeping at the grandeur of Allah's dazzling magnificence, crafted by the hands of men. As the abundance of reddish-golden maple leaves flickered onto the yellow earth, serendipity washed over my being.

The advice the learned physician had so eloquently expressed earlier had made perfect sense. A sense of bromance for Fahrib took hold of me. Unexpectedly, I reached over and planted a lingering kiss on Fahrib's lips. Astonished by my unanticipated action, the marquis looked on in amazement. The sheik, taken by surprise, was as bewildered as our companion. He did not know how to react to my sudden, impassioned outburst. Before he could utter a word, I imbedded another kiss on the doctor's lips. He did not withdraw. Instead, our lips stayed locked in a passionate embrace.

I, for one, did not know what had come over me. Neither did the Arab. Neither of us pulled away until the marquis forged a fraudulent cough, *"Uhh Hmmm!"* he voiced phlegmatically. *"I'm still here, boys. Do you need a moment to yourselves?"*

We pulled away instantaneously. I did not know how to respond to that remark. Fahrib did the talking: *"That won't be necessary. I think we should be heading back to join our entourage."*

We prattled on much about nothing on our journey back to the golden pavilion. By then, the Arab and I had already forged an unspoken bond that only the two of us could chronicle in our implicit lives' journals.

Before I was called upon to take position in the *Chamber of Dharma Waters* for my *Sacred Sex in Sacred Places* session with Guy and Yuri, my jealousy of Keiko had miraculously vanished. In its place was veneration and reverence for the young man and my Valet. As per the sheik's advice, I had made it a point to befriend Keiko. True to Fahrib's advice, the Eurasian also possessed jealousy and envy like everyone else. As he had mentioned, every one of us is harnessed by an unseen connecting thread, and that is the cosmic order of the human race. Keiko was indeed not just an extension of me, but of all humanity.

71

The Pleasure Garden

"A man falls in love through his eyes, a boy through his ears."
Woodrow Wyatt

Early June 2013

I was finally ready to reply to Dr. Arius after pondering for a few days how best to respond to his gibberish message. I wrote:

Hello Dr. A.S.

I hope this email finds you well. Walter and I continue to pray for your recovery. Although I have only known you for a little more than a year, we had become pen pals. I'm grateful for your kind assistance in helping me locate Oscar and, in an indirect way, trace Andy. You are very kind to perform a case study of my young life even though we have not met.

I understand it is tiring for you to battle your disease, yet your credence and faith in **A Harem Boy's Saga** *is a powerhouse of conviction for me to continue documenting my autobiography. I look forward to your recovery so we can continue our regular correspondence. I miss hearing your words of encouragement and friendship. If we lived in closer proximity, we would have visited you and your lovely companions, Pepsi and Cola, sooner. We* *hope to meet you in the not-too-distant future when we travel to Europe next year.*

Do email me when you are feeling better. I greatly cherish our communications.

Best of health, my friend!
XOXOXO
Young.

1967

The Rakuen Ochaya

On the night we were to depart Kyoto for Paris and London, the prince had requested Takioko to introduce our entourage to the finest *Ochaya* (tea house) in the city. Although there were numerous ochayas at *hanamachi* (flower street) in the geisha district of this ancient city, Takioko escorted us to the Rakuen Ochaya (Pleasure Garden Tea House).

There is a major difference between an *ochaya* and *chashitsu* (tea room). Although the former's literal meaning is 'tea house', ochayas do not serve tea, except as an ordinary beverage. Rather, they are exclusive pleasure establishments. They are open only to established patrons and their guests. Since Takioko's father, Mr. **Fujikawa** was a patron of the Pleasure Garden, our entourage was welcomed by the house's *taikomochi*, the Japanese equivalent of a court jester, Orutsu.

In an ochaya, patrons are provided private spaces to be entertained by *geikos* (geishas) and *maikos* (geisha apprentices) during and after an extravagant meal.

In general, geishas are not affiliated with a particular ochaya. They are hired from an *okiya* (a geisha house) to entertain, converse, flirt sensually, serve food and beverages, play traditional musical instruments, sing, play games, and dance. An ochaya typically does not prepare food, but customers may order **in house** catering or **à la carte** dishes from a variety of restaurants within the geisha district.

The **Rakuen Ochaya**'s signage hung in the middle of the main entrance, above the *noren* (Japanese entrance curtain) of a large house. Although most ochayas are licensed by the city and cater to a discreet clientele, the front entrances are nondescript but not particularly secretive.

Orutsu greeted us with warm pleasantries before beckoning us to follow him to a spacious room with a stage at one end. We removed our shoes and left our personal belongings with the staff before entering the tatami floor chamber. Comfortable kimonos were also provided to prepare us for a gratifying evening at the Garden.

As soon as we were seated and drinks were ordered, the taikomochi began his ribaldrous storytelling, peppered with racy heterosexual jokes and risqué gay, lesbian and transgender double entendres. Although Orutsu's jokes were spoken in Japanese, another English speaking *houkan* (the formal name for *taikomochi*), Sukoji, interpreted them in English. Still, many were lost in translation. The majority of us, who spoke no Japanese, did not find his japes witty or humorous. The only two who found the jester funny were Takioko and Gabrielli, who spoke Japanese. The lawyer came close to rolling on the mat in delirious laughter.

As soon as our drinks appeared, so did the ornately dressed and made-up geishas and their maikos. It was difficult to tell the sex and age of these entertainers; they wore white makeup with redder than red lipstick and possessed demure, passive demeanors that traditional Japanese culture would consider seductively provocative.

I was hypnotized by their genteel movements, delicate hand gestures, elaborate costumes, wigs, makeup and accessories. I was not the only one who seized the opportunity to apprehend these rare beauties with my automatic camera; our two professional photographers also whipped out their cameras to snap away at these decorous mortals of the night. Little did we suspect that as the evening progressed, some of these savoir-faires would transform themselves into erotic *oirans* (courtesans or women-of-pleasure), and not all was what met the eye.

Conversation with Takioko

No sooner had our scrumptious meal been served on handcrafted porcelain dishes than the beautiful geishas and their maikos started performing a series of traditional dances, playing Japanese classical musical instruments and singing love ballads of yore. Under the strings of unperturbed serenity, my Valet and I had a chance to ask our guide, seated next to us, *"Is this place a bagnio?"*

"What's a bagnio?" the Japanese asked, looking puzzled.

My chaperone resumed, *"A bordello, otherwise known as an 'Oriental prison'."*

"Good god! No! This is a registered traditional tea house; it is not a brothel!" the lawyer exclaimed, offended. He continued, *"These beauties are not common prostitutes. They are superior hostesses and entertainers, specialized in the art of entertaining men..."*

I blurted, *"You mean, like courtesans. Are they mistresses or kept women by wealthy aristocratic men?"*

My sudden interjection seemed to have thrown our guide off guard before he resumed, *"Well, eh... Some of them may be mistresses, but first and foremost, they are versed in the arts of beauty and refinement. Nothing at all like prostitutes."*

Andy emphasized, *"They are like mysterious birds of paradise. I'm sure many heterosexual men are captivated by their intrinsic exoticism."*

The lawyer seemed to take my lover's proclamations as an approbation to his proud culture. He murmured, *"You may be surprised by what you'll find under their exterior deportment."*

"What do you mean?" I questioned excitedly.

He grinned and said nothing until he finished chewing a mouthful of food. *"Well, my pretty ikemen (twink), you'll soon find out, won't you?"*

I looked at him, puzzled, not knowing the meaning of 'ikemen'. He continued gobbling mouthfuls of food. I decided to ask Sukoji what 'ikemen' meant when I had the chance.

An abundance of both subtle and obvious flirtations went on during and after dinner, when the geishas were pouring our drinks and serving food. The Middle Easterners in our group were indeed having a fun time, not to mention our European contingent. The only persons who were distant from these provocative indispositions were Ludovic, Ikram, the baron, Andy, Mario and me. Since the six of us were oriented toward males, we found ourselves chatting with each other while the rest were entertained by the coy and bashful geishas. Our Arab friends in particular relished the geikos' and maikos' attentiveness, especially after they were informed by the two taikomochis that the maikos' *Mizuage* (which literally means 'a hoisting from water' and metaphorically means 'loss of virginity of a maiko') would soon be auctioned to the highest bidder. Since our Arab contemporaries had a cultural history of bidding to deflower virgins, they were more than ready to bid for this opportunity.

Mizuage

When it came time for the auction, the houkans announced, *"This is a traditional ceremonial rite of passage for maikos in our geisha community. Her onee-*

san ('older sister') will exercise the symbolic gesture of cutting the topknot of her maiko's hair to signify that she is ready to come of age as a geisha.

"For each of our three maikos, it is an important initiation rite to enter womanhood by offering her virginity to the highest bidder for an evening with them. Please do not worry about future relationships with our maikos once your function of deflowering her is served." He added, *"Let me be clear that the amount of financial contribution acquired from your bidding for the maiko's mizuage will be used to promote her debut as a geisha. This is not to be misconstrued as an act of prostitution. Your generosity is a gift for her to emerge from her cocoon, to metamorphose into a beautiful butterfly. Before we begin the bidding, let me extend my warm thanks on behalf of the three maikos to our beneficent patrons for their generosity."*

The Bidding

Prince P, Sheik Fahrib, Wazir Thabit, Habibi Aziz, Vicomte Charles, Marquis Mathieu and Takioko were that evening's magnanimous bidders. The rest of us watched with interest as the bids went higher and higher. My Valet turned to my professor and asked, *"Is it legal to pay to deflower maikos in this day and age? I thought this tradition was abolished."*

The learned Gabrielle answered softly, *"As far as I'm aware, this practice was outlawed some years ago."*

My guardian continued with curiosity, *"Why is it happening as we speak?"*

"Don't forget, Andy, this practice has been around for centuries. Customs are difficult to eliminate overnight, even if they have been outlawed. It may take years or decades to dissipate. It may even go undetected or disappear underground, like the bidding for the best 'batche' at the Sekham," my teacher advised.

Aziz bid the highest for the first maiko on the auction block, followed by Vicomte Charles for the second. Before the final maiko went on the auction platform, the taikomochis heralded jestingly, *"Sakura, our final maiko is a unique specimen. Unlike Yukisan and Sukisan, who are both pretty lasses, Sakura on the other hand possesses the best of all elements that any male or female will find satisfactory.*

"Which of you benevolent benefactors will be the first to delight in Sakura's jollies?"

The count and the baron had joined in the final bid. They obviously wanted to compete to be the benevolent benefactor to deflower this virgin she-male. I reasoned that the doctor's participation in this bidding war was for another opportunity to be intimate with His Highness. He knew his best friend would not leave him out of the picture if another **ménage à trois** or orgy were to follow. To me, that was the scope of Fahrib and P's intimacies. Their cultural and religious upbringing had ingrained in them that an adult homosexual relationship was a sin.

Between us, Andy and I betted on whom the grand prize would go to. The loser would perform any task the winner desired.

I guessed the sheik, while Andy championed His Highness. True to form, it was P who outbid the rest.

I felt that the bidders had wanted to 'give face' to the prince; after all, he had hosted our entire stay in the Land of the Rising Sun and was also the principal patron of our projects. As in chess, the players knew when to advance or retreat. Therefore, it was an astute and calculated move on the players' part to give P the winning hand.

I had guessed correctly; the prince invited none other than the sheik to participate in a **ménages à trois**.

As to our private wager, it was now stalemate between my opponent and me.

72

No. 11 Place Des Etats-Unis

*"You attract people with the qualities you display.
You keep them with the qualities you possess."*

Bernard Tristan Foong

1967

Paris

     Prince P was one of those people who did not like to see my Valet and me depart after our three-month service at the Quwah. He detained us by insisting we accompany his entourage to Paris to view potential Carousel sites. It was after much hassle and jostle by Wazir Thabit, Sheik Fahrib and Gabrielli that he finally relented and flew us back to Heathrow Airport, one day after we were scheduled back at Daltonbury Hall. If he'd had his way, we would be staying another term in his service.
     Fahrib convinced His Highness that he would see us after our Christmas and New Year holidays; after all, he had handed his application in to the E.R.O.S. board for membership. He did not mention to my Valet or me that our service would be required when E.R.O.S. approved his application. The sheik's outstanding **résumé**, plus P, Thabit and another fellow Arab members' recommendations, was more than sufficient to get him into our secret society with flying colors.

Although at the time my chaperone and I were not aware of where we would be stationed after Quwah, we had strong suspicions that our next assignment would be at the sheik's household. During the short period we had been in each other's company, I had become the doctor's confidant.

Like the prince, I too had fallen in love with Paris. As much as I'd like to return to Daltonbury Hall in time for the students' annual Christmas Ball, I was glad to spend a couple of days in this enchanted metropolis. This time around, the prince had his assistants book us into the Four Seasons Hotel George V, located at number 31 Avenue George V, Paris.

No sooner had we checked into our suites than we were whisked off to no. 11 Place des États-Unis, the magnificent residence of Vicomtesse Marie-Laure de Noailles, for a party she had arranged to entertain His Highness and his entourage. Since her untimely demise in 1971, this resplendent building has been converted into Le Maison Baccarat (the Baccarat headquarters). Today, it houses the brand's luxury boutique, its gallery museum and an in-house restaurant. The Vicomtesse's original ballroom of exceptional craftsmanship is now the setting of the maison's most beautiful achievements: Art de Vivre, Jewelry and Accessories, as well as its sparkling legendary collections.

During the Vicomte and Vicomtesse ownership, this three thouand-square-meter home was dedicated to the painters, writers and musicians of her era.

Her artistic and social skills extended far beyond the accumulation of fine art objects to the people she associated herself with. Her lavish party of interesting guests from international walks of life was legendary, and welcoming His Highness, the guest of honor that evening, was no exception to the rule.

At 11 Place des États-Unis

As the evening progressed, my chaperone and I were introduced to a certain Count Guy Philippe Henri Lannes de Montebello, whose aristocratic lineage stretched back to the Marquis de Sade. In the early winter of 1967, de Montebello was working as an assistant curator within the Department of European Paintings at the Metropolitan Museum of Art in New York. He was visiting his aunt, the Vicomtesse, when his uncle Vicomte Charles introduced us: *"Guy, meet my friends from England. They are in Paris for a day before returning to their boarding school. This young man here,"* he said, directing his gaze at me, *"is planning to study fashion. I'm sure you'll have a lot in common since you are highly educated and well versed in art history..."* Just as soon as he introduced us, he was pulled away by other guests, leaving his nephew in our company.

After formal greetings, Guy said, *"I was in London before visiting Aunt Marie-Laure. When I'm in London, I love visiting Liberty's. Are you familiar with the store?"* Before either Andy or I could comment, he asserted, *"It was opened by Arthur Lasenby Liberty in 1875. He named it East India House. His brilliant idea of importing oriental style goods, especially fabrics, trims and accessories, to the English public, was a hit. He was an immensely successful solicitor of the artistic patronage, the likes of George Frederick Watts, James Whistler, and Frederick Leighton."*

I chimed before he could continue, *"Doesn't Liberty's produce their own oriental and medieval-inspired fabrics and prints?"*

"You're a keen observer, young man. Originally, Liberty was part of the 'Aesthetic Movement', brought about by artists and writers. It was a counterculture movement against what they saw as the dehumanization of the Victorian Industrial Age of steam power, industry, and mass production."

I chirped, *"In our art history class, we did learn about the Aesthetic Movement. The Pre-Raphaelite Brotherhood was created by Dante Gabriel Rosetti, William Holman Hunt, and John Everett Millais, if I'm not mistaken."*

The curator smiled and said, *"That's correct. These artists and designers favored a less restrictive culture that relied on handcrafted goods. They preferred clothing styles that were simple, elegant, and beautiful, based on the designs of the late Middle-Ages. These styles were the rage among their followers; it was not unlike our current hippie movement.*

"'Beauty for the sake of beauty' was their motto. **Art was meant to be beautiful, but that view did not reflect political or moral attitudes of the time."**

My Valet queried, *"Did this movement extend to architecture and engineering?"*

"Of course it did. There are many fine examples of the aesthetic architecture all over Europe." De Montebello added, *"Sometimes it is difficult to differentiate the Aesthetic Movement from the Art Nouveau and the Craft Movement. These various schools of thought have similar origins and were often influenced by one another, as often portrayed in* literature, fine art, furniture, metalwork, ceramics, stain glass, textiles, and wallpapers.*"*

"What are the similarities?" I asked.

"All three movements argue that art is not supposed to be utilitarian or useful in any practical sense. Instead, the artistic experience is a fully autonomous and independent aspect of human life. Thus, art should exist solely for its own sake. Therefore, they're sometimes referred to as 'Les Arts Décoratifs', or as the English call it, 'The Decorative Arts'.*"*

My Valet inquired, *"Can you give me some examples of architectural and engineering feats from these movements?"*

"*Unfortunately, the two of you are leaving Paris tomorrow; otherwise, I'd be happy to show you some fine examples of these three movements in the city and in Prague, Brussels and New York. Contact me when you return; I'll be delighted to show you some of these aesthetically pleasing works of art. Although I am based in New York, I travel frequently within Europe for my job with the Metropolitan Museum,*" the assistant curator proposed.

"*That would be splendid. I am a big architectural and engineering fan. I'll definitely take you up on your offer to see examples of 'Les Arts Décoratifs', especially when accompanied by an expert art historian such as yourself.*"

"*I'm sure Young will love to learn more about the costumes, fashions and accessories from these periods. Fashion is his passion,*" my guardian remarked.

Before we left the Count's presence, we exchanged contact information. I was pleased to know that there were some things my lover and I shared in common.

Potential Carousel Sites

The following morning, our entourage of six trooped off with the Aga Khan's realtor to view the three potential Carousel sites. Two were located at the ninth arrondissement while the last was situated in the Latin Quarter. The second venue held the best promise for all involved. It was a large, old-fashioned derelict dance hall. In its heyday, from the 1920s to before the Second World War, it had been a cabaret club that could rival any of its decadent Berlin clubs. After the war, it was converted into a pornographic cinema that catered largely to an underground gay audience, which was there to cruise, do drugs and have illicit sex.

At Vicomtesse de Noailles party, P, Ikram, Andy and I were introduced to Monsieur Fabrice Emaer, nicknamed 'The Prince of the Night'. He was a Parisian nightclub impresario and knew the major premier nightspots in the city. Marie-Laure planned to have him manage the Paris Carousel, and he had expressed interest in the project. Emaer and Ikram hit it off as soon as they were introduced. Besides being handsome and charming, Fabrice was also knowledgeable about Parisian nightlife, which endeared him to the kaneeth especially when it came to the seedier side of gay life. Like P's sadistic younger brother, Hamad, Ikram was beguiled by the sordidness of the Parisian gay lifestyle, to which "The Prince of the Night" was more than happy to introduce the interior designer.

I saw great potential in this theatre venue, even though it would have to be completely overhauled. There were beautiful art nouveau architectural elements that could be preserved and incorporated into Carousel.

Fabrice Emaer

Francis Paul Emaer grew up in Wattrelos, near Lille in northern France. His father, a traveling salesman for the local spinning mills, met an untimely death, leaving the family impoverished.

At seventeen, Emaer left home and traveled to North Africa and the French Riviera before settling in Paris. He had changed his name to the more elegant Fabrice while working as a stylist and make-up artist. Before long, the charismatic charmer breezed his way into Parisian high society; hence his presence at Marie-Laure's party.

He had opened his first dance club, "Le Pimm's Bar," in 1964. It soon evolved into the premier gay club on Saint-Anne Street, situated in the heart of the gay neighborhood near L'Opera, amidst an abundance of bars, bathhouses, and bordellos frequented nightly by gay locals and visitors alike. His clientele consisted exclusively of gay men who were there to cruise.

In 1967, he was already planning to start a high-end dance club. He said in one of our numerous meetings, *"The greatest innovation of my club idea is that it will be defined by glamour, not homosexuality. Everyone will be included - gay, straight, undecided. You don't have to be rich, you don't have to be famous, but you do have to be beautiful."* Emaer himself did fit the bill. His good looks and open personality endeared him to many. When his DJ friend, Guy, took over at the turntables, the Carousel and his future clubs became the 'epicenter of disco', attracting the international young and beautiful. On any given night, visitors might see the bad-boy artist Francis Bacon, Nureyev, the ballet régisseur, Mick and Bianca Jagger, the talk-of-the-town musician and his then lovely wife, Andy Warhol, the leading Pop Art figure, or the young, trendy designers Karl Lagerfeld, Yves Saint Laurent and Kenzo.

Unfortunately for Carousel, Fabrice left after a year of service before starting his very own 'Le Sept', more famously known as 'Club Sept'. This leading impresario ventured into a bigger and brighter horizon by creating the legendary 'The Palace,' which rivaled New York's Studio 54 during its heyday in the late 70s and early 80s.

His departure from Carousel proved to be a major blow to the Parisian Carousel. In less than twenty-four months, the Paris branch finally closed its doors in the year 1971, while the Japanese enterprise continued in full swing until the early 80s.

For my minor contribution to this short-lived but exciting Parisian dance establishment, His Highness had generously rewarded me with thirty thousand dollars. This financial gift did not included the abundance of other gratuities and jewels showered upon Andy and me during our time at the Quwah household. My time spent with His Highness was indeed a once-in-a-lifetime experience.

73

Naughty Bad Boys

"Let's be naughty and bad. That'll save Santa the trip."
Bernard Tristan Foong

1967

Back at Tolkien Brotherhood

It was mid-afternoon when Andy and I arrived at Daltonbury Hall. After the regular check-in procedures for returning exchange students, my Valet was returned to Yates Fraternity while I was assigned to share a room at Tolkien Brotherhood with a Junior named Albert and a Scottish 'big brother', Coilin. Albert was on a three-month sabbatical from his last Middle Eastern household in Jeddah, Saudi Arabia. He had returned to Daltonbury Hall for a break from the extensive travelling. His previous Valet, Jimmy, had accompanied another Junior back to Jeddah, leaving Albert in Coilin's care. Although I had much in common with Albert, our good-looking temporary BB was more reserved, speaking only when spoken to. I couldn't tell if he was a regular Daltonbury Hall 'big brother' or an E.R.O.S. recruit. Albert didn't have a clue either. The Junior confided that during the three months he had been under Coilin's supervision, the BB had remained scrupulous and reticent in regard to his personal matters.

Since I was in school for a week before students broke for our annual winter holidays, I did not pay much attention to Coilin's punctiliousness. I was simply happy to see my friends John, Samuel and Duc after several months' absence.

Conversation with John

John, like me, had just returned from a household service in Riyadh. Since Albert, John and I had many interesting stories to exchange, we met after class for a snack at the Hobbit. Just then, Coilin entered the canteen alone. He greeted us cordially before sitting at the bar to savor his pints. I couldn't help but whisper, *"John, is Coilin an E.R.O.S. member?"*

My friend replied, *"I haven't a clue. I can find out."*

"How?" I queried. *"We can't ask him directly. If he's not one of us, he may get suspicious and ask questions about the society. We are not supposed to draw attention to E.R.O.S. We could get in trouble."*

The reformed bad boy gave me a mischievous grin before answering, *"I have ways of finding out. If you'd like to know, the two of you will have to play along with me."*

I exclaimed, *"Isn't it unethical to pry into our BBs' private affairs?"*

The Portuguese/Filipino smiled cheekily, *"We'll get to know this BB's little secrets in less time than you'd expect."*

"What's up your sleeves, you artful dodger?" Albert vociferated.

John patted our backs, leaned across and whispered into our ears. When he finished, he decreed rakishly, *"We'll meet at lunch tomorrow, and I'll fill you in with the details."*

By the time the three of us pulled our hooked pinkies away from each other, our secret agreement was already sealed.

Pre-birthday Romp

Since my birthday fell on December 8th and Albert's on December 20th, our close-knit chums decided to organize a pre-birthday celebration for both of us. My roommate and I, accompanied by Coilin, Andy, Duc, Samuel and John, hit *Bear & Boar,* a local pub. Although Juniors and Freshmen could not order alcoholic beverages, we could enter a tavern when accompanied by our BBs. We trotted off to the *Bear and Boar* for a boys' night out. The pub was already filling up with regulars and a sprinkling of weekend tourists. We and some other students from Daltonbury Hall were having a relaxing evening, chitter chattering about our school's latest gossip. After ordering a round of drinks, John inquired of Coilin, *"Which part of Scotland are you from?"*

The BB answered with the word, *'Glasgow'.*

"What's it like in Glasgow?" the Senior continued.

"Expanding by the minute," he responded without saying more than was necessary.

Albert queried inquisitively, *"You've been my 'big brother' for nearly three months, yet I don't know much about you or your family background."*

"There is nothing worth knowing about me or my family," he gulped down a glass of beer before replying.

I enquired, *"What kind of business is your dad involved in?"*

He did not answer until John offered to buy him another round of beer. When John returned with double pints in hand, the Scotsman was more than ready to swig down mouthfuls before responding, *"My dad is in the* shipbuilding, heavy industrial engineering and bridge-building business."

Upon hearing Coilin's pronouncement, Andy pricked up his ears immediately. He questioned, *"Is it a family business?"*

"Yes," the BB replied while guzzling down his third glass of beer. Little did he, Andy, Duc or Samuel realize that the Senior had added a couple drops of LSD to his drinks.

Duc purchased the next round, which Coilin swilled down as quickly as it was placed on our table. My Valet continued to snoop, *"Are your dad's ships and bridges built in Glasgow? I'm fascinated by these kinds of engineering marvels."* He was obviously dishing for an invitation to visit Coilin's family firm.

The Scotsman had relaxed considerably since entering the drinking establishment. *"Yes. Dad's construction factories are based in and around various parts of Scotland. If you are interested, you're welcome to return home with me during the holidays. I'm sure dad will be happy to show you the tricks of his trade. He wants to groom me and my brother to take over the family business. Personally, I've no interest in this line of work,"* he declared.

Andy jumped at the opportunity. *"That would be superb. I'll definitely take up your offer to visit your family's enterprise, possibly during our spring or summer holidays. Young and I will be in Spain when school breaks for our winter holidays. We've been invited to visit some friends in Barcelona and France. We'll be returning to London to ring in the New Year with Young's uncle, James,"* he declared.

As the evening progressed, Coilin became merrier and uninhibited. By his fifth round, he was talking gibberish. Before we knew it, he had climbed onto one of the pub's benches and was belting aloud the Scottish rendition of Happy Birthday to Albert and me. Before he could finish singing his nonsensical song, he threw up all over himself before collapsing in a heap on the floor. Astonished by such unscrupulous impropriety, Andy and Duc speedily dragged the drugged drunkard away from the tavern and back to our dorm. Although both BBs wanted to stay to make sure Coilin was alright, John, Albert and I assured them that we were more than capable of attending to our big brother's needs in case he threw up again or required our assistance in getting to the bathroom. Before Andy and Duc left for the night, they had stripped off Coilin's filthy clothes and scrubbed him clean before tucking the naked man securely into bed. Little did they suspect that our mischievous trio had concocted this devilish scheme to play a sexual prank on this taciturn big brother!

Manhandling Coilin

As soon as Andy, Duc and Samuel left, we set to work. Albert and I began **spurring** our BB's organ with our expert oral stimulations while John's nippy fingers galvanized and twitched his nipples with artful subtlety. Before long, his manhood was throbbing against his heaving washboard abdomen. We took turns suckling, nibbling and caressing his lithe physique. The Scotsman was out like a light. He didn't make any effort to brush away our continued arousal. We certainly had no intention of awakening this guzzler.

The Senior spread his legs apart and went to town lapping and swathing our big brother's dangling scrotum while Albert and I took turns to suckle his bublousness and munch at his manly nipples. I lifted his hands above his head and went to town sniffing, inhaling and licking the man's hairy armpits. Although the occasional moaning sounds emanated from the intoxicated victim, he made no effort to move. Our stiffnesses were bobbing unrelentingly from this reticent foreplay.

John signaled us to roll the unconscious man on his stomach. We did as was instructed. Before I knew it, our honcho had spread Coilin's derriere apart and delved his seductive tongue into his anal orifice. He rimmed desirously at the pinkish opening, spitting several wads of saliva into the man's anus before his prodding fingers wiggled its way into the puckered crevice. We were surprise that Coilin's buttocks had tilted slightly off the bed in reciprocation of the invading fingers. His muscular bottom was twitching to John's rhythmic jabs as if clamoring for further intrusion.

This titillating milieu sent Albert and me teetering for what was to happen next. Our roguish leader spit on his hardness. Without hesitation he thrust his length into the man, causing him to groan woozily for a brief second. John froze for a moment for the man's dubiety to subside before he besotted his backside with slow, cushy movements. The BB soon drifted back to deep slumber. The Senior gave us a nefarious wink to denote that all was under control and we could once again proceed without hindrance. The sight of our inebriated big brother being compromised by the puckish bad boy sent Albert and me to uncontrollable heights of erotic ecstasies. Kneeling at either side of our ganger, we jerked our erections to rapturous orgasmic releases. Albert's **copious**ness coated John's organ as he continued plowing into the receiving hollow. The erotic exaltations triggered me to deposit my seed onto the slippery anal recess. Moans of blissful jubilations sent the impish sprite over the threshold. He blew his creamy mass deep within the palpitating gape that was already filled with Albert's and my unrestrained profusions.

Our coltish gaffer was the first to lick up the accumulations before we shared the heap in a three-way kiss. Albert couldn't wait to clean up the remaining leftovers between our big brother's crack. I was the last to swab clean the delirious dribbling tell-tale remnants before our big brother awoke from his bootylicious dream of sensual and sexual erotica.

The Day After

By the time the chapel's wake-up bells tolled the next morning, Albert and I had shot out of our dorm room to the communal showers. We did not encounter Coilin until late that evening, when we had already retired to our individual beds.

Andy and I had visited Dr. Hunton, at 'The Rabbit Hole' (our school's clinic) that afternoon, for our regular check-up. Nurses Mary and Felicia were happy to see us before ushering us individually into the examination room. We received clean bills of health.

Over dinner, John pulled me aside when Andy and our friends were out of earshot. He announced, *"Shit! I think I have crabs. You and Albert better pay a visit to The Rabbit Hole to make sure you haven't been infected by those darn things."*

I chirped, *"Doctor Hunton gave me a clean bill of health this afternoon. Are you sure you have them?"*

"My groin has been itchy since our liaison," the Senior declared.

"Have you informed Albert?" I queried.

"No! You are the first person I told," he stated.

"I was with Albert this morning during communal shower and he didn't mention anything about his pubes being itchy," I commented before exclaiming, *"What are we going to do? Shouldn't we inform Coilin? I hope he didn't catch the creepy crawlies. You certainly gave him a good pounding last night."*

"Shit, shit, shit! I'm paying the doctor a visit right now. If you see Albert, ask if he has any symptoms," the

naughty boy advised before disappearing towards the direction of The Rabbit Hole.

I did not see Albert until I returned to my dorm room. Since Coilin was nowhere in sight, I had my chance to talk to the Junior. *"John told me he may have crabs. He went to The Rabbit Hole for a check-up. Do you have any symptoms?"* I asked, concerned.

"No, I feel fine. What about you?"

"I'm fine. Doctor Hunton gave me a clean bill of health this afternoon," I responded.

"Do you think Coilin has it? He does have a sprinkle of hair on his ass which I find very sexy. But if he has crabs, it's definitely not sexy," the Junior professed.

"Have you spoken with him today?" I queried.

"I saw him in passing. He did look at me suspiciously but said nothing extraordinary."

An alarming thought flew through my mind. *"If John has crabs, how are we going to break the news to our big brother? He'll have a fit if he finds out we took advantage of him while he was drunk, let alone secretly dosed with LSD,"* I declared anxiously.

"Don't start panicking until we hear what John has to say after his visit to the doc. It's only speculation at this juncture," Albert rendered.

"You're right! There's nothing we can do until we get an update from the Senior," I dittoed.

We pretended to be asleep when we heard the Scotsman enter the room. We dared not look at our big brother, in case he suspected something was amiss.

74

Cupid's Disease

*"And, after all, what is a lie? 'Tis but
The truth in masquerade."*
Lord Byron

1967

Err Oh!

Coilin finally cornered Albert and me as we were dashing out of our room for our morning communal shower. Our big brother questioned, *"Why are the two of you avoiding me? What's up your sleeves, you devils?"*

"Nothing," I lied.

He looked at us suspiciously before adding, *"If I find out you are lying, I'll send the two of you for discipline at the school's detention center."*

Albert and I looked him in the eye before we uttered, almost in unison, *"As you are aware, end of term examinations are in a couple of days. We are busy studying at the library."*

Albert added, *"We're not avoiding you. You are an excellent big brother and thank you for being concerned of our wellbeing."* He was obviously buttering up our guardian to soften his dubious stance.

I chimed, *"We had a number of assignments to complete for our professors; that's why you didn't see much of us yesterday."*

I detected a canny smile on his face. *"I want to see both of you during lunch break. Meet me at Canterbury at noon,"* he directed.

Albert and I nodded. *"We'll be at the cafeteria,"* we answered.

As soon as Coilin disappeared into the shower stall, my roommate whispered, *"Damn! Do you think he knows what happened?"*

I speculated, *"He seemed to accept our answers earnestly. I detected a sagacious smile when he asked us to meet him at noon."*

"Why do you think he wants to see us? Do you think he has crabs too?" the Junior queried.

"I don't know! By the way, have you heard from John about his diagnosis?" I questioned.

"I haven't a clue. We better find him as soon as we get out of class, during tea break," he asserted. *"We have to get our alibis straight in case Coilin asks further questions."*

I stated, *"I'll look for him after class and get him to join us during break."*

With that comment, we disappeared in different directions to get ready for morning tutorials.

Crabs or No Crabs?

I found the Senior exiting the lecture hall when I caught up with him. *"John! Wait!"* I shouted to the lad. Surprised to see me, he announced chirpily, *"Hi there, I've been meaning to find you. What's up, pal?"*

"You tell me! What did the doctor say?" I tweeted.

"He said I'm dying a slow death." John gave me a devious look.

"Be serious. What did the doctor diagnose?" I pressed.

"He said I'm dying of Cupid's disease. I have three months to live," the bad boy falsified with a grim pretense.

I opined with concern, *"No! You are not serious. You're pulling my leg. Besides, I've never heard of such a thing as Cupid's disease."*

"He gave me three months to live at most!" John sighed. *"I'll die of bladder failure. I'll explode from not being able to urinate,"* he fabricated, *"The pain is very bad; it's like cupids' arrows being shot up my cock and balls. That's why it's called Cupid's disease."*

"Are you really dying?" I exclaimed. *"Wait a minute,"* I continued to question. *"You made no mention of your itching symptoms. What did the doctor say about that?"*

Before I could inquire further, the bell rang for our next class. I ran towards the direction of my classroom as I shouted, *"Meet Albert and me at the cafeteria during tea break."*

Tea Break

As soon as I saw Albert enter the Canterbury, I rushed over to him. *"Terrible news! John has Cupid's disease, and he's been given three months to live,"* I divulged.

"I find that hard to believe. Are you sure he's not bamboozling you with his trickery? You know he's a prankster," the Junior stated unflinchingly.

I voiced in seriousness, *"He was resolute. The doctor diagnosed him with Cupid's disease."*

"What in hell is Cupid's disease? I've never heard of such an ailment."

"That's what he called it when I saw him in between classes. You can ask him when we see him. He's meeting us here," I replied.

Just as I was finishing my sentence, John's hands wrapped around our shoulders before he spoke, *"What are you going to ask me?"*

We shrieked at the thought of a diseased lad wrapping his arms around us. We writhed free, trying not to seem ill at ease. The Senior, sensing my paranoia, admonished, *"Are you afraid you'll catch my malady? Here, let me give it to you."* He proceeded to maul us waggishly.

My roommate and I screeched as we tried desperately to avoid physical contact with the diseased Rabelaisian. The more we parried, the bolder he became, until our unscrupulous commotion caused a couple of BBs to give us an earful and shush us out of the Canterbury. John chased us around the campus corridors, threatening to transmit the deadly virus for eluding him when he needed our friendship most, especially after we had pledged to stay loyal to each other.

The bell had struck again for students to resume class. Needless to say, we did not find out the truth about our friend's illness.

At the Canterbury

My heart was thumping a mile a minute when Coilin walked into the Canterbury. Albert had not appeared. My BB saw me queuing in the food line.

He asked, *"Is Albert here?"*

I looked around to see if the Junior had arrived. He was nowhere to be found. Unbeknown to me he was hiding behind a partitioned corner table, observing the Scotsman and me.

No sooner had I sat down than Coilin occupied the seat across from me. He stared at me but did not utter a word. I was beginning to get nervous. I dared not look at him; instead, I gobbled my food as fast as I could. I was anxious to get away. Coilin watched me intently while I ate. As soon as I had finished my last morsel, he began, *"Since I'm here alone with you,"* he said and paused, *"How far along are you in preparation for your upcoming exams?"*

Since I didn't think he wanted to see Albert and me to discuss our studies, I was thrown off track by his query. *"Not bad. I'm spending most of my time studying at the library. Haven't you noticed?"* I threw in the question to test Coilin's reaction.

"That's good, boy. If you require my assistance in your schoolwork, don't hesitate to ask. I'll be happy to help you."

In the short period of time I'd known this big brother, he'd always been reserved and a little standoffish. Now, he was offering to help me with my schoolwork. Something didn't seem right. *"Thank you. I'll take up your offer if I need help,"* I answered.

He added, *"I'm good at most subjects, especially math and biology. I know these are not your forte. I'm happy to assist if you have problems in these particular areas."*

Although my antsiness was eating at me, I showed no outward apprehension. I did my best to remain collected, but I dared not look him in the eye throughout our conversation. I sneaked a peek at him when I thought he wasn't looking. There was a contented smile on his face, as if he'd had an internal revelation.

"Thank you, sir. I'm sure I'll require your help soon. Math and science are not my strong suits."

"Well then, I'll help you with your studies after class tomorrow evening. Meet me at our dorm room," my BB affirmed.

Double Meanings

Before I could respond, he had already confirmed our five P.M. appointment. Changing the topic, he queried, *"You must think I'm an alcoholic?"*

Before I could respond, he continued, *"Contrary to what you perceive of us Scotsmen, it's in our blood to consume our spirits. We are pretty aware of our surroundings, even though we seem drunk outwardly."* He gave me a Cheshire cat's grin and winked. I remained quiet. He added, *"I know more than you think I do."* His remark left an unsettling knot in my stomach. I couldn't help thinking, 'Where are Albert and John when I need them? Am I being abandoned to face this dilemma on my own? Is this what it was like for John after my roommate and I left him to face his medical predicament alone?' By now, I was conscience-stricken on all counts – disloyalty to Coilin and John, not to mention the times I had hidden the truth from Andy. My inner guilt was manifesting internally, but I put on a brave face in front of the big brother.

The Scot commented, *"I had a fantastic time at your pre-birthday celebration. I enjoyed that you guys did all the dirty work."*

"Like scrubbing and cleaning up your mess," I revealed.

"And more," he declared, now grinning.

I was worried about what the man was going to say next. I turned to look at the entrance, wishing that Albert would miraculously appear. The BB resumed, *"I... like it."*

My curiosity was getting the better of me. *"What do you mean?"* I probed.

He gave me a sly grin but did not answer my question before taking a swig of beer. *"When I was growing up in Glasgow, I had several friends from school. There were times when we played doctors and patients. You know what I mean?"* He suddenly felt self-conscious. After a silence, he spoke, *"You boys are good at what you do."*

"What are we good at?" I pretended not to understand what he was referring to.

"When I was your age, we had no idea what we were doing," he muttered uncomfortably, expecting me to comprehend the double meanings of his questions. The man was obviously embarrassed about his sexuality. From that moment, I knew he wasn't an E.R.O.S. recruit. I decided to play dumb now that I had a better grasp on the situation.

I uttered, *"Oh! You mean, identifying the various parts of the human anatomy."*

My statement seemed to retreat him into his shell. He looked at me, wondering if he should continue the dialogue. He finally said with uncertainty, *"I enjoyed what you guys did the other night."* He looked embarrassed.

I decided to put the blame on the Senior. *"We were doing John's bidding. Just having some fun,"* I babbled.

He swallowed another mouthful of beer before maundering, *"I know. I like the sensation..."* By now, he had difficulty finishing his sentences. I finished it for him by nodding.

There was another long pause. He gulped down his glass of ale and got up to leave. Before he departed, he rasped, *"I'll see you tomorrow at five. Bring your mates if you wish."*

Diagnosis

By the time I arrived at the Hobbit, John and Albert were already seated at a corner table in the dining hall.

They waved me over. As soon as I had set my dinner tray on the table, the Senior began to pick at my plate's vegetables. Abashed by this indecorous gesture, I clamored vociferously, *"Get you filthy hands off my food."*

Amused by my uproar, he crowed moronically, *"Are you afraid of catching my disease?"*

He ducked to evade my slapping hand. *"You are already infected, you cocksucker,"* he pooh-poohed.

Albert came to my succor. *"Don't let this scoundrel fool you with his Cupid's disease baloney. He is toying with your gullibility."*

"You mean he fooled us into believing he had this stupid Cupid's disease?" I tutted, annoyed. I reached across to slap the side of his head. Once again, he dodged my smack. He chortled.

I barraged a string of curses at him before demanding an explanation. *"What in the world did you have on your wretched groin that made you itch? I hope you do die within these three months, bastard!"*

The picaroon burst out in unruly laughter. Albert spoke on his behalf, *"He had heat rash around his balls and inner thighs. Doctor Hunton gave him some soothing ointment and sent him on his way. This bugger is neither suffering from crabs nor dying."*

Before the Junior could continue, John gurgled, *"I tricked you!"*

"I bet there is no such thing as Cupid's disease," I hissed at the vagabond.

"Cupid's disease is slang for Gonorrhea. That, I swear, is the truth. If you don't believe me, you can ask Dr. Hunton yourself." The prankster crossed his heart and clasped his hands together as if in prayer.

By the time dinner was over, I had forgiven the Senior. I didn't bring up what had transpired between Coilin and me during our lunch meeting, and Albert did not press me. The Junior appeared oblivious to his no-show.

75

Mirrors of the Soul

*"The face is the mirror of the mind,
And eyes, without speaking,
Confess the secrets of the heart."*

Saint Jerome

December 1967

Daltonbury Hall School Library

While I was busy preparing for my end-of-term examinations, Andy was equally busy meeting with the school's student counselor, discussing engineering universities in the Southern Hemisphere. The week at Daltonbury Hall had been hectic, and I didn't see much of my Valet. I was deep in concentration in the library when a hand tapped my shoulder. My guardian stood beside me. He whispered, *"Come out to the hallway. I want to speak with you."*

I followed him to a quiet area. As soon as we sat on a bench, he said, *"I haven't seen much of you. How are you coping with your studies?"*

"I'm busy in the library every day. I'm doing fine," I replied.

Andy queried, *"Do you need help with your mathematics and science?"*

I blurted without thinking, *"Coilin is giving me private lessons this evening."*

Andy looked at me curiously, as if there was more to my statement. He queried, *"Your BB was quite reticent before; why the sudden interest in helping with your studies? Is there more to that story?"*

I shrugged my shoulders as if I hadn't a clue. He remarked, *"When and where are the two of you meeting? I'll be there. Two minds are better than one when guiding you in your schoolwork."*

I answered honestly, *"I'm meeting him at my dorm room at five P.M. I presume he is just being a helpful big brother, although he did ask me to bring my pals."*

"Who have you asked?"

"No one thus far," I declared.

My guardian enquired, *"Does Albert need help with his studies too?"*

"I don't know... I can ask him when I see him during recess."

"Do ask. I'll be happy to lend a guiding hand if he requires my help," Andy iterated with a quirky grin.

Although I did not confront my Valet, I had a feeling that my lover, besides being an amenable BB, was also interested in bedding my roommate. I nodded that I would pass on his message when I saw Albert.

At the Hobbit

Albert was dining alone at the canteen when I saw him. I jumped straight to the point as soon as I sat across from him, *"Andy asked if you need help with your schoolwork. He'll be happy to lend a guiding hand if you require private tutorials."*

He seemed startled by my message before responding, *"That's very kind of your Valet."*

I commented, *"Coilin and I are meeting at five P.M. to go over my mathematics and science lessons."*

"Coilin offered to help you with your studies?" my roommate questioned. *"He has never offered to assist me in the three months I've been under his care."* He looked at me suspiciously before exclaiming, *"What's going on between the two of you?"*

"Nothing!" I voiced. *"In fact, he specifically told me to ask you and John to join us at five P.M. We are meeting at our dorm room."*

The Junior chirped, *"Does he know we took advantage of him?"*

I pretended I didn't have a clue. *"I don't know. By the way, why didn't you show during lunch at the Canterbury yesterday? You could've asked him yourself,"* I stated.

"What did he say to you?"

I feigned ignorance. *"He offered to help me with studies so I could cope with my upcoming examinations. I'm to bring you and John if you guys require support.*

"If you are curious to find out what's on our big brother's mind, turn up at five. You can ask him yourself," I taunted.

"Is John going?" he questioned.

"I haven't seen him yet to ask. You can tell him if you locate him before I do," I voiced. *"Are you coming?"*

The inquisitive Junior did not commit. *"Maybe; maybe not. I'll see how my day goes."* After hesitating for a moment, he asked, *"Is Andy going to be there?"*

"Turn up at the appointed hour, and all will be revealed," I cajoled.

At the Dorm Room

At five P.M. sharp, Albert and I were at our dorm room with our big brother Coilin. As soon as we had sat at our respective writing desks, our BB wasted no time in getting us started. He had not expected Andy to join us – the knock on the door startled him. Although the Scotsman behaved professionally, there were times when his hand would casually brush against my thighs. He was obviously testing my reactions to his physical contacts. I made no sign of shying away; neither did I encourage him.

Coilin had assigned himself to help me while Andy worked with the Junior at his writing desk. To my eyes, my Valet seemed overly attentive to Albert's progress. Since our respective escritoires were located on opposite sides of the room and our backs faced each other, I couldn't see them. Throughout the lesson, I had an inkling that something was playing out behind me. I did not turn around to see what was happening. I concentrated solely on listening to my BB's tutelage. As our lessons progressed, so did his physical contact. Occasionally, he glanced in my Valet's direction. As he leaned closer and closer to me, I could feel his breath on my neck. His hand inched higher and higher up my thigh. His deliriousness was affecting my concentration and my libido. I decided to brush my hand across his crotch nonchalantly to test his reaction. I felt his sweltering protuberance palpitating beneath his pants.

Not having the opportunity to see what had occurred behind my back, my big brother suddenly caught hold of my wrist and inserted my palm inside his unzipped trousers, onto his throbbing bulge. Taken aback by this turn of events, I did not remove my hand. With a bold move, he slithered his trousers and underwear halfway down his thighs, exposing his lengthy engorgement for me to behold.

I didn't know how my Valet and my roommate would react to this pervious act. Little did I suspect that Albert's head was already bobbing up and down on my Valet's manhood while he sat spread eagle, relishing the Junior's excellent fellatio.

Coilin pushed me onto his thickness, choking me in the process. He gripped my head tightly as he shoved his organ down my throat. I had little choice but to inhale his pubic masculinity. I was at once impressed with and befuddled by this sudden onslaught from this inhibited big brother. I had no idea what had overcome him; all I could concentrate on was the job at hand. Like any A-list Bahriji student, I did what I know best: give and to receive pleasure in any way, shape, or form. In this instance I suckled, blew and nourished the bublousness that was now leaking precum from its aroused slit.

With his palms folded behind his head, my Valet had relaxed onto the chair. He was enjoying Albert's gurgling feed on his erect curvaceousness. He made no effort to grasp the boy's head, unlike the nervous Scotsman, who was afraid that I might lose my attention to his thumping hardness. The Junior was relishing my guardian's upturned appendage with abandon.

It dawned on me that my lover and my roommate had had the hots for each other all along. Their veiled amorousness had eluded my detection until this moment.

When Andy lifted the boy onto the bed, his nakedness concealed the Junior as they French kissed passionately. Stirred by this erotism, Coilin had thrown caution to the wind. His professed heterosexuality seemed to have evaporated from watching this sensual foreplay. His eyes glued to my Valet, he mirrored my lover's every move. He, too, lifted me onto the bed to participate in unrestrained decadence. He stripped me bare as I straddled my big brother as Albert did Andy. As much as I basked in this tantalizing four-way liaison, my jealousy had once again raised its head. Time and again, I had promised my lover that I would subdue the green-eyed monster, yet this abominable beast kept materializing, even when I did not expect it. Now, it loomed large in my mind as the Scotsman prepared me to accept his unbridled manhood and Albert readied to receive my lover's anal impaler.

I was torn by ecstasy and jealousy simultaneously. The duo's unconditional amativeness galvanized and exasperated my person all at once. Their emotional display of fervent copulation only fueled my seething fury. I wanted to ride my lover like Albert rode him. I was ripped apart by my raging resentment. I decided to spite my lover. I rode the Scotsman with acrimonious intensity, as the Junior was riding my beloved. Coilin, thinking I loved rough play, enshrouded his largeness forcibly into my shuddering hollow as his perpetual plowing impaled me into provocative sobs of agonizing propensities. My jealousy had driven me to stupefied insanity. I wanted to demonstrate to Andy the solicitous confusion that was eating at my heart and craving for his attention. In truth, I cared not to share him with another. His love was mine and mine alone.

As for Coilin, his inexperience in the art of lovemaking did nothing to satisfy my revengeful provocations. His premature ejaculation only left me unfulfilled and disgruntled. My lover pleasured the Junior to the point of no return; the boy shot his copiousness onto Andy's heaving chest. My chaperone, always in tune with my requisites, had guesstimated my jealous aggravations. As soon as the Junior released his anal grip on Andy's drumming member, my guardian lifted the Scotsman's legs onto his muscular shoulders. He plunged into the man with all his might. Astonished by this unforeseen incursion, the big brother lay passively beneath my lover. He had no choice but to receive each invading stroke from my retaliatory lover. He had secretly longed for a repeat performance of the other evening's foray, when John had tarnished his maleness into a heap of submissive degradation. In private, he coveted to be outstripped of his machismo. His womanizing wantonness was only a superficial cover-up for his dormant homosexuality. Under peer pressure, he had cloaked himself in, becoming a reserved, taciturn man. It was of little wonder that over these past couple of days, I detected a certain contentedness on his otherwise sullen personality.

Every stroke of my Valet's domineering pounding brought him closer to orgasmic liberation; yet to avenge the Scotsman's crassness towards me, my beloved was battering the man's bottom tenaciously. He cupped Coilin's mouth so his excessive squealing could not alarm the dorm's residents.

With a restrained outburst, my lover pulled out of the big brother. He discharged his voluptuousness onto my twinkling orifice, coating my anal opening with overflowing lushness before thrusting his pulsating firmness into my core. He continued jamming every inch of himself into my person, sending electric tremors down my quivering spine. I could no longer hold off my liquid youthfulness; jets of pulsating amorousness flew above my head and onto Andy's perspiring face. Rivulets of seminal perspirations flowed from our brows as our French kisses rekindled our divinity, returning us to our Garden of Eden, where love knows no boundaries.

76

The Boy Who Wouldn't Grow Up

"I'm not a villain. I've never hurt anyone. I'm just a tawdry character who explodes now and again."
Oliver Reed

1967

Hurrah! Exams are over

With our end-of-year examinations out of the way, it was time to celebrate the last few days of our winter term. As per Daltonbury Hall and Hattonfield Abbey's annual tradition, our schools' glee club together with their performing arts society had bucked heads to put on that year's Christmas pantomime of *Peter Pan*. Traditionally, males in British pantomime cross-dress to play female roles and vice versa. The role of Peter went to a big sister from Hattonfield Abbey. My current and ex-roommates competed for the co-starring role of Wendy. Albert, an active member of the glee club, beat out a number of his contemporaries, including Samuel, to be Peter's romantic interest. The Freshman, being an excellent actor won the role of Tinker Bell from nine other contenders. As was written by J.M. Barrie, the fairy is Peter's best friend and is often jealously protective of him.

Although I knew Albert fancied my chaperone to be his permanent lover, I had no idea that Samuel was also vying for my Valet's affection. Throughout my year with

Andy, I'd grown to take him for granted, never suspecting, at my young age, that others in the peripheries would connive to steal my lover, least of all my best pals. Neither did I suspect that the self-professed 'straight' big brother Coilin was also secretly enamored by my Valet's sexual prowess. He desired my guardian to be his surreptitious fuck buddy, which would never happen on a long term basis; Andy preferred twinks like me and my boyish roommates. Little did I suspect that my lover would soon proffer an unorthodox proposal that would challenge my conventional mindset of one-on-one love. Back then, I was simply living life, glad that my examinations were over and looking forward to new and exciting adventures on the not-too-distant horizon.

At Rehearsals

Unbeknown to me, Samuel was maneuvering to outshine the unwary Albert at every turn during pantomime rehearsals. On the surface, Sam played the role of the tinkling fairy to perfection, but when it came time to get the 'Lost Boys' to shoot fake arrows at the gender-bending Wendy, a.k.a Albert, the Freshman would secretly replace the faux arrowheads with sharpened darts that would cause injury to their human target. At one of the rehearsals, a couple of these honed arrows hit Wendy's arm and leg, sending the bleeding Junior to the Rabbit Hole for care. Of course, nobody knew who the culprit was; no one detected or suspected the innocent-looking Tinker Bell, who acted as if he hadn't a clue to the identity of the prankster. The miscreant was never flagged. Instead, the entire cast was chastised by the glee club and performing arts professors, Dr. Peabody and Madam Noel respectively. They gave the members a stern warning that if such insolence should repeat itself, the hoodlum would be sent to the headmaster or headmistress for punishment. These warnings did not deter the impish Sam from crafting other capers against the Junior.

At dress rehearsal on the afternoon before opening night, the spoiled and jealous Tink blew a handful of talcum powder directly into Wendy's eyes, temporary blinding the boy. When the cross dresser screamed and scrambled for help amidst a sea of beguiled actors, he was again hauled off to the Rabbit Hole for medical aid.

The Freshman feigned confusion, saying that someone had replaced his harmless fairy dust with the white powder and that he had unintentionally blown the particles directly into the Junior's eyes (after all, Wendy was supposed to have his eyes closed).

This time around, Dr. Peabody and Madam Noel called in headmaster Higgins and headmistress Abbott. They announced that if the perpetrator who had swapped the fairy dust to talcum powder did not reveal him or herself, the entire cast would clean the schools' toilets for a week, forfeiting a week of their Christmas and New Year holidays from their respective schools in the process. A deadly silence fell over the troupe, yet nobody came forward to shoulder the blame. As much as our school's authorities warranted the offender to disclose himself or herself, the show had to go on – the audience and guests were the schools' contributing patrons and distinguished parents. They would certainly not take kindly to their respective school boards if their children were detained, especially during this festive season.

The sardonic Freshman had one final stunt to pull. It happened on the opening night of *Peter Pan*, also known as *The Boy Who Wouldn't Grow Up*.

Opening Night

Although I knew my Valet had volunteered as a stage hand in the pantomime, I had not envisioned that one of the reasons for his participation was to spend time with Albert. In my mind, Andy had eyes only for me. Little did I suspect he also coveted my roommate, much like he had me when I was under Nikee's care.

I had not inferred that the clock had been set in motion for reassessment in our relationship. It was growing to become more complex, and I was growing with it. After all, this was the era of free love, free speech, and everything else, especially in contemporary music, art and youth culture. As we moved into 1968, a new generation with strange new vibrations experimented with love-ins in all forms. Our friends, Andy and I were no exception to the rule, whether we belonged to the Enlightened Royal Oracle Society or not. We, together with our coevals, were swept along in the currents of time, where conventional propositions gave way to unorthodox sexual evolutions. It worked for a time, until emulousness heaved havoc in the face of sexual liberations. Andy's love for me never waned, and neither did mine for him throughout our harem years. We faced many challenges, yet he remained steadfast in his promise to me. Unfortunately, it was I who broke the camel's back.

Panto Etiquettes

In December, Christmas decorations were dusted off and scattered throughout the school hall for the Christmas Ball on the evening after the production of *Peter Pan*.

As per tradition, unwritten etiquette and social codes went with this kind of production. Unlike a regular play, stage musical or opera, during which the audience is more reserved, a Christmas panto lives and dies off audience participation, especially when it came time to hiss or make catcalls such as *"Oh yes you will!"* or *"Oh no you wouldn't!"* or boo and jeer at the villains. Although I could never understand the satire that went with a pantomime, that year I let my hair down and went for it, shouting, sneering and singing along to cheer on my actor pals.

More often than not, hidden sexual innuendos such as *"Has anyone seen Dick?"* or *"How ginormous is it?"* are scripted into the dialogue at moments when the adult audience would understand its double meanings. In many instances, Freshmen or Freshwomen or their little brothers and sisters were not yet aware that language could have such hidden codes. They were likely mesmerized by the fantasy sets, sequined costumes and sparkling stage lights.

It was also customary to proceed backstage to congratulate the actors at the end of the show. Unfortunately, this was not the case at the 1967 Daltonbury Hall's production of *Peter Pan*.

The Show

The few months I had been away, Samuel had matured considerably. Though he was once shy and coy, he had become sure and assertive. He was aware that his physical assets could win him whatever he desired. If left unchecked, his pride could boil over and make him cocky. Luckily, Duc was there to keep him in check if his fiery personality got too heated for his own good. As much as Andy fancied the Freshman, he knew to pace himself, as Sam was under Duc's tutelage as a potential E.R.O.S. candidate. Until the appropriate time, the Freshman was his big brother's 'property', not to be tampered with unless Duc invited Andy or me as trainers for his charge.

Sam, on the other hand, had no idea about this unspoken E.R.O.S. rule. After our forest rendezvous three months ago, Sam had longed for a replay of our four-way liaison. Like Albert, he had become infatuated with my guardian and was desperately clamoring for my Valet's attention. Andy, being an honorable gentleman, had kept a polite distance whenever the boy exhibited signs of desiring more than friendship. Out of frustration, Samuel unleashed his vindictiveness against Albert, an easy target. In his limited understanding, we had Andy's affection, and he felt left out of our intimate fraternity. Although Duc did his best to convince the boy that this wasn't the case without revealing that he was under E.R.O.S. recruitment surveillance, Samuel's injured ego had gotten the better of him, and his tawdriness could cost him acceptance into E.R.O.S.'s inner sanctum. At the moment before the show began, he was readying to unbridle his trickery on 'pretty' Wendy.

In the beginning, the performance proceeded without any hitches. The responsive audience shouted, booed, ahhed, jeered and cheered at all the right moments – that was, until the villainous Captain Hook captured, bounded and blindfolded our 'sweet' heroine, Wendy. She was forced onto the gangplank by the cadaverous Hook and about to be cast to the crocodiles when, suddenly, an explosive sound shot across the hall. One of the ship's cannons had been detonated, sending the Captain and Wendy tumbling off the plank onto the fake ocean. If it had gone according to plan, Wendy would have fallen into a trap door on the stage floor, landing on several padded mattresses. Unfortunately, this was not the case.

The crowd went silent. We heard only the groaning sounds from the spot where Hook and Wendy had landed. The first-aid crew rushed to their rescue posthaste as the billowing smoke cleared onstage. They were rushed to the Rabbit Hole on stretchers. No-one, backstage or front stage, had any idea how the cannon had been fired. We were informed later that an accident had occurred, and that the cannon went off accidentally. Once again, foul play was not suspected and the felon went undiscovered.

As soon as the commotion died down, the show had to go on. Wendy's understudy was installed. Now that

Albert was out of the picture, smirking little Tinker flew around stage on his harness, steered by none other than my lover and Valet, Andy. For the time being, Tinker Bell had accomplished his circuitous scheme of eliminating his frenemy, even if it had caused collateral damage along the way.

Duc, Coilin and I went backstage to congratulate the actors on a job well done, but we were eager to visit my friend and roommate. Luckily, no bones were broken on either the actor or actress. They suffered minor concussions and were soon released to their respective dormitories.

Tinker's scheme backfired on him – Andy, Coilin and I spent the next couple of days attentively attending to Albert's every need. Divine intervention had sanctioned time for the four of us to better familiarize ourselves with one another.

77

We Need to Talk, Young Man. We Need to Talk!

"In any relationship, you have to open yourself up and accept others."
Bernard Tristan Foong

1967

Yuletide preparations

Andy, Samuel, Duc and I had signed up to assist the decorating committee for our school's Yuletide Ball. Daltonbury Hall's auditorium was decked out in sparkling tinsel, Christmas ornaments and Yuletide trinkets. Of course, the main feature was the freshly cut twelve-foot spruce pine, which had arrived thirteen days before the premiere of Peter Pan.

As I was dusting off the festive decorations, I couldn't help reminiscing about my time at the boathouse with Nikee on the night of the Christmas Ball. Tears began welling in the corners of my eyes. I missed Nikee. It had been almost two years since I'd lost my virginity to my handsome big brother. Andy, sensing my pensiveness, came over to console me. *"Are you all right?"*

I glanced at my cherished Valet and broke into tears. He wrapped me in his muscular arms to soothe my nostalgia. He sighed, *"Young, tell me what's the matter."*

I stared at my lover without uttering a single syllable. Evocative poignancies rushed to the front of my mind. All eyes turned in my direction as I burst into mournful sobs. Andy, not knowing what had caused this delirium, led me outside for a breath of fresh air. *"Tell me what's bothering you, young man. I can't help you if you don't tell me why you're crying,"* he iterated.

"I don't know why I'm missing Nikee all of a sudden. I love my ex-big brother," I chirped.

"Hush, my pretty boy. Shush, don't cry. I'm here for you," my lover knelt in front of me as I sank onto the frosty ground. He held my face and kissed me on my lips. Some of the boys in the hall saw us kiss. They cheered from behind the windows. Andy lifted me off the wet grass, brushing the snowflakes from my backside. He held my hand as we walked away from the auditorium in silence. I guided him towards the boathouse jetty where Nikee and I had sat a couple years ago. My Valet must have guessed what was going through my mind. As soon as we sat on the warm blankets he had gathered from the boathouse, he brushed the wetness off my face before planting another loving kiss in my mouth. I stirred.

Words were not required as we sat in introspective silence, watching the winter's sun sink below the horizon. Our love was sufficient to warm the chill that surrounded us. My eyes never left Andy's scrutinizing gaze. I reached my hand into his bomber jacket, feeling his pulsating heart. His adoration for me was as potent as it had been the first time I had invited him into my bed. I felt for him as I had for Nikee. Now, I was sitting by the same wooden pier once again with my lover, except the boy wasn't my ex-BB but my Valet, the man whose unconditional love had exceeded all my expectations.

This time around, it was I who made the first move. I reached my slender hands into his muscular chest, brushing my fingers against the hairs that covered his manliness. Our proximity stirred in us a sensual urgency that needed no justification. We were in love, and love knows no boundaries. Andy reciprocated my every gesture. We, like Siamese twins, were one; we would and could not survive without the other. We fed off each other's affinity as if it were blood. Our pulsating hardness gyrated in unison to the rhythmic call of the wild. Behind the fabric coverings that concealed our modesty, we were also each preposterously envisioning another: I my initial sexual relationship with Nikee and Andy his besotted Albert. Unbeknownst to me, my lover was cogitating the correct moment to deliver his bohemian proposal to me. For now, we were simply hypnotized by our intimacies. His postulation would have to wait.

Heightened by our burning passions, our fevered eroticism had seduced us to strip bare in the midst of this winter landscape. Concealed by a woolen blanket, we cajoled naked as a single entity electrified by the warmth of lubricious carnality. The chance of being discovered by passersby served only to intensify our homo concupiscence to intransigent defiance. This was our incognizant way of rebelling against conventional attitudes towards the love that dared not speak its name. After all, it was the dawning of the Age of Aquarius, when gay men would want to be seen, heard and be respected. We no longer desired to hide in the shadows of conformity. Andy and I were coming into ourselves in more ways than one. We, like many others of our genre, were demanding change; our lovemaking that winter's evening was simply a means to an end.

The Spies

Little did we know that the two observers hiding quietly nearby were the potential E.R.O.S. recruit and his trainer, Duc.

Samuel had tailed to see why I was weeping. Duc, on the other hand, had cautioned his charge to leave us alone, but the boy had insisted. Since the BB could not persuade him to stay put, he tagged along. He deliberated that it would be valuable for his little brother to learn through observation. Sam was erotically enamored by Andy's and my unbridled sexuality. Little did Duc suspect that his irreproachable-looking charge was secretly striving for my lover's affection. Worst of all, his scheming puerility would no doubt injure his potential acceptance into the Enlightened Royal Oracle Society. Like Nikee before him, the BB was recording his little brother's conduct for presentation to the E.R.O.S. selection board.

My lover's and my accumulative orgasmic cries led us to rummage deeply into our inner conflicts, until now camouflaged by our stoic denial. Although Andy knew I was missing Nikee, he did not deduce that I was fantasizing about my ex during our heated passion. Neither did I surmise that my lover was imagining me as Albert as he pistoned his way to the point of no return. Our previous, undemanding attraction had whirled us into a complicated position. Our unconditional love would soon be put under scrutiny by none other but by ourselves.

We lay quietly in each other's arms. We made no motion to leave until the night owl beckoned our return to the warmth of our respective chambers. I wanted to stay with Andy and he with me, but duty waived our impulsiveness. We parted ways reluctantly. We would be together again in less than a couple days, when we would depart for Spain to visit our other lover, Oscar, and his new lover, Alfonso.

At the Ball

Coilin looked staggeringly handsome in formal dress (and so did the rest of my friends). Once again, I donned the three-piece evening ensemble that Uncle James had gifted me when I first arrived at Daltonbury Hall. Throughout the jubilant festivities, the females from our sister school never failed to congregate around the good-looking beaus from their brother school. As usual, Coilin and Duc had garnered an assembly of big sisters and female Juniors. So had Albert and Samuel, who had a flair for attracting admiring Freshwomen into their expanding retinues. As much as I enjoyed dancing with the females, I was pining for Andy's presence. I kept watch over the receiving line as each attendee's name was announced upon arrival. Finally, the footman promulgated aloud, *"Mr. Andy Finchenstein."*

Standing above the staircase was the strikingly handsome Valet. No sooner did he reach the bottom of the curved staircase than a bevy of ladies gathered to greet and to introduce themselves to my lover. I, like the females, was awestruck by my attractive guardian. When none of them were watching, he gave me an acknowledging wink. I felt privileged that this gorgeous man had eyes for me – that was until I noticed Andy's beguiling stare never vacillated from Albert's direction, even though the Junior was vividly engaged in animated conversation with his giggling posse. Albert, sensing my Valet's inconspicuous gaze, would make discreet eye contact with the grinning beau while he, too, was busily chatting with his admirers.

Jealousy

Jealousy roared. Unlike Yuletide two years ago, when I'd had to leave the stifling hall for a breath of fresh air, that night I had to leave this festive playground to save myself from my incendiary self. I needed time to cool my displeasure in this disparaging winter wonderland that, a few days ago, had stirred a euphoric nostalgia of my time with Nikee. I walked aimlessly, not knowing where I was heading until the boathouse loomed before me. I found myself sitting on the edge of the wooden pier, mulling over my relationship with my guardian.

Deep in thought, I did not notice the man creeping up behind me until he touched my shoulder. I leaped to my feet from astonishment. In the darkened landscape, I could not make out who the intruder was. I stood stupefied.

"Sorry I scared you," he apologized.

I did not reply. He spoke again, *"Why aren't you enjoying yourself at the Ball, young man?"*

I stared into the darkness. All I could make out was a well-dressed man in evening attire. Still I could not see his face. He continued, *"Why are you alone by the pier when the Yuletide celebration is in full swing? Are you all right?"*

Then, I recognized the voice. It was Duc. He had shadowed me when I left the auditorium. I uttered, as graciously as I could muster amidst the despondency that was devouring my sanity, *"I'm fine, sir."*

"You don't sound fine to me," he probed. *"Tell me, Young, what's troubling you?"*

I tried to change the subject. I asked, *"Aren't you having a fun time in the hall? I saw you talking with a group of girls. They are charmed by you."*

He did not respond. Instead, he led me to a nearby bench before he answered. *"I'm not here to talk about me. I'm here to make sure you are all right."*

As much as I wanted to confide to the big brother the jealousy that was consuming my person, I remained silent. That was until he iterated again, *"Big brothers are here to assist little brothers. Whatever you disclose to me will be confidential. You should know that without me having to remind you, especially among E.R.O.S. recruits."*

I plucked up the courage and murmured, *"I am confounded by jealousy."*

Duc did not reply. After a pause, he cupped my hands in his and looked directly into my eyes. He said, *"There are several routes I take when I'm confronted by the green-eyed monster."*

He had grabbed my attention. I questioned, *"What are the options?"*

"Choice number one is to allow yourself to become buddies with that anxiety and fear – to conspire with these negative feelings to validate their story of hurt and anger. You see, Young, part of us denies that these feelings have been provoked by jealousy, and we often look outward at the person or moment that set off the trigger. We search for something to blame and to project our emotional muck onto. This can lead to combative communication and frustrating fights or quarrels with your lovers."

I remarked without hesitation, *"I wanted to pick a fight with Albert..."* Before I could continue, I knew I had revealed too much of my inner turmoil. I quickly changed the subject and added, *"I'm sorry I interrupted. Please go on."*

Duc peered at me. He was obviously trying to decipher the reason I was jealous of the Junior. He commented, *"Choice number two is to acknowledge the jealousy for what it is and to follow the feelings. You have to understand, Young; jealousy is typically more about the past than it is about the present. Jealousy is often the manifestation of our past wounds, abandonment or insecurity. It shows up along with fear and anxiety. It is an illusory protection from getting hurt. Those past negative experiences live in the body and eventually form a pattern or story that we use as a coping mechanism. If we allow ourselves to listen quietly and follow the feelings instead of reacting to them, that story often unfolds, and more often than not the negativity will dissipate."*

I chimed, *"Easier said than done."*

The man gave me a musing smile before declaring, *"I have had time to process my personal feelings of jealousy. Along the way, I've had some great partners whom I felt I trusted. There are times when these old feelings still crop up. Instead of reacting or blaming my partner, I take these opportunities to go inward. I take a deep breath to connect to the truth of who I am in that moment, and I realize that there is more to me than those negative feelings. I make it a point to acknowledge my feelings and give myself space to move through them. Like you, I feel the hurt, the anger, the sadness. I release it in that moment. I give myself permission to let go of the past and open into the present."*

He added, *"From that present moment, I can be clear of what my needs are without the influence of my past relationships and hurt. Through this clarity, I can then express my needs to my partner and share my feelings from a loving and compassionate place."*

I voiced, *"Andy taught me some techniques to subdue jealousy, yet when push comes to shove, I fail miserably."*

The BB scruffed my hair. *"My dear boy, navigating jealousy takes practice. The journey is not necessarily easy. When we choose the path of awareness, we step into a full range of emotions that can emerge – sadness, anger, hurt, anxiety and fear. When we encounter these emotions and recognize them, we are forcing them to relinquish their control for us to move forward to a lighter, happier and more secure place.*

"For me, passing through these challenging moments helps me connect to a deeper sense of my true self. It is an emotional and spiritual opening for me. The Tantric path is one of celebrating the full spectrum of life – releasing judgment of good and bad. To embrace it all is part of the journey toward radical self-acceptance and ecstatic love," he mused assertively.

"In other words, you are saying that I don't have to deal with jealousy. All I need to do is to acknowledge it, accept it, and through my acceptance, the green-eyed monster will set me free?" I asked.

Before Duc could give me an answer, Andy miraculously appeared. He walked towards us. Stopping in front of me, he reached to pull me to him. *"We need to talk, young man. We need to talk."*

78

Auld Land Syne

"I don't need a crowded ballroom; everything I need is here. If you're with me, next year will be the perfect year."
Dina Carroll

Auld Lang Syne

This Scottish song title translates into English as *'Old Long Since'*, or, more idiomatically, *'Long Long Ago'*, *'Days Gone By'* or *'Old Times'*. Consequently, *'For auld lang syne'*, as it appears in the first line of the chorus, might be loosely translated as *'For (the sake of) old times'*. For old times' sake, I remember the various characters I've met throughout the course of my third household, the Quwah.

Andy and I did 'Talk the Talk' and 'Walk the Walk.' It is an episode in and of itself, which is revealed in ***A Harem Boy's Saga – IV – Metanoia***.

Time spent with Oscar, Alfonso, Mary and her then companion Jewel in Spain was both fun filled and educational. That week, we visited many places of interest in Barcelona and the nearby region of Andorra. That holiday was the last time I saw Oscar.

During my numerous fashion sojourns, I had the opportunity to see Mary. Shortly after our Spanish vacation, the model had parted ways with Alfonso, and though they saw little of each other, they remained friends.

I had guessed correctly: Mary was indeed a lesbian. The last I heard of her, she was in a relationship with a female model whom Mario had photographed regularly for French Vogue in the early and mid-seventies.

> *Should old acquaintance be forgot,*
> *And never brought to mind?*
> *Should old acquaintance be forgot,*
> *And old lang syne?*

My answer to these first few lines of Robert Burns lyrics would be a resounding 'no'. I have never forgotten the big brothers who nourished and nurtured me throughout my boarding school years, especially Nikee, Oscar, Duc, and of course, Andy. Their unconditional love, together with their steadfast tutelage, instilled in me a sense of civic duty. As a result, I've come to respect those with whom I have crossed paths.

Duc

Besides being Samuel's notable BB, Duc served as my surrogate Valet when I encountered difficulties with my lovers. During the three months I was stationed at my fifth household, I lived in close proximity with this erudite scholar, turning to him often for advice. More often than not, he far exceeded his BB duties, helping me come into my spiritual self with ease and grace.

Toward the latter part of 1968, Duc went on to study psychology at the best university in the Netherlands, The University of Groningen. That was the last news I heard of this enlightened big brother.

> *And surely you'll buy your pint cup!*
> *And surely I'll buy mine!*
> *And we'll take a cup o' kindness yet,*
> *For auld lang syne.*

Coilin

We visited Coilin in Scotland during the 1968 Spring-term break. In the time I knew this big brother, he continued to struggle with his drinking and his sexuality. He tried to gain endearments from my Valet, but to no avail. Andy already had his hands full and did not wish to cause further complications, especially when it came to conducting a clandestine erotic relationship with a man who lived a self-imposed carnal lie.

The Scotsman left Daltonbury Hall in the summer of 1968 for New York City. While he was visiting relatives, he became actively involved with the United Nations International Children's Emergency Fund (UNICEF). The man did not return to the United Kingdom; he travelled far and wide, assisting in humanitarian and developmental efforts for underprivileged children and destitute mothers in developing countries. The last I heard of Coilin was that he was assisting in the rebuilding efforts in war-torn Nigeria during the early months of 1971. This BB's cup o' kindness flowed to every corner of the earth, where, for old times' sake, he is deeply cherished by his little brother, *moi*.

> *We two have run about the slopes,*
> *And picked the daisies fine;*
> *But we've wandered many a weary foot,*
> *Since auld lang syne.*

Both my tutors, Monsieur Alain Dubois and Signor Gabrielli Marciano Castrogiovanni, took over the reins from my fourth Household teacher, Takioko, whenever the opportunity arose. I am forever indebted to these two learned men for passing to me their intellectual and academic knowledge. They allowed me to grow into a well-rounded individual for whom preconceived discriminations do not equate to shrewd perspicacity.

Monsieur Alain Dubois

In 1969 Monsieur Dubois obtained his doctorate degree. His years of Zentology research had earned him a PhD degree in the field *of* Progressive Sensuality and Sexuality Studies. I never saw or heard from my erudite professor after he secured tenureship at the Bahriji School, where he was an alumnus.

Ikram

I continued to work with the kaneeth on Carousel. Makut, Ebram and Khatum remained his loyal chaperones. Together, the Arab and I had many fun and difficult times. I survived each trying moment as long as I was the relenting anticipant. When all was said and done, Carousel was Ikram and Prince P's project. They had the final say. I was a sounding board to provide suggestions and recommendations when called upon. I was an apprentice, and I knew better than to allow my pride to stand in the way of the epileptic's egotistical endeavors. I'm simply thankful for the opportunity to witness Carousel's fruition.

Ludovic Makmud Albriem

The gay Muslim did garner sufficient funding to start his GLBT mosque in Paris. His charisma along with his stylish grace and youthful countenance enabled him to move in aristocratic circles wherever he went. Along his life's journey, he encountered many wealthy, mature gentlemen who would be more than happy to take him under their wings. As others did in generations before him, he carved out a comfortable living being a 'kept boy'.

Throughout my service in the other harems, Ludovic was like a seasoned bumblebee, fluttering from one bloom to the next, resting temporarily at one chateau before taking flight to the next castle.

Through the grapevine, I learned of the man's untimely demise. He was thirty-eight when he fell victim to the 'gay cancer' during the early years of the AIDS crisis.

Bryanna

The model, being in the fashion and beauty business, and I, an aspiring fashion designer, ran about the à la mode slopes, picking plentiful 'daisies' along the way. Her 'daisies' were men of substance and women of influence. Mine were simply suave, wealthy and titled gentlemen I had the effrontery to meet during my harem services. Mario, Bryanna and I wandered many a weary foot as we navigated through the ever-changing international fashion arena.

Finally, this eccentric woman fell in love with her prince charming, a wealthy entrepreneur in the beauty industry. She relinquished her modelling career in 1970 to be mother to two young boys from her husband's previous marriage. Mario, Andy and I visited the model in Zürich to attend her intimate wedding ceremony. That was the last time I saw this transsexual beauty outside of international fashion pages.

We two have paddled in the stream,
From morning sun till dine;
But seas between us broad have roared
Since auld lang syne.

Prince P

As judicious as His Highness was when it came to financial and business accruements, he was also mutable and unpredictable when it came to the spur-of-the-moment decisions. As exhilarating as this idiosyncrasy was at my young age, I was also aware of the perils that went alongside it.

He was indeed a generous man and showered Andy and me with many expensive gifts and monetary gratuities. Unfortunately, his lack of patriotism to his country of birth was not appreciated by his father, Isa bin Salman Al Khalifa. Exasperated with family feuding and power scheming, he made France his permanent home in 1970, returning to his country of birth only when protocol demanded his presence.

I continued to work closely with His Highness during Carousel's inception. I was often on loan from his loyal friend, Sheik Fahrib. The lives of these two men had become inextricably intertwined.

Out of defiance for his family, P married Anastasie. The marriage lasted for a year before the New York model forged her mark within the modelling circle. Away from her American values, she was tired of living in a male-dominated society. Before their separation, she bore His Highness a male heir. As soon as she served her divorce papers, the problem of custody arose. Their bickering led to an outright war; the boy was kidnapped and spirited away to Manama by his Arabian grandmother, Fatima, the queen dowager. The battle lasted for years after I left harem services. Although I have no idea how it ended, I did learn that this fiasco brought the prince and the sheik closer together.

His Highness did remarry. This was told to Andy and me when we visited Baron Pierre at Chateau Rouge in the summer of 1969.

Sheik Abdul Mutmud bin Fahrib

Dr. Fahrib was accepted into the Enlightened Royal Oracle Society as a distinguished patron in early 1968. Andy and I were one of the first batch of foreign exchange students to serve in his 'makeshift' household. Initially, Andy and I were deployed to an Amsterdam townhouse that the sheik had bought as a getaway for his personal use – that was until the physician was comfortable enough to inform his wives of our existence. Only then were we invited to the *Salamalekum* (Peace be with you) mansion in Sharjah, a city in United Arab Emirates.

My Valet and I got on well with his wives. As was often the case, fashion spoke a thousand words, and it became an invisible connection between the two burka-wearing ladies and me. As soon as I earned their trust, I was invited into their female inner sanctum. I had seemingly – and unconsciously – taken on the role of a kaneeth. Acting in an advisory capacity as their stylist and interior decorator, I travelled with them on their extensive shopping sprees. This further solidified my comprehensive understanding of the international fashion and art scenes.

The sheik, the prince, Andy and I often went paddling in the stream from morning until dusk. Sometimes, I tagged along as they competed in international yacht races since auld lang syne. It was a dream come true, especially for my Valet, whose love for water sports never waned.

> *And there's a hand my trusty friend!*
> *And give me a hand o' thine!*
> *And we'll take a right good-will draught,*
> *For auld lang syne.*

The Marquis

I capitulated to the Marquis' persistent advances by giving in to this generous friend; that was before he moved on to greener pastures with his other conquest. Mathieu rewarded me and my guardian handsomely, and so did his trusted friend, the magnanimous Baron Pierre.

Whenever the 'cats' were out of sight, the 'mice' came out to play. This certainly rang true for the three aristocratic 'mice': the baron, the marquis and the vicomte.

The Baron

During the few years I had come to be acquainted with the baron, he had changed partners every three to six months, just like a seasonal designer wardrobe. In the summer of 1969 when the Frenchman invited Andy and me to visit his chateau, he was infatuated with a good-looking seventeen-year-old named Jesus, a Puerto Rican boy whom he had met in a bar when on holiday in none other than Puerto Rico. He had transported this exotic urchin all the way to France, romanticizing that he was the 'one' in his life. Of course, it did not work out. Before long he was onto the next and the next and the next until, I'm sure, he permanently ran out of breath trying to catch the next beautiful butterfly.

Vicomte Charles

As I read in a tabloid, his passing in 1981 was survived by two children. In the short time we had become acquainted, I had great respect for the man and his wife. Although Marie-Laure passed eleven years prior to his demise, they had both contributed greatly to furthering French art, literature and film, especially the writings of the late Marquis de Sade, who was a close relative of the Vicomtesse. Although the Vicomte and I were not attracted to each other sexually, he did on occasions solicit the services of my other E.R.O.S. counterparts. Out of respect for Marie-Laure, his trysts were often conducted with discretion and secrecy, away from the noisy paparazzi and gossip columns.

> *For auld lang syne, my dear,*
> *For auld lang syne,*
> *We'll take a cup of kindness yet,*
> *For auld lang syne.*

For auld lang syne, I'm sure my female peers and their big sisters went on to pursue productive careers, much like my other big brothers and their little brothers. I never saw Elizabeth, Matumi, Didee or Karina after my Quwah service.

Dr. A. S. Finckenstein

Last but not least, I raise a toast to my dear friend, Dr. A. S., whom I've never met and never will have the opportunity to meet. I learned of his passing through his Facebook page. It was also on this page that we connected two years ago when I was searching for Andy, my ex-Valet. We became pen pals.

Instead of Andy, he located my other long lost BB, Oscar, on my behalf. For this I raise my glass of gratitude to all my acquaintances, old or new, and especially to this special man, whose cup of kindness overflowed with generosity. May he never be forgotten but be remembered for as long as he survives within these pages.

Young.

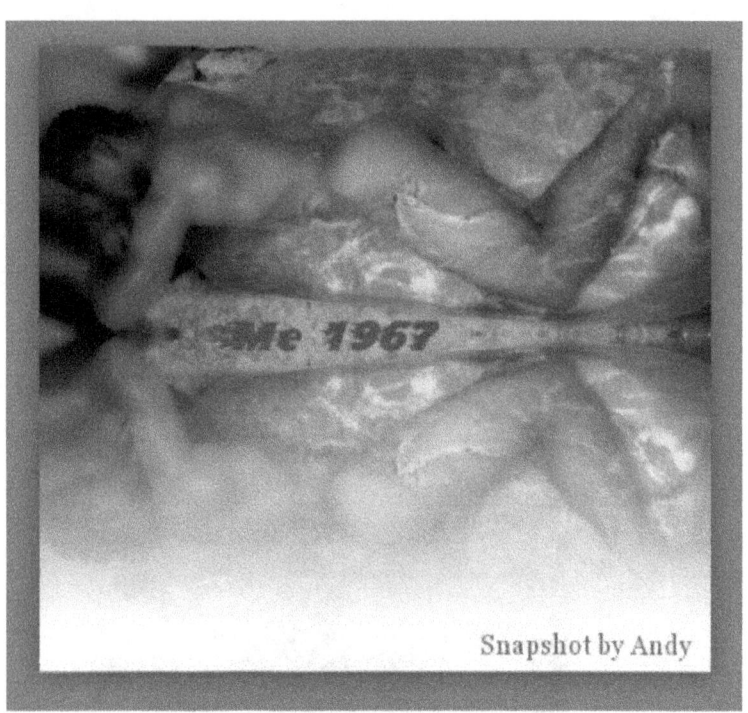

Author's Bio

Bernard Foong is, first and foremost, a sensitivist. He finds nuance in everything. To experience the world he inhabits is an adventure which is mystical, childlike and refreshing. He has a rare ability to create beauty in a unique fashion. His palettes have been material, paint, words and human experiences.

By Christine Maynard (screenwriter and novelist).

Bernard Tristan Foong alias Young, is an accomplished fashion designer. After graduating from The Royal College of Art, London, England; he worked as an in-house bridal wear designer for Liberty's of London for four years.

The Hong Kong Polytechnic/University offered Mr. Foong a fashion design professorship for the next six years. He was a founding member of The Hong Kong Fashion Designer's Association. Consultant to numerous fashion companies in Hong Kong; ranging from lingerie, furs, womens-wear designs to his specialty: romantic and ethereal bridal ensembles.

During his lecturing sojourn in the United States of America, he was recruited by The University of Wisconsin, Madison as an associate fashion professor. He was also a visiting lecturer at The Minneapolis College of Art, Minnesota.

In 1994 to 1996, The Singapore Temasek Polytechnic recruited Mr. Foong to organize the school's fashion design and merchandising department. He was also the acting fashion development manager for Parkson Grand department stores in Kuala Lumpur, Malaysia.

The designer was offered a scholarship to complete his Master in Theatre Costuming at The University of Hawaii in 1996. Since then he has made Hawaii his home. He resides in the beautiful island of Maui with his life partner of sixteen years, Mr. Walter Bissett and their *'Goddess'* daughter, Ms. Kali Durga (a fluffy Himalayan).

He is a full-time writer and is currently working on his fourth book, the sequel to **Initiation, Unbridled** and **Debauchery**.

A Harem Boy Saga is a series of seven books, documenting the designer's life.

Acknowledgements

In January 2011, an interminable urge overtook me to document a segment of my adolescent life which had been kept secret for forty-two years. I was compelled by an unseen power to write *A Harem Boy's Saga*.

Ms. Marji Knowles, a friend and confident, intrigued by my story, encouraged me to proceed. Not only did she offer me assistance in editing my manuscript, she also provided sound advice and suggestions throughout my writing process. I am grateful for the months of hard work she devoted to **A Harem Boy's Saga – Book I – Initiation.** Her cogent arguments spearheaded my determination to complete the first in a series of *A Harem Boy Saga*.

Ms. Christine Maynard, my editor in chief manifested from Louisiana. She is a genius in keeping my youthful voice intact while transforming my story onto the pages of **Initiation** and **Book II – Unbridled**. I have grown to cherish and love this amazing woman during the months we spent editing. We laughed, cried, and sometimes cursed but forgave, as we cleaned and scrubbed this manuscript to perfection. We have since become close friends. A quote by William Blake:

"Opposition is true friendship."

In the process of editing **Unbridled**, I've the privilege to come to know my other editor, Ms. Ellen Fishbein from New Jersey who had since moved to the 'Big Apple'. I appreciate her patience and perseverance in editing **Book III – Debauchery** after months of dedication to this what appears to be a never-ending project. She did a superb editing job and provided valuable suggestions to improve my writing skills. For this I am thankful and grateful for her help.

I'm indebted to Ms. Emerantia Antonia Parnall-Gilbert (my Literary Agent – Gilbert Literary Agency). Besides providing me with valuable advice, she also found me my current publisher – Solstice Publishing to publish *A Harem Boy's Saga* series. Her unfaltering support and faith in my writing gave me the incentive to continue on this long and winding road to complete my seven books series. Ms. Parnall-Gilbert is currently approaching movie, television and stage production producers to have A Harem Boy's Saga made into a film, TV miniseries and/or a stage musical.

I also like to thank Ms. Melissa Miller – Solstice Publishing for her credence in my memoirs and to Ms. KateMarie Collins (Solstice Publishing editor-in-chief) for devoting time to format and upload A Harem Boy's Saga to the international distributions sites.

Not forgetting my dear friend, Mr. Robert DeNigris who took time from his busy schedule to proofread Debauchery's manuscript. Mahalo Bob! You are a gem.

At this juncture, I would like to say, a big "Thank You" to all my friends and supporters who continue to support my revelations during the past years of grueling work, before **Initiation**, **Unbridled** and **Debauchery** came to fruition.

Last but not least, I am deeply appreciative to my life partner, Mr. Walter Bissett for his resolute support, encouraging me to tell my story truthfully. In his words;

"The truth will set you free."

Young.

young@aharemboysaga.com
www.aharemboysaga.com

www.ingramcontent.com/pod-product-compliance
Lightning Source LLC
Chambersburg PA
CBHW070916180426
43192CB00037B/1157